Making the Revolution

Many treatments of the twentieth-century Latin American left assume a movement populated mainly by affluent urban youth whose naïve dreams of revolution collapsed under the weight of their own elitism, racism, sexism, and sectarian dogmas. This book demonstrates that the history of the left is much more diverse. Many leftists struggled against capitalism and empire while also confronting racism, patriarchy, and authoritarianism. The left's ideology and practice were often shaped by leftists from marginalized populations, from Bolivian indigenous communities in the 1920s to the revolutionary women of El Salvador's guerrilla movements in the 1980s. Through ten historical case studies of ten different countries, *Making the Revolution* highlights some of the most important research on the Latin American left by leading senior and up-and-coming scholars, offering a needed corrective and valuable contribution to modern Latin American history, politics, and sociology.

Kevin A. Young is Assistant Professor of History at the University of Massachusetts, Amherst. He is the author of *Blood of the Earth: Resource Nationalism, Revolution, and Empire in Bolivia* (2017).

D1211305

Making the Revolution

Histories of the Latin American Left

Edited by

KEVIN A. YOUNG
University of Massachusetts, Amherst

CAMBRIDGE
UNIVERSITY PRESS

University Printing House, Cambridge CB2 8BS, United Kingdom

One Liberty Plaza, 20th Floor, New York, NY 10006, USA

477 Williamstown Road, Port Melbourne, VIC 3207, Australia

314–321, 3rd Floor, Plot 3, Splendor Forum, Jasola District Centre,
New Delhi – 110025, India

79 Anson Road, #06–04/06, Singapore 079906

Cambridge University Press is part of the University of Cambridge.

It furthers the University's mission by disseminating knowledge in the pursuit of
education, learning, and research at the highest international levels of excellence.

www.cambridge.org
Information on this title: www.cambridge.org/9781108423991
DOI: 10.1017/9781108539449

© Cambridge University Press 2019

First published 2019

Printed in the United Kingdom by TJ International Ltd. Padstow Cornwall

A catalogue record for this publication is available from the British Library.

Library of Congress Cataloging-in-Publication Data
NAMES: Young, Kevin A., editor.
TITLE: Making the revolution : histories of the Latin American left / edited by Kevin A.
Young, University of Massachusetts, Amherst.
DESCRIPTION: Cambridge ; New York, NY : Cambridge University Press, 2019. |
Includes bibliographical references and index.
IDENTIFIERS: LCCN 2019004816| ISBN 9781108423991 (hardback : alk. paper) |
ISBN 9781108439251 (paperback : alk. paper)
SUBJECTS: LCSH: Social movements – Latin America. | Revolutionaries – Latin
America. | Right and left (Political science) – Latin America.
CLASSIFICATION: LCC HN110.5.A8 M327 2019 | DDC 303.48/4–dc23
LC record available at https://lccn.loc.gov/2019004816

ISBN 978-1-108-42399-1 Hardback
ISBN 978-1-108-43925-1 Paperback

For Jeffrey, and all revolutionaries who didn't live to see the world they deserved.

– KY

Contents

Figures

Contributors

Marc Becker is Professor of Latin American history at Truman State University. His research focuses on the history of the Latin American left. His publications include *The FBI in Latin America: The Ecuador Files* (2017), *Twentieth-Century Latin American Revolutions* (2017), *Pachakutik: Indigenous Movements and Electoral Politics in Ecuador* (2011), and *Indians and Leftists in the Making of Ecuador's Modern Indigenous Movements* (2008).

O'Neill (Nelly) Blacker-Hanson (Ph.D., University of Washington) has published and taught extensively on the Cold War era in Mexico. A social historian, her work is based on archival materials in Guerrero and Mexico City, as well as interviews with participants in Guerrero's opposition movements of the 1960s–1970s. She has published articles as well as book reviews on the subject. She is currently a scholar-in-residence at the University of New Mexico.

Barry Carr is Emeritus Professor at La Trobe University, Melbourne, Australia. His research interests have included the labor and agrarian history of Mexico and Cuba, the development of Marxism and Communism in Latin America, the history of tourism and leisure in Mexico in the period 1880–2015, and the development of transnational networks of radicals, revolutionaries, activists, and exiles in the Greater Circum-Caribbean, 1920–1940.

Michelle Chase is Assistant Professor of History at Pace University and author of the book *Revolution within the Revolution: Women and*

Gender Politics in the Cuban Revolution, 1952–1962 (2015). She has written about contemporary Cuba for *The Nation, Jacobin, Boston Review*, and *NACLA*. Her work has been supported by the American Association of University Women, the Lyndon B. Johnson Foundation, and the New Jersey Council of the Humanities.

Forrest Hylton is Associate Professor of Political Science at the Universidad Nacional de Colombia, Medellín. He studies power, politics, and authority among the Aymara in modern Bolivia and the Wayúu in colonial New Grenada, in relation to markets, states, and empires. He is revising a manuscript entitled *Specters of Race War: Indian Communities, the Federal War of 1899, and the Regeneration of Bolivia*, and with Sinclair Thomson is coauthor of *Revolutionary Horizons: Past and Present in Bolivian Politics* (2007).

Betsy Konefal is Associate Professor of History at the College of William and Mary, specializing in twentieth-century Latin America and histories of race/ethnicity, human rights, and oppositional politics. Her first book, *For Every Indio Who Falls: A History of Maya Activism in Guatemala, 1960–1990* (2010), was named *Choice* "Outstanding Academic Title." She is currently working on a study of liberation theology and student-led organizing in the Guatemalan highlands.

Aldo Marchesi (Ph.D., 2012, New York University) is Associate Professor at the Universidad de la República (Montevideo, Uruguay). He has been working extensively on the recent history of the Southern Cone. In recent years his work has focused on the history of the radical left during the 1960s and 1970s in the region. His most recent work is *Latin America's Radical Left: Rebellion and Cold War in the Global 1960s* (2018).

Margaret Power is Professor of History at Illinois Institute of Technology. She has authored or coedited the following titles: *Right-Wing Women in Chile: Feminine Power and the Struggle against Allende* (2002); *Right-Wing Women: From Conservatives to Extremists around the World* (2002); *New Perspectives on the Transnational Right* (2010); and *Hope in Hard Times: Norvelt and the Struggle for Community during the Great*

Depression (2016). Her current research focuses on the Puerto Rican Nationalist Party and its transnational networks across the Americas. She coedited an issue of *Radical History Review* on Puerto Rico.

Diana Carolina Sierra Becerra is a Postdoctoral Fellow for the project "Putting History in Domestic Workers' Hands," a collaboration between Smith College and the National Domestic Workers Alliance. In 2020, she will take up her position as an Assistant Professor in the History Department at the University of Massachusetts Amherst. She is currently revising a book manuscript about the praxis of revolutionary women in El Salvador.

Kevin A. Young is Assistant Professor of History at the University of Massachusetts Amherst. He is the author of *Blood of the Earth: Resource Nationalism, Revolution, and Empire in Bolivia* (2017) and coauthor, with Tarun Banerjee and Michael Schwartz, of the forthcoming book *Levers of Power: How the 1% Rules and What the 99% Can Do About It*.

Editor's Note

Chapters 1, 2, and 5 appeared previously in somewhat different form, and are reproduced here with permission. See Forrest Hylton, "Tierra común: Caciques, artesanos e intelectuales radicales y la rebelión de Chayanta," in *Ya es otro tiempo el presente: Cuatro momentos de insurgencia indígena*, by Forrest Hylton, Félix Patzi, Sergio Serulnikov, and Sinclair Thomson (La Paz: Muela del Diablo, 2003), 127–87; Barry Carr, "Identity, Class, and Nation: Black Immigrant Workers, Cuban Communism, and the Sugar Insurgency, 1925–1934," *Hispanic American Historical Review* 78, no. 1 (1998): 83–116; Kevin A. Young, "The Making of an Interethnic Coalition: Urban and Rural Anarchists in La Paz, Bolivia, 1946–1947," *Latin American and Caribbean Ethnic Studies* 11, no. 2 (2016): 163–88.

Financial support was provided by the Office of the Vice Chancellor for Research and Engagement, University of Massachusetts Amherst, to cover the Duke University Press reprint fee of $550 for Chapter 2.

All editor's royalties from the sale of this book will be donated to the Museo de la Palabra y la Imagen (Museum of the Word and the Image) in San Salvador. See www.museo.com/sv for information.

Cover photo by Mike Goldwater (Chalatenango, El Salvador, 1984). Used with permission.

Unless otherwise noted, throughout the book, all non-English sources have been translated by the chapter's author or translator.

Abbreviations

(For archival abbreviations see footnotes)

ACG	Asociación Cívica Guerrerense/Civic Association of Guerrero (Mexico)
ACNR	Asociación Cívica Nacional Revolucionaria/National Revolutionary Civic Association (Mexico)
AFP	Atlanta Federal Penitentiary (United States)
AMES	Asociación de Mujeres de El Salvador/Association of Women of El Salvador
CCF	Congress for Cultural Freedom/Congreso por la Libertad de la Cultura
CDHES	Comisión de Derechos Humanos de El Salvador/Human Rights Commission of El Salvador
CIA	Central Intelligence Agency (United States)
CIG	Central Intelligence Group (United States)
CLAM	Congreso Latinoamericano de Mujeres/Congress of Latin American Women
CMCLAL	Congreso de Mujeres Cubanas por la Liberación de América Latina/Congress of Cuban Women for the Liberation of Latin America (Cuba)
CNOC	Confederación Nacional Obrera de Cuba/National Workers' Confederation of Cuba
COB	Central Obrera Boliviana/Bolivian Workers' Central
CPUSA	Communist Party USA
CSLA	Confederación Sindical Latinoamericana/Latin American Trade Union Confederation

CUC	Comité de Unidad Campesina/Committee for Peasant Unity (Guatemala)
DFS	Dirección Federal de Seguridad/Federal Security Agency (Mexico)
DINA	Dirección de Inteligencia Nacional/National Intelligence Directorate (Chile)
EGP	Ejército Guerrillero de los Pobres/Guerrilla Army of the Poor (Guatemala)
ELN	Ejército de Liberación Nacional/National Liberation Army (Bolivia)
FAD	Federación Agraria Departamental/Departmental Agrarian Federation (Bolivia)
FAR	Fuerzas Armadas Rebeldes/Rebel Armed Forces (Guatemala)
FARC	Fuerzas Armadas Revolucionarias de Colombia – Ejército del Pueblo/Revolutionary Armed Forces of Colombia – People's Army (also known as FARC-EP)
FBI	Federal Bureau of Investigation (United States)
FDMC	Federación Democrática de Mujeres Cubanas/Democratic Federation of Cuban Women
FEI	Federación Ecuatoriana de Indios/Ecuadorian Federation of Indians
FMC	Federación de Mujeres Cubanas/Federation of Cuban Women
FMLN	Frente Farabundo Martí para la Liberación Nacional/Farabundo Martí National Liberation Front (El Salvador)
FOF	Federación Obrera Femenina/Women Workers' Federation (Bolivia)
FOL	Federación Obrera Local/Local Workers' Federation (Bolivia)
FPL	Fuerzas Populares de Liberación Farabundo Martí/Farabundo Martí Popular Liberation Forces (El Salvador)
ILD	International Labor Defense (United States)
JCR	Junta de Coordinación Revolucionaria/Revolutionary Coordination Board
MIR	Movimiento de Izquierda Revolucionario/Revolutionary Left Movement (Chile)

MLN-T	Movimiento de Liberación Nacional Tupamaros/Tupamaros National Liberation Movement (Uruguay)
MNR	Movimiento Nacionalista Revolucionario/Nationalist Revolutionary Movement (Bolivia)
OAS	Organization of American States/Organización de Estados Americanos
OLAS	Organización Latinoamericana de Solidaridad/Latin American Solidarity Organization
ORPA	Organización Revolucionaria del Pueblo en Armas/Revolutionary Organization of People in Arms (Guatemala)
OSS	Office of Strategic Services (United States)
PCC	Partido Comunista de Cuba/Cuban Communist Party
PCE	Partido Comunista del Ecuador/Communist Party of Ecuador
PCP	Partido Comunista Puertorriqueño/Puerto Rican Communist Party
PDLP	Partido de los Pobres/Party of the Poor (Mexico)
PGT	Partido Guatemalteco del Trabajo/Guatemalan Workers' Party
PIR	Partido de la Izquierda Revolucionaria/Revolutionary Left Party (Bolivia)
PNPR	Partido Nacionalista de Puerto Rico/Puerto Rican Nationalist Party
POR	Partido Obrero Revolucionario/Revolutionary Workers' Party (Bolivia)
PPD	Partido Popular Democrático/Popular Democratic Party (Puerto Rico)
PRT-B	Partido Revolucionario de los Trabajadores – Bolivia/Bolivian Revolutionary Workers' Party
PRT-ERP	Partido Revolucionario de los Trabajadores – Ejército Revolucionario del Pueblo/Revolutionary Workers' Party – People's Revolutionary Army (Argentina)
PSE	Partido Socialista Ecuatoriano/Ecuadorian Socialist Party
PSP	Partido Socialista Popular/Popular Socialist Party (Cuba)
SNOIA	Sindicato Nacional de Obreros de la Industria Azucarera/National Union of Sugar Industry Workers (Cuba)
UAG	Universidad Autónoma de Guerrero/Autonomous University of Guerrero (Mexico)

UFC	United Fruit Company
UFR	Unidad Femenina Revolucionaria/Revolutionary Women's Unity (Cuba)
UNIA	United Negro Improvement Association
URNG	Unidad Revolucionaria Nacional Guatemalteca/ Guatemalan National Revolutionary Unity
WIDF	Women's International Democratic Federation
WIRE	Women's International Resource Exchange (United States)

INTRODUCTION

Revolutionary Actors, Encounters, and Transformations

Kevin A. Young

Long after the end of the Cold War, certain specters still haunt discussions of Latin America's twentieth-century left: the charismatic strongman, the communist ideologue slavishly subservient to the Kremlin, the middle-class youths who, "mesmerized" by the 1959 Cuban Revolution, grabbed guns and took to the hills, oblivious to the wishes of the poor rural populations into which they parachuted. The typical leftist was, for one critic, "elitist, internationalist, arrogant, and unrealistic."[1] Another writer, critiquing the Salvadoran rebels of the 1980s, describes them as middle- and upper-class individuals who were "dogmatic, sectarian," and "narrowly militaristic," and who showed a "disdain for ordinary people." In El Salvador and elsewhere, militant leftist movements gained mass support only through the use of coercion, fear, and appeals to "anti-Americanism" and other "irrational" feelings.[2] These critiques often echo the discredited *dos demonios* narrative of the Cold War, according to which "left- and right-wing extremists" terrorized Latin American populations.[3] Sometimes Washington is still cast

---

* Thanks to Diana Sierra Becerra and Sinclair Thomson for feedback on this introduction.

[1] Jorge G. Castañeda, *Utopia Unarmed: The Latin American Left after the Cold War* (New York: Knopf, 1993), 16; Michael Radu, "Introduction: Revolution and Revolutionaries," in *Violence and the Latin American Revolutionaries*, ed. Michael Radu (New Brunswick, NJ: Transaction, 1988), 7 (second quote). *Internationalist* is, of course, intended as a pejorative.

[2] Yvon Grenier, *The Emergence of Insurgency in El Salvador: Ideology and Political Will* (Pittsburgh, PA: University of Pittsburgh Press, 1999), 89, 70, 26; Radu, "Introduction," 8.

[3] Jonathan C. Brown, *Cuba's Revolutionary World* (Cambridge, MA: Harvard University Press, 2017), 15. See also David Stoll, *Between Two Armies in the Ixil Towns of Guatemala* (New York: Columbia University Press, 1993); Hal Brands, *Latin America's Cold War* (Cambridge, MA: Harvard University Press, 2010). In every country but Peru right-wing

as an earnest force of restraint that "promoted moderation over rightist and leftist ideology and violence."[4]

Critiques of the left are not limited to conservative circles. Many progressive observers have stressed the traditional left's class reductionism, authoritarian decision making, and domination by urban, male, *mestizo* (mixed-race) leaders who failed to understand the complexity of oppression in their countries.[5] One typical scholar writes that "the various Lefts have been historically and notably silent on questions of ethnicity and race."[6] Progressives may celebrate the Zapatista rebels and other "new" left movements that emerged starting in the late twentieth century, but they tend to view older left movements in more negative terms.

These progressive critiques are much more grounded in reality than the conservative ones. Many leftists have indeed been deeply flawed, both personally and politically. Yet the history of the Latin American left is more diverse than these critiques tend to imply. As recent scholarship has begun to highlight, many twentieth-century leftists struggled against class exploitation and imperialism while also confronting racism, patriarchy, and other oppressions, and while seeking to build more democratic organizations and societies. Revolution, for them, meant not just the seizure of state power or a change in property relations, but also a series of other transformations in social life. Many were flexible, self-reflective, and open to critique. And rather than seeking to graft "foreign" ideologies onto their societies, they tried to adapt ideas like Marxism, anarchism, and feminism to their particular national contexts.

These practices and visions did not merely emanate from formal leaders. The contributors to this volume understand the formation of the left

---

violence (almost always aided by the United States) greatly outweighed violence by the left, and was far more often directed against civilians. For a corrective see Greg Grandin and Gilbert M. Joseph, eds., *A Century of Revolution: Insurgent and Counterinsurgent Violence during Latin America's Long Cold War* (Durham, NC: Duke University Press, 2010).

[4] Russell Crandall, *The Salvador Option: The United States in El Salvador, 1977–1992* (New York: Cambridge University Press, 2016), 10.

[5] For instance Charles R. Hale, *Resistance and Contradiction: Miskitu Indians and the Nicaraguan State, 1894–1987* (Stanford, CA: Stanford University Press, 1994); María Josefina Saldaña-Portillo, *The Revolutionary Imagination in the Americas in the Age of Development* (Durham, NC: Duke University Press, 2003); Jocelyn Viterna, *Women in War: The Micro-processes of Mobilization in El Salvador* (New York: Oxford University Press, 2013); Florencia Mallon, "Beyond Colonialism: Race and Ethnicity in the Mobilization of Indigenous People," *LASA Forum* 48, no. 2 (2017): 17–19.

[6] Deborah J. Yashar, "The Left and Citizenship Rights," in *The Resurgence of the Latin American Left*, ed. Steven Levitsky and Kenneth M. Roberts (Baltimore, MD: Johns Hopkins University Press, 2011), 192.

as a contested historical process in which rank-and-file actors and external constituencies, not simply top party leaders, played vital roles. Oppressed groups within the left, or whom the left sought to organize, often exercised important influences on left ideology and practice. Leftist women and indigenous people, in particular, helped reshape leftist politics in a number of the cases examined here, but their interventions are often ignored in studies that emphasize the left's sexism and racism. Uncovering the negotiations over power, platforms, and everyday practices on the left is essential to an accurate understanding of past revolutionaries' successes and failures. Those stories, in turn, hold important lessons for peoples struggling for emancipation in the twenty-first century. Learning the lessons of the past requires revisiting the history of the Latin American left with fresh eyes, unencumbered by Cold War categories and other blinders.

DEFINING THE LEFT

In broad terms, the left might be defined to include all those who work for equity in one or more realms of society: the economy, the home, the community, and the polity. It is often defined much more narrowly, to include only those who self-identify as socialist, communist, or anarchist. This restrictive definition fails to include the countless organizations, communities, and individuals who fight for a more egalitarian society but for various reasons do not formally affiliate with the left. It misses, for instance, the radical Zapatista peasant movement in Mexico in the 1910s. It misses the Zapatista-inspired movement led by Rubén Jaramillo a few decades later, which confronted capitalism and autocracy but did not directly identify as socialist.[7] It misses labor activists around Latin America who were not explicitly anti-capitalist but who struggled against capitalist power in meaningful ways. And it misses many movements of indigenous people, Afro-descendants, women, and other groups, which are often portrayed as strictly "identity" movements despite their incorporation of class demands.[8] Many such movements have sought revolutionary changes, whether or not they have self-identified as revolutionary

---

[7] Tanalís Padilla, *Rural Resistance in the Land of Zapata: The Jaramillista Movement and the Myth of the Pax Priísta* (Durham, NC: Duke University Press, 2008).

[8] This tendency to separate class from identity is especially common in scholarship on indigenous movements. It is also apparent in much of the broader literature on "new" social movements and in postmodern and subaltern studies scholarship that stresses fragmented experiences rather than class.

and whether they have been armed or unarmed. The point is not to claim all movements of the oppressed for the left. In fact, the self-identified Left (with a capital *L*) has often been behind the curve of popular resistance, as some of this book's chapters emphasize. Rather, this broader definition of the left is a more or less objective one based on egalitarian goals and values.[9]

The tendency to draw a sharp distinction between class and identity is largely a product of Cold War repression and of the neoliberalism imposed by business, governments, and financial institutions since the 1970s. During the Cold War those who threatened capitalist interests were threatened with torture and death (and often still are). Meanwhile, neoliberal policies of austerity, privatization, and deregulation further undercut labor unions and working-class solidarity. By erecting higher barriers to collective material empowerment, right-wing terror and neoliberalism pressured movements to emphasize ethnic, gender, and other non-class identities.[10] By the 1990s many scholars and research funders had gone even further, concluding that class and political economy were passé.

Recent scholarship on the left has begun to challenge the distinction between class and identity, in two major ways. First, it has shown that the categories themselves are closely intertwined. Non-class identities have implications for the class structure, for instance when racism informed the United Fruit Company's hiring practices and shaped workers' interactions with each other.[11] Conversely, changes in property relations or economic policy help to reshape other hierarchies, as when the Chilean agrarian reform of the early 1970s unwittingly exacerbated gender conflicts in

---

[9] Of course, many movements are progressive in some ways and conservative in others. But in most cases, a movement's core demands place it mostly on either the right or left side of the political spectrum.

[10] See for instance Charles R. Hale, "Does Multiculturalism Menace? Governance, Cultural Rights and the Politics of Identity in Guatemala," *Journal of Latin American Studies* 34, no. 3 (2002): 485–524; Carol Anderson, *Eyes off the Prize: The United Nations and the African American Struggle for Human Rights, 1944–1955* (Cambridge: Cambridge University Press, 2003); Lesley Gill, *A Century of Violence in a Red City: Popular Struggle, Counterinsurgency, and Human Rights in Colombia* (Durham, NC: Duke University Press, 2016). For some movements this change of emphasis was mostly a strategic discursive choice made under great duress, while for others it reflected a deeper ideological shift.

[11] Phillipe I. Bourgois, *Ethnicity at Work: Divided Labor on a Central American Banana Plantation* (Baltimore, MD: Johns Hopkins University Press, 1989); Cindy Forster, *The Time of Freedom: Campesino Workers in Guatemala's October Revolution* (Pittsburgh, PA: University of Pittsburgh Press, 2001), 16, 18.

peasant households.[12] Second, movements themselves have often combined economic and noneconomic demands. Recent scholars have uncovered neglected histories of leftists who attacked multiple forms of oppression simultaneously. Visions of indigenous and black liberation were present in some leftist movements in the Andes, Central America, and the Caribbean long prior to the rise of more visible indigenous and black movements in the late twentieth century. Often these visions were promoted by indigenous and black leftists themselves.[13] In parallel fashion, leftist women often insisted on merging socialism and anti-imperialism with feminist demands. Whether or not they embraced the feminist label, they practiced a more holistic revolutionary politics than standard narratives imply.[14] Similar stories can be found in other parts of

---

[12] Heidi Tinsman, *Partners in Conflict: The Politics of Gender, Sexuality, and Labor in the Chilean Agrarian Reform, 1950–1973* (Durham, NC: Duke University Press, 2002).

[13] Greg Grandin, *The Last Colonial Massacre: Latin America in the Cold War* (Chicago, IL: University of Chicago Press, 2004); Joanna Crow, "Debates about Ethnicity, Class and Nation in Allende's Chile (1970–1973)," *Bulletin of Latin American Research* 26, no. 3 (2007): 319–38; Marc Becker, *Indians and Leftists in the Making of Ecuador's Modern Indigenous Movements* (Durham, NC: Duke University Press, 2008); Jeffrey L. Gould and Aldo A. Lauria-Santiago, *To Rise in Darkness: Revolution, Repression, and Memory in El Salvador, 1920–1932* (Durham, NC: Duke University Press, 2008); Iván Molina Jiménez, "Afrocostarricense y comunista: Harold Nichols y su actividad política en Costa Rica," *Latinoamérica: Revista de Estudios Latinoamericanos* 46 (2008): 141–68; Betsy Konefal, *For Every Indio Who Falls: A History of Maya Activism in Guatemala* (Albuquerque: University of New Mexico Press, 2010); Gerardo Rénique, "'People's War,' 'Dirty War': Cold War Legacy and the End of History in Postwar Peru," in *A Century of Revolution*, ed. Grandin and Joseph, 309–37; Steven J. Hirsch, "Anarchist Visions of Race and Space in Northern Perú, 1898–1922," in *In Defiance of Boundaries: Anarchism in Latin American History*, ed. Geoffroy de Laforcade and Kirwin Shaffer (Gainesville: University Press of Florida, 2015), 261–80; Alfonso Salgado, "'A Small Revolution': Family, Sex, and the Communist Youth of Chile during the Allende Years (1970–1973)," *Twentieth Century Communism* 8 (2015): 62–88; Anne Garland Mahler, "The Red and the Black in Latin America: Sandalio Junco and the 'Negro Question' from an Afro-Latin American Perspective," *American Communist History* 17, no. 1 (2018): 16–32.

[14] Deborah Levenson-Estrada, "The Loneliness of Working-Class Feminism: Women in the 'Male World' of Labor Unions, Guatemala City, 1970s," in *The Gendered Worlds of Latin American Women Workers: From Household and Factory to the Union Hall and Ballot Box*, ed. John D. French and Daniel James (Durham, NC: Duke University Press, 1997), 208–31; Tinsman, *Partners in Conflict*; Rosario Montoya, *Gendered Scenarios of Revolution: Making New Men and New Women in Nicaragua, 1975–2000* (Tucson: University of Arizona Press, 2012); Michelle Chase, *Revolution within the Revolution: Women and Gender Politics in the Cuban Revolution, 1952–1962* (Chapel Hill: University of North Carolina Press, 2015); Diana Carolina Sierra Becerra, "Insurgent Butterflies: Gender and Revolution in El Salvador, 1965–2015" (Ph.D. diss., University of Michigan, 2017).

the world. In the US context, the contributions of black Southern communists during the Great Depression, radical women of color in the 1970s, and gay and lesbian anti-imperialists in the 1980s are now being rediscovered. Like much new work on Latin America, recent studies of the United States left have highlighted the remarkable radical coalitions that have sometimes emerged across lines of racial, gender, and sexual difference.[15] These studies suggest that the familiar distinction between class and identity movements distorts the ways that many activists understood their own efforts.

Also unwarranted is the firm distinction often made between leftists and nationalists – another binary that was central to Cold War counter-insurgency. Some critics continue to echo Cold War discourse by depicting the historic Latin American left as blind transmitters of foreign ideologies, ignorant of national realities if not traitors to national interests. But recent scholarship has moved beyond national borders to illuminate the genuinely transnational dimensions of labor and leftist history.[16] This book expands on this work, particularly by examining leftists' negotiation of national identities and internationalist solidarity. Many of the chapters highlight the ways that leftists tried, with varying levels of success, to bring international ideas into dialogue with national political cultures.

---

[15] Robin D. G. Kelley, *Hammer and Hoe: Alabama Communists during the Great Depression* (Chapel Hill: University of North Carolina Press, 1990); Jennifer Guglielmo, *Living the Revolution: Italian Women's Resistance and Radicalism in New York City, 1880–1945* (Chapel Hill: University of North Carolina Press, 2010); Moon-Kie Jung, *Reworking Race: The Making of Hawaii's Interracial Labor Movement* (New York: Columbia University Press, 2010); Maylei Blackwell, *¡Chicana Power! Contested Histories of Feminism in the Chicano Movement* (Austin: University of Texas Press, 2011); Amy Sonnie and James Tracy, *Hillbilly Nationalists, Urban Race Rebels, and Black Power: Community Organizing in Radical Times* (Brooklyn, NY: Melville House, 2011); Emily K. Hobson, *Lavender and Red: Liberation and Solidarity in the Gay and Lesbian Left* (Berkeley: University of California Press, 2016).

[16] Aviva Chomsky, *Linked Labor Histories: New England, Colombia, and the Making of a Global Working Class* (Durham, NC: Duke University Press, 2008); Gilbert M. Joseph and Daniela Spenser, eds., *In from the Cold: Latin America's New Encounter with the Cold War* (Durham, NC: Duke University Press, 2008); Gerardo Leibner and James N. Green, eds., *Latin American Perspectives* 35, no. 2 (2008); Leon Fink, ed., *Workers across the Americas: The Transnational Turn in Labor History* (New York: Oxford University Press, 2011); Jessica Stites Mor, ed., *Human Rights and Transnational Solidarity in Cold War Latin America* (Madison: University of Wisconsin Press, 2013); de Laforcade and Shaffer, eds., *In Defiance of Boundaries*; Ernesto Semán, *Ambassadors of the Working Class: Argentina's International Labor Activists and Cold War Democracy in the Americas* (Durham, NC: Duke University Press, 2017); Aldo Marchesi, *Latin America's Radical Left: Rebellion and Cold War in the Global 1960s* (New York: Cambridge University Press, 2018).

The assumption that the left does not understand race, nation, gender, religion, or other social identities is partly a reflection of the tendency to equate the left with its formal, publicly recognized leadership. Most studies of the Latin American left have focused on top leaders and intellectuals, for understandable reasons: they are undeniably important and relatively easy to study.[17] Despite the explosion in social or "bottom-up" history since the 1970s, the study of the left (with some stellar exceptions) has lagged behind in this regard.[18] Even studies that try to highlight the role of common people in revolutionary processes often take a flat view of the left, identifying it entirely with its visible leaders and implying mass indifference or opposition to leftist governments and organizations.[19]

Studies of top leadership have made important contributions to our knowledge, but they also miss a great deal. A fuller understanding of the left must also consider the diverse thoughts and experiences of rank-and-file participants, supporters, sympathizers, and even bystanders and opponents, in addition to those of the formal leadership. The interactions within and among these various constituencies shaped

---

[17] Robert J. Alexander, *Communism in Latin America* (New Brunswick, NJ: Rutgers University Press, 1957); Michael Löwy, ed., *Le marxisme en Amérique Latine* (Paris: La Découverte, 1980); Sandra McGee Deutsch, "Gender and Sociopolitical Change in Twentieth-Century Latin America," *Hispanic American Historical Review* 71, no. 2 (1991): 259–306; Castañeda, *Utopia Unarmed;* Timothy P. Wickham-Crowley, *Guerrillas and Revolution in Latin America: A Comparative Study of Insurgents and Regimes since 1956* (Princeton, NJ: Princeton University Press, 1993); Barry Carr and Steve Ellner, eds., *The Latin American Left: From the Fall of Allende to Perestroika* (Boulder, CO: Westview, 1993); José Aricó, *La hipótesis de Justo: Escritos sobre el socialismo en América Latina* (Buenos Aires: Sudamericana, 1999); Carlos Aguirre, ed., *Militantes, intelectuales y revolucionarios: Ensayos sobre marxismo e izquierda en América Latina* (Raleigh, NC: A Contracorriente, 2013).

[18] An early exception was Peter Winn's *Weavers of Revolution: The Yarur Workers and Chile's Road to Socialism* (New York: Oxford University Press, 1986). Recent works include George Ciccariello-Maher, *We Created Chávez: A People's History of the Venezuelan Revolution* (Durham, NC: Duke University Press, 2013); Chase, *Revolution within the Revolution;* Joaquín M. Chávez, *Poets and Prophets of the Resistance: Intellectuals and the Origins of El Salvador's Civil War* (New York: Oxford University Press, 2017); Marian E. Schlotterbeck, *Beyond the Vanguard: Everyday Revolutionaries in Allende's Chile* (Berkeley: University of California Press, 2018).

[19] For example, some of the scholarship on the Cuban Revolution that purports to take a bottom-up approach understates the extent of genuine support for the Castro government after 1959, implying that Cubans in general opposed the regime or that their allegiance was the result of manipulation. See Susan Eva Eckstein, *Back from the Future: Cuba under Castro*, second ed. (New York: Routledge, 2003); Lillian Guerra, *Visions of Power in Cuba: Revolution, Redemption, and Resistance, 1959–1971* (Chapel Hill: University of North Carolina Press, 2012).

the left in myriad ways. Sometimes the influence of grassroots pressures was direct, as in the 1980s when indigenous peasants in Chiapas, Mexico, chastised the urban guerrillas who arrived in their lands with vanguardist pretensions and rigid conceptions of class struggle, in a productive clash of visions that led to the forming of the Zapatista National Liberation Army.[20] Other times it was indirect, as in 1975 when the radical Catholicism of Salvadoran peasants moved the leaders of the country's leading guerrilla faction to renounce their prior insistence on atheism.[21] Attention to these encounters, dialogues, and conflicts – the *process* of revolutionary history – is a common feature in the chapters that follow.

This book does not merely seek to challenge dismissals of the left by uncovering a few interesting counterexamples. Nor does it seek to replace negative stereotypes with a romanticized history that glosses over the left's many real flaws. Rather, we want to go beyond simplistic Cold War narratives, including those sometimes found on the left, and work toward a deeper understanding of its complex and diverse history. Wherever possible, we trace the impacts of the debates and conflicts. Many of the encounters examined here had important consequences, helping to define the left and even the broader society. Even when defeated or suppressed, dissident voices sometimes exerted long-term impacts, with their demands partially reflected in the victors' future platforms and practice. This dynamic often prevailed even within vanguard parties, which generally only enjoyed mass support when the leaders accepted a significant degree of popular initiative.

Why have the narratives critiqued in this book proven so enduring, and why have scholars only recently begun to challenge them? I have hinted at some of the likely reasons: the methodological tendency to focus on formal leadership, the often subconscious ideological residue of the Cold War, institutional and cultural pressures within academia, and the spread of an individualistic understanding of "identity politics" that empties the term of its original anti-capitalist meaning.[22] All these factors remain strong decades

---

[20] Adela Cedillo Cedillo, "El suspiro del silencio: De la reconstrucción de las Fuerzas de Liberación Nacional a la fundación del Ejército Zapatista de Liberación Nacional (1974–1983)" (Master's thesis, Universidad Nacional Autónoma de México, 2010); Christopher Gunderson, "The Provocative Cocktail: Intellectual Origins of the Zapatista Uprising, 1960–1994" (Ph.D. diss., City University of New York, 2013).

[21] Marta Harnecker, *Con la mirada en alto: Historia de las FPL a través de sus dirigentes* (San Salvador: UCA, 1993), 64–65.

[22] See the interview with Barbara Smith, one of the term's originators, in *How We Get Free: Black Feminism and the Combahee River Collective*, ed. Keeanga-Yamahtta Taylor (Chicago, IL: Haymarket, 2017), esp. 60–66.

after the Cold War's end. By the same token, however, events since 1991 have also shaped historical research in more fruitful ways. The emergence of highly visible movements of peasants, indigenous and Afro-descendant communities, feminists, environmental defenders, the urban poor, and LGBTQ people has generated a new interest in those same actors in the pre-1991 era. Those actors take center stage in much of the new research, while the urban labor unions and political parties that were long the focus of left history are decentered. Sometimes this alternative focus has shed further light on the left's ethnocentrism and other shortcomings, but in other cases it has yielded new findings that compel us to rethink traditional narratives. In this sense, movements of the post–Cold War era have *possibilized* (as one might say in Spanish) the new lines of historical inquiry and revisionist arguments sampled in this book.[23]

THE CHAPTERS

The case studies that follow represent some of the most innovative recent work on the history of the Latin American left. They span a broad geographic and temporal scope, reflecting the diversity of the left itself. While the book is far from comprehensive, it does seek to cover a wide range of countries, eras, and experiences. The chapters cover four major periods in the left's history: (1) the aftermath of the 1917 Russian Revolution, when Communist parties proliferated and diverse rebellions took place, sometimes featuring unprecedented interethnic alliances; (2) the Popular Front and early postwar period of 1935 through the early 1950s, characterized by interclass alliances in the war years followed by renewed left mobilization and state repression of leftists in the early Cold War; (3) the aftermath of the 1959 Cuban Revolution, which inspired revolutionary struggles from Mexico to Argentina; and (4) the wave of renewed revolutionary ferment concentrated in Central America in the 1970s and 1980s.

The Russian Revolution had deep impacts in Latin America. For one, it led to a decline in the influence of anarchists, who had pioneered many of the region's first labor unions, and a corresponding rise in Marxist influence on the left. Whereas anarchists eschewed party politics and the quest

---

[23] Among scholars of modern Latin America, Bolivian sociologist René Zavaleta Mercado had an especially keen awareness of how contemporary events can lead to a productive rethinking of the past. See for instance his *Towards a History of the National-Popular in Bolivia*, trans. Anne Freeland (Calcutta: Seagull, 2018), and Luis Tapia, *The Production of Local Knowledge: History and Politics in the Work of René Zavaleta Mercado*, trans. Alison Spedding (Calcutta: Seagull, 2018).

for state power, the Bolshevik triumph in Russia appeared to signal the promise of state-oriented strategies. Communist parties cropped up around Latin America, a trend hastened by the 1919 formation of the Communist International, or Comintern.[24]

One of the most interesting features of the 1920s and early 1930s were the left's attempts at interethnic organizing. In 1928 the Comintern began to emphasize the role of racial or "national" oppression alongside that of class, and also called for worker–peasant alliances against local feudal and capitalist forces.[25] This new orientation influenced Latin American communists. But perhaps just as important was the relative independence of many Marxists from the Soviet Union during these years. In contrast with the later Stalinist period, many Latin American Marxists espoused a fluid and creative approach to revolutionary organizing that sometimes entailed new alliances among the oppressed. A striking example is the massive 1927 agrarian revolt in southern Bolivia analyzed by Forrest Hylton in Chapter 1. Crucial to the revolt was an alliance between urban socialists, primarily artisans and intellectuals, and rural indigenous communities. Hylton shows that the alliance was based on a shared antipathy to predatory landlords and local officials. Also central was the demand for rural education, which the insurgents understood to be closely linked to the struggle for land and democracy. Although the revolt was suppressed, it stands as a major example of radical interethnic mobilization that declared war on capitalism, racism, and authoritarianism.

The Great Depression sent Latin America's oligarchic export economies into crisis, triggering large-scale revolts by workers and peasants in Cuba, El Salvador, Mexico, and elsewhere. In many of these cases the newly formed Communist parties played important organizing roles, sometimes expanding their prior political analysis and strategy to take into account racial oppression.[26] Many communists reached out to

---

[24] In keeping with standard usage, terms like *communist* and *socialist* are capitalized throughout this book when they refer to specific parties or organizations, and left in lowercase when they denote a more general ideological orientation.

[25] Marc Becker, "Mariátegui, the Comintern, and the Indigenous Question in Latin America," *Science & Society* 70, no. 4 (2006): 450–69. Much of the literature on the so-called Third Period (1928–35) emphasizes its sectarianism; see for example Manuel Caballero, *Latin America and the Comintern, 1919–1943* (Cambridge: Cambridge University Press, 1986). But it was also a period of creative and radical movement-building in many places.

[26] Gonzalo Sánchez, "Los bolcheviques del Líbano," in *Ensayos de historia social y política del siglo XX* (Bogotá: El Áncora, 1984), 11–111; Barry Carr, "The Mexican Communist Party and Agrarian Mobilization in the Laguna, 1920–1940: A Worker-Peasant

groups they had previously scorned in the hopes of building radical popular alliances that could put the nail in capitalism's coffin. Barry Carr's chapter on Cuba (Chapter 2) shows that Communists were the most vocal opponents of the anti-immigrant xenophobia that was enveloping Cuban society at both the elite and popular levels. While initially somewhat disdainful of black migrants from Jamaica, Haiti, and other Caribbean locations, the party had shifted its approach dramatically by 1933 and recruited a new cohort of militant black organizers. Black workers played a vital role in the sugar insurgency of late 1933, in which workers occupied dozens of plantations and mills in rural Cuba. Carr is careful not to overemphasize the role of the Communist Party, however, stressing also the "tradition[s] of struggle" and autonomous initiative of rank-and-file workers.[27] Here, as elsewhere, the course of rebellion was shaped by a dialogical encounter between the self-identified Left and the informal left.

A different type of alliance appeared during the Popular Front and World War II years, as many communists renounced class struggle and allied with more conservative forces against the threat of fascism. The war also brought closer economic, political, and military ties between Washington and most Latin American governments, including the growth of a military and intelligence apparatus that directed its energies not only against fascists – who were not very numerous or powerful in most of the region – but against leftists, whose cooperation against fascism would not spare them capitalists' wrath in the postwar period. Following a brief democratic opening at war's end, US–allied governments unleashed a wave of repression against domestic leftists and progressives, justifying their crackdowns through the rhetoric of Cold War anti-communism.[28] This juncture, spanning the late 1930s through the early 1950s, is the setting for the chapters by Becker, Power, and Young.

Marc Becker's account of the Ecuadorian indigenous movement (Chapter 3) highlights the US Federal Bureau of Investigation's (FBI's) wartime surveillance of the left, but also the vital dynamics that FBI spies missed. Despite being one of the most active and militant political forces in the country, the Ecuadorian Federation of Indians mostly escaped the

---

Alliance?" *Hispanic American Historical Review* 67, no. 3 (1987): 371–404; Gould and Lauria-Santiago, *To Rise in Darkness.*

[27] See also Barry Carr, "Mill Occupations and Soviets: The Mobilisation of Sugar Workers in Cuba, 1917–1933," *Journal of Latin American Studies* 28, no. 1 (1996): 129–58.

[28] Leslie Bethell and Ian Roxborough, eds., *Latin America between the Second World War and the Cold War, 1944–1948* (Cambridge: Cambridge University Press, 1992).

FBI's spy apparatus. Racism blinded FBI agents to the realities of indigenous political action in the countryside. Becker shows, though, that Indian activists did indeed "advance their own agendas, both alone and in collaboration with sympathetic urban allies." This history of indigenous–*mestizo* cooperation has remained hidden in part due to the biases of state agents and reporters who failed to document it.

US intelligence agents were much more attuned to the threat of Puerto Rican dissidents, who suffered imprisonment and other repression at the hands of their colonial overlord. In Chapter 4, Margaret Power analyzes the complex and evolving relationship among nationalists and communists both on the island and in the United States. While the Nationalist Party was not officially anti-capitalist, it was in some respects more radical than its Communist counterparts, particularly in its demand for national liberation. Power traces transnational debates over political platforms and vision, focusing on the personal encounters between a handful of Nationalists and Communists. She shows that the friendships among these activists played an important role in shaping their political thought and practice in the 1940s and early 1950s. The left, she notes, is not simply "an impersonal response to oppressive structures in society." Understanding it requires us to go beyond "the official transcript" by paying careful attention to interpersonal relationships, in addition to ideas and analysis.

Personal relationships were likewise essential in the alliance that arose between urban and rural anarchists in La Paz, Bolivia, in 1946 – another instance of interethnic collaboration among radicals, this time driven by demands for labor rights, autonomy, and education. In Chapter 5, I highlight several factors to explain the growth of the alliance: the urbanites' flexibility and belief in organizational federalism, the rural activists' own past history of autonomous mobilization, and the work of coalition brokers who straddled the urban–rural, Indian–*mestizo* divide. Those factors enabled the anarchists to take advantage of a temporary political opening in 1946. The opening slammed shut in 1947, when the movement was all but extinguished by state repression.

The third period covered in the book, stretching from 1959 until the early 1970s, has been the subject of many scholarly studies. The Cuban Revolution itself has inspired thousands of books and articles, though overwhelmingly focused on the leadership of Fidel Castro and Che Guevara. Michelle Chase's study (Chapter 6) breaks with this pattern, using new archival sources to uncover the role of progressive and radical women in the early development of the revolution. Chase focuses on the

Cuban women who attended an international women's conference in Santiago, Chile, in November 1959. The conference was a key site of debate over Cuban women's visions for the revolution, and also plugged the Cuban attendees into a transnational network of radical women. Chase uses the conference to reassess the state-backed Federation of Cuban Women (FMC), founded the next year. By analyzing the roles of diverse women in the process, she challenges the common argument that the FMC was "merely a top-down mass organization established by the revolutionary leadership to ensure women's support."

Among the many reverberations of the Cuban Revolution was the way it gave hope to radicals across the so-called Third World, inspiring numerous guerrilla campaigns in Latin America alone. Many of these campaigns were short-lived and easily repressed. Aldo Marchesi's chapter sheds light on how activists in Argentina, Bolivia, Chile, and Uruguay made those ill-fated decisions. In Chapter 7, Marchesi traces the emergence of a militant transnational political culture, influenced by the "new" left of the 1960s, that critiqued existing leftist currents and embraced armed struggle as the only way forward. His subjects dramatically underestimated the obstacles to revolution, however. They placed extreme stress on the importance of ideology, which led them to attribute all setbacks to "ideological weakness" and to adopt counterproductive remedies. Like the book's other authors, Marchesi stresses the role of political culture in shaping the left's actions, but he shows how, in this case, those actions proved detrimental to the left's prospects.

The leftist opposition in the southwestern Mexican state of Guerrero offers an instructive contrast. Unlike the Southern Cone militants, Guerrero's leftists garnered considerable popular support. In Chapter 8, O'Neill Blacker-Hanson shows how Genaro Vázquez, Lucio Cabañas, and other leftists made astute use of the Mexican state's own weapons, namely its educational system and the radical promises of the 1910 revolution. They drew from Marxism, but they also framed their struggle in terms of Mexico's own revolutionary nationalism. Blacker-Hanson describes Vázquez and Cabañas's non-dogmatic application of Marxist ideology to their local context, though she also asks whether their eventual shift away from nationalist discourse may have cost them some popular support. In any case, the Mexican state suppressed the threat through a "dirty war" that murdered hundreds of guerrillas and civilians in the early 1970s, the full details of which are only beginning to come to light.[29]

---

[29] O'Neill Blacker, "Cold War in the Countryside: Conflict in Guerrero, Mexico," *The Americas* 66, no. 2 (2009): 181–210; Alexander Aviña, *Specters of Revolution: Peasant*

By the early 1970s the number of active Latin American guerrilla struggles
had declined, due to their suppression by militaries and right-wing death
squads and perhaps also to the 1970 electoral triumph of Chilean socialist
Salvador Allende.[30] However, the 1973 US-backed military overthrow of
Allende signaled that neither Washington nor Latin American elites would
tolerate a democratic transition to socialism. Despite its long record of
formal democratic rule, Chile joined the ranks of countries ruled by savage
military regimes. Few dictatorships were as repressive as those in Central
America, which witnessed the growth of guerrilla insurgencies in Nicaragua,
El Salvador, and Guatemala. Central America exemplifies the profound
asymmetries of violence and power between left and right in twentieth-
century Latin America: while the left sometimes committed human rights
abuses, they were infrequent and relatively mild compared to the mass
slaughter, torture, rape, and disappearances perpetrated by right-wing
forces.[31] Moreover, the right possessed the formidable advantages of state
power, US support, and control over the economy and media.[32]

The Central American revolutionary movements were shaped by more
than just state repression, though. Their growth and political trajectory were
contested, dynamic processes shaped by rank-and-file revolutionaries, guerrilla commanders, and outside entities like the state.[33] Betsy Konefal's study
of Guatemala (Chapter 9) highlights the extent to which human choices and

---

Guerrillas in the Cold War Mexican Countryside (New York: Oxford University Press,
2014). For a broader account see Gladys McCormick, "The Last Door: Political Prisoners
and the Use of Torture in Mexico's Dirty War," *The Americas* 74, no. 1 (2017): 57–81.

[30] The Allende period has generated exciting new research over the past two decades. In
addition to sources cited above, see many recent articles in the Chilean–Russian journal
Izquierdas (www.izquierdas.cl/).

[31] According to survivor testimonies, the right in El Salvador and Guatemala committed at
least 85 and 93 percent of violent attacks, respectively. See UN Security Council, Annex,
*From Madness to Hope: The 12-Year War in El Salvador: Report of the Commission on
the Truth for El Salvador* (New York: United Nations, 1993), 35–36; Comisión para el
Esclarecimiento Histórico, *Guatemala: Memoria del silencio* (Guatemala City: CEH,
1999), 5: 42, 52.

[32] Some assert that Cuban and Soviet aid to Latin American leftists after 1959 was on a par
with US and other foreign aid to the right, but this claim is easily refuted. Tellingly, Brands
tries to support the claim by listing a series of Cuban and Soviet monetary transfers from
the Castro government to Latin American guerrillas, but in no case did the transfers
exceed $1 million (*Latin America's Cold War*, 42). US aid to El Salvador alone averaged
well over $1 million *per day* during the country's twelve-year civil war.

[33] Dirk Kruijt, *Guerrillas: War and Peace in Central America* (London: Zed, 2008);
Konefal, *For Every Indio*; Montoya, *Gendered Scenarios*; Chávez, *Poets and Prophets*;
Sierra Becerra, "Insurgent Butterflies."

relationships shaped the country's revolutionary movement. Elsewhere Konefal has shown how Maya activists pushed the armed left to incorporate anti-racism and cultural demands into the revolutionary struggle. Many Mayas participated in the guerrilla struggle, while others became deeply disillusioned with *ladino* (non-indigenous) leftists for de-emphasizing ethnic identity and culture.[34] Her chapter here adds another layer to this analysis. She uses a riveting tale about the state's kidnapping of a Maya revolutionary, Emeterio Toj, to explore the role of personal trust in political relationships. When Toj escaped and tried to return to the guerrillas, they would surely have taken him for a spy if not for the intervention of a particular commander, whose prior experience in Maya villages helped him determine that Toj had not betrayed the movement.

The importance of human choices and actions is also evident in Diana Sierra Becerra's study of radical women in El Salvador's FMLN guerrilla coalition in Chapter 10, which challenges those who dismiss the FMLN as sexist, class-reductionist, and excessively focused on military struggle. By expanding the focus beyond the top commanders, Sierra Becerra shows that rank-and-file women, including civilians, were vital players in the political organizing work that undergirded the FMLN's military strength. Taking up arms did not signify the abandonment of grassroots organizing and educational work. Perhaps most importantly, many revolutionary women developed a feminist consciousness and practice in the course of wartime struggles, and they succeeded in influencing gender relations in the guerrilla territories. This story challenges Cold War binaries that pit armed struggle against feminism and feminism against socialism.

HISTORY AND THE RADICAL IMAGINATION
IN THE TWENTY-FIRST CENTURY

Why dwell on this history? Haven't post–Cold War developments fundamentally changed the region? Is the left even relevant in today's context of neoliberal globalization, when the very idea of utopias invites scorn from intellectuals and politicians, and when talk of socialism – at least in the radical sense of working-class control of the economy – is often derided as an archaic "leftover" of a bygone era?[35]

---

[34] Konefal, *For Every Indio*.
[35] Castañeda, *Utopia Unarmed*; Jorge G. Castañeda and Marco A. Morales, eds., *Leftovers: Tales of the Two Latin American Lefts* (New York: Routledge, 2008).

Latin America has indeed changed since the peace accords and demo-
cratizations of the late twentieth century, with many strategic implications
for the left. The route of armed struggle appears entirely futile; even the
Colombian FARC disarmed in 2016. Conversely, the electoral sphere is
more open to the left than at any prior point, with a raft of left-leaning
("Pink Tide") governments elected since 1999. At the same time, however,
capitalists have retained enormous power. Even modest progressive
reforms still face unremitting hostility from elite sectors, who possess
formidable power to block or hinder them, either through overt opposition – including successful coups in Haiti, Honduras, Paraguay, and
Brazil – or by shifting their investments elsewhere. The promoters of
neoliberalism have taken steps to lock in their own reforms and insulate
economic policy from democratic input, tying the hands of any would-be
progressive reformers. The result in most Latin American countries has
been a shallow version of democracy in which many of the vital questions
about institutions and policies are beyond the control of the electorate.[36]

Furthermore, the social landscape in which the twentieth-century left
grew has been greatly eroded. In most countries the organized left is a shell
of its former self, reduced through a combination of overwhelming state
terror in the 1970s and 1980s and the neoliberal restructuring that has
weakened labor unions. At a broader cultural level, the consolidation of
the neoliberal order and urban consumerism have corroded social bonds
and contributed to the depoliticization of popular sectors. High levels of
urban crime and violence across the region are both consequences and
causes of these trends.[37] In turn, street crime has helped fuel a resurgence
of right-wing parties that stoke "law-and-order" sentiment, most notably
with the 2018 election of the neofascist Jair Bolsonaro as president of
Brazil.

Far from rendering the left obsolete, though, the changes of recent
decades make it more relevant than ever. The Pink Tide of the early
twenty-first century resulted from massive public condemnation of poverty, inequality, and the neoliberal economic policies that exacerbate
them. Once in power, left-leaning governments adopted significant, albeit

[36] William I. Robinson, *Promoting Polyarchy: Globalization, US Intervention, and Hegemony* (Cambridge: Cambridge University Press, 1996); James E. Mahon, Jr., *Mobile Capital and Latin American Development* (University Park: Pennsylvania State University Press, 1996); John Crabtree and Francisco Durand, *Peru: Elite Power and Political Capture* (London: Zed, 2017).
[37] See especially Deborah T. Levenson, *Adiós Niño: The Gangs of Guatemala City and the Politics of Death* (Durham, NC: Duke University Press, 2013).

quite modest, policy changes that reduced poverty and injustice and asserted a degree of independence from the imperial centers. Most centrist and right-wing politicians, meanwhile, still support the basics of neoliberalism and lack a minimally viable project for addressing the region's profound economic, social, and ecological problems.[38]

The Pink Tide governments have succeeded in some ways and failed in others. Certainly they have not been as radical as many leftists had hoped, and the anti-capitalist aspirations of many leftist leaders have visibly waned since the 1970s and 1980s. Yet to the extent that these governments have faltered, the reason is not an excess of radicalism but rather their inability or unwillingness to confront capitalist power and political exclusion in more aggressive ways. Those governments' shortcomings hardly invalidate the importance of the left. In fact, the apparent stagnation of many Pink Tide projects only confirms the need to revisit some of the vibrant radical debates that took place in eras past.[39]

Collectively, the stories in this book are important for at least two reasons. First, there is value in simply uncovering hidden histories of resistance to oppression. As historian Jeffrey Gould writes, "In a world in which the very idea of fundamental social change has become chimerical, where elementary forms of human solidarity seem utopian," past examples of solidarity, courage, and creativity "should be excavated and remembered."[40] Glimpsing these forgotten moments can enhance our capacity for political action, combating the temptation to succumb to

---

[38] In this regard the strategies of center and right parties today are revealing: candidates tend to de-emphasize their neoliberal beliefs, instead garnering support by promising to stamp out crime and corruption and by riding waves of popular discontent with economic problems for which they and their sponsors are largely responsible.

[39] Among many good works on the twenty-first-century left see Emir Sader, *The New Mole: Paths of the Latin American Left* (London: Verso, 2011); Jeffrey R. Webber and Barry Carr, eds., *The New Latin American Left: Cracks in the Empire* (Lanham, MD: Rowman and Littlefield, 2013); Richard Stahler-Sholk, Harry E. Vanden, and Marc Becker, eds., *Rethinking Latin American Social Movements: Radical Action from Below* (Lanham, MD: Rowman & Littlefield, 2014); Ciccariello-Maher, *We Created Chávez*, and *Building the Commune: Radical Democracy in Venezuela* (London: Verso, 2016); Jeffery R. Webber, *The Last Day of Oppression, and the First Day of the Same: The Politics and Economics of the New Latin American Left* (Chicago, IL: Haymarket, 2017); Dario Azzellini, *Communes and Workers' Control in Venezuela: Building 21st Century Socialism from Below* (Chicago, IL: Haymarket, 2018); Steve Ellner, ed., *Latin America's Pink Tide: Breakthroughs and Shortcomings* (Lanham, MD: Rowman & Littlefield, 2020).

[40] Jeffrey L. Gould, "On the Road to 'El Porvenir': Revolutionary and Counterrevolutionary Violence in El Salvador and Nicaragua," in *A Century of Revolution*, ed. Grandin and Joseph, 116.

cynicism at a time when violence, deprivation, ecological destruction, and impunity for the perpetrators often seem overwhelming and inevitable. One of capitalism's greatest triumphs in the Cold War was to suppress the belief that a fundamentally different order is possible. For that reason alone, the radical ambitions of past leftists, and their attempts to put those ideas into practice, deserve our attention.

Beyond just celebrating past resistance, the book also seeks to inform current-day political practice by critically engaging with the thought and actions of twentieth-century leftists. Past struggles for emancipation offer many important lessons, both inspiring and cautionary. One such lesson, implicit in many of the chapters that follow, is that the left has been most successful – and most revolutionary – when it has maintained internal democracy, self-reflexivity, and humility vis-à-vis the constituencies it seeks to organize. Readers are invited to engage with our arguments and draw their own lessons.

I

Common Ground

Caciques, *Artisans, and Radical Intellectuals in the Chayanta Rebellion of 1927*

Forrest Hylton

Marx, with all the fire of his thought, has illuminated all subsequent revolutions. But Marxism itself has never produced a revolution. Rather, that has occurred when Marxism has looked to national history for the hidden roots of revolution.

– René Zavaleta Mercado[1]

On the afternoon of July 25, 1927, a young shepherdess set fire to a hillside on Florentino Serrudo's estate, launching the greatest insurrection of indigenous peasants in Bolivia since the Federal War and indigenous revolts of 1899.[2] Summoned by the sign of Santiago, the powerful Catholic warrior and patron saint of Spain, some 300 *comuneros*

* I thank Marcus Rediker, the late Michael Jiménez, the late William Roseberry, Sinclair Thomson, and Greg Grandin for their critical feedback; Erick Langer for sharing sources and encouraging this project; and Kevin Young for the spadework of translation and editing. This chapter is an abridged translation of "Tierra común: Caciques, artesanos e intelectuales radicales y la rebelión de Chayanta," in *Ya es otro tiempo el presente: Cuatro momentos de insurgencia indígena*, by Forrest Hylton, Félix Patzi, Sergio Serulnikov, and Sinclair Thomson (La Paz: Muela del Diablo, 2003), 127–87.
[1] "Ni piedra filosofal ni summa feliz," in *El Estado en América Latina* (La Paz: Los Amigos del Libro, 1990).
[2] On 1899 see Ramiro Condarco Morales, *Zárate, "el temible" Willka* (La Paz: Talleres Gráficos, 1965); Marie-Danielle Demelas, "Sobre jefes legítimos y 'vagos,'" *Historia y Cultura* 8 (1985): 51–73; René Zavaleta Mercado, *Lo nacional-popular en Bolivia* (Mexico City: Siglo XXI, 1986), 96–179; Tristan Platt, "The Andean Experience of Bolivian Liberalism, 1825–1900," in *Resistance, Rebellion, and Consciousness in the Andean Peasant World, 18th to 20th Centuries*, ed. Steve J. Stern (Madison: University of Wisconsin Press, 1987), 280–323; Pilar Mendieta Parada, "Entre el caudillismo y la modernidad: Poder local y política en la provincia de Inquisivi: El caso de Mohoza (1880–1889)" (Master's thesis, CESU-CEBEM, 2000).

(communal landholders) from surrounding *ayllus* (communities), led by those of the Jaiguari *ayllu*, descended upon the valley to occupy the estate. The insurgents began celebrating the feast of Santiago, ritualistically taking possession of the land of their ancestors and of the fruits of their own labor. Twenty-four hours later, on the night of July 26, the Jaiguari insurgents led three other *ayllus* and the tenant farmers from the estate of Andrés and Sixto Garnica in two more land takeovers.

Andrés Garnica gave a detailed description of the July 26 takeovers in a denunciation supporting the charges against the Indian leaders, which included "assault, attacks, destruction, arson, [and] theft on the Tambillos, Murifaya, and Peaña estates." Armed with "clubs, knives, and other weapons," they attacked the house where Garnica and his wife Encarnación slept.[3] With "hard blows," Garnica reported, "they laid waste using iron bars and farm tools, plus axes, picks, and hoes, and broke doors and windows to the point of leaving no trace of them."[4]

Garnica survived, despite having been tried and found guilty by the insurgents, but other landlords did not. According to Honorato Romero de Ocurí, the Jaiguari *comuneros* killed, and ate the heart of, Julio Berdeja as part of a ritual sacrifice. Near the Purpuri sanctuary honoring *Tata* Santiago, the patron of mountain spirits and shamans, they buried his bones "in the Kuntur Nasa mountain along with *q'uwa* [an herb] and other fragrances," and reciting an incantation "so that he would give them courage and continued triumphs."[5] With the arrival of the *Pachakutic* the insurgents turned the world upside down, putting it right-side up and restoring the balance of the Andean Catholic cosmos; they took both literal and symbolic possession of their territory.[6] They had waited until July 25, the day when taxes were due, and when the greatest numbers would be concentrated in the region due to the arrival of llama herders.

When the Chayanta rebellion ended, some 10,000 indigenous peasants had taken part in property seizures, acts of arson, and other forms of collective resistance in four of the nine Bolivian departments, as part of an

---

[3] *Sublevación indigenal* (1927), 1: 41, Archivo y Biblioteca Nacionales de Bolivia, Sucre.

[4] Ibid., 1: 30.

[5] Quoted in Fernando Montes, *La máscara de piedra: Simbolismo y personalidad aymaras en la historia*, second ed. (La Paz: Armonía, 1999), 381. For more testimony on ritual cannibalism see *Sublevación indigenal*, 2: 19.

[6] See Montes, *La máscara de piedra*, 209–66. Pachakutic is an Aymara term that means to return proper balance to the earth and cosmos in time and space by overturning existing structures of oppression. In Jesuit Ludovico Bertonio's vocabulary of Aymara (1612), the term is associated with a time of judgment.

uprising that spread across the southern countryside between late July and late August.[7] By the time the army and courts had "pacified" the rebellion, over 300 rebels and several landlords had died in battle. Around 200 *caciques* (indigenous community leaders) had been captured and taken to Sucre, the judicial capital of the country, where, given little food and water, they were confined to await sentencing.[8]

In 1927 the trope of the Indian "criminal" was often used in newspapers, government reports, and landlords' correspondence. Andrés Garnica and his brother Sixto referred to the "*comuneros* of the *ayllus* of Socopoco, Jaiguari, Sorotoco, and Chirarque" as "plotters and conspirators, organized in gangs of criminals."[9] However, a more novel trope also appeared in the counterinsurgent discourse: "communism."[10] Garnica accused the Indians of "preaching that all the estates belonged to their Inca ancestors, that the current owners had usurped them and it was therefore necessary to take everything by force."[11] This was one of the first elite allegations of communist-inspired revolt in Bolivian history, which, as Herbert Klein notes, "indicated a growing concern amongst the upper classes with a potential rising tide of extreme radicalism on the far left."[12] The year before, Gustavo Navarro, alias Tristán Marof, who was accused of having led the Chayanta rebellion, had published his book *La justicia del inca*, a homage to the "socialist" ancient indigenous civilizations that also predicted a social revolution that would restore Bolivia's Indians to their prior glory.[13]

---

[7] Erick Langer gives a figure of 10,000 based on prefectural reports from Chuquisaca department; "Andean Rituals of Revolt: The Chayanta Rebellion of 1927," *Ethnohistory* 37, no. 3 (1990): 229. The Ministry of Government gave figures anywhere between 12,000 and 50,000; see Angela Grünberg, "The Chayanta Rebellion of 1927, Potosí, Bolivia" (Ph.D. diss., St. Antony's College, Oxford, 1996), 132.

[8] After forty days in prison under these conditions they started a hunger strike; Grünberg, "Chayanta Rebellion," 140.

[9] *Sublevación indigenal*, 1: 40.

[10] During and after the Chaco War with Paraguay (1932–35), "communism" would become the official explanation for all rural unrest. René Danilo Arze Aguirre, *Guerra y conflictos sociales: El caso rural boliviano durante la campaña del Chaco* (La Paz: CERES, 1987), 22.

[11] *Sublevación indigenal*, 1: 40. Contrary to what Garnica alleged, I have found no evidence that the insurgents invoked Inca symbols.

[12] Herbert Klein, *Parties and Political Change in Bolivia, 1880–1952* (Cambridge: Cambridge University Press, 1969), 97. For an earlier rebellion in La Paz department, see Roberto Choque Canqui and Esteban Alejo Ticona, *Sublevación y masacre de 1921, Jesús de Machaqa* (La Paz: CIPCA, 1996), 147.

[13] *La justicia del inca* (Brussels: Edición Latino Americana, 1926).

By exploring the connections between indigenous *caciques* and the radical urban artisans and intellectuals accused of mobilizing them, this chapter takes seriously the fears that Chayanta generated among the upper class, state officials, and the international press. Although creole elites distorted the nature and aims of Indian mobilization, the dreaded alliance – among *caciques*, urban artisans, and Socialist Party intellectuals – was not merely a paranoid illusion. The chapter goes beyond accounts focused on elite discourses of counterinsurgency, as well as those that assert the complete autonomy of the indigenous peasantry. Instead it examines the dynamics of mobilization, the formation of alliances among *caciques*, artisans, and intellectuals, and the state response.[14]

The rebels from Jaiguari in fact testified to the power of the sacred Andean sphere while also invoking republican laws, suggesting that they did not view these two sets of principles as mutually exclusive: they practiced anthropophagy, but also paid homage to republican legal norms by obtaining titles for the lands they occupied. They saw land titles as a result of longtime indigenous resistance to land theft, and their *caciques* used them as a way of asserting their own legal authority on the local level. On July 30, the same day that the Jaiguari *ayllu* led a takeover of the Guadalupe estate and ate the heart of the estate owner, Jaiguari's secretary of education, Saturnino Choque, arrived in Sucre at the house of Manuel Michel, the "Cacique General" of Sucre and Potosí.[15] Choque entered the house carrying the land titles that had belonged to Andrés Garnica, presenting them to the eleven other *caciques* who had gathered there for a meeting.

Four days later, on August 3, police raided Michel's house and arrested the twelve *caciques* inside, accusing them of rebellion and subversion, and seizing many of the documents on which this chapter is based. By the time of the raid, several prominent artisans and radical intellectuals had also been arrested in connection with the uprising, and more would be detained in the coming days.[16]

Saturnino Choque's journey to the meeting of *caciques* highlights four key aspects of the Chayanta rebellion: the demand for the restoration of

---

[14] I thus challenge one of the main assumptions of subaltern studies: the idea that elites and popular actors operate in distinct political realms. I argue that all operated within a single social totality, and that there is a history of political alliances between Indians and non-Indian opposition that predates 1927. See for instance Ranajit Guha, *Dominance without Hegemony: History and Power in Colonial India* (Cambridge, MA: Harvard University Press, 1997), xii.

[15] *Sublevación indigenal*, 1: 38–39; 2: 100.   [16] Ibid., 1: 5–6, 9v, 12.

indigenous lands, the rebels' emphasis on education, the political alliances they formed, and the demand for political representation. Prior historians have examined some of these elements. What has not been adequately understood are the ties that bound the *caciques* to urban organizers – tailors, lawyers, and writers – with whom they shared a commitment to redistribute wealth and property, build rural schools, and reestablish communal ownership of the land under the control of the *ayllus*.

The Chayanta rebellion had many precedents. It followed decades of indigenous legal battles to reclaim usurped lands, and also built on regional traditions of ritual war and sacrifice.[17] The insurgents combined pre-Incan forms of community struggle and claims-making – as expressed in the sacrifice and burial of Julio Berdeja – with colonial norms about the proper relation between people and the sovereign and a commitment to preserving the Indian community as a corporate entity holding land in common. The *caciques* renewed the anticolonial ideas and practices of revolution that had been forged in the 1780s and again in the 1890s. They used republican concepts of citizenship, rights, and legal equality to denounce what they called slavery. In 1927 they also drew upon revolutionary ideas like direct democracy, alliances among oppressed sectors, and resistance to state policies – of which they had more practical knowledge than their urban allies did. While the language of engagement with both allies and the state was Spanish, the conceptualization of historical change was clearly indigenous.

Numerous state officials highlighted the "communist" element to explain the revolt. But despite their claims of a national-level communist conspiracy, the leadership was exercised at the local and regional levels. The rebels sought autonomy for the *ayllus* – communal control over lands and political officials – by means of trials and ritual sacrifices, but only after legal means had proven ineffective. This was not a movement controlled "from outside" or "from above" by communists, in Eric Hobsbawm's terms.[18] Saturnino Choque's trip to the house of Manuel Michel shows that Marcelino Burgos, who served as judge and executioner in the Guadalupe valley from July 27 to July 30, recognized Michel's authority in the Sucre and Potosí region. In other words, the Chayanta rebellion was directed by a chain of *caciques* with Manuel Michel in Sucre and Marcelino Burgos in the Guadalupe valley. The urban radicals did not lead the

---

[17] Tristan Platt, *Los guerreros de Cristo: Cofradías, misa solar y guerra regenerativa en una doctrina Macha (siglos XVII–XX)* (La Paz: Plural, 1996).

[18] E. J. Hobsbawm, "Peasants and Politics," *Journal of Peasant Studies* 1, no. 1 (1973): 11.

movement, contrary to the allegations of landlords, journalists, and certain government officials.

However, prior to the rebellion there were important connections between the two groups that merit a closer look. Government officials in charge of suppressing, investigating, and analyzing the rebellion were correct to explore the links among *caciques*, artisans, and radical intellectuals in Sucre and Potosí, though they were unable to understand them as evidence of a genuine political coalition. As Olivia Harris and Xavier Albó have argued, the Bolivian left at the time was making a concerted attempt "to fuse Marxism and *indigenismo*," and thus "the moment was very conducive to such coalitions."[19] While they did not direct the rebellion either ideologically or tactically, urban radicals figured prominently in the context in which it developed. Unlike their Indian comrades, they had skills, as well as access to printing presses, that they could utilize within the dominant creole-*mestizo* society. They put their skills and presses in the service of the insurgent *caciques* in May and June 1927, prior to the rebellion. The documents that the police seized from Michel in the August 3 raid, plus Michel's testimony before a district prosecutor on August 10, indicate the importance of the ties between the network of *caciques* and the most radical wing of the Bolivian labor movement in the first half of 1927.

In the next section I review press reports and trial testimonies on Chayanta, locating the rebellion within a cycle of struggle that began in 1914. In the third section I examine the connections among Manuel Michel and the local leaders known as "school mayors," and the struggle for land, schools, and local power. The fourth section discusses the history of alliances between *caciques* and urban activists from the mid-1920s until the 1927 revolt, showing that elite fears of collaboration were not without basis. In the conclusion I discuss Chayanta's role in the crisis of the oligarchic republic, as evidenced by the state responses that the revolt generated.

Given the miscommunication and distrust that divided indigenous-peasant movements from workers in Latin America between the 1930s and 1980s, the Chayanta rebellion deserves close scrutiny. The revolt failed to become a revolution due to fierce repression and the absence of a complementary insurrection by urban artisans, as well as its limited scale. But Chayanta nonetheless had national, and even international,

---

[19] Olivia Harris and Xavier Albó, *Monteras y guardatojos: Campesinos y mineros en el norte de Potosí* (La Paz: CIPCA, 1986 [1975]), 68–69.

repercussions. It also illuminates historical possibilities that were suppressed in later decades, demonstrating that neither the "new" social movements nor the "new" left are as new as we often think.

CHAYANTA IN HISTORICAL PERSPECTIVE

Although previous studies of Chayanta neglect the communist alliance among *caciques*, artisans, and radical intellectuals, for both Bolivian and international reporters it was often the key element, since they viewed the indigenous insurgents as an unthinking mass incapable of organizing their own resistance, who blindly followed the directions of "outside agitators."[20] An Associated Press article appearing on the front page of the *New York Times* noted that the "rising is blamed on reds." The article began: "Armed with clubs and slingshots, 80,000 descendants of the ancient Inca Indians are on the warpath ... slaying whites, burning farmhouses and endeavoring to destroy every vestige of the white man's civilization."[21]

The *Times* article's claim of a race war echoed the reports that the Bolivian Ministry of Government and Justice had already published in the La Paz press. The idea that race war was central to an "Incan" revolution was also expressed by landlord Andrés Garnica and repeated in debates in the Bolivian Senate. By mid-August, the Bolivian government and the national and international press had agreed on the framing of the Chayanta uprising as both a communist threat to the capitalist order and a race war. For the counterinsurgent state, the "race war" trope was the most effective way to politically discredit its adversaries and justify its repression.

The south, which included the country's major mining center, faced the "Indian threat": the cities of Oruro and Sucre were located in "the centre [*sic*] of the disturbed region" (Figure 1.1). By mid-August provisions were growing scarce, and the Potosí railroad then under construction was threatened as the uprising spread.[22] Troops arrived to carry out what the government called "pacification." At stake were the tens of millions of dollars that the Bolivian government owed US creditors.[23] From the perspective of financiers, foreign investors, the US government, and

---

[20] On this trope in the discourse of counterinsurgency, see Ranajit Guha, *Elementary Aspects of Peasant Insurgency in Colonial India* (Durham, NC: Duke University Press, 1999), 222–25.

[21] "80,000 Inca Indians Revolt in Bolivia," *New York Times*, August 13, 1927, 1.

[22] "Indian Rebellion Spreads in Bolivia," *New York Times*, August 14, 1927, 5.

[23] Herbert Klein, *Bolivia: The Evolution of a Multi-Ethnic Society* (New York: Oxford University Press, 1982), 79.

FIGURE 1.1 Bolivia.
Source: Forrest Hylton and Sinclair Thomson, *Revolutionary Horizons: Past and Present in Bolivian Politics* (London: Verso, 2007). Reproduced with permission of Verso.

Bolivian political and economic elites, the uprising threatened the center of capitalist accumulation in the country: the mining-railroad complex. Perhaps that is why the *New York Times* followed events so closely.

According to the *Times*, the uprising had two fundamental causes: "dissatisfaction over the distribution of land, coupled with instigation on the part of agitators." The paper nonetheless reassured readers that "the white man's civilization" would be protected from the contagion that the indigenous insurgency represented, since Bolivian troops had access to weapons made in the United States and England: "The rebels, despite their preponderant numbers, are no match for the soldiers, who are splendidly trained and equipped with the most modern war material. Consequently it is expected that the movement will be stamped out, although perhaps not before many lives have been sacrificed."[24] The article did not specify *whose* lives would be sacrificed, but reported that 100 Indians had died and many injured in a single battle, whereas only two soldiers had died as a result of that battle.[25] Its explanation, meanwhile, reflected a simplistic materialist analysis, citing the two simple causes already mentioned: land ownership and communist agitation.

Across the border in Puno, the Peruvian army reinforced its base, fearing that the conflict might traverse national borders as Túpac Amaru's 1780 revolt had.[26] The Bolivian army, with thousands of soldiers stationed in La Paz, was haunted by the specter of Túpac Katari. Elites throughout the southern Andes apparently believed that the anticolonial leaders who had been executed long before were going to return "as millions."[27] For the first time since the 1899 rebellion, when southern insurgents had destroyed the railroad, foreign investment in infrastructure was also threatened. And as the *Times* noted, there was an exodus of large landlords to the cities, and "fears are voiced by officials that if the movement reaches La Paz it might easily assume the nature of a catastrophe."[28]

However, unlike real catastrophes, the Chayanta uprising began after decades – in fact, centuries – of community organization and agitation against land expropriation, which utilized both the legal system and direct action. After the Liberal Party triumph in 1899, a group of defeated regional elites that included Andrés and Sixto Garnica, Nicanor Serrudo, and Julio Berdeja had expanded their landholdings at the expense of Indian communities which would become active centers of

---

[24] "80,000 Inca Indians Revolt."

[25] The *Times* may have been referring to an August 6 battle in which almost a hundred Indians were killed. See Manuel Diez Canseco, *Memoria de Gobierno y Justicia presentada al H. Congreso Nacional de 1927 por el Ministro Doctor Manuel Diez Canseco* (La Paz: Litografías e Imprenta Unida, 1927), 296.

[26] See Marie-Daniele Demelas, "Darwinismo a la criollo: Darwinismo social en Bolivia, 1880–1910," *Historia Boliviana* 1, no. 2 (1981): 55–82; Brooke Larson, "Andean Highland Peasants and the Trials of Nation-Making during the Nineteenth Century," in *The Cambridge History of Native American Peoples: South America*, ed. Frank Salomon and Stuart B. Schwartz (Cambridge: Cambridge University Press, 1999), 3: 563.

[27] The famous last words of Túpac Katari, executed in La Paz in 1781, were reportedly, "I will return as millions."

[28] "Indian Rebellion Spreads."

the Chayanta movement. Serrudo and Berdeja had occupied public offices in order to enrich themselves, and all of them – Serrudo, Berdeja, and the Garnica brothers – had been accused of raping the wives and daughters of the tenants living on their estates. Valley communities struggled not only to reclaim their lands but also to stop sexual violence and end the forced labor that they called "slavery." Thus the insurgents' program reflected the multiple grievances and concerns of the tenant farmers.

The July 27 trial at Jaiguari included testimony about the amount, intensity, and wages of estate work. Tenants accused Andrés Garnica of buying sheep at artificially low prices, selling goods at exorbitant ones, engaging in abusive rent practices, and frequently insulting them.[29] Tenant farmer José González said the landlords exploited peasants through taxes, forced labor, and rack-renting. He reported that "all the land rents and taxes go up each year" and that "he buys sheep from us at artificially low prices [*un precio que no vale*]."[30] Another laborer testified that "if a sheep dies, we have to pay him for a large adult sheep," and that "it costs us one *boliviano* to transport goods to Sucre on a donkey, but he pays us just 40 cents." Furthermore, "he makes us work from dawn to dusk and for just 30 cents, and he works us like his slaves."[31]

The experience of exploitation under the system of oligarchic capitalism varied by gender. Life on the Garnicas' haciendas was even more oppressive for women than for men, as the ever-present risk of sexual assault suggests. Three tenant women accused Andrés Garnica of rape. One, "Dolores Villacortes, an older married woman," testified that he "tried to abuse her, offering her five *bolivianos*," but "she refused." Another elderly woman, Timotea Micaco, testified that Garnica habitually assaulted both married women and girls who tended sheep and cattle in the fields. The widow Juana Torres added that Garnica took advantage of the wives and girls who did domestic labor in his house, forcing them to have sex with him and punishing those who refused: he would "forcibly summon the female *pongos* [captive laborers] to his house and commit abuses" against them.[32] The rape of female tenants (who were, of course, sisters, daughters, and wives) threatened the already limited power of the male domination – understood in terms of patriarchal honor – that the male tenants exercised over the sexuality and reproductive lives of the women in their homes.

---

[29] *Sublevación indigenal*, 1: 41.   [30] Ibid., 2: 101.   [31] Ibid., 2: 103.
[32] Ibid., 2: 101v–102.

This crisis was exacerbated by what Tristan Platt has called "the first agrarian reform" in Bolivia, the large-scale expropriation of indigenous lands that began in earnest in the 1880s. As US geographer George McCutchen McBride noted in 1920, "The extinction of the communities is becoming more rapid each year, particularly since the construction of railroads has stimulated the development of industries, commerce, and agriculture, increasing the demand for farming land."[33] After 1910 this process gave rise to rebellions like Chayanta as well as a national network of indigenous community leaders, the *caciques apoderados*, who struggled against wealthy landlords who had dispossessed entire communities. The *caciques* in Chayanta participated in this network, using an 1883 law that reaffirmed the validity of colonial-era land titles in republican courts.[34] The Chayanta rebellion should be understood as the culmination of this indigenous resistance going back to the 1880s.[35]

The *caciques'* strategy involved five elements: the search for colonial land titles for the expropriated lands; direct communal resistance to land surveyors; refusing to perform forced labor on the haciendas; the public denunciation of local authorities' abuses; and the establishment of rural schools. At times their resistance erupted into outright rebellion, starting with the 1914 uprising that began in Pacajes province and spread to four other provinces in the department of La Paz. The rebels of 1914 sought to confront land usurpation, forced labor, and the corruption of local officials. They demanded that communities themselves be allowed to name their own representatives. Thus they sought to recoup their land and to win back political power at the local level.[36] In similar fashion, struggles for local democracy and indigenous schools eventually led to the 1921 uprising at Jesús de Machaqa. Though the state unleashed a massacre in response, the repression exposed the emptiness of its *indigenista* rhetoric,

---

[33] George McCutchen McBride, *The Agrarian Indian Communities of Highland Bolivia* (New York: Oxford University Press, 1921), 27.

[34] Tristan Platt, *Estado boliviano y ayllu andino: Tierra y tributo en el norte de Potosí* (Lima: Instituto de Estudios Peruanos, 1982), 73–111; Silvia Rivera Cusicanqui and Taller de Historia Oral Andina (THOA), *Ayllus y proyectos de desarrollo en el Norte de Potosí* (La Paz: Aruwiyiri, 1987), 47; THOA, *Santos Marka T'ula, el cacique apoderado de las comunidades de Qallapata* (La Paz: THOA, 1984); Juan Félix Árias (Waskar Ari Chachaki), *Historia de una esperanza: Los apoderados espiritualistas de Chuquisaca, 1936–1964* (La Paz: Aruwiyiri, 1994).

[35] Silvia Rivera Cusicanqui, *"Oprimidos pero no vencidos": Luchas del campesinado aymara y qhechwa, 1900–1980* (La Paz: Hisbol/UNRISD, 1984), 37.

[36] Rivera Cusicanqui, *"Oprimidos pero no vencidos"*, 43–44, 47.

and was unsuccessful in quelling the growing resistance. Smaller uprisings soon proliferated, particularly in the south.

As early as 1923, the Garnica brothers' problems with their tenants and with neighboring *comuneros* led them to request government forces to protect Peaña and Murifaya, estates the insurgents would seize in 1927. Over the next three years, several nearby landlords also complained that tenants were refusing to work or pay rent, claiming that they were in fact the "exclusive owners" of the properties. Similar claims appeared in many tenant legal petitions. Already in these years the *caciques* were apparently in contact with each other, organizing schools, demanding the return of their lands, and starting to establish their own local authority.[37]

Indigenous resistance after 1910 sometimes used violent means, but legal means were a much more common way of trying to reclaim lands and halt the abuses of local authorities. *Caciques* often traveled hundreds of miles in search of old land titles. However, their preference for legal means did not stop them from organizing violent revolts against landlords and local authorities when the legal strategy proved ineffective.[38]

LAND, LOCAL AUTHORITY, AND THE POLITICS OF EDUCATION

Chayanta must also be understood in the context of the emergence of national-popular politics in the 1920s. In 1921 the Republican Party ousted the Liberal Party in a coup, placing Bautista Saavedra in power.[39] The Republican opposition was composed of elites excluded from power by the Liberals in La Paz, as well as popular sectors formally excluded from political participation: artisans lacking clientelistic ties to the Liberals, *caciques* of indigenous communities, and an incipient but growing proletariat including workers in the transport, textile, communications, construction, and mining industries. With the end of World War I and the formation of the Third International, new revolutionary ideas began to have influence among portions of the Bolivian labor movement.

---

[37] Grünberg, "Chayanta Rebellion," 195–214.

[38] Rivera Cusicanqui and THOA, *Ayllus y proyectos*, 49–57. On this combination of legal and extralegal means in Bolivian history see also Sergio Serulnikov, *Subverting Colonial Authority: Challenges to Spanish Rule in Eighteenth-Century Southern Andes* (Durham, NC: Duke University Press, 2003).

[39] Marta Irurozqui, "Partidos políticos y golpe de estado en Bolivia: La política nacional-popular de Bautista Saavedra, 1921–1925," *Revista de Indias* 54, no. 200 (1994): 145.

The rhetoric of Saavedra and the Republicans promoted the virtues of solidarity and cooperation in place of liberal individualism, flirting with anarchist and socialist ideas in an effort to co-opt the new radical forces appearing in the wake of the war. The Saavedra administration blamed landlords, priests, and local government officials for the problems in the countryside and proposed strengthening the central government as the solution. State-funded schools would make the Indians into citizens and would help them defend themselves against creoles and *mestizos* in the courts. Education, understood in paternalistic "civilizing" terms, would incorporate the Indian into the nation.

Although *caciques* had proposed literacy campaigns in 1900, and liberal governments had built some rural schools in the 1910s, only in 1919 did the *caciques apoderados* begin to foreground the demand for education. That year they also called for a nationwide demarcation of lands, seizing on a legislative proposal that Saavedra introduced in Congress. They insisted that education was essential to the land struggle, and in their quest for it they would seek to forge new alliances with members of creole-*mestizo* society, including government officials.[40] The *caciques* sought to take advantage of proposals from above in order to advance proposals from below, by using the central government to discipline rural landlords.

Although President Saavedra repressed labor strikes and indigenous uprisings, starting in 1923 he mounted a rhetorical attack against the large landlords who had come to dominate the countryside during the Liberal era. He accused Liberal landlords of being abusive, unproductive, and obstacles to national progress. This campaign included the promotion of national education in rural locales. In 1923 Saavedra issued an Executive Decree on Indian Literacy. Along with land, education was the source of greatest conflict, because it threatened the unchecked power of the landlords over indigenous communities by introducing central state authority for the first time. Since Saavedra quickly lost the support of the regional oligarchs, he tried to use rural communities and the proletariat as levers to implement the central government's decrees in local contexts.[41] He thus

---

[40] Marta Irurozqui, "Ebrios, vagos y analfabetos: El sufragio restringido en Bolivia, 1826–1952," *Revista de Indias* 56, no. 208 (1998): 731–37. The *caciques* believed that the Republicans would help them recover their stolen lands. Instead, the new government massacred Indian rebels who tried to reclaim them. The same mistaken expectation had led an earlier generation of *caciques* to rise up in support of the Liberal Party against the Conservatives in the 1890s.

[41] Irurozqui, "Partidos políticos," 143–48.

opened a political space that was quickly filled by the *caciques apoderados* and the most radical segment of the labor movement. These forces grew increasingly independent of the government's oversight, demanding land, education, and political and economic freedom, as the next section will show.

Many of the *caciques* came either from *ayllus* like Jaiguari – strong, intact, and close to areas of hacienda expansion – or from those that had been dispossessed. Manuel Michel came from one, Soreche, that had been evicted after the Liberals defeated the Conservatives in the 1899 war (thanks to Indian participation on the Liberal side). The *ayllus* that Michel represented had "sold" fourteen times as much land as any other nearby *ayllu* in the quarter-century that followed the Liberal victory.[42] They even lacked corn to exchange with their kinfolk who migrated back to the area each May from the highlands in accordance with the agricultural and religious calendar. As George McCutchen McBride said of the area, "Here practically all the land that is sheltered and well enough watered to make maize cultivation possible has already passed out of aboriginal possession."[43] Land dispossession and its corollaries, labor exploitation and sexual violence, led to local protests and to greater coordination with protest networks in other regions like La Paz, as well as with radical activists from the southern labor movement like Rómulo Chumacero, Gustavo Navarro, and Víctor Vargas Vilaseca.

Hacienda expansion in the valley disrupted the agricultural and religious calendar that regulated the rhythms of rural life, unsettling the *ayllus'* relationship with their land, their relatives, and the Andean Catholic cosmos. *Ayllu* subsistence in Chayanta was guaranteed through exchanges among familial networks of agricultural products from different microclimates, with the schedule based on Catholic holidays. In the Copavilque valley, one important center of the rebellion, communities from all five Bolivian departments involved in the uprising – Oruro, La Paz, Chuquisaca, Potosí, and Cochabamba – had lands, a fact that helps explain the revolt's broad geographic reach.

Education, as noted, was the most novel aspect of the insurgents' demands. In the weeks prior to the July 1927 uprising, Michel and his secretary, Saturnino Navarro, wrote letters to other *caciques* and local officials in which they stressed the role of education in the creation of a better future. As they saw it, education was a means of Indian self-

---

[42] Platt, *Estado boliviano y ayllu andino*, 130, 133.
[43] McCutchen McBride, *Agrarian Indian Communities*, 19.

defense and emancipation. As we will see below, urban educators and activists like Rómulo Chumacero and Víctor Vargas had a similar concept of education as a means of self-liberation. Both movements saw education as the only way to ensure the real political participation of the exploited classes and races in national life.

On July 18, 1927, Manuel Michel, acting in his capacity as chief *cacique* of Chuquisaca department, alongside education commissioner Agustín Saavedra, nominated Camilo Yali as "school mayor" for the Tarabuco region.[44] Michel and Saavedra urged Yali to "take decisive action to promote Indian literacy by founding free rural Indian schools," and to solicit "moral and, especially, economic resources" from parents to build and maintain the schools.[45] Yali then designated Germán Yucra the *cacique* of Mojocoya, a "title that helped me organize the schools," Yucra later testified.[46] The nominations of Yali and Yucra were both approved by the rector of the University of Chuquisaca, who had the legal power to grant licenses to indigenous schools in the department.

Through education, Michel and Saavedra sought to build "a new country where truth and justice for all prevail."[47] Two days before the Chayanta rebellion began, the *caciques* wrote to Camilo Yali again, citing the university rector as an ally in their struggle for education.[48] Michel and Saavedra ordered Yali to show their letters to local parents and explain to them "in *Quechua*" the role of the "school mayors." They emphasized that "each indigenous parent should reflect" on how "we have lived for so long, and continue to live, in the darkest and most shameful ignorance. We have no understanding of life, country, or society; we are truly half-animal . . . .the Republic in its hundred years of existence has not been able to remedy the condition of the disinherited Indian." For Michel and Saavedra "the only way of saving ourselves from the dark veil of ignorance that covers our eyes" was "to build education centers."[49] Given that these statements were made two days before the biggest uprising since 1899, the use of the word "ignorance" should be read as

---

[44] McCutchen McBride found Tarabuco to have "some of the strongest communities in the republic." Ibid., 20.

[45] *Sublevación indigenal*, 2: 32.   [46] Ibid., 2: 23v.   [47] Ibid., 2: 32.

[48] They reminded Yali that "the school mayor is *required* to make efforts to establish schools and to give weekly reports to the Cacique [Michel] and education commissioner [Saavedra]." Community members were not allowed to decline a nomination to a public position, and their work was supervised to ensure its completion. See the testimony of Matías and Felipe Reinaga in ibid., 2: 16–17.

[49] Ibid., 2: 17.

a discursive strategy in which the *caciques* used dominant stereotypes to reject exploitation and neocolonial domination. In light of the insurgency that followed, the fact that they called themselves "half-animal" can only be understood as an effort to bring about a "country where truth and justice for all prevail."

The *caciques* who met in Michel's house at the end of July discussed both education and the land takeovers. They agreed to establish schools in each village of Potosí and Chuquisaca. The day of the police raid, Michel told his secretary that "I handed over the [recovered] property to the *ayllu* and to all the *ayllus*, both in Pocoata and Macha, so they will be its owners, and to the Jaiguari tenants I gave the eight *arrienderos* [strips of land]."[50] Clearly Michel measured his authority not by his ownership of land but by his ability to determine the use of the occupied land. His statement also suggests the degree of programmatic and tactical unity between tenant farmers and communities in the region.

The *caciques* also discussed the alliances that they had formed with urban radicals Gustavo Navarro and Alberto Murillo, based on a shared commitment to obtaining rural education, locally designated authorities, and the recovery of communal lands. Saturnino Choque, Jaiguari's "commissioner for the founding of schools," described the basis for the alliance:

Alongside Michel's arguments about the reclaiming of our lands and the need to start schools conducive to that goal, Secretary General Saturnino Navarro made the same arguments and, since he was the only one who knew how to read and write, he read aloud some printed materials … that almost always came to the same conclusion: that it was our obligation to work together to recover our lands, with severe punishments for those who refuse to take part either personally or by paying dues.[51]

Saturnino Navarro, who had served as Michel's secretary since 1926, stated: "I read them the news, [including] a paper in which Alberto Murillo Calbimonte and Gustavo Navarro attest that the *cacique* Manuel Michel had attended the workers' congress held in Oruro [in April 1927] and that he belongs to the Socialist Party."[52] Education served to bridge rural communities, urban radicals, and the central government, who all agreed that Indians must learn to read and write. But violent opposition by landlords and local officials hindered any potential literacy campaign.

---

[50] Ibid., 2: 104.   [51] Ibid., 2: 9v, 16v.   [52] Ibid., 2: 13.

The landlords had reason to oppose indigenous education, given that the *caciques* wanted to educate Indians to recover their stolen lands and elect their own local authorities. Prior to the rebellion, the Minister of Government and Justice, Manuel Diez Canseco, reported that "hundreds of school buildings have been built in recent years" due to Indians actively "request[ing] the necessary help of public officials." Unlike landlords, Diez Canseco hailed this process as auguring "the incorporation of the Indian into national life" as "a good citizen."[53] The *caciques* took advantage of the paternalistic and assimilationist attitudes of officials like Diez Canseco, successfully invoking the cause of education in order to garner the central government's support against regional and local elites.

By the end of May, however, Socialist Party activists including Michel and Navarro were calling for the immediate overthrow of the government. The letter that Michel wrote to President Hernando Siles upon Michel's capture on August 3 must have reinforced state officials' beliefs about "communist" influence, since Michel referred to Murillo, Navarro, and Chumacero as "*compañeros*," and mentioned their organizing to establish schools. The letter suggests the importance that Michel, as General *Cacique* of Chuquisaca and Potosí, ascribed to the alliance between the *caciques* and the urban radicals:

We have learned that our *compañeros* Navarro, Chumacero, Murillo, and others are said to be inciting us to revolt, simply because they have helped us protest the many injustices of which we are victims. They, like many others, have luckily understood the need to side with the indigenous race, and they do so selflessly, giving us good advice, showing us the authorities to whom we should direct our demands, and generally seeking our improvement, especially in the education that we need. Above all, honorable Sir, we are fully convinced that state authorities, landlords, and the lettered class are tenaciously opposed to our children learning to read. So should we remain silent when our only supporters are persecuted? Have they done wrong by promoting our literacy, by standing up to the landlords, by starting an Indian Defense League? The ignorance in which [elites] keep us is the reason for our slavery, and those who seek to free us from it are righteous and human.[54]

Between April and August of 1927 the *caciques*, led by Michel, had linked up with the urban radicals of the Socialist Party. When Michel was forced to testify, rather than hiding or renouncing the connection with his Socialist Party comrades, he declared his loyalty to them. The insurgent

[53] Diez Canseco, *Memoria*, 172.   [54] *Sublevación indigenal*, 2: 96.

caciques of Chayanta welcomed coalitions with "righteous and human" allies who wanted to work toward self-determination for the *ayllus*.

ELECTIONS, ALLIANCES, AND INSURGENCY

On April 18, 1927, Michel and the *caciques* met in Oruro with the teacher, organizer, tailor, and political propagandist Rómulo Chumacero, plus the writer and organizer Gustavo Navarro and the labor educator Víctor Vargas. Vargas and Chumacero had met earlier that decade, and Vargas now attended the congress to represent the Ferrer School, a workers' school that Chumacero had founded in 1922. The relationship between them and the *caciques* had started in 1923, when Vargas and radical lawyers Alberto Murillo and Ricardo Daza had begun working with Michel's education commissioner, Agustín Saavedra, and with the other indigenous authorities in Copavilque, with whom they were now attending the Oruro labor congress. Daza and Michel had met in 1924, and thereafter worked together trying to reclaim territories in Tomoyo and Moromoro using colonial titles dating from 1552. They also collaborated to build rural schools and denounce the abuses committed by landlords and local officials.[55]

Thus, for four years before the Chayanta rebellion, the *caciques* had been working with the urban radicals accused of directing them. In their effort to build an alliance between socialists and the *caciques* movement, Navarro, Murillo, and Chumacero tread the common ground plowed earlier by Víctor Vargas, Manuel Michel, Agustín Saavedra, and Ricardo Daza. By the time of their 1927 meeting in Oruro, the *caciques* and urban radicals were partners, even comrades.[56]

When a state investigator interrogated Michel about his "work of subversion" and demanded the names of leaders and accomplices, Michel mentioned the national labor congress he had attended in Oruro, and also mentioned three or four prior meetings in Chumacero's house in Sucre.[57] He stated that although he had not understood much of the Spanish spoken during the congress, he had taken part just the same: "I spoke up to say that we are victims of incredible abuses and that government authorities do not help or protect us." When the interrogator demanded more information, Michel recounted that he had collected

[55] Ibid., 2: 11, 171, 178.
[56] Ibid., 2: 14v, 178–87. See also Grünberg, "Chayanta Rebellion," 181.
[57] *Sublevación indigenal*, 2: 5, 6v, 11v, 14–14v, 92–94, 97.

dues from local residents to fund school construction and land reclamation efforts. He had paid small sums to Daza and other lawyers.[58] Michel also authorized other community officials throughout Sucre and Potosí to collect dues in the weeks leading up to the rebellion.[59] The dues linked communities and their *caciques* to Michel, and Michel to Ricardo Daza, Alberto Murillo, and other urban lawyers.

The discussion at Chumacero's house in early April 1927 revolved around schools and the trip to Oruro later that month for the national labor congress. Saturnino Mamani, an indigenous official in Copavilque, testified that "Chumacero talked to us about schools, telling us that we could only recover our lands if we learned to read, at which point the *cacique* Manuel Michel spoke up and said the same."[60] Mamani also met the "tall and skinny" Gustavo Navarro, who told the *caciques* that "soon everything will belong to us and we'll no longer pay taxes." Chumacero, as President of the upcoming labor congress, and Navarro, the secretary-general of the recently formed Socialist Party, invited the *caciques* to speak in Oruro.[61]

Like Chumacero and Navarro, Michel was a member of the Socialist Party, and he addressed the 150–300 delegates ("a mixture of indigenous people and gentlemen") who attended.[62] As the quotation suggests, ethnic and class hierarchies did not vanish as a result of joint political work. It would be hard to overstate the hierarchies that divided the Bolivian working class at the time. A minority were urban, literate, independent artisans. The rest were poorer, illiterate noncitizens whom the "respectable" artisans accused of lowering wages.[63] Socialists attempted to overcome hierarchy and build equitable relations between the labor movement and the *caciques*. While they succeeded only partially, the fact that Michel was invited to speak at least indicates that Chumacero and the other organizers of the congress recognized the importance of Indians in the growth of the national labor movement.[64]

---

[58] Ibid., 2: 14–15.   [59] Ibid., 1: 25; 2: 21v–22v, 205.   [60] Ibid., 2: 6v.

[61] Ibid., 1: 8–8v; 2: 5v, 6v, 11v, 22v, 92–94.

[62] Ibid., 2: 5v, 11v, 14v. Different sources give widely varying estimates of the number of attendees.

[63] Rossana Barragán, "Los múltiples rostros y disputas por el ser mestizo," in *Seminario mestizaje: Ilusiones y realidades* (La Paz: MUSEF, 1996), 88–89.

[64] They apparently made much less effort to overcome patriarchy. The overall absence of women in the archival sources on Chayanta – save for victims of sexual assault and wives demanding freedom for their imprisoned husbands – suggests that patriarchal relations were the dominant current within the movement. There were, however, feminist countercurrents in the 1920s, most notably the Federación Obrera Femenina (Women Workers'

The April labor congress was an historic event. Herbert Klein notes that here "the class struggle for the first time was openly espoused by the worker movement, and a major programme of political and labour action against the capitalist classes was adopted." Guillermo Lora adds that "perhaps for the first time land expropriation" for the benefit of "rural communities and families" was discussed, and that the delegates "agreed to create a major plan for indigenous education."[65] The congress's documents described Indian and worker liberation in the same terms: "Indian liberation will be the work of the Indian himself, just as workers' redemption will be the work of workers themselves."[66] Such phrasing suggests that the labor activists most closely linked to the Chayanta movement – with the possible exception of Gustavo Navarro – did not consider themselves an enlightened vanguard of creoles and *mestizos* who should control Indians for their own good. Although there were sharp differences among delegates regarding relations between unions and parties, the anarcho-syndicalist workers and the Socialist Party militants agreed on a vision of agrarian collectivism based on the *ayllu* structure and a strategy based on direct action.[67]

Michel left the congress with two documents, later seized in the raid, that reveal the shared program of the *caciques* and the urban radicals. The first, a certificate written by Alberto Murillo and signed by Gustavo Navarro, authorized Michel to publicize the congress's resolutions in the countryside. The various resolutions called for "the distribution of lands to the Indian population," the organization of the "indigenous class" into councils within the departmental labor federations, and the "creation of indigenous schools." They proclaimed that "landlords cannot obstruct worker organizing in the countryside." The certificate instructed Michel "to lead [rural] workers in the struggle for their rights."[68] In the second document, issued at Michel's request, Murillo and Navarro warned: "if the Indian rises up against injustice, it is due to

Federation) in La Paz. See Ineke Dibbits, Elizabeth Peredo Beltrán, and Ruth Volgger, *Polleras libertarias: Federación Obrera Femenina, 1927–1964* (La Paz: Tahipamu, 1986).

[65] Klein, *Parties and Political Change*, 97; Guillermo Lora, *Historia del movimiento obrero boliviano, 1923–1933* (La Paz: Los Amigos del Libro, 1970), 24 (penultimate quote from Víctor Vargas Vilaseca).

[66] Quoted in Lora, *Historia del movimiento obrero*, 25. Statement written by Víctor Vargas Vilaseca.

[67] Silvia Rivera Cusicanqui, "Breve historia del anarquismo en Bolivia," in *Los artesanos libertarios y la ética del trabajo*, ed. Zulema Lehm Ardaya and Silvia Rivera Cusicanqui (La Paz: THOA, 1988), 33.

[68] *Sublevación indigenal*, 2: 95.

extreme despotism."[69] Clearly the *caciques* used their allies in the labor movement as a political counterweight and source of legitimacy before landlords and local officials, even when they were trying to strengthen their relations with the central government.

A copy of the second document was directed specifically to the "corresponding authorities," urging them to implement the resolutions of the recent labor congress.[70] Was this a situation of dual power in the countryside? Did the *caciques* think that the labor congress had enough weight in national politics to grant them authority and threaten local government officials? The evidence suggests that the insurgent *caciques* had come to see themselves as the legitimate political authority in the countryside even before the uprising.

The urban Socialists' political program helped them build a coalition with the *caciques*. Gustavo Navarro, in his 1926 pamphlet *La justicia del inca*, was the first to publicize the slogan "Land to the people, mines to the State," which would become a widespread rallying cry in the decades that followed.[71] More important than the slogan, though, was the spread of socialist ideas and their resonance with indigenous struggles. Navarro's pamphlet of course cited Marx, Lenin, and the example of the Russian Revolution, but it also described the *ayllus'* efforts to recover their lands and found schools as part of the socialist struggle. The same argument appeared in the Socialist Party's 1927 platform, which Navarro and Murillo published in Potosí on May 1. The platform called not for the immediate overthrow of capitalism, but for reforms including the setting up of agrarian cooperatives under popular control, progressive taxation, an eight-hour workday, and a stronger state role in strategic economic sectors like mining and petroleum.[72]

The Socialists combined images of Inca revolution with a vision of broader social transformation. In the 1920s Navarro spoke more about the return of the Inca than about the development of the productive forces in the economy. He and Chumacero wrote about economic freedom, but not in the liberal sense of the term, which in Bolivia meant the violent destruction of the *ayllu*, forced labor, and the rape of Indian women. For them it meant instead access to land, as suggested by the title of Chumacero's newspaper, *Tierra y Libertad*. Chumacero praised Mexican anarchist Ricardo Flores Magón for his "great dream of winning *freedom* alongside *land* for his people."[73]

---

[69] Ibid., 2: 99–99v.   [70] Ibid.   [71] *La justicia del inca*, 32.
[72] *Sublevación indigenal*, 2: 213.
[73] Quoted in Lehm Ardaya and Rivera Cusicanqui, eds., *Los artesanos libertarios*, 104n11.

Instead of trying to apply an abstract and Eurocentric teleology of proletarian revolution to the Bolivian context, both Navarro and Chumacero sought to reckon with the country's historical specificity. Their definition of the proletariat was broad and fluid, more akin to that of the anarchists than to the Leninist one that would take hold in the 1930s. The Socialists included Indians, students, workers, and "men of good conscience" in their category of the "full Bolivian proletariat."[74] The proletariat encompassed those enslaved not only by capitalists but by "departmental, provincial, and cantonal authorities, as well as by clergy and military officers."[75] And the Socialists understood that, given the importance of local government officials in mediating between communities and the central government in Bolivia, community control over those local officials was just as important as the recovery of lands.

Socialist organizers also sought to provide *caciques* with ways to make themselves heard directly, without others speaking on their behalf. The official party newspaper, the *Boletín del Mitayo*, invited workers and Indians to submit their complaints to a newly created Indian Defense League and to publish them directly in the paper. The first issue published a complaint lodged by fifty-six *caciques* against local authorities, landlords, and mine-owners, in which the authors said that they lived in "conditions worse than slaves" and denounced their "cruel and inhuman" treatment at the hands of the estate- and mine-owners.[76]

The Socialist Party prioritized the fight against local abuses, but it also sought "a new socialist State in which there are no oppressors nor oppressed, stuffed nor starving, powerful nor powerless, privileged nor ignorant."[77] They wanted to abolish hierarchical distinctions of all kinds, including those between the lettered class – of which they were a part – and illiterate Indians, their allies. They had a strong libertarian foundation that defined oppression and liberation in broad and social terms, rather than narrow and sectoral ones.

In June 1927 this revolutionary vision led the Socialists in Potosí and Sucre to take an insurrectionary turn. Did they think Indian communities were ready for all-out rebellion? If so, why did they not try to organize urban uprisings in Sucre and Potosí? We might speculate that they had an overly voluntarist and millenarian vision of history. They expected that the Chayanta uprising would serve as a spark for a series of urban insurrections that they could inspire via their propaganda, despite the

[74] *Sublevación indigenal*, 2: 213.   [75] Ibid., 2: 99–99v.   [76] Ibid., 2: 199–199v.
[77] Ibid., 2: 213.

lack of a strong working-class base at the national level. For instance, one party statement directed that "revolutionary propaganda should be intensified through all means, both legal and illegal, until we triumph."[78] They were not alone in their excessive optimism: throughout the world, the revolutionary left thought the end of capitalism was just around the corner.

There was no uprising of radicalized workers in Potosí and Sucre, nor elsewhere in Bolivia. But elites' fears had come true throughout the region's rural areas. The documents seized from Manuel Michel's house on August 3 confirmed that "communism" had indeed infected the countryside.

CONCLUSION

While the government officials who investigated the Chayanta rebellion cited revolutionary agitation as one of its causes, they placed the ultimate blame on the "three plagues of the indigenous class": priests, landlords, and the local officials known as *corregidores*.[79] In contrast with prior indigenous revolts, the state responded to the Chayanta insurgency by promoting the reconfiguration of local power relations via reforms. The federal government blocked further hacienda expansion in the south and replaced corrupt local officials. "Land to the people," first advocated by Gustavo Navarro in 1926, would in the 1930s become an obligatory slogan for aspiring politicians. And while it imprisoned and persecuted urban radicals, the Bolivian government also began to promote an official labor movement.[80] Moreover, the Siles government's lenient treatment of captured rebels was unprecedented: in October 1927 Siles declared amnesty for all 184 Indians imprisoned during the revolt, including the *caciques*, proclaiming that the uprising had its roots in exploitation at the hands of the three plagues.[81] The oligarchic state was much less immune to popular pressures in the 1920s than previous studies have implied. Its relatively flexible response to Chayanta challenges the firm distinction that historians often make between the eras before and after the Chaco War (1932–35), which is commonly considered the decisive historical

---

[78] Ibid., 2: 210.   [79] Diez Canseco, *Memoria*, 170.
[80] Guillermo Lora, *A History of the Bolivian Labour Movement, 1848–1971*, ed. Laurence Whitehead, trans. Christine Whitehead (Cambridge: Cambridge University Press, 1977), 145–46.
[81] Grünberg, "Chayanta Rebellion," 138; Arze Aguirre, *Guerra y conflictos sociales*, 24; Platt, "Andean Experience of Bolivian Liberalism," 329.

turning point in the first half of the century.[82] In some ways the "national-popular" period of Bolivian history began in the 1920s.

What explains the state's shift toward paternalism as a new means of counterinsurgency? Perhaps a new cohort of officials in the army and the executive and judicial branches, who had lived through the Liberal period, now decided that growing indigenous resistance necessitated a new and more stable rural order as a foundation upon which to build the nation.[83] By 1927, perhaps, they were in a position to implement some of their "enlightened" policies. Certainly the appearance of new elements in the repertoire of Indian insurgency set off louder alarms than prior revolts had, with the fear of a nationwide communist alliance now conjuring images of a social revolution in the future.

As this chapter has shown, some years before the violent uprising of 1927, rural *caciques* and radical artisans and intellectuals in the cities of Sucre and Potosí had formed a political alliance based on a shared commitment to rural education, communal land ownership, and redistribution of wealth and power. Officials in the Siles government understood the danger that this alliance posed to mining and agrarian capitalism in the country. After Chayanta they took measures to destroy it, maintaining a state of siege in the late 1920s, even as they also sought to check the power of the landlords. The alliance soon disintegrated. Leandro Condori Chura, the scribe of the famous *cacique apoderado* Santos Marka T'ula, later described the distance between the *caciques* and the labor movement. By the late 1920s and early 1930s, he recalled, "among workers there was a lack of understanding of the Caciques' practices."[84] The alliances among workers, peasants, and intellectuals that did form in the 1930s and 1940s were suppressed in the 1950s and 1960s by a "revolutionary nationalist" strategy of counterinsurgency that pitted workers against peasants. The gulf between city and village, between labor movement and indigenous-peasant movement, would not be bridged again until the rise of the *katarista* movement in the 1970s, and then only temporarily.[85]

The Chayanta rebellion and the alliance that lay behind it were not exceptional in Latin America at the time. In various places in the early decades of the century, especially in the Andes, urban activists built

---

[82] The most classic example of this argument is Klein, *Parties and Political Change.*
[83] See for instance Diez Canseco, *Memoria,* 283–310.
[84] Esteban Alejo Ticona and Leandro Condori Chura, *El escribano de los caciques apoderados/Kasikinakan puriarkunakan quillqiripa* (La Paz: Hisbol/THOA, 1993), 99.
[85] Rivera Cusicanqui, *"Oprimidos pero no vencidos,"* 124–71.

alliances with peasants, both *mestizo* and Indian, and viewed "the agrarian and indigenous question" as integral to building the working-class movement. These incipient alliances sought to erase ethnic and class hierarchies in order to build a more democratic and participatory society. What set southern Bolivia apart was the scale of the 1927 insurrection, as well as the state reforms that followed after its repression.

2

Identity, Class, and Nation

Black Immigrant Workers, Cuban Communism, and the Sugar Insurgency, 1925–1934

Barry Carr

In the period between independence (1902) and revolution (1959), immigrant workers were a vital force in Cuba's sugar and tropical fruit industries. The largest single group came from Spain (especially the northern provinces of Galicia and Asturias) and from the Canary Islands. But land shortages and the fragility of the sugar industry, which made life difficult for post-emancipation rural folk in several nearby island societies, also created circumstances that induced emigration to Cuba from the rest of the black Caribbean. The boom in Cuba's sugar industry, driven by rising

* I am grateful for comments by Avi Chomsky, Ron Harpelle, Dario Euraque, and the anonymous reviewers of the *Hispanic American Historical Review*, where this chapter first appeared. Since its original publication in 1998 the number of studies of British West Indian and Haitian immigration to Cuba has grown considerably. A small sample of this literature includes Matthew Casey, *Empire's Guestworkers: Haitian Migrants in Cuba during the Age of US Occupation* (Cambridge: Cambridge University Press, 2017); Gillian McGillivray, *Blazing Cane: Sugar Communities, Class and State Formation in Cuba, 1868–1959* (Durham, NC: Duke University Press, 2009); Jana K. Lipman, *Guantánamo: A Working-Class History* (Berkeley: University of California Press, 2008); Robert Whitney and Graciela Chailloux Lafitta, eds., *Subjects or Citizens: British Caribbean Workers in Cuba, 1900–1960* (Gainesville: University Press of Florida, 2013); Frances Peace Sullivan, "'Forging Ahead' in Banes, Cuba: Garveyism in a United Fruit Company Town," *New West Indian Guide* 88, nos. 3–4 (2014): 231–61; Anne Garland Mahler, "The Red and the Black in Latin America: Sandalio Junco and the 'Negro Question' from an Afro-Latin American Perspective," *American Communist History* 17, no. 1 (2018): 16–32; Gerald Horne, *Race to Revolution: The US and Cuba during Slavery and Jim Crow* (New York: Monthly Review, 2014); Lara Putnam, *Radical Moves: Caribbean Migrants and the Politics of Race in the Jazz Age* (Chapel Hill: University of North Carolina Press, 2013); Jorge L. Giovannetti-Torres, *Black British Migrants in Cuba: Race, Labor and Empire in the Twentieth-Century Caribbean, 1898–1948* (Cambridge: Cambridge University Press, 2018).

prices and increases in US investment during World War I, as well as by stories of fabulous wages, attracted immigrants from Haiti, Jamaica, Barbados, Grenada, Puerto Rico, Aruba, and Curaçao. By the early 1930s there were between 150,000 and 200,000 Caribbean immigrants (*antillanos*) in Cuba.[1]

By the late 1920s, however, the welfare of these immigrants was under attack by the threatening anti-imperialist and racist discourses provoked by a worldwide economic crisis that culminated in the Great Depression. The movement for cultural and economic renewal that transformed literary and political life in the neocolonial republic contained a strident critique of the forces that were "diluting" Cuban national identity. Anti-imperialism and defense of *cubanidad* were, therefore, often accompanied by opposition to black immigrant labor because Cubans linked (correctly) the drive to recruit *antillanos* to US sugar capital. The regime of Gerardo Machado y Morales (1925–33) responded to the new nationalism by initiating the repatriation of Haitian and British West Indian workers at the end of the 1920s. But the most dramatic moves to Cubanize labor and repatriate Caribbean workers were introduced by the brief revolutionary government of Ramón Grau San Martín, which came to power shortly after the collapse of the Machado regime. The actions of the Grau administration demonstrated how far the drive for social and economic justice could strengthen chauvinism and elicit support from Cuban-born workers of all races for measures directed against immigrants.[2]

Anti-immigrant sentiment and economic crisis came together in a powerful blend just as a wave of worker mobilizations, culminating in a massive general strike in Havana and other cities in early August 1933, overwhelmed the Machado dictatorship. Popular insurgency also determined the fate of the leftist Grau San Martín government, which briefly ruled Cuba between September 4, 1933, and January 10, 1934. The

---

[1] Ken Post, *Arise Ye Starvelings: The Jamaican Labour Rebellion of 1938 and Its Aftermath* (The Hague: Martinus Nijhoff, 1978), 43–44, 118; Franklin W. Knight, "Jamaican Migrants and the Cuban Sugar Industry, 1900–1934," in *Between Slavery and Free Labor: The Spanish-Speaking Caribbean in the Nineteenth Century*, ed. Manuel Moreno Fraginals, Frank Moya Pons, and Stanley L. Engerman (Baltimore, MD: Johns Hopkins University Press, 1985); Rolando Alvarez Estévez, *Azúcar e inmigración, 1900–1940* (Havana: Ed. de Ciencias Sociales, 1988); Elizabeth McLean Petras, *Jamaican Labor Migration: White Capital and Black Labor, 1850–1930* (Boulder, CO: Westview Press, 1988), esp. chap. 8; Michael L. Conniff, *Black Labor on a White Canal: Panama, 1904–1981* (Pittsburgh, PA: University of Pittsburgh Press, 1985); Lancelot S. Lewis, *The West Indian in Panama: Black Labor in Panama, 1850–1914* (Washington, DC: University Press of America, 1980).

[2] Alejandro de la Fuente, "Two Dangers, One Solution: Immigration, Race, and Labor in Cuba, 1900–1930," *International Labor and Working Class History* 51 (1997): 7–29.

inauguration of Grau's "Government of 100 Days" failed to halt the popular mobilizations, which in part were driven by the Cuban Communist Party (PCC) and its allies. Without a mass base capable of defending its program – partly the result of the bitter hostility shown toward it by Cuban Communists – the radical government was unable to consolidate its position. Finally, the combination of an aggressively hostile and interventionist US government in alliance with the army strongman, Fulgencio Batista, secured the collapse of the Grau administration in the middle of January 1934.

Sugar workers were at the center of the mobilizations that helped to shape political outcomes during the second half of 1933. From August to October 1933, field and mill workers seized thirty-six sugar mills and estates, and in a number of cases the occupations adopted the form of worker and peasant councils, or soviets.[3] The motivation behind mill seizures and occupations was very complex. The Great Depression and government attempts to stabilize prices by restricting the amount of land dedicated to the cultivation of sugarcane had drastically shortened the length of the sugar harvest (*zafra*), ruining sugar planters and creating havoc for field and mill workers. Sheer hunger motivated some of the rural insurgency, particularly the seizure of warehoused sugar and food stocks. In other cases, occupations and worker militancy were driven by rumors that mills would not grind in the 1933–34 season. Large-scale unemployment and the sudden appearance on town and city streets of tens of thousands of sugar workers, many of them native-born black people and Caribbean *braceros* (temporary migrant workers), increased the elite's apprehension of the risk of social unrest and gave a distinct racial inflection to the threat of subversion by the subaltern classes. The exclusionary aspirations of the new nationalist mood met with resistance from two quarters: the Cuban branches of the United Negro Improvement Association (UNIA) of Marcus Garvey, and the PCC.

While the UNIA's challenge to a multiethnic *cubanidad* constituted a call for black "racial pride," Cuban Communists promoted alliances that emphasized class rather than ethnicity or nationality. The anti-imperialist revolution that the PCC called for would be made by workers and peasants of all

[3] Barry Carr, "Mill Occupations and Soviets: The Mobilisation of Sugar Workers in Cuba, 1917–1933," *Journal of Latin American Studies* 28, no. 1 (1996): 129–58; Angel García and Piotr Mironchuk, *Los soviets obreros y campesinos en Cuba* (Havana: Ed. de Ciencias Sociales, 1987); Efraín Morciego Reyes, *El crimen de Cortaderas* (Havana: Unión de Escritores y Artistas de Cuba, 1982); Octaviano Portuondo Moret, *El soviet de Tacajó: Experiencias de un estudiante de los años 30* (Santiago de Cuba: Ed. Oriente, 1979); Ursinio Rojas, *Las luchas obreras en el central "Tacajó"* (Havana: Editora Política, 1979).

nationalities and ethnicities.[4] Both the Garveyites and the Communists attempted to address certain needs of the *antillano* population. Garveyism, while ostensibly adopting conservative positions in labor–capital conflicts, became a resource that British West Indian workers employed to defend themselves when conditions worsened in the 1920s. But by the time labor insurgency exploded in 1933, the UNIA was a shadow of its former self. The PCC, in contrast, viewed class struggle as the motor of history, and by late 1933 its cadres were already a significant force in the labor movement. More importantly for the *antillanos*, Cuban Communists were the staunchest opponents of the anti-immigrant policies initiated by the Grau government, which came to power after the 1933 revolution.

This chapter begins by discussing the racial dimensions of the nationalist and anti-imperialist discourse that developed in the 1920s and early 1930s. After examining the relationship between Caribbean immigrants and the PCC, it explores the ways in which both black English-speaking immigrants and Haitians responded to the labor mobilizations of the summer and fall of 1933. While the nationalist thrust of the 1933 revolution undoubtedly promoted interethnic mistrust and even outright conflict, the heightening of class conflict in the sugar zones frequently drew immigrant and Cuban-born workers into a common struggle. No such pan-ethnic solidarity occurred in the major strike that shook the Atlantic coast of Costa Rica the following year – and it is this contrast between the Cuban and Costa Rican cases that shapes the conclusion to this essay.

ANTI-IMMIGRANT DISCOURSE

During the 1920s anti-immigrant discourse linked *antillano* workers to disease, unfair competition, and a general dilution of *cubanidad*. Elite attacks on black immigrants, however, were directed as much against Cuba's "indigenous" black population, Afro-Cubans, as against *antillanos*. Paradoxically, these attacks may also have promoted the integration of Afro-Cubans into national society by discouraging black Cubans from engaging in political practices and self-definitions that were based on their identity as people of color.[5] A particularly virulent opposition to black

---

[4] On Garveyism in Cuba, see Rupert Lewis, *Marcus Garvey: Anti-Colonial Champion* (London: Karia Press, 1987), chap. 7; Pedro Pablo Rodríguez, "Marcus Garvey en Cuba," *Anales del Caribe* 7–8 (1987–88): 279–301.

[5] Aviva Chomsky, "West Indian Migrant Workers and the Development of National Identity Myths in Cuba and Costa Rica, 1898–1959," paper presented to the New England Historical Association, April 23, 1994.

separatism had been a powerful trope in Cuban nationalist discourse among Cubans of European and African origin ever since the frenzied suppression of the 1912 rebellion, a revolt that had been launched by the Partido Independiente de Color (Independent Party of Color).[6] The idea of a Cuban nation that stood above class was, moreover, firmly anchored in the multiethnic character of the mobilizations that had driven the final struggles for independence in the 1890s.

Anti-immigrant views were not only articulated by politicians and members of the plantocracy and cane-farmer (*colono*) class. Intellectuals, social activists, and certain sectors of an increasingly self-conscious working class also developed their own similar rhetoric.[7] Fernando Ortiz, the pioneer ethnographer whose early writings on Cuba's black population influenced a generation of researchers on *afrocubanidad,* shared many of the prejudices of the elite of his era. His early writings were influenced by a concept of racial hierarchy in which black people were constructed as "morally primitive," sensuous, close to nature, and prey to irrational fears and taboos. Ortiz spoke warmly of the virtues of Italian and Spanish immigrants and warned that black immigration on a massive scale might bring unhealthy and criminal elements to the island. His warnings reflected the medicalization of social thought that shaped the attitudes of racists and reformers alike during the period from 1880 to 1920.[8]

Cuban anti-imperialist discourse was also deeply influenced by fears of Antillean immigrants, whose movements to and from Cuba were attributed to foreign domination of the sugar industry. In journals like the *Revista de Avance* (1927–30), nationalist fear of a diluted *cubanidad* was accompanied by unflattering and inaccurate references to the inferior nature of Caribbean workers.[9] Ramiro Guerra y Sánchez, the economic nationalist and defender of the *colonos* (tenant farmers), considered the importation of Antillean labor to be the most noxious consequence of the

---

[6] Aline Helg, *Our Rightful Share: The Afro-Cuban Struggle for Equality, 1886–1912* (Chapel Hill: University of North Carolina Press, 1995).

[7] Dr. Jorge Le Roy y Cassá, *Inmigración anti-sanitaria* (Havana: Dorrbecker, 1929); Luis Mariano Pérez, "La inmigración jamaiquina desde el punto de vista social, económico y sanitario," *La Reforma Social* (Havana) (October 1916): 391–97.

[8] On the same discourse in Brazil, see Dain Borges, "'Puffy, Ugly, Slothful, and Inert': Degeneration in Brazilian Social Thought, 1880–1940," *Journal of Latin American Studies* 25, no. 2 (1993): 238–56.

[9] Francine Masiello, "Rethinking Neocolonial Esthetics: Literature, Politics, and the Intellectual Community in Cuba's *Revista de Avance*," *Latin American Research Review* 28, no. 2 (1993): 3–31.

rise of the sugar latifundium.[10] Thus, as in other Caribbean and Central American societies such as Costa Rica, anti-imperialism took sometimes contradictory guises. It could eschew a radical critique of class inequalities and promote the concept of a Cuban nation "above" class, a position that could be adopted from either a conservative or liberal perspective. Or anti-imperialism could be linked to the mobilization of the subaltern classes of all colors and nationalities, a position most clearly advocated by the Cuban Communist Party.[11]

Nevertheless, pessimism regarding the impact of Antillean immigration on Cuban racial identity also penetrated the political left. In the late 1920s and early 1930s, the progressive intellectual and historian Emilio Roig de Leuchsenring, a member of the Grupo Minorista (Minority Literary Group) and the Liga Anti-Imperialista (Anti-Imperialist League), campaigned against immigrant labor, arguing that the *bracero* trade was part of the heritage of slavery and the sugar elite's search for profit through low wages.[12] Opposition to immigration had also been a strong theme within Cuban worker organizations ever since the 1870s and 1880s, when tobacco workers, to take the most important example, felt threatened by employers' preference for immigrants from Spain.[13] The embarkation of over half a million Spaniards for Cuba between 1902 and 1925, added to the concurrent recruitment of several hundred thousand Caribbean *braceros* to work in the sugar industry, represented a major challenge to the nascent labor movement's struggle to roll back employer control over the workplace. Since Cuban laborers were particularly worried that the government and employers might use *antillanos* as strikebreakers, their vociferous activism in favor of immigration control is not surprising.[14]

---

[10] Ramiro Guerra y Sánchez, *Sugar and Society in the Caribbean: An Economic History of Cuban Agriculture* (New Haven: Yale University Press, 1964), 141–49. See also Alvarez Estévez, *Azúcar e inmigración,* 186–93.

[11] The Cuban case can be usefully contrasted with the experience of Costa Rica. On Costa Rica, see Aviva Chomsky, *West Indian Workers and the United Fruit Company in Costa Rica, 1870–1940* (Baton Rouge: Louisiana State University Press, 1996), esp. chapters 8–9.

[12] Emilio Roig de Leuchsenring, *Historia de la Enmienda Platt: Una interpretación de la realidad cubana* (Havana: Instituto Cubano del Libro, Ed. de Ciencias Sociales, 1973).

[13] Jean Stubbs, *Tobacco on the Periphery: A Case Study in Cuban Labour History, 1860–1958* (Cambridge: Cambridge University Press, 1985); Gerald Poyo, *"With All, and For the Good of All": The Emergence of Popular Nationalism in the Cuban Communities of the United States, 1848–1898* (Durham, NC: Duke University Press, 1989), 107–08.

[14] Jorge Ibarra, *Cuba, 1898–1921: Partidos políticos y clases sociales* (Havana: Ed. de Ciencias Sociales, 1992), 155–66.

BLACK IMMIGRANTS, POLITICS, AND
THE LABOR MOVEMENT

The political and organizational dimensions of Caribbean immigration have been little studied, in part because writers on this period have assumed that Caribbean *braceros* were not active in the labor struggle given that they set themselves apart from, and were marginalized by, their politically active Cuban-born fellow workers. Immigrants were – the argument goes – reluctant to organize and thereby risk further ostracism and repression. In addition, the *braceros* have also been stereotyped as possessing a culturally derived disposition to differentiate themselves from the local workforce. Finally, it is alleged that the high labor turnover among immigrant workers meant that they had little time to forge the bonds of solidarity that would have linked them more closely with Cuban-born laborers.

The divisive impact of language differences as well as regional and local cultural variation must not be underestimated. But given the political agitation and union organizing that increasingly characterized the sugar industry over the period from 1930 to 1935, it would be very surprising if Caribbean *braceros* had not been touched in some way by the heightened class conflict. While most British West Indian workers were temporary residents, by the early 1930s some Jamaicans had become Cuban citizens. At the port of Nuevitas, for example, the leaders of the longshoremen and stevedores were mostly Jamaican and Haitian, like much of the town's labor force, and most of these immigrants were also Cuban citizens.[15] There is also definite evidence of British West Indian involvement in union activities and radical politics. Back in Jamaica, former immigrant workers with experience in Cuba were among the pioneers of Marxism. Hugh Clifford Buchanan, "the first Jamaican Marxist," had worked in Cuba in the 1920s, where he had been a member of the Garveyite UNIA and "almost certainly had at least indirect contacts with the Communist party."[16]

Jamaicans performed low-status field work, but their higher literacy and political nous as compared with other *antillanos* earned them the respect of employers and, therefore, promotion to higher-paying jobs.

---

[15] E. A. Wakefield, U.S. Consul, Nuevitas, March 17, 1931, Havana Post Records, Part 10, 1931, 800 Cuba, "Report on Political Situation in Nuevitas Consular District," Record Group (hereafter RG) 84, U.S. National Archives and Records Administration (hereafter NARA).

[16] Post, *Arise Ye Starvelings*, 5–6.

Due to their "superior personal hygiene and education," British West Indians and Puerto Ricans were frequently given the most highly prized jobs both in the sugar yards, or *bateyes* (where they were employed in skilled and semiskilled jobs, for example as sugar dryers, stevedores, and guards), and on the railroads (where they worked as mechanics and electricians).[17] Large numbers of British West Indians, especially women, also worked as servants for the foreign managerial elite, where their English was much appreciated by overseas managers. Of the 65,000 British West Indians working in Cuba in 1930, approximately 25,000 were domestic servants while 15,000 were skilled tradesmen working in a wide variety of sectors.[18]

Jamaicans and other English-speaking West Indians in Cuba had a reputation for being literate, aware of their rights, and knowledgeable about how the diplomatic support of British consuls could help them deal with employers and the Cuban authorities.[19] "Nothing is too trivial for a Jamaican to bring to the notice of a Legation," insisted a British diplomat rather testily in 1924. "My first few weeks here were far from pleasant," the same official remarked, "I remember arriving each morning at the office to find it blocked with aggrieved niggers."[20] The frustration and self-confidence of British West Indian workers were such that during the early 1920s it was estimated that 90 percent of the work handled by the British Consulate-General in Santiago de Cuba and 75 percent of the total business processed in 1924 by the British legation in Havana dealt with matters brought up by Jamaican residents. Eventually, London created a special post in its Santiago consulate, partly financed by the Jamaican colonial government, to handle concerns raised by Jamaican immigrant workers.[21]

The literacy of British West Indians distinguished them not only from the almost entirely illiterate Haitian *braceros*, but also from the largely unlettered Cuban laborers who were mostly employed as agricultural

---

[17] A. Aurelio Portuondo to Manuel Rionda, "Immigration into Cuba (Jamaicans and Haitians)," January 25, 1924, RG II, S10C, f. 38, Braga Collection, University of Florida, Gainesville (hereafter UFBC); Gerard Smith to Higinio Fanjul, July 10, 1917, Series 1, Smith, Gerard F., 1917 (Francisco Sugar Co.), UFBC; Rojas, *Luchas obreras*, 52.

[18] T. J. Morris to Foreign Office, March 7, 1930, A2177/2177/14, FO 371, Public Records Office, London (hereafter PRO).

[19] Lewis, *West Indian in Panama*, 69–72.

[20] Morris to J. Vansittart, March 12, 1925, A1667/22/14, FO 371, PRO.

[21] Morris to London, October 15, 1929, K12335/6657/214, FO 369, PRO, enclosing a 1924 dispatch by a Mr. Gainer; L. Haggard to London, "Treatment of West Indian Immigrants in Cuba," June 8, 1923, A3865/23333/14, FO 371, PRO.

laborers in the sugar fields. A presidential envoy, Dr. Rogelio Pina y Estrada, who investigated conditions among black immigrant workers in 1934, concluded that "it is difficult to find [a Jamaican] who cannot read or write."[22] The resulting self-confidence of anglophone workers was frequently construed as arrogance by government authorities in Cuba and other countries such as the Dominican Republic.[23] British diplomats often expressed the same views. A lengthy memorandum on the situation of West Indians in Cuba prepared by the embassy in Havana stated:

> The ignorance and quarrelsome character of the British West Indian is proverbial. Aggressive and impotent, he does nothing to adapt himself to his surroundings and is welcome nowhere. The more humble Haitian is much more successful in avoiding trouble. In addition, the coloured British community is disunited and has no idea of cooperation and self-help. Ignorant of the language, they are dragged before the courts and sentenced, their witnesses unheard.[24]

Literacy apart, the self-confidence of British West Indians may also have been shaped by the fact that many of them had already been exposed to a world far beyond the Caribbean. Some migratory workers had fought with the British army in World War I, a fact that was well known to employers and representatives of the Cuban state.[25] A Jamaican, Hubert Stulz, allegedly assaulted by police at the Manatí mill in 1924, had formerly been a soldier in the West Indian Regiment and had served with General Allenby in Palestine.[26] The first large contingent of Barbadians to leave for Cuba were all ex-soldiers whose emigration applications were prioritized by British colonial authorities.[27] Moreover, British West Indian *braceros* in Cuba frequently vaunted their military service in correspondence sent to British diplomats and colonial office officials. The *braceros'* indignant letters often mentioned their loyal service to the British crown while relating the ill-treatment they had received at the hands of Cuban authorities. British West Indian

[22] "Informe rendido por el Dr. Rogelio Pina y Estrada al Hon. Sr. Presidente de la República y al Consejo de Secretarios sobre la inmigración haitiana y jamaicana," June 29, 1934, p. 7, Secretaría de la Presidencia, 121/84, Archivo Nacional de Cuba (hereafter ANC).

[23] Patrick E. Bryan, "The Question of Labor in the Sugar Industry of the Dominican Republic in the Late Nineteenth and Early Twentieth Centuries," in Moreno Fraginals, et al., *Between Slavery and Free Labor*, 245.

[24] Haggard to London, "Treatment of West Indian Immigrants in Cuba."

[25] Trowbridge to Manuel Rionda, January 8, 1919, Travelling Book 20, p. 97, RG II, Series 3, vol. 27, UFBC.

[26] "Brutal Treatment of West Indians in Isle of Cuba," *Negro World*, January 31, 1925, 2.

[27] Basil Maughan, "Some Aspects of Barbadian Emigration to Cuba, 1919–1935," *Journal of the Barbados Museum and Historical Society* 37 (1985): 241, 244–45.

workers were known to ostentatiously display war medals on their clothing and this practice, which infuriated Cuban officials, was the occasion
for frequent assaults on immigrants by Guardias Rurales.[28]

At first sight these expressions of loyalty to the British army, an institution that had systematically discriminated against black soldiers, relegat-
ing them to menial support tasks and denying them equality of treatment
with frontline soldiers, seem surprising. They may even invite allegations
of British West Indian workers' "accommodation" to the colonial order
that rest on assumptions about the "false consciousness" of Caribbean
immigrants. But working in a country where differences in language and
cultural heritage estranged *braceros* from mainstream society must have
been a profoundly alienating experience for migratory workers from
Jamaica and the other islands of the British Caribbean. In these circumstances a sense of community necessarily had to be constructed from
outside the experience of participating in Cuban society, even when the
main point of reference, Britain and the Empire, elicited mixed feelings.
The references to crown, imperial loyalty, and Britishness, then, may have
been manifestations of a "much-needed self-valorization in the face of
comprehensive rejection."[29]

These occasional demonstrations of membership in the Empire reveal
the extreme plasticity of Jamaican and British West Indian identity in an
alien setting. Jamaican *braceros,* it seems, could clearly choose when and
when not to be "British."[30] In any case, appeals by British West Indians to
the moral and legal authority of the crown flowed quite naturally from
a long-standing element in the Jamaican radical tradition, according to
which the intervention of the imperial center was often invoked, sometimes successfully, against the unpopular actions of the colonial regime or
local planter society.[31] It would be wrong, therefore, to interpret these
expressions of loyalty to the crown and imperial authority as signaling
simple acceptance of the colonial order, as has been argued in regard to
Jamaican labor emigrants in Costa Rica and Panama.[32]

[28] Great Britain, Foreign Office, *Further Correspondence between His Majesty's
Government and the Cuban Government Respecting the Ill-Treatment of British West
Indian Labourers in Cuba* (London: His Majesty's Stationery Office, 1924), 22.

[29] Jerry White, *The Worst Street in North London: Campbell Bunk, Islington, between the
Wars* (London: Routledge & Kegan Paul, 1986), 106.

[30] Ibid.

[31] Abigail Bakan, *Ideology and Class Conflict in Jamaica: The Politics of Rebellion*
(Montreal: McGill-Queen's University Press, 1990), 16–17, 83–85.

[32] For a contrasting argument concerning West Indian reputation and behavior on the
UFC's banana estates in Costa Rica and Panama, see Philippe I. Bourgois, *Ethnicity at*

Haitians predominated in field work. They worked mostly as cane cutters, although initially employers argued that they were not as efficient as native-born Cuban cutters.[33] Haitians frequently bore the brunt of discriminatory treatment and violence from Cuban authorities, but they were much less likely than their British West Indian counterparts to appeal to their government for diplomatic help. In one revealing incident in 1924, two Haitians working on the Santa Rosa section of the Río Cauto mill (near Bayamo) were killed during a fight with the administrator and overseer, precipitated by the Haitians' decision to leave the mill at a time of acute labor shortage.[34] Ill-treatment of Haitians was so bad that in July 1928 the Haitian government issued a decree that temporarily prohibited emigration to Cuba.[35] Collective action by Haitian workers to protest poor wages and working conditions, although less common than among Jamaicans, was reported to have occurred on several occasions. A strike of cane cutters at the Mercedita mill in March 1928, for example, was almost entirely composed of Haitians, who protested against the mill's miserly payment of 60 cents for each 100 *arrobas* cut.[36]

While Jamaican *braceros* were often accorded a degree of grudging respect, contemporary accounts are replete with cruel and mocking responses to Haitians. This was exemplified by the sarcastic, grandiloquent, and ridiculous nicknames bestowed on them, such as "Pedro el Grande," "Aleíbiades el Magnífico," "Judas Crocante," and "Cerveza Tropical." Haitians were often given the names of former Cuban presidents like Menocal, José Martí, or José Miguel, or labeled with animal epithets such as *buey* (ox). Generally,

---

Work: Divided Labor on a Central American Banana Plantation (Baltimore, MD: Johns Hopkins University Press, 1989). Bourgois argues that the heritage of slavery and a rigid racial social structure in Jamaica meant that Jamaican laborers "more readily endured a social order that legitimized inferior treatment, housing and pay based on phenotypes" (51).

[33] Rojas, *Luchas obreras*, 52; Juan Pérez de la Riva, "Cuba y la inmigración antillana 1900–1931," in *La república neocolonial: Anuario de estudios cubanos*, ed. Juan Pérez de la Riva et al. (Havana: Instituto Cubano del Libro, Ed. de Ciencias Sociales, 1979), 2: 26–27, 48; Alvarez Estévez, *Azúcar e inmigración*, 79–80.

[34] *Gaceta Oficial* (Havana), May 27, 1932, 9889–91. On Haitian migrants to Cuba, see Mats Lundahl, "A Note on Haitian Migration to Cuba, 1890–1934," *Cuban Studies* 12 (1982): 21–36; José Millet, "Presencia haitiana en el oriente de Cuba," in Université des Antilles et de la Guyane, Centre d'Etudes et de Recherches Caraibéennes, *Cuba et les Antilles: Actes du Colloque de Pointe-à-Pitre (3–5 décembre 1984)* (Talence: Presses Universitaires de Bordeaux, 1988), 105–17.

[35] Subsecretario de Estado to Secretario de Estado, August 30, 1928, Secretaría de la Presidencia, ANC.

[36] *El Heraldo de Cuba* as cited by *Cuba Today*, March 9, 1928, 3.

Haitians were referred to only by first name, a custom of naming that underscored their status as "children." Without legally registered surnames, many Haitian *braceros* became, in effect, legally disenfranchised. And when they were not mocked, Haitians were treated as objects of fear. Terrifying stories of Haitian ferocity and occult activities circulated widely in the countryside.[37] References to the "primitive" religious customs, witchcraft, and voodoo practices of the Haitians were common. In his memoirs, the sugar worker Ursinio Rojas recalls how his mother was terrified by the Haitians and Jamaicans who lived in the barracoons at Francisco – all of whom spoke "foreign languages." The young Ursinio would be locked up for safety when the foreigners passed the family house.[38]

Along the continuums of "civilized practices" and "racial quality," Haitians were relegated to last place. More common, though, was the naked racism typical of the moral panic that gripped many Cubans. According to an article that appeared in *El Heraldo de Cuba* in 1922, "In the province of Oriente, Haitians are devotees of witchcraft [*brujería*], contaminating black Cubans in an atavistic leap backwards in time. They practice the superstitious 'Vodu' cult which is full of black magic . . . and [are] led by a priest known as 'papa Bocú.'"[39] Even leftist observers employed racial stereotypes about Haitian workers, seeing their alleged failure to develop a rich associational culture (of the kind that British West Indians created) as undermining respectable modes of class struggle, which supposedly required self-discipline and a concern with self-improvement, education, and solidarity. Carleton Beals, the American radical journalist and writer, argued that "the Haitian immigrant is atrociously backward," and referred to "a great flood of ignorant black labor from Haiti and Jamaica."[40]

These elaborate representations of "Haitianness" developed at a time when Cuban ignorance of Haitian conditions was overwhelming. Hardly anything was known about the Haitian background of the laborers who provoked such scorn and derision. Certainly there was no awareness of the historical circumstances from which the flood of Haitian peasants sprang. Employers and government officials seemed unaware of Haitian responses to the United States' occupation of the immigrants' homeland and of the militant peasant response to marine brutality, mounted by the

[37] Jesús Guanche and Dennis Moreno, *Caidije* (Santiago: Ed. Oriente, 1988), 22–23.
[38] Rojas, *Luchas obreras*, 24.
[39] Oscar Zanetti and Alejandro García, eds., *United Fruit Company: Un caso del dominio imperialista en Cuba* (Havana: Ed. de Ciencias Sociales, 1976), 248.
[40] Carleton Beals, *The Crime of Cuba* (Philadelphia, PA: J. B. Lippincott, 1933), 58, 406.

caco guerrilla forces of rebel leader Charlemagne Péralte. Haitians were, by the Cuban plantocracy's definition, supremely ignorant and super-stitious, a discursive theme that was central to the racist and contemptu-ous treatment of Haiti that permeated debates and writings about the first black-ruled republic in the Americas. That some Haitian immigrant work-ers, the descendants of the Caribbean peasantry with the longest tradition of autonomy, might have participated in political and guerrilla struggles in Haiti never occurred to opinion makers and planters.[41]

But Haitians were not simply victims of persecution and exploitation. It can also be argued that the layers of discrimination that enveloped Haitian immigrants provided them with a powerful way of asserting their difference and securing respect – a respect born out of the awe and even fear with which Cubans viewed them. Haitian workers were clearly not engaging in respect-able forms of class struggle or exhibiting respectable forms of masculinity. Instead, they were responding to the derision and hostility of Cuban eco-nomic and cultural elites by defending their worth through ostentatious displays of the traits for which they were condemned by their critics. In the eyes of Cubans, Haitian immigrants engaged in a series of practices that surrounded them in a halo of mystery: their reputation for *brujería* and magic; the barely understood world of Haitian *vodú* (a religious practice, long associated with slave and post-emancipation forms of black solidarity, that Haitians brought to Cuba and that was eventually assimilated by broad layers of the peasant population of eastern Cuba); the Haitians' use of Kréyol (the oral language of most rural Haitians); and even the association between Haitians (represented as *negros brutos* by Cubans) and savagery.[42] Haitians knew how to exploit their sinister reputation to heighten the cultural separa-tion between themselves and the Cuban-born population. And when all else failed, they could use fear of the "exotic" and "savage" to secure respect and minimize harassment. Moreover, their prestige in matters of magic and herbal medicine could earn Haitians the respect of fellow workers and even *colonos*.[43] In other words, Haitians could turn marginality into an asset.

---

[41] On Haitian resistance to the US occupation, see Kethly Millet, *Les paysans haïtiens et l'occupation américaine d'Haïti, 1915–1930* (La Salle: Collectif Paroles, 1978).

[42] See the comments of a Jamaican worker interviewed in the 1970s: "Haitians are stupid and brutal; I've seen a Haitian kill for a cent, for one cent! He sticks the knife right in the gut." Morciego Reyes, *El crimen*, 158; Julio Angel Carreras, *Esclavitud, abolición y racismo* (Havana: Ed. de Ciencias Sociales, 1985), 119–20.

[43] Joel James, José Millet, and Alexis Alarcón, *El vodú en Cuba* (Santo Domingo; Santiago de Cuba: Ediciones Centro Dominicano de Estudios de la Educación; Casa del Caribe, 1992), 79–80.

COMMUNISTS, UNIONS, AND BRITISH WEST INDIAN WORKERS

The scanty literature on the political and cultural affiliations of British West Indian workers in Central America and the Caribbean has tended to present these labor migrants as cultural and political isolates, working and acting on the margins of the societies in which they were inserted. This is not to suggest, as many writers have argued, that these workers were always passive. The evidence of British West Indian labor militancy on the United Fruit Company (UFC) estates in Costa Rica and Panama between 1910 and 1924 suggests quite the opposite. Nevertheless, at least in Central America, the militancy of British West Indians seems to have declined over time. Racial animosities between black and Hispanic workers, deliberately cultivated by the UFC, as Philippe Bourgois's analysis of the UFC in Panama and Costa Rica convincingly demonstrates, made it very difficult to achieve interethnic solidarity among workers. As a result, attempts by the Costa Rican Communist Party to attract black support failed and black participation in the important 1934 strike on the UFC's Costa Rican estates was minimal.[44] Nevertheless, comparative evidence strongly confirms that after World War I the most consistent attempts to mobilize and recruit Afro-Latin Americans were made by Communist parties.[45]

Evidence of the participation of black immigrants in Cuban labor unions is difficult, but not impossible, to find. One revealing case is that of Enrique (Henry) Shackleton, probably a Jamaican or Barbadian, who was secretary of the Unión de Obreros Antillanos de Santiago de Cuba (Union of Antillean Workers of Santiago de Cuba), which he represented at the Second National Labor Congress in Cienfuegos in February 1925. Shackleton also participated in the commission that drafted the statutes of Cuba's first national labor federation, the Confederación Nacional Obrera de Cuba (National Workers' Confederation of Cuba, CNOC). A few months later, Caribbean delegates including Shackleton attended the Third Labor Congress in Camagüey, where the Unión de Obreros Antillanos delivered an extensive report on immigration and its consequences.[46] Another black union leader was Sandalio Junco, the

---

[44] Bourgois, *Ethnicity at Work,* 52–61.
[45] George Reid Andrews, *Blacks and Whites in Sao Paulo, Brazil, 1888–1988* (Madison: University of Wisconsin Press, 1991), 304 n.53.
[46] Alvarez Estévez, *Azúcar e inmigración,* 149–53. For Shackleton's correspondence with the governor of Jamaica in 1924 concerning conditions of West Indian blacks in Cuba, see

PCC's first Negro affairs specialist (and later the founder of Cuban Trotskyism) who, in claiming that the union was created by the Communists, evidenced the strong ties that were felt to exist between Communist organizing and black participation in labor unions.[47]

The PCC's vision of ethnic and immigration issues reflected the position of the Comintern's Third Period.[48] Inaugurated by the Sixth Congress of the Comintern in 1928, the Third Period was seen as the final crisis of world capitalism. The bankruptcy of reformist political and workers' organizations would create opportunities for revolutionary and Communist-led attacks on capitalism. This would require Communists to halt collaboration with social democrats, socialists, and radical nationalists and build an independent base within mass movements by establishing "dual" unions. The sectarian tone of the Third Period has been blamed (with good reason) for isolating Communists from political and industrial organizing work in the mainstream. Less well acknowledged is the fact that the "class against class" line also obliged Communists to identify new constituencies that would gain them prestige and support. This policy shift was clearly reflected in the new emphasis on building support among the labor force of the Caribbean fruit and sugar enclaves, with their large communities of black immigrant workers. Naturally, the Third Period decision to privilege class over rival loyalties such as nation and race also made practical sense in multinational, multiethnic, and multilingual societies like Cuba.[49]

Maughan, "Some Aspects," 252–53; Garner to Foreign Office, London, April 23, 1924, A 2903/13/14, FO 371, PRO; and the petition (dated April 1, 1924) signed by Shackleton and addressed to the governor of Jamaica. Shackleton claimed that 2,500 working men and women had signed the petition. He also appears on a 1930 list of Cubans and foreigners who were involved in "propagating Communism." The report notes his expulsion (but there is no date provided). See "República de Cuba: Policía Secreta Nacional, 'Relación de extranjeros y cubanos que se dedican a la propagación del comunismo,'" in F. T. F. Dumont to Secretary of State, December 2, 1931, 837.00B/42, RG 59, NARA.

[47] *Bajo la bandera de la CSLA: Resoluciones y documentos varios del Congreso Constituyente de la Confederación Sindical Latinoamericana efectuada en Montevideo en mayo de 1929* (Montevideo: Impr. La Linotipo, 1929), 174–75.

[48] Pedro Serviat, *El problema negro en Cuba y su solución definitiva* (Havana: Editora Política, 1986), 110–15.

[49] On the Cuban Communists in the early 1930s, see Barry Carr, "From Caribbean Backwater to Revolutionary Opportunity: Cuba's Evolving Relationship with the Comintern, 1925–1934," in *International Communism and the Communist International*, ed. Andrew Thorpe and Tim Rees (Manchester: Manchester University Press, 1998), 234–53.

As part of its turn to the left, the Comintern called for stronger action against racial discrimination and for energetic campaigns to recruit black workers. In July 1929, it created an organization of black workers, the International Trade Union Committee of Negro Workers, headquartered in Hamburg and affiliated with the Red International of Labor Unions (Profintern). Cuba was represented on the executive committee and was featured prominently in its monthly journal, *The Negro Worker*.[50] Caribbean Communists, especially the Trinidadian George Padmore (head of the Profintern's Negro Workers' Bureau), played a key role in establishing the new organization. The committee tried to organize immigrant workers, especially the "new current of slaves," the label Comintern officials attached to the migratory workers employed by the mainly US-controlled sugar and fruit companies in Central America and the Caribbean.[51] Visits by the US-based, but Surinam-born, Communist Otto Huiswood to Jamaica and Cuba (and his attempt to enter Haiti) in 1930 were probably linked to the new Profintern initiative and to the international work of the recently organized Negro Department of the National Executive Committee of the US Communist Party (CPUSA), which Huiswood headed.[52] West Indian seamen and dockers, especially those who were members of the Marine Workers Industrial Union, were entrusted with the work of carrying propaganda to Caribbean ports.[53]

Among the new slogans of the Communist movement was the call for black self-determination. Black people, it was argued, constituted an oppressed nation in societies such as the United States and Cuba, in which, in certain regions, they actually constituted a majority. Some Communists opposed the actual separation of black peoples into new states as well as radical demands that in certain areas with a large black population (such as parts of the United States) 50 percent of jobs be reserved for black workers. However, in the middle of 1930 the Comintern's Negro Commission adopted a more radical interpretation of the new line, insisting that the CPUSA's slogan should be "The Right of

---

[50] Philip S. Foner and James S. Allen, eds., *American Communism and Black Americans: A Documentary History, 1919–1929* (Philadelphia, PA: Temple University Press, 1987), 150–51; Eastern Secretariat, "The Position of the Negro Race and the Proletarian Movement," 495/r55/87, Russian Center for the Preservation and Study of Documents of Recent History, Moscow (hereafter RTsKhIDNI).

[51] *Bajo la bandera de la CSLA*, 178.

[52] Eastern Secretariat, Report on the West Indies by Otto Huiswood and George Padmore, January 24, 1931, 495/r55/98, RTsKhIDNI; Post, *Arise Ye Starvelings*, 5.

[53] Eastern Secretariat, Re: Proposals on Initiating Activities in the British West Indies, February 26, 1931, 495/155/98, RTsKhIDNI.

Self-Determination of Negroes in the Black Belt," a policy that would include "the right of negroes to exercise governmental authority in the entire territory of the Black Belt, as well as to decide upon the relations between their territory and other nations."[54]

The CPUSA's line was replicated within the Cuban Communist Party, as revealed by the latter's use of the term "Franja Negra," a direct translation of the CPUSA's "Black Belt."[55] Beginning in 1930, the PCC campaigned for black self-determination in the southeastern portion of Oriente province (Baracoa, Guantánamo, Santiago de Cuba, La Maya, Songo, Caney, Cobre, San Luis, and Palma Soriano), where black people formed a majority of the population.[56] Self-determination was a loose concept, but the PCC made it clear that it could involve the creation of an independent state, if that was the express wish of the black masses in the Franja Negra.[57] The party also called for antiracist work to be carried out in the cities alongside struggles against racial discrimination and the deportation of foreign black workers, especially Haitians.[58] The Communist-influenced CNOC line on employment went so far as to demand the employment of equal numbers of black and white workers.[59]

The Communist Party's decision to plunge into organizing the sugar sector was also driven by Comintern advice. Since the sugar industry was considered the most proletarianized segment of Cuban capitalism, an international strategy of "class against class" made no sense in countries

---

[54] Harvey Klehr and William Thompson, "Self-Determination in the Black Belt: Origins of a Communist Policy," *Labor History* 30 (1989): 354–66; Mark Naison, *Communists in Harlem during the Depression* (Urbana: University of Illinois Press, 1983), 17–114; Robin D. G. Kelley, *Hammer and Hoe: Alabama Communists during the Great Depression* (Chapel Hill: University of North Carolina Press, 1990), 13–15, 17, 37–38, 122.

[55] The PCC's stance was in fact shaped by a member who had returned to Cuba after several years in the United States; see "Testimonio: Preguntas y respuestas sobre los años 30: Fabio Grobart en la escuela de historia," *Universidad de la Habana* 100 (1973): 135.

[56] Louis A. Pérez, Jr., *Lords of the Mountain: Social Banditry and Peasant Protest in Cuba, 1878–1918* (Pittsburgh, PA: University of Pittsburgh Press, 1989), 131–32.

[57] "Testimonio: Preguntas y respuestas," 136–37; Alberto Arredondo, *El negro en Cuba, ensayo* (Havana: Ed. "Alfa," 1939), 82.

[58] Serviat, *El problema negro*, 116–21; "Resolución sobre el trabajo entre los trabajadores negros," in *IV Congreso Nacional Obrero de Unidad Sindical: Resoluciones y acuerdos sobre la estructura orgánica de la CNOC* (Havana: CNOC, 1934), 69–73; see the article signed "Luis," "Cómo comprender el derecho a la autodeterminación de la población negra de Cuba y la lucha por su aplicación práctica," *Bandera Roja*, April 18, 1934, 3.

[59] See the column "Lucha diaria" in the PCC newspaper *Bandera Roja*, February 22, 1934, 2; SNOIA, *La zafra actual y las tareas de los obreros azucareros* (Havana: SNOIA, 1933), 18.

where Communists neglected the key proletarian sector. Given the social and ethnic structure of central and eastern Cuba, targeting sugar workers necessarily obliged unions and parties to engage with both native-born and immigrant black people on a massive scale. Logically, a Communist Party that was the leading edge of a largely black labor force might be expected to show a dramatic increase in the number of its black members.

However, it is not clear how close the PCC was to Cuba's black population in practice. The long delays in targeting unionization of the sugar industry certainly affected the party's work. In early 1931 the PCC admitted that there were "very few negro workers" and that there were "practically no negroes in the Party . . . although one-third of the population is negro."[60] This statement may have been an exaggeration, designed to sharpen the case for an aggressive campaign to recruit black members, but the claim is partially supported by the evidence of confidential PCC reports available in the recently opened Comintern archives. In its early years the party clearly underestimated the political potential of Antillean migrant workers from the British West Indies and from Haiti who (in 1929) it described as having "a cultural level below that of Cuban workers and no tradition of struggle or organizational [activity] . . . they are docile material ready for exploitation."[61]

As late as September 1932, the Caribbean sub-bureau of the Confederación Sindical Latinoamericana (Latin American Trade Union Confederation, CSLA) acknowledged that its weakest work was among Caribbean immigrant workers; it urged the CPUSA to use its influence within the Marine Workers Industrial Union to circulate propaganda and provide secure travel for Comintern and Caribbean party cadres.[62] The Comintern archives provide us with a glimpse of some of the obstacles that stood in the way of organizing across national and color lines. There were frequent reports of white nervousness concerning the impact of massive recruitment of black union members. A 1932 report on youth work reported that the PCC had not organized dances in Havana for a year because black members would have participated; the Santa Clara branch of the Communist Youth League, moreover, had called for a halt to recruitment since half its membership was already black.[63] But even with these fears, and despite the

[60] O. Rodríguez, "Our Present Tasks in Cuba," *The Communist* (New York) (June 1931): 524.

[61] Profintern, 354/7/389, RTsKhIDNI.

[62] Profintern, 534/4/427, anonymous report addressed to "Herrn Alexander," 10/9/32, RTsKhIDNI.

[63] "Report on the Work in Cuba and Mexico Given to LAB" (signed "Eduardo"), July 19, 1932, 495/105/61, Cuban Party, RTsKhIDNI.

Communists' mishandling of the Havana general strike in August 1933, which helped precipitate Machado's downfall, by the end of 1933 the party's energetic involvement in the sugar strikes and mill occupations had speeded up the recruitment of black workers.[64] Leading cadres included a number of black figures, some of whom would soon become prominent Communist leaders. The earliest and best known was Blas Roca, a shoemaker from Manzanillo, who after 1934 was general secretary of the party and editor of its newspaper, *Bandera Roja*. Early black Communists also included Martín Castellanos, primarily responsible for developing the thesis of black self-determination in Cuba; Sandalio Junco, a baker who was accused of Trotskyism and expelled from the party in 1932; and a young black sugar worker from the Nazábal mill, Antolín Dickinson Abreu, editor of *El Obrero Azucarero*, the magazine of the CNOC-affiliated Sindicato Nacional de Obreros de la Industria Azucarera (National Union of Sugar Industry Workers, SNOIA).[65]

In 1934 the PCC proudly claimed that it was predominantly made up of black workers.[66] This was clearly an overstatement. While fourteen of the sixty-seven delegates at its April 1934 second congress were black (as were seventeen out of the forty-five delegates who attended the first conference of the party's Communist Youth League in May), party documents also noted that its organization in black villages and *barrios* was very poor.[67] Nevertheless, the ethnic composition of the party's newly elected Central Committee indicated a marked improvement in the representation of people of color holding leadership positions; out of twenty-three

---

[64] The Communist Party was at the center of the Havana general strike of August 1–10 that helped topple Machado, although the PCC neither initiated the strike nor directed the movement. In mid-strike the PCC leadership agreed to negotiate with the now desperately isolated Machado and, in return for the legalization of the party and other concessions, offered to use its influence to order a return to work. Havana workers did not heed the Strike Committee's call and the origins and impact of the "August Mistake" became the center of what is still a highly sensitive issue in Cuban historiography. See Carr, "From Caribbean Backwater to Revolutionary Opportunity."

[65] Osvaldo Torres Molina, *Apuntes para la historia del movimiento comunista, obrero y campesino en Matanzas, 1869–1958* (Havana: Editora Política, 1984), 63–68; Tomás Fernández Robaina, *El negro en Cuba, 1902–1958: Apuntes para la historia de la lucha contra la discriminación racial* (Havana: Ed. de Ciencias Sociales, 1990), 134–4.

[66] Partido Comunista de Cuba, *Hacia las luchas decisivas por el poder soviético: Resolución sobre la situación actual, perspectivas y tareas, adoptada por el Segundo Congreso del Partido Comunista de Cuba, celebrado a fines de abril de 1934* (Havana: Partido Comunista de Cuba, n.d.), 23.

[67] "Simón" a "Querido Nicolás," May 25, 1934495/105/104, Cuban Party, RTsKhIDNI; Blas Roca, "Oriente, fuente estratégica de la revolución," *Bandera Roja*, May 1934, 9.

members, eight were *negros* and two were *mulatos*.[68] Moreover, the PCC's determination to reach immigrant workers was being signaled on nearly every occasion. *Bandera Roja*'s practice of publishing materials in English and French clearly indicated the organization's interest in reaching British West Indian and (less realistically in view of their high levels of illiteracy) Haitian workers.[69]

Cuban Communists also targeted discrimination in social and cultural spheres, including within labor unions. For example, in January 1934 the Fourth Congress of the CNOC called on unions to include both black and white workers in dances and sporting events, demands that suggest that discriminatory behaviors were widespread. The Communists were most successful when they supported the efforts of black people to defend their cultural autonomy and resist the dominant social order. A striking but rare example of the PCC's understanding of the cultural dimension of Afro-Cuban politics occurred in the fall of 1933, when cadres in the party's Oriente region campaigned to overturn the prohibition of "African" popular dancing that had been decreed by municipal authorities in Santiago de Cuba, the site of the island's renowned carnival.[70]

Explicit attention to the rights of black workers, especially the slogan calling for self-determination in the "Black Belt," aroused controversy. Party sources suggest that the abstract notion of the Franja Negra never took root among workers of color and offended non-black workers. Indeed, non-Communist left-wingers thought that the emphasis on race was irresponsible and only served to divide workers. Cuban anarchists and, in particular, Trotskyists criticized the CNOC and SNOIA policy of advocating complete parity between black and white workers among union officeholders, arguing that it was contributing to a "race war."[71] Other labor movement activists argued that despite the exclusionary and racist politics of the post-independence era, the Franja Negra notion ignored the fact that the 1895–98 independence war had forged a single Cuban nation and united all ethnic groups.[72]

---

[68] "Informe de Bell sobre el II Congreso del PCC," May 5, 1934, 495/105/98, Cuban Party, RTsKhIDNI.

[69] For the English and French notices, see *Bandera Roja*, March 6, 1934, 2.

[70] "La cuestión nacional en Cuba," November 10, 1934, 495/105/95, Cuban Party, RTsKhIDNI. See also Fernández Robaina, *El negro en Cuba*, 135–38.

[71] *Nuestra Palabra* 2, no. 16 (1935): 2. See also Bernardo Rodríguez, "Temas alrededor del IV Congreso Obrero en la Habana," *Adelante*, January 26, 1934, 10; and *Programa del partido bolchevique leninista* (Havana: Impr. O'Reilly, 1934), 40.

[72] "Testimonio: Preguntas y respuestas," 138.

More importantly, the PCC's defense of immigrant workers challenged important elements of Cuban nationalism. The rebirth of Cuban nationalism in the 1920s, along with its anti-imperialism and calls for self-discovery, contained a strong racial element. The radical nationalist critique of the dominant role played by US and foreign capital in the sugar industry had understandably emphasized the links between foreign capital, the importation of Caribbean *braceros*, and the resulting downward pressure on wages and dilution of *cubanidad*. Therefore, when the Communists decided to attack ethnic and racial chauvinism, they offended the very same constituency that the left was trying to win over and risked confrontation with a powerful current of opinion shared by Cubans who embraced progressive politics. Indeed, when the first stirrings of the Popular Front reached Cuba at the end of 1934, the PCC gratefully seized the opportunity to begin toning down its line on the Franja Negra, abandoning the concept completely during the following year.

The ultraleftism of the Third Period also obstructed the party's plans to recruit more Afro-Cuban members. It was precisely the marginalized and impoverished black unemployed who were likely to be among the main beneficiaries of the new nationalist labor legislation, especially in areas where Afro-Cubans constituted a large part of the labor force and competed with Caribbean workers in a depressed labor market.[73] Afro-Cubans enthusiastically applauded the 50 percent legislation implemented in the fall of 1933, judging by the size and composition of the demonstrations that greeted the passage of the law; they also demanded an increase from 50 to 80 percent in the employment of native-born workers.[74] Anger over leftist opposition to the nationalist measures led mobs to storm *El País,* the only Spanish-language newspaper employing operatives affiliated to the CNOC, after the Havana paper had opposed nationalist labor legislation.[75] Communists of color also became the targets of urban violence.

Finally, pan-ethnic solidarity was undermined by several other new laws, such as those banning foreign workers from leadership positions in unions. Street fights erupted in Havana when nationalist organizations

---

[73] David Booth, "Cuba, Color and the Revolution," *Science & Society* 11 (1976): 149. Booth is wrong, however, in his reference to the PCC's "hesitant approval" of the Ley del 50%.

[74] This was true of the December 15 demonstration; Enrique Lumen, *La revolución cubana, 1902–1934: Crónica de nuestro tiempo* (Mexico City: Ediciones Botas, 1934), 156.

[75] Samuel S. Dickson to Secretary of State, December 26, 1933, 837.00/4571, RG 59, NARA.

"volunteered" to implement the legislation, sometimes with the tacit approval of government ministries. Members of the nationalist organization that called itself the Comité Supremo del 50% (Supreme Committee of the 50 percent), for example, visited the offices of labor unions suspected of opposition to the nationalist laws and physically ejected foreign-born leaders, replacing them with native Cubans.[76]

REPATRIATION, ETHNIC CHAUVINISM, AND THE 1933 REVOLUTION

The ethnic nationalism of the Grau San Martín government flourished in an environment in which racial tension had been steadily increasing. Anti-immigrant measures had already been initiated by Machado. In an attempt to neutralize concern over unemployment and undermine the nationalist critique of official immigration policy, the Machado government favored native Cubans in employment. Public works contracts were altered to stipulate that 50 percent of workers employed in government projects be Cuban-born.[77] More dramatically, in the late 1920s the government began deporting West Indian workers.[78] Lack of financial resources, however, limited the government's ability to implement this preferred option. As a result, officials of the Machado regime tried to coerce foreign embassies into covering the costs of repatriation and, in the end, these costs were frequently borne by foreign governments.[79] Thus, in the summer and winter of 1931 and at the beginning of 1932, US Navy vessels repatriated 700 Puerto Ricans and a large number of Virgin Islanders, while a Jamaican government scheme helped finance the return of some 40,000 of its citizens between 1930 and 1933.[80] Jamaican

[76] *Cuba Today,* December 21, 1933, reporting information that had appeared in the newspaper *Ya.*

[77] Noble Brandon Judah to Secretary of State, March 8, 1929, enclosing report by Frederick Todd, Cuba Embassy Post Records, Part 16, 1929, 855 Immigration 1929, RG 84, NARA.

[78] The repatriations began in 1928, when 17,742 Caribbean workers left Cuba (voluntarily and through compulsion). Edward Nathan, US Consul, Santiago de Cuba, to Secretary of State, "Emigration and Deportation of Colored Population from Eastern Cuba," June 7, 1928, 837.5538/8, RG 59, NARA.

[79] In the summer of 1931, the British Embassy managed to frustrate attempts by field officers of the Cuban Department of Labor, assisted by rural guards, "to stir up discontent among West Indian labourers on the sugar plantations in Oriente and indirectly to force this Legation to undertake the wholesale evacuation of the British elements among them." Sir J. Broderick to Sir John Simon, April 4, 1932, FO 371, PRO.

[80] Edwin Schoenrich, US Consul, Santiago de Cuba, to Secretary of State, September 3, 1931, 837.504/336; November 5, 1931, 837.504/374; and State Department to US

workers were relatively fortunate. Workers from other islands, such as those
from the Leeward Islands group and Barbadians (most of them employed at
the Chaparra estate), did not receive equivalent aid from their colonial
governments to help with the costs of repatriation.[81]

Nevertheless, the major factor that led to the expulsion of Caribbean
labor from the plantations was the collapse of sugar prices and the drastic
shortening of the *zafra*. In the Nuevitas area (on the north coast of
Camagüey province), employers were already trying to replace Jamaicans
and Haitians in field work during the 1931 *zafra*.[82] Conditions at the
Chaparra estate deteriorated to such an extent that over 500 British West
Indians begged assistance from the British Embassy, complaining that

there is no progress ... starvation has taken place and a famine is threatening the
island right now. So before many of us should die of starvation and calamities, we
are putting our distress to the mother country, asking her for some kind of
assistance by which we may be able to leave this island of Cuba. We are just like
the children of Israel in the land of Egypt.[83]

Ethnic and interethnic sensitivities, therefore, were already in
a heightened state when the Grau San Martín government unveiled its
social and economic legislation.[84] The two most dramatic manifestations
of the new government's economic and ethnic nationalism were an
October 18 decree banning further immigration of Jamaican and
Haitian workers, and a November 18 decree calling for the nationalization of the workforce – the so-called Ley del 50%.[85] A parallel decree
obliging unions to appoint only Cuban-born individuals to leadership
positions also created resentment – especially among those unionists
who recalled how, in the early 1930s, *machadista* officials had blamed

Consul, Santiago de Cuba, January 2, 1932, 837.504/376 (all in RG 59, NARA). The
scale of British West Indian distress was indicated by the huge volume of correspondence
passing through the British consulate general in Santiago de Cuba. In 1929 alone the
secretary handled an average of twenty-nine letters a day; Morris to Foreign Office,
March 7, 1930, A2177/2177/14, FO 371, PRO.

[81] See the April 30, 1931, petition from George J. Carlyle (a native of Antigua) attached
to M. A. Jacobs to British Embassy, Havana, K7511/7084/214, FO 369, PRO.

[82] E. A. Wakefield, "Political Situation in Nuevitas Consular District," February 6, 1931,
Havana Post Records, Part 10, 1931, 800 Cuba, RG 84, NARA.

[83] See the petition signed by M. A. Jacobs and British West Indian subjects resident at the
Chaparra mill, K7511/7084/214, FO 369, PRO.

[84] Among the pro-worker measures were laws limiting the working day and recognizing
unions. At the very end of the Grau government, Decree 117 set a new minimum wage for
cane cutting, loading, and hauling, which would be 50 cents per 100 *arrobas* as opposed
to the 30 cents and less paid during 1933.

[85] Pérez de la Riva, "Cuba y la inmigración antillana," 70–73.

unemployment on the actions of foreign-led unions. As in Brazil, where Getúlio Vargas's newly formed Ministry of Labor had passed (with strong Afro-Brazilian support) a law calling for the nationalization of labor in 1931, labor-market competition by foreign-born workers was also the scapegoat for a perceived "social problem" within Cuba. In both countries, nativist and xenophobic rhetoric infected black and white laborers, even though there was no Afro-Cuban equivalent of the quasi-fascist Brazilian Black Front of the early and mid-1930s.[86]

The ethnic and national policy of the 1933 revolution did not break with the previous regime's stand; Grau continued Machado's policy of repatriating foreign workers. In the cities the main victims were the Spanish immigrant workers who dominated the utilities and commercial sectors as well as the railroads and urban tram systems. Jewish artisans were also targeted.[87] In rural areas, however, *antillanos* bore the brunt of the nationalist assault. The expulsions followed the passage of a law decreeing the repatriation of all foreigners who were out of work or without resources.[88] Although in theory the Grau government restricted repatriation to indigent workers, who were given a token two pesos upon their departure, numerous abuses against employed workers were committed.[89] As under Machado, raids and deportations were initiated by the Guardia Rural. And during the last twelve days of November, *antillanos*, particularly Haitians, were tracked down in Oriente province by bounty hunters eager to collect the rewards that had been promised to those who helped in their capture.

Candidates for repatriation were chosen arbitrarily. They included Haitians who were employed in the sugar or coffee sectors, as well as others who were small landowners. Many of the Haitian coffee cultivators in the Santiago de Cuba and Guantánamo areas had lived in Cuba for over fifteen years.[90] Cases abounded in which deportees lost belongings, animals, and wages or other monies owed them. They often had to sell their earthly possessions for a pittance – providing juicy pickings for employers,

---

[86] Andrews, *Blacks and Whites*, 147, 151–55.

[87] Thomas F. O'Brien, *The Revolutionary Mission: American Enterprise in Latin America, 1900–1945* (Cambridge: Cambridge University Press, 1996), chapters 8–9; Robert M. Levine, *Tropical Diaspora: The Jewish Experience in Cuba* (Gainesville, FL: University Press of Florida, 1993), 52–59.

[88] Translation of Decree 2232 attached to E. Schoenrich, "Repatriation of Haitians by Cuban Government from Santiago de Cuba, November 22, 1933," November 28, 1933, 837.504/427, RG 59, NARA.

[89] Alvarez Estévez, *Azúcar e inmigración*, 216–17.

[90] *Adelante*, December 3, 1933, 15–16.

merchants, and local functionaries – which gave rise to the assertion that the repatriations constituted a second *"zafra"* for the lucky few.[91] Haitian workers who had been particularly active in unions or labor agitation, especially those who had been active participants in the sugar insurgency of August through October, were singled out for attention by foremen, *colonos,* and mill owners.[92] Most of the deportees were not even allowed to alert their families or collect their belongings before being moved to deportation centers in Santiago. The first load of human cargo left Santiago on November 22, on board a Cuban steamer, the *Julián Alonso,* carrying 995 Haitian deportees. Fidel Castro, then a seven-year-old Santiago schoolboy, recalled the sad spectacle of Haitian deportees leaving Santiago on a similar ship.[93]

The PCC and CNOC attacked the labor nationalization laws as a fascist attempt to divide workers and make scapegoats of foreign-born *braceros.*[94] The Communists' suspicions were certainly well founded, to judge by the many cases in which Cuban-born workers (including Afro-Cubans) helped round up Haitians. At the Alto Cedro mill, workers celebrated the capture of Haitians before assaulting Jamaican workers with chants of "Next time it will be your turn."[95] In some areas Guardias Rurales bought the cooperation of Cuban-born workers with payments of 20 cents for each Haitian captured.[96] Communist Party activists reluctantly admitted that Cuban-born black workers were frequently indifferent to the repatriation of *antillanos,* whom they considered to be of an "inferior race" and even "savages." The nationalization of labor laws had caught the PCC by surprise and had created havoc in the party's organizational work among native-born black people.[97]

[91] Letter from Dr. Cristóbal Baro, *Adelante,* May 25, 1934, 4, 9; *El Obrero Azucarero (Organo Central del SNOIA),* June 1, 1934, 1.

[92] *El Obrero Azucarero,* June 1, 1934, 8; Pérez de la Riva, "Cuba y la inmigración antillana," 72.

[93] Frei Betto, *Fidel and Religion: Conversations with Frei Betto* (Sydney: Pathfinder Press, 1986), 83. In his 1995 conversations Fidel Castro criticized Grau's nationalist labor legislation and the inhuman and cruel nature of the deportations.

[94] Some recent Cuban writers have tried to downplay this opposition; see Serviat, *El problema negro,* 113.

[95] *Adelante,* December 5, 1933, 4, 9; Leví Marrero, "Los horrores de los feudos azucareros: Cazando haitianos en la región oriental," *Bohemia,* March 25, 1934, 62.

[96] *Daily Worker* (New York), January 4, 1934, 4.

[97] "Juan" to "estimados compañeros," December 2, 1933, 495/105/68, Cuban Party, RTsKhIDNI; Reunión del Grupo Sindical con el Secretariado del Partido, October 12, 1933, 495/105/80, Cuban Party, RTsKhIDNI; "Actas de la Conferencia Celebrada en La Habana a los siete días del mes de diciembre de 1933 en preparación del Congreso del

In itself, the Ley del 50% did not specifically target the sugar industry; indeed field labor was explicitly excluded from its provisions. In response to protests by foreign-owned sugar companies, foreign technicians were also exempted, as were 200 Chinese workers of the UFC whose job it was to sew up gunnysacks of sugar after they had been filled.[98] A survey of eight sugar mills conducted by the British Embassy in the summer of 1934 revealed that while some British West Indians were being discharged, the number of repatriations as a result of the Ley del 50% was smaller than expected. This is not so surprising. Overall employment levels in the sugar industry had fallen substantially during the Depression and the pool of potentially deportable workers was, therefore, much reduced. More importantly, from the mid-1920s British West Indians had drifted from the countryside to permanent residence and employment in cities and towns. A large percentage never returned to the cane fields, where the repatriation campaign was focused.[99]

The Ley del 50% unquestionably divided working-class communities and weakened solidarities based on both class and ethnicity. Once again, native-born Afro-Cubans were among the most enthusiastic supporters of the labor nationalization actions.

IMMIGRANTS AND WORKER ACTIVISM IN THE LABOR INSURGENCY OF 1933

Morris of Lykes Brothers tells a good story. He saw a negro in the street with a red flag so he stopped his car and called the negro over and asked him if he were a Communist. The negro proudly said "sí señor." Morris enquired as to just what a Communist might be. The negro stopped and thought a second and then said "un hombre muy guapo con una bandera roja" [a brave man with a red flag].[100]

PCC," p. 8, 495/105/70, RTsKhIDNI. Nevertheless, on occasions (as in the sugar center of Morón) the party was able to mobilize a cross-ethnic coalition against the nationalist labor legislation. See Cuban Party, 495/105/68, "Simón" to "Querido Johnny," December 30, 1933, 495/105/68, Cuban Party, RTsKhIDNI.

[98] Samuel S. Dickson to Secretary of State, December 22, 1933, 837.00/4570, including F. T. F. Dumont, "Memorandum re: United Fruit Company," December 20, 1933, RG 59, NARA.

[99] Rees to Foreign Office, London, August 8, 1934, A6831/211/4, FO 371, PRO; Harris to Foreign Office, London, March 11, 1925, A/1667/22/14, FO 371, PRO, transmitting a report prepared by H. T. Dignum. See also Grant Watson to Foreign Office, London, February 21, 1934, A82031/211/14, FO 371, PRO.

[100] Ruby Hart Phillips, *Cuban Sideshow* (Havana: Cuban Press, 1935), 176.

When the energies of the labor movement were unleashed in the summer of 1933, Afro-Cubans were prominent among the working men and women who flexed their collective industrial muscle and tested the new order. Foreign and domestic observers noted an increase in the self-confidence of Afro-Cubans following the overthrow of Machado.[101] Black soldiers were prominent in public displays of anti-imperialist fervor, especially in Havana. During a demonstration on September 14, called by the Anti-Imperialist League to protest US interventionism, a black soldier created a sensation when he pledged the support of his fellow soldiers in any move taken to prevent the landing of US troops.[102] Observers were also struck by the prominent role Cuban-born blacks played in promoting and enforcing the Ley del 50%. Afro-Cubans were at the head of the crowds that worked their way through Havana streets in early January 1934, confronting shopkeepers and owners of small businesses who had not implemented the labor nationalization law.

North American diplomats and journalists, clearly unprepared for the explosion of political statements by black workers of all nationalities, expressed resentment when confronted by evidence of heightened black and Antillean assertiveness. Sumner Welles, the US plenipotentiary and *éminence grise* of Cuban politics during the summer and fall of 1933, was outraged when an American citizen en route to the Miranda mill was obliged to obtain a pass "from a Jamaican who signed himself as corporal of the Red Guard."[103] A more measured response to British West Indian sympathy with the revolutionary fervor sweeping the streets and fields came from the *New York Times* correspondents in Havana, somewhat taken aback by their Jamaican servants' warm response to the efforts being made to unionize domestic labor. The wording of one diary entry ("John, being Jamaican, is quite keen on looking out for his personal rights") says a good deal about contemporary expectations concerning Jamaican behavior.[104]

---

[101] "Negroes were among the leaders in seizing sugar properties and making exorbitant demands on mill managers. Moreover, following the revolt of the sergeants, the percentage of Negro officers and enlisted men in the Cuban army greatly increased." See Foreign Policy Association, *Problems of the New Cuba: Report of the Commission on Cuban Affairs* (New York: Foreign Policy Association, 1935), 33.

[102] *Daily Worker*, September 15, 1933, 1; Lionel Soto, *La revolución del '33* (Havana: Pueblo y Educación, 1985), 3: 81.

[103] Sumner Welles to Secretary of State, September 30, 1933, 837.00B/83, RG 59, NARA.

[104] Phillips, *Cuban Sideshow*, 147.

Away from the cities, reports of the *antillanos'* role in the sugar industry actions of 1933 are contradictory. Post-1959 Cuban historiography
has presented a uniform and unproblematic treatment of this issue,
according to which relations between black and white workers, native
and foreign-born, were generally shaped by class solidarity.[105] The contemporary evidence, however, does not support such an undifferentiated
reading of events. It is clear that Cuban-born workers did not expect
immigrants, especially Haitians, to be in the front line of unionization or
political action. On the other hand, Haitian workers had certainly
defended themselves when wages and working conditions began to collapse in the early 1930s. In mid-January 1932, Haitians and Jamaicans
protested pay cuts by refusing to begin cutting cane at the US-controlled
Cunagua mill.[106] Moreover, one of the earliest actions in which the PCC
and CNOC were successful was a movement of 300 Haitian coffee pickers
in Bueycito (near Manzanillo) in December 1932.[107] Despite these incidents, Cuban Communists were clearly taken aback by the scale of *antillano* involvement in the sugar insurgency. As the most experienced of the
Comintern envoys to Cuba in the early 1930s noted in a confidential
December 1933 report:

It is clear that in Havana we were terribly ignorant of the persecution of *antillano*
workers, before and after the Ley del 50%. In fact, in past years when we discussed
sugar work we believed that this was difficult and that the main obstacles were the
Haitian and Jamaican workers whom we could not reach because they spoke
English or patois. But our assumption was built on complete ignorance ... .
Haitian and Jamaican workers demonstrated a high degree of combativeness in
the recent labor struggle. They fought more like members of a slave rebellion who
had nothing to lose. In many mills they were in the front line of the struggle.[108]

Generalizations about the behavior of Haitian and Jamaican immigrants
abound. Lionel Soto, the Cuban historian and diplomat, maintained that
Haitians and Jamaicans proved difficult to mobilize in the first wave of
union organization and strike activity, from January to March 1933.[109]
This view did not go unchallenged. A contemporary observer, the
Communist Party leader and theoretician Rubén Martínez Villena,

---

[105] This, for example, is the view of Alvarez Estévez in his excellent book, *Azúcar
e inmigración,* 150.
[106] *Cuba Today* 8, no. 268 (1932): 5, citing *El Mercurio* (Havana).
[107] *El partido comunista y los problemas de la revolución en Cuba* (n.p.: Comité Central del
Partido Comunista de Cuba, 1933), 18, 38.
[108] "Juan" to "estimados compañeros," December 2, 1933.
[109] Soto, *La revolución del '33,* 2, 161.

celebrated the establishment of cross-ethnic unity, insisting that Jamaican workers had refused to act as strikebreakers at several mills during the first strike wave of 1933.[110] The Cuban Communist's account, written in New York before he returned to Cuba, can be viewed as a comforting endorsement of the Comintern's advocacy of agitation among black laborers, including immigrants. Another near-contemporary account of black labor militancy, based on extensive field research and interviewing, was the *Problems of the New Cuba* (drafted in 1934 by a US panel of New Deal academics), which noted that "negroes were among the leaders in seizing sugar properties and making exorbitant demands on mill managers."[111] Finally, an examination of lists of sugar workers imprisoned in Havana in mid-October reveals many Anglo surnames, a sure sign of the presence of a British West Indian contingent.[112]

Foreign businessmen also thought that Jamaican and Barbadian immigrants were prone to "red" activities, even if they qualified their comments with the familiar reservations about workers acting "under duress" and being provoked by "outside agitators." A correspondent for a leading sugar industry journal wrote in late October 1933 that "there would have been a great deal less difficulty … if it were not for the presence of large numbers of negro laborers from other parts of the West Indies … who have displayed much more tendency to join in extreme movements than have the Cuban workers."[113] At the Estrella mill, the English office manager told the British Embassy that thirty Jamaicans had joined the strike movement although, he added, all but half a dozen had done so "under compulsion."[114] At Manatí (in the northwestern corner of Oriente province), the British chief engineer reported that the "wildest" of the men who descended on the mill to press their demands were "Jamaicans and Spaniards."[115] The identification of *antillano* workers with labor militancy was sufficiently widespread for a manager of the UFC to inform a US

---

[110] Rubén Martínez Villena, "Las contradicciones internas del imperialismo yanqui en Cuba y el alza del movimiento revolucionario," in *Rubén: Antología del pensamiento político*, ed. Josefina Meza Paz (Havana: Ed. Arte y Literatura, Instituto Cubano del Libro, 1976), 443; Luis Ortiz, "El empuje revolucionario de las masas termina con la dictadura machadista," *Mundo Obrero* (New York) (August–September 1933): 12–13, 21. See also *Daily Worker*, July 26, 1933, 5.

[111] Foreign Policy Association, *Problems of the New Cuba*, 33.

[112] *Ahora*, October 18, 1933, 1.   [113] *Facts about Sugar* (November 1933): 415.

[114] A. Hopton Jones to Grant Watson, September 16, 1933, in Watson to London, September 20, 1933, A7120/255/14, FO 371, PRO.

[115] Grant Watson to Foreign Office, London, September 19, 1933, A7118/255/14, FO 371, PRO.

Navy officer that his company would benefit from the Ley del 50% because it "gives them an opportunity to weed out the known radicals and undesirables."[116] Since sugar companies were in general hostile toward Grau's nationalist labor laws, this was a remarkable admission.

A more careful examination of the evidence concerning *antillano* responses to the labor insurgency reveals a much messier picture. Evidence of Haitian worker unrest always caught observers' attention. At Tánamo (in northeastern Oriente province), a newspaper correspondent who attended a meeting of workers called by the union noted with surprise how even the Haitian cutters spoke out.[117] On the other hand, a SNOIA conference document implied that the complex ethnic composition of the sugar labor force was an obstacle to united action. The presence of Haitians at the Delicias and San Germán mills in Oriente province, it noted, "makes work more difficult."[118] In the same vein, the report acknowledged that once the era of black immigration had ended in 1930 and 1931, the resulting increase in the number of white workers employed in the sugar mills had "facilitate[d] struggle."[119]

But "Granda," a delegate from the SNOIA's National Bureau to the Santiago regional conference of the sugar workers' union in September 1933, reported that UFC workers of all races and nationalities at Banes had joined with Jamaicans and Haitians, and that together they had formed a common bloc and participated in the red militias.[120] At the Río Cauto mill, Jamaicans had been enrolled in the strike movement. The same thing happened with the strike committee at the Mabay mill.[121] At Cayo Juan Claro, in Oriente province, Jamaicans and "Dutch" workers (presumably from the islands of Aruba and Curaçao) took part in strike action. At Miranda (also in Oriente province), Jamaicans and Haitians were reported to be among the leaders of protest activity in various *colonias*.[122] Jamaicans and Haitians at the América mill (Oriente province) were said to be members of the SNOIA. Among "communists" arrested in early October in the Chaparra-Delicias zone in Oriente province were several British West Indians.[123] In October, British West Indian workers also appear to have

---

[116] Commanding Officer to Commander, Special Service Squadron, "Subject: Visit of USS *Reuben James* to Nipe Bay, 5–12 Dec. 1933," December 12, 1933, Cuba Embassy Reports, Part 12, 800, Cuba Reports from Ships. Commanding Officer, USS *Reuben James*, Nipe Bay, RG 84, NARA.

[117] *Adelante*, September 14, 1933, 10.   [118] Rojas, *Luchas obreras*, Annex 3, 178.

[119] Ibid., 179.   [120] Ibid., Annex 5, 184.   [121] Ibid., 186.   [122] Ibid., 189, 191.

[123] Commanding Officer USS *Dupont*, October 8, 1933, to Commander, Special Service Squadron, "Subject: USS *Dupont*, Station File at Puerto Padre, Cuba from 27 Sept. to 7

been active at Jaronú, where a worker from St. Lucia, Walter Cyril, was killed by the Guardia Rural during a striker-led demonstration.[124]

Eyewitnesses to the occupation of the Senado mill recalled no conflict between white and black workers. Rather, they noted the key role played by a Jamaican worker, Jaime Brown, who claimed to have fought in World War I and may have been a member of the Cuban Communist Party.[125] Finally, it is significant that ten of the victims of the massacre perpetrated by soldiers at Senado on November 18 were Haitians and one, Elijah Sigree, a Jamaican.[126]

A detailed account of developments at the Báguanos and Tacajó mills during September 1933 (written from a management perspective) also suggests that Antillean workers did not shy away from labor activism; they certainly warranted particular attention from US observers. Maurice Leonard, administrator of the Punta Alegre Corporation, referred to the harassment of his managers "by mobs of crazily excited Haitians and Jamaicans, as well as by Cubans and Spaniards."[127] The occupation of the Punta Alegre mill was allegedly led by a Haitian nicknamed "Cerveza Tropical." During the mill occupation, West Indian workers pulled up the railroad lines to prevent troops from arriving. They also tried to prevent the Cuban navy from disembarking sailors at the docks of Punta San Juan.[128] Jamaican workers had played an active role from the beginning of the occupation of the Báguanos mill: "Before noon a group of 20 Jamaican workmen with sticks appear[ed], and compel[led] the female servants of private homes to leave their work." The women servants mentioned in this report may also have been Jamaicans, given the popularity of employing English-speaking British West Indians in domestic service. The management and nonunionized staff of Báguanos were constantly threatened by reports that the strike committee would be strengthened by the impending arrival of thousands of Haitians from Tacajó.[129]

Oct. 1933," October 4, 1933, Cuba Embassy Post Records, Part 12, 800 Cuba 1933 – Reports from Ships, RG 84, NARA.

[124] Grant Watson to Foreign Office, January 27, 1934, A1389/1389/14, FO 371, PRO.

[125] Morciego, *El crimen*, 46–53.

[126] Marrero, "Los horrores," 62. On the killing of Sigree, see Watson to Foreign Office, London, December 13, 1933, A63/63/14, FO 371, PRO.

[127] Maurice Leonard to Edward L. Reed, October 6, 1933, in Welles to Secretary of State, October 11, 1933, 837.00/4207, RG 59, NARA.

[128] Carlos González Echevarría, *Origen y desarrollo del movimiento obrero camagüeyano* (Havana: Ed. de Ciencias Sociales, 1984), 86–87.

[129] "Memorandum Re: Central Báguanos strike," in Welles to Secretary of State, October 11, 1933, 837.00/4207, RG 59, NARA.

CONCLUSION

As we sort through the complex responses of *antillanos* to the strikes and mill occupations of 1933, some tentative conclusions emerge. It is clear that Haitians and Jamaicans did not stand aside from the mobilizations; indeed there is considerable evidence of active participation by *antillanos*. There is, therefore, a sharp contrast between the behavior exhibited by Caribbean workers in Cuba during 1933 and the stance adopted by British West Indian workers in the tropical fruit enclaves of Central America. In Costa Rica, for example, *antillano* workers did not heed the call to drop their tools in the great 1934 strike against the UFC, despite calls for interethnic unity by sections of the (by Cuban standards very weak) forces of the left.[130] In Costa Rica, the Communists were unable to build a following among immigrants and the strikers were almost entirely Hispanic workers.

In both the Cuban and Costa Rican cases, *braceros* and locally born workers were competitors in an appallingly depressed labor market. Similarly, there were strands of ethnic chauvinism in the anti-imperialist and nationalist projects that enveloped the labor movements of the two societies. The contrast between the behavior of *antillano* workers in Cuba and Costa Rica may be explicated by the relative strength of the forces advocating a radical, non-chauvinist version of anti-imperialism in the two countries. In Cuba, the participation of the Communist Party was a critical factor both in the formation of the island's first national sugar workers' union (SNOIA) and in the coordination, if not the execution, of the most important strikes and occupations. This meant that the impact of the nationalist and racist discourse that constructed *antillano* workers as the enemy of *cubanidad* could, on many occasions, be blunted or over-turned by appeals to class solidarity. In Costa Rica, at the time of the UFC strike, the Communist Party had only been in existence for three years; for this reason its presence on the Atlantic Coast was weak and its impact on labor militancy less consequential than in Cuba. Nevertheless, the contrast between the two cases should not be exaggerated. In Cuba, as in Costa Rica, racially charged jingoism served to divide the labor force along lines of nationality.

---

[130] Ronald Harpelle, "The Social and Political Integration of West Indians in Costa Rica: 1930–1950," *Journal of Latin American Studies* 25, no. 1 (1993): 107; Bourgois, *Ethnicity at Work*, 108–09.

The difference in *antillano* behavior also appears to have been a function of the contrasting socioeconomic profiles of the two *bracero* groups. In the Costa Rican case it has been argued that *antillano* aloofness was a product of the fact that many British West Indian immigrants had become small landowners by the early 1930s and preferred to support the UFC rather than the strikers and their allies among medium-sized national banana producers.[131] By contrast, *antillano* workers in Cuba did not grow significant amounts of sugar for processing in the mills, although many *braceros,* especially Haitians, did cultivate small plots as a way of surviving the increasingly lengthy *tiempo muerto* between harvest seasons.

But it was the differing contents and contexts of the Cuban and Costa Rican labor actions that encouraged and constrained the involvement of *antillanos.* In Cuba, worker effervescence during the summer and fall of 1933 was intimately linked to the temporary disintegration of the bourgeois political order. The collapse of the Machado regime on August 12 was followed, a little over three weeks later, by a sergeants' revolt and the disintegration of army discipline over large areas of the island. These events rendered the normal repressive forces inoperative or weak during the early stages of the strikes and mill occupations. This temporary collapse of the old order gave sugar workers opportunities to reverse the rhythms of everyday life – with strikers expelling and humiliating mill owners and managers while at the same time creating parallel structures of organization, policing, and production. In the Cuban case, insurgency took the form of physical occupations of the mills and mill properties, and this allowed for more radical breaks with the past than strikes could provide. In these circumstances, a large proportion of the sugar labor force and its families were sucked into the vacuum left by the temporary abdication of managerial and state authority. *Antillano* workers moved (and sometimes were swept) into the spaces opened up by the insurgency. Neutrality was rarely a viable option. In Costa Rica, however, the mobilizations did not exceed the limits of a strike, albeit a militant one, and the worker actions on the Atlantic Coast did not coincide with a crisis of the Costa Rican political system.

---

[131] This is the view of Bourgois, *Ethnicity at Work*, and Chomsky, *West Indian Workers*.

3

Indigenous Movements in the Eye
of the Hurricane

Marc Becker

Sociologist Andrés Guerrero has famously examined how nineteenth-century liberal legislation in Ecuador created a "ventriloquist's voice" that mediated Indigenous expressions of resistance to exclusionary governing structures.[1] An oft-repeated assumption is that in political struggles Indigenous voices disappear, and we are left with the actions of intermediaries who purportedly spoke in defense of subaltern rights but in reality only desired to advance their own political, social, and economic interests. In essence, this perspective alleges that these intermediaries added another layer of exploitation to an already marginalized and silenced population. Careful studies, however, reveal that Indigenous activists did advance their own agendas, both alone and in collaboration with sympathetic urban allies. These examinations highlight the problematic nature of Guerrero's choice of metaphor, as ventriloquists' dummies are inanimate, with no sentience or consciousness of their own. In contrast, this chapter emphasizes the agency of hidden actors as they sought to advance their political agendas. A larger problem is the lack of written archival documentation that typically forms the basis for a scholarly examination of the past, and these absences complicate the recovery of subaltern voices. Typically this lack of sources is not the fault of local organic intellectuals, but rather a function of the racist and sexist attitudes of the members of a dominant class who did not find Indigenous peoples' thoughts and actions worthy of preservation.

[1] Andrés Guerrero, "The Construction of a Ventriloquist's Image: Liberal Discourse and the 'Miserable Indian Race' in Late 19th-Century Ecuador," *Journal of Latin American Studies* 29, no. 3 (1997): 555–90.

One stunning example of the disregard for rural communities emerges in an examination of US surveillance of leftist activists in Latin America during the 1940s. During World War II, the Federal Bureau of Investigation (FBI) assigned about 700 agents to the region through a program called the Special Intelligence Service. The original justification for their presence was to combat German Nazi influence in Mexico, Brazil, Chile, and Argentina, although the program quickly became focused on countering communist activities, which was always FBI Director J. Edgar Hoover's main concern.[2] These endeavors followed in the tracks of previous US military and diplomatic surveillance of leftist activities and foreshadowed that of the Central Intelligence Agency (CIA) in the postwar period.

Despite the US security apparatus' stated concern about subversive movements, and even as officials conducted heightened intelligence-gathering efforts against urban leftists, they missed some of the most significant political organizing efforts. Neither the FBI nor embassy officials submitted to Washington substantive reports on the foundation of the Federación Ecuatoriana de Indios (Ecuadorian Federation of Indians, FEI) in 1944 or its subsequent organizing efforts. As evidence of this negligence, the FBI was unable to identify Dolores Cacuango, the most important Indigenous leader from the 1940s, when she participated in a 1943 anti-fascist meeting and then served as the Indigenous representative to the resulting anti-fascist committee.[3] In May 1947, shortly after the departure of the FBI, the US embassy in Quito reported that the principle direction of the Partido Comunista del Ecuador (Communist Party of Ecuador, PCE) efforts appeared to be in support of "Youth movements and Indian activities," but the diplomats failed to include any specific details in their lengthy ten-page report.[4] Officials also consistently

---

[2] Marc Becker, *The FBI in Latin America: The Ecuador Files* (Durham, NC: Duke University Press, 2017).

[3] J. Edgar Hoover to Adolf A. Berle, Jr., "Communist Activities in Ecuador," January 26, 1944, Record Group (hereafter RG) 59, 822.00B/78, U.S. National Archives and Records Administration (hereafter NARA), College Park, Maryland. Cacuango was well known locally for her activism. One hacienda owner, for example, complained about "the *famous* Dolores Cacuango" organizing Indigenous workers on his estate. See C. Anibal Maldonado to Manual Villacis, Hda. Muyurco, October 9, 1946, Correspondencia Recibida (hereafter CR), M-H, Julio-Diciembre 1947, p. 32, Archivo Nacional de Medicina del Museo Nacional de Medicina "Dr. Eduardo Estrella," Fondo Junta Central de Asistencia Pública, Quito (hereafter JCAP) (emphasis in original).

[4] George P. Shaw to Secretary of State George Marshall, "Report on Recent Communist Activities in Ecuador," June 12, 1947, no. 5312, RG 59, 822.00B/6–1247, NARA.

downplayed the political role of women, and Afro-Ecuadorians are almost completely absent from US intelligence reports.

Philip Agee, in his report on CIA activities in Ecuador two decades later, only mentions in passing a massive December 1961 FEI march that provided an impetus for a sweeping agrarian reform several years later.[5] In a 2008 interview shortly before his death, Agee claimed ignorance of the highly active and militant Indigenous organizing efforts that took place during his time in the country.[6] George Jones, a political officer in the US embassy in Quito in the 1960s, similarly acknowledged that diplomats "had very little relationship with the Indians." He confessed, "There was nobody in the Embassy who could speak any of the Indian languages and in defense of that, precisely because they had no role in the system, no influence on the system, it was a very low priority for us."[7] Despite this lack of attention, the FEI is significant both for its contemporary advance of agrarian issues, and for how it laid the groundwork for subsequent social-movement organizing strategies. The absence of scrutiny of the FEI, one of the first pan-ethnic federations in Latin America, reveals much about the narrow assumptions and nature of US intelligence-gathering efforts. That lack of imperial interest in subaltern mobilizations contributed to the development of a distorted understanding of the left that emphasizes urban and male actors to the exclusion of Indigenous and female militants. The recovery of these subaltern voices is critical for a fuller and more accurate understanding of the Latin American left.

SUBALTERN VOICES

The US intelligence apparatus was not alone in ignoring marginalized voices. Ecuadorian archives are just as silent when it comes to preserving Indigenous actions. Subaltern voices appear sporadically, and it requires a laborious and time-consuming review of documents before one accidentally stumbles across them. For example, in 1935 an abusive administrator evicted the Indigenous laborer Ildefonso Quimbiamba from the government-owned

---

[5] Philip Agee, *Inside the Company: CIA Diary* (New York: Bantam Books, 1975), 212. See Marc Becker, *Indians and Leftists in the Making of Ecuador's Modern Indigenous Movements* (Durham, NC: Duke University Press, 2008), 131.

[6] Philip Agee, Jaime Galarza Zavala, and Francisco Herrera Arauz, *The CIA Case against Latin America*, Historical Archive, Notebook No. 2 (Quito: Ministry of Foreign Affairs and Human Mobility, 2014), 94.

[7] Interview with George F. Jones, August 6, 1996, www.adst.org/OH%20TOCs/Jones,%20George%20F.pdf (accessed May 7, 2018).

Santo Domingo de Cayambe hacienda. With nowhere else to go, Quimbiamba settled on a piece of land, known as "Ancho Callejón," that the rural dwellers in the area understood to be communal land. The heirs of the recently deceased oligarch Gabriel García Alcázar, son of the famous nineteenth-century conservative president Gabriel García Moreno, claimed the land was part of their Chaguarpungo hacienda.[8] The conflict did not appear out of nowhere. The rural residents in the *parroquia* (parish) of Juan Montalvo had long been engaged in struggles with neighboring hacienda owners over land rights. Ten years earlier, their leader Jesús Gualavisí had formed the Sindicato de Trabajadores Campesinos de Juan Montalvo (Peasant Workers' Union of Juan Montalvo), the country's first peasant union. He served as its secretary-general from its founding in 1926 until his death in 1962.

Gualavisí was born in 1867 on the Changalá hacienda in Cayambe, and was well known "for his activities of being a social agitator among the Indian class." According to government officials, local leaders followed Gualavisí's orders.[9] In addition to being one of the earliest and most important Indigenous leaders in Ecuador, Gualavisí also played a key role in bringing rural demands to the attention of socialists in Quito. He represented his peasant union at the May 1926 founding congress of the Partido Socialista Ecuatoriano (Ecuadorian Socialist Party, PSE), and in fact protests in the countryside provided an impetus for the party's creation. Gualavisí assumed a position comparable to that of Manuel Quintín Lame Chantre, a contemporary Indigenous leader from the Cauca region of Colombia who similarly possessed a "double consciousness" in that he embraced a strong ethnic identity as well as many of the cultural and legal norms of Western civilization. Quintín Lame's approach facilitated alliances with other activists who were fighting for social justice and for an end to oppression.[10] Historian Oswaldo Albornoz argues that Gualavisí's

---

[8] C. Rotelly Ch. to Ministro de Previsión Social, November 15, 1935, and César Jarrín E. to Ministro de Previsión Social, January 14, 1936, both in Caja 183, Carpeta 5, Archivo del Ministerio de Previsión Social, Archivo Intermedio, Quito (hereafter AMPS).

[9] Juan Francisco Sumárraga to Director, Junta Central de Asistencia Pública, March 21, 1946, in CR, Segundo Semestre, Segunda Parte, 1946, p. 1555, JCAP.

[10] Brett Troyan, *Cauca's Indigenous Movement in Southwestern Colombia: Land, Violence, and Ethnic Identity* (Lanham, MD: Lexington Books, 2015). Also see Gonzalo Castillo-Cárdenas and Manuel Quintín Lame Chantre, *Liberation Theology from Below: The Life and Thought of Manuel Quintín Lame* (Maryknoll, NY: Orbis Books, 1987), and Diego Castrillón Arboleda, *El indio Quintín Lame* (Bogota: Tercer Mundo, 1973). The reference to "double consciousness" is from W. E. B. Du Bois, *The Souls of Black Folk* (New York: W.W. Norton, 1999), 11.

personal experiences and observations made him sympathetic to communism. They led him to adopt the Marxist tools of class analysis in order to understand the exploitation of the Indigenous masses and to combat the injustices they faced.[11] He believed that the communists could give organizational expression on a national level to the Indigenous peoples' local demands.

In 1935, Gualavisí mobilized his community to defend Quimbiamba's right to remain on the plot of land he had claimed. Gualavisí lined up community members to testify on Quimbiamba's behalf and contacted their lawyers in Quito for copies of colonial land titles. As happens all too often, the archival record does not contain the resolution of the case. The last item in the file is a carefully typed letter on official paper, with the appropriate stamps and Gualavisí's signature, which asks the minister of social welfare to return the documentation that the community members had presented to prove their property rights. A ministerial official typed a response on the letter indicating that if the documentation was found the government would return it as requested. Apparently, the documentation that the community needed to prove their case had been either lost or misplaced, because a handwritten note in the margin simply stated "*no se encuentra*": the documentation could not be found.[12]

Gualavisí's political engagement extended beyond his local community. In October 1943, the police in Quito arrested Raymond Mériguet, a French communist and leader of Ecuador's anti-fascist movement. Among a flood of letters in his defense were at least two from Gualavisí. One was addressed to the minister of government, and argued that Mériguet's imprisonment was an error "because antifascists should not be persecuted, but rather supported by the government."[13] A second letter was a handwritten missive to Mériguet in prison in Tulcán, encouraging him to stay strong until he could once again breathe fresh air.[14] These communications indicate Gualavisí's active engagement with broader

---

[11] Oswaldo Albornoz Peralta, "Jesús Gualavisí y las luchas indígenas en el Ecuador," in *Los comunistas en la historia nacional*, ed. Domingo Paredes (Guayaquil: Editorial Claridad, S.A., 1987), 155–88.

[12] Jesús Gualavisí to Ministro de Previsión Social, May 6, 1936, Caja 183, Carpeta 5, AMPS.

[13] Jesús Gualavisí, "Comité Antifascista de Juan Montalvo," *Antinazi* 2, no. 28 (January 20, 1944): 4–5.

[14] Raymond Mériguet Cousségal, *Antinazismo en Ecuador, años 1941–1944: Autobiografía del Movimiento Antinazi de Ecuador (MPAE-MAE)* (Quito: R. Mériguet Cousségal, 1988), 309.

political issues beyond those that immediately influenced his local community.

Agustín Vega similarly became enmeshed in leftist politics as an outgrowth of his involvement in local struggles. From a young age, hacienda administrators had forced Vega to pasture animals in the high *páramo* (alpine tundra) grasslands above the Tigua hacienda in Cotopaxi. At the age of eighteen, he demanded a small plot of land called a *huasipungo* as partial payment for his work on the estate, but the *mayordomo* (overseer) refused and the disagreement came to blows. Vega escaped to the neighboring town of Quevedo, where he encountered labor activists. Through them, he met Ricardo Paredes, the secretary-general of the PCE in Quito, who was already working with Gualavisí and other Indigenous activists such as Dolores Cacuango, Tránsito Amaguaña, and Ambrosio Lasso. With their support and encouragement, Vega returned to Tigua. Hidden in canyons under cover of night away from the watchful eyes of hacienda owners, Vega began to organize the community to fight for an end to abuses, the termination of endless debts, and access to land. In September 1929, Tigua workers pressed governor Gustavo Iturralde to force the hacienda owner to address these issues. When the *hacendado* refused, 300 Indians paralyzed work on the estate. The governor sent police to restore order, and they fired their weapons into the peacefully assembled crowd, killing ten protestors, including a pregnant woman. Vega escaped into the *páramo*. From exile, he wrote to the national congress denouncing attempts to silence workers, demanding justice, and requesting a return of the workers' possessions.[15]

Indigenous workers on the neighboring government-owned Zumbahua hacienda turned to the socialist lawyer Gonzalo Oleas for assistance in a long, drawn-out fight over wages and working conditions. Typically, Oleas signed the petitions he drafted in the name of the illiterate workers, but when the legal correspondence was on behalf of a local Indigenous activist such as Vega who knew how to read and write, that person would sign the document as well. At one point when Oleas was not

---

[15] Julio E. Moreno to Contralor General, September 10, 1929, no. 690, Ministerio del Interior, Sección Gobierno, Libro de Varios Autoridades, Julio a Setiembre 1929, #3, p. 438, Archivo General del Ministerio de Gobierno, Quito; Agustín Vega Tipan, María Vega, Pedro Toaquiza, and others, "Tremenda matanza indígena en Tigua," *La Hoz* 1, no. 2 (September 11, 1930): 2; Celso Fiallo and Galo Ramón, *La lucha de las comunidades indígenas del cantón Pujilí y su encuentro con el pensamiento comunista* (Quito: Documento CAAP, 1980), 3–4; Jean G. Colvin, *Arte de Tigua, una reflexión de la cultura indígena en Ecuador* (Quito: Abya Yala, 2004), 19.

available, Vega took it upon himself to write to the minister of social welfare. Vega stated that in Oleas' absence it would be "in the interests of my constituents" to retain "a lawyer who can enforce the rights of workers and for that reason … we have hired Dr. Bernardo Aguilar."[16] Similar to Gualavisí's correspondence, this letter was typed on official paper with the appropriate stamps and Vega's signature. Neither Gualavisí nor Vega had legal training, but both were literate, and both were experienced organizers who understood quite well how to navigate the legal system to their advantage.

At other times, Vega simply used his position as a local organizer to send the government a list of demands. Four years after the massacre on the Tigua hacienda, Vega complained that the ongoing problems of abuse had still not been addressed. "Mr. Minister," Vega wrote in representation of the peons on the hacienda, "you know perfectly well that as workers we cannot continually be abandoning our agricultural labors that provide the root of our lives to come to the capital." He begged for urgent attention to their just demands.[17] Another letter ended with a rhetorical flourish: "We wait for justice and attention to our demands. We live in abject poverty and slavery, worse than beasts of burden. We are no longer able to resist the exploitation to which we are subjected."[18] Vega signed the letters in representation of other Indigenous workers who did not know how to write. As an organic intellectual, Vega had become an intermediary who used his skills to advance local community concerns.

Both Gualavisí and Vega challenge assumptions that Indigenous activism was controlled by urban leftist "ventriloquists" who subordinated Indigenous issues to external demands that reflected purely class or economic interests. Their actions as well as those of many of their contemporary counterparts have been largely ignored, both in the popular imagination and in the academic literature. Much of what we know of their activities is thanks to random and isolated traces that they left in the archival record. We have even less documentation from those who did not know how to read and write, and most of the evidence of their activities is

---

[16] Agustín Vega to Ministro de Previsión Social, April 19, 1939, Caja 178, Carpeta 7, AMPS. Also see Marc Becker, "Gonzalo Oleas, Defensor: Cultural Intermediation in Mid-Twentieth-Century Ecuador," *Journal of Latin American Studies* 43, no. 2 (2011): 237–65.

[17] Agustín Vega to Ministro de Gobierno y Previsión Social, March 5, 1933, Caja 203, Carpeta 26, AMPS.

[18] Agustín Vega to Ministro de Gobierno y Previsión Social y Trabajo, August 8, 1935, Caja 203, Carpeta 16, AMPS.

from unsympathetic outsiders. The nature of these sources has contributed to distorted understandings of their political participation.

HIDDEN IN PLAIN SIGHT

The US intelligence apparatus never placed much importance on understanding rural organizing efforts, nor even attempted to counter the potential threat that they might represent. A 1931 report on communism in Ecuador concluded that it was "more difficult to obtain definitive information on" Indigenous social movements than any other subject. It was apparent that the communists were dedicating significant resources to mobilizing Indigenous communities, but the author of the report had received conflicting information as to whether they had made "no progress because of the indolence and century-old sense of subjugation of the race," or if they were "making alarming progress." The report indicated Ecuadorian government concern for "outside agitation" in Indigenous communities, but understood the threat in terms of communists stirring up racial hatreds against the whites rather than mobilizing a class struggle to overcome systematic exploitation and exclusion.[19]

More than a decade later, the FBI similarly denigrated communist attempts to "infiltrate" Indigenous communities as having met with very little success.[20] The Office of Strategic Services (OSS) provided an equally derogatory depiction of Indigenous communities, describing them as an "inert and oppressed element" and a "large but traditionally inarticulate sector of the population."[21] Together with the lingering feudalistic tendencies in the land tenure system, the country's greatest social problem was "the abject condition of the Indians, living in ignorance and in extreme poverty and neglect."[22] The inward-looking nature of the traditional hacienda system in the Andean highlands meant that it contributed

---

[19] William Dawson to Secretary of State (Henry Stimson), January 29, 1931, despatch no. 150, pp. 15–17, RG 59, 822.00B/24, NARA.

[20] Hoover to Berle, "Communist Activities in Ecuador," 5.

[21] United States Office of Strategic Services (OSS), "Preliminary Analysis of Elements of Insecurity in Ecuador," November 4, 1941, *O.S.S./State Department Intelligence and Research Reports, Part XIV, Latin America, 1941–1961* (Washington, DC: University Publications of America Inc., 1979), Microfilm Reel VIII, p. 15; OSS, "The First Half Year of the Velasco Ibarra Administration in Ecuador," November 28, 1944, in ibid., 2.

[22] OSS, "Political Developments and Trends in the Other American Republics in the Twentieth Century," October 1, 1949, *O.S.S./State Department Intelligence*, Microfilm Reel II, p. 51.

little either to Ecuador or the global economy. As such, neither the OSS nor the FBI thought that rural communities represented a serious threat to US. economic interests, especially as these were expressed in expanding banana production on large coastal plantations. In fact, US officials were at times more concerned with a conservative and backward-looking oligarchy that hindered the emergence of a capitalist mode of production than they were with leftists who pressed for progressive, modernizing reforms.

In February 1944, the FBI estimated that out of a total population of 3 million people in Ecuador, only about 100,000 – government employees or wealthy individuals – took an active interest in politics. An additional half-million people from the lower middle class only became politically engaged when their economic livelihoods were endangered. "The remaining 70% of the population," the FBI report concluded, "are Indians who have never shown any interest in or exerted pressure in Ecuadoran politics."[23] Rather than reflecting reality, such statements highlighted the racism of both FBI agents and upper-class Ecuadorian society. The agents' disdain for rural Ecuador may also reflect their preference for their urban, middle-class surroundings. They spent most of their time in the cities and expressed little interest in venturing into the countryside. Their comfortable lifestyle further separated them from rural residents, and perhaps gave them an unconscious stake in downplaying the importance of rural mobilizations.

Half a year later, in August 1944, Indigenous representatives from across Ecuador gathered in the Casa del Obrero (Workers' Center) in Quito to found the FEI to fight for their social, economic, and political liberation. The creation of one of the first national-level Indigenous federations in Latin America took place in the aftermath of a May 28, 1944, revolution that removed a repressive regime from power and ushered in a period of optimism that there would be deep changes in society. Reflecting the left's warm relations with the new government, long-time Indigenous leader Dolores Cacuango welcomed the country's president José María Velasco Ibarra as the honorary president of the congress. Activists discussed their problems and drew up plans to address them. The congress approved a list of thirty-three demands that encompassed a broad range of issues, including an insistence on complete freedom of organization in rural communities. Delegates also called for humane

---

[23] Hoover to Berle, "Political Conditions in Ecuador," February 14, 1944, no. 64-33001-322, pp. 3–4, RG 59, 822.00/1626, NARA.

treatment of hacienda workers, abolition of forced labor, creation of a Ministry of Indigenous Affairs, provision of adult education as well as schooling for Indigenous children, compliance with the 1938 labor code, and free medical treatment. Most of these demands revolved around political and economic issues.[24]

Delegates to the FEI's founding congress drafted a popular program of social reform that revealed the presence of dramatically forward-looking views on ethnic and economic issues. The federation expressed a desire to:

1. Gain the economic emancipation of Ecuadorian Indians;
2. Raise the Indians' cultural and moral level while conserving whatever was good in their native customs;
3. Contribute to national unity;
4. Establish links of solidarity with all American Indians.[25]

The first goal indicated that the FEI would engage economic issues in the context of a class struggle, but with a focus on a specific ethnic population. Rather than replacing local ethnic identities with a homogenized *mestizo* national identity, leaders advocated for a preservation of the uniqueness of Indigenous cultural identities. Although the FEI was organizing a class struggle, militants did not ignore the presence of racism or deny the importance of ethnicity. The strong articulation of ethnic language and demands disrupts academic models that assert an evolution from class-based organizations before the 1960s to ethnic federations in the 1970s, finally culminating in ethnic nationalities in the 1980s. Organizational statements challenge assumptions that the FEI "did not have ethnic demands."[26] Ideologies of class-consciousness, ethnic identities, and oppressed nationalities were all present at the formation of the FEI.

Aspects of this mission statement could also be interpreted as expressing paternalistic and assimilationist attitudes, particularly in situating the value of Indigenous communities in terms of their contributions to "national unity." And who would decide which aspects of Indigenous culture were worth keeping? This language could be read as an indication that a subtly Western-centric thinking influenced the drafters of the

---

[24] Becker, *Indians and Leftists*, 82–84.
[25] FEI, *Estatutos de la Federación Ecuatoriana de Indios* (Guayaquil: Editorial Claridad, 1945), 3.
[26] Guillermo de la Peña, "Etnicidad, ciudadanía y cambio agrario: Apuntes comparativos sobre tres países latinoamericanos," in *La construcción de la nación y la representación ciudadana, en México, Guatemala, Perú, Ecuador y Bolivia*, ed. Claudia Dary and Guillermo de la Peña (Guatemala City: FLACSO, 1998), 45.

statement, whether they were urban communists or Indigenous activists. Alternatively, it could indicate the presence of a frank and sophisticated understanding that all cultures contain positive and negative elements, hence the need for "intercultural" exchanges. Either way, the statement reflects the reality that the FEI emerged within the context of broader discussions, including those among international solidarity movements.

US intelligence-gathering operations largely ignored the founding of the FEI. An OSS report simply noted that Velasco Ibarra sent his leftist minister of education Alfredo Vera to the congress to explain the government's education program.[27] This absence of interest was the case even as Ecuador's newspapers, which often provided the source of information for intelligence reports, noted the federation's activities and organizational goals.[28] The FBI's agents were apparently unaware of or unconcerned with the FEI's resonance in rural communities across the country. Delegates returned home from the Indigenous congress newly inspired to fight for their rights. For example, Julio Miguel Páez, the administrator of the state-owned Moyurco and San Pablo-urco haciendas in Cayambe, long a center of communist agitation, complained that the situation he faced was growing worse by the day. The peons refused to obey orders, claiming that the haciendas belonged to them and that they would work when they wanted and only for their own personal benefit. Instead, Páez complained, his workers were always traveling to Quito or the city of Cayambe for meetings. He claimed that he was in danger of losing the wheat harvest because the peons refused to work. If the government did not intervene, he warned, the country's agricultural production would be harmed.[29] These rumblings in rural areas remained entirely off the FBI's radar.

A year later, FBI agents reported that Communist leader Ricardo Paredes "continues to use his combined capacities as Functional Representative of the Indians and leader of the Communist Party to good advantage in increasing the popularity of the Communist Party activities among the Indians." Without giving many details, the FBI referenced a series of "clashes between Indian agricultural workers and hacienda owners" at the beginning of 1945. Paredes visited those sites

---

[27] OSS, "The First Half Year of the Velasco Ibarra Administration," 5.

[28] "Estatutos de la Federación de Indios están en estudio del Ministerio de Previsión Social," *El Día* (Quito), November 8, 1944, 8.

[29] Gregorio Ormaza to Ministro de Previsión Social y Asistencia Pública, August 17, 1944, Oficio no. 116-M, Comunicaciones Dirigidas "M," Segundo Semestre 1944, JCAP.

"presumably in his capacity as Functional Representative of Indians." Rather than interrogating the actions of rural activists, the agency's focus remained on their urban allies. The FBI was concerned about the fact that the Communist Party had funded Paredes' trip to the rural communities and that a member of the PCE's central committee (probably Luis F. Alvaro) had accompanied him.[30]

The "clashes" referenced in the FBI report were uprisings that had swept through the provinces of Chimborazo, Cotopaxi, and Pichincha in the first weeks of 1945 and in some cases had led to massacres of Indigenous activists. Newspapers recounted the organizing efforts, with wealthy property owners publicly denouncing "the Indigenous agitation created by the communist Paredes and his henchmen." From the floor of the national assembly, Paredes vocally denounced the abuses perpetrated against Indigenous peasants. The minister of social welfare blamed the unrest on "the interference of people who claim to be defenders of the Indigenous race but are no more than exploitative *tinterillos* [informal lawyers] who continue to incite Indigenous leaders."[31] Rural activism had acquired a very public tone in Ecuador, but its importance still did not register with foreign intelligence agencies.

A February 1945 FBI summary of communist activities noted in passing that "several Indian uprisings have occurred during January, and Communist leaders are said to have been instrumental in instigating these uprisings," a development that FBI Director J. Edgar Hoover also highlighted when he forwarded the findings to the Department of State. The report continued by observing that Paredes "has been named on several occasions as being connected with these uprisings."[32] Yet the brevity and vagueness of the FBI's references to political turmoil, together with the agency's failure to investigate the uprisings, highlights the lack of significance it attributed to Indigenous activism.

[30] J. Edgar Hoover to Frederick B. Lyon, "Dr. Ricardo A. Paredes (Romero) Ecuador Communist Activities," October 11, 1945, no. 100–337879-4, RG 59, 822.00B/ 10–1145, NARA. "Functional representatives" were senators whom the constitution allowed various interest groups (including schools, the media, agriculture, commerce, labor, and the military) to appoint to promote their interests in congress.

[31] "Versión oficial de levantamiento de los indígenas en el anejo Sanguicel," *El Comercio* (Quito), January 13, 1945, 1, 11; "Prodújose levantamiento de indígenas de cantón Cayambe contra la autoridad," *El Comercio*, January 30, 1945, 1, 2; "Artículos relacionados con el derecho de propiedad aprobó la Asamblea," *El Comercio*, January 31, 1945, 1.

[32] J. Edgar Hoover to Frederick B. Lyon, "Communist Activities in Ecuador," March 14, 1945, no. 64-200-212-72, RG 59, 822.00B/3–1445, NARA.

A subsequent FBI memo reported with a certain amount of sensationalism that the January "uprisings have been on a scale never before witnessed in the country and consequently, they have caused considerable comment." As if it had been engaged in serious detective work beyond what a casual observer could accomplish simply by reading the morning papers, the FBI "definitely identified" Paredes as well as Alvaro and Oleas "as individuals connected with these uprisings." As for Paredes,

It is known that the Indians have a profound respect for him and often act under his direct orders. He is believed to have sent several letters to Indians in various sections of the country, in which he advised them that they could further their cause by uprisings.[33]

The FBI created a narrative in which Indigenous communities were inert and responded only to the instigation of "outside agitators."

To support this case, the FBI pointed to an open letter to the minister of government that Paredes had published in the August 4, 1945, issue of the Communist newspaper *Bloque*, in which he denounced massacres in rural communities. For the agency, the letter was illustrative of the propaganda use that Paredes was making of his combined positions as party leader and legislator. It translated an extensive passage from the letter that stated in part:

In the rural regions of the Sierra during the past few months there has been unleashed a wave of furious persecution of the Indians. In this space of time public force has effected three massacres of defenseless and peaceful Indians in San Cuisel, Province of Chimborazo; Panyatug, Province of Cotopaxi; and in Shacundo, Province of Bolivar. Treacherous crimes without any justification. All in order to satisfy the landowners and aid in the exploitation of the Indians.[34]

Historian Oswaldo Albornoz later commented that the authorities attempted to cast a veil over these "cowardly and infamous" acts, "and leave the criminals unpunished, as if the lives of the fallen Indians meant nothing." A failure to investigate the massacres or prosecute the perpetrators led Albornoz to conclude that "the life of the Indians was a trivial thing for the wealthy landowners and their government allies."[35] He argued that government officials intentionally and deliberately ignored

---

[33] Hoover to Lyon, "Communist Activities in Ecuador," March 14, 1945. See also Hoover to Lyon, "Dr. Ricardo Paredes Communist Activities – Ecuador," April 20, 1945, no. 100–337879-2, RG 59, 822.00B/4–2045, NARA.

[34] Hoover to Lyon, "Dr. Ricardo A. Paredes."

[35] Oswaldo Albornoz Peralta, *Las luchas indígenas en el Ecuador*, second ed. (Guayaquil: Editorial Claridad, 1976), 96–97.

these abuses, and the FBI echoed their perspective. The bureau reported
that the military's response to the uprisings led to injuries and deaths, but
agents only mentioned military casualties and not those suffered by rural
community members.

In contrast, the FBI's agents reported that PCE activist Enrique Gil
Gilbert secured a seat on the Tribunal of Constitutional Guarantees to
investigate landowner abuses in Indigenous communities because "the
Communist Party does not dare risk allowing the Indians to feel that
they have been betrayed or neglected."[36] The FEI had a membership of
22,000 out of a population of more than one-and-a-half million
Indigenous people living in the highlands. In an internal memo, FBI
Director J. Edgar Hoover reported that Gil Gilbert had stated, "This is
a tremendous force if we get them under our control," and that he had
argued that "much of our future force will be the Indian Federation."[37]
Without a sizable urban proletariat rooted in industrial production on
which to build its party, the Communists turned instead to rural communities and appealed to their interests in an attempt to establish a strong
base of support. For this reason, Gil Gilbert dedicated much energy to
strategizing with the FEI leadership in pursuit of legal action against the
perpetrators of the massacre, even as his statements might betray a certain
degree of paternalism.

In his letter in *Bloque*, Paredes provided specific details on each case, in
what the FBI termed "a very lurid and one-sided manner." He requested
that the imprisoned individuals be freed and those responsible for the
massacres be punished. Paredes closed the letter with a call for "justice for
those who form the majority of the Ecuadoran population." The
Communists helped Indigenous concerns attain a visibility that they
otherwise would not have had. The FBI particularly objected to Paredes'
depiction because he blamed the massacre on the *"guardia civil"* or civil
guards, whom the bureau had helped train as a replacement for the
militarized police (*carabineros*) that insurgents had defeated in the
May 1944 revolution.[38]

Also notable was the FBI's subtle racism, expressed in denying agency
to the rural activists and only focusing on the subversive actions of urban

---

[36] Shaw to Secretary of State (James Byrnes), "Communism in Ecuador," November 9,
   1945, no. 3663, pp. 2–3, RG 59, 822.00B/11–945, NARA.
[37] Hoover to Lyon, November 15, 1945, no. 100–335694, pp. 9–10, RG 59, 822.00B/
   11–1545, NARA.
[38] Hoover to Lyon, "Dr. Ricardo A. Paredes."

Communists. The FBI stressed to the point of distortion the activity of the FEI's urban allies in the rural struggles. For example, the bureau transmitted a quote from the August 19, 1945, edition of *Bloque*:

> Thanks to the efforts of the Communist Party which created the Federation of the Ecuadoran Indians, the indigenous movement of Ecuador has entered into a new phase of organization and of reasserting the rights of the Indians to enter into civilized life. They are events that signalize [*sic*] the significance in Ecuador. The indigenous movement assumes aspects of incalculable importance.[39]

According to the FBI, the article in *Bloque* indicated that Paredes would give a series of lectures starting on August 21, 1945, "dealing with the transcendental aspect of the indigenous movement." Paredes would deliver the talks at Calle Flores 11, the usual meeting place of Quito's branch of the PCE. The report closed with the comment that "The general public is invited to the lectures," a public which presumably included FBI moles.[40]

The FBI's informant also reported Paredes to be principally responsible for the FEI's newspaper *Ñucanchic Allpa* (Kichwa for "Our Land"), which published articles in both Spanish and Kichwa. The FBI characterized the paper as "intended primarily for Indian consumption," adding that it was "written in a vein of vigorous agitation of the Indian working class." The informant identified Paredes as the author "of a good percentage of the articles which set forth glowing accounts of efforts and intentions of the Communist Party for the betterment of the Indians." The FBI agent pointed to an article in the July 20, 1945 issue of *Ñucanchic Allpa* that discussed the formation of the "Comité de Defensa Indígena," the FEI's legal defense committee, which included Luis Alvaro as secretary-general and Paredes as a committee member. Other than complaining about the committee stirring up the rural masses, the FBI did not provide details on its actions.[41] Unfortunately, activists rarely preserved publications such as *Ñucanchic Allpa* or *Bloque*, and few copies are to be found in libraries. Occasionally copies made their way into police files, where researchers would subsequently discover them.[42] Otherwise, we are left mainly with fragments of the publications referenced in other sources, including FBI surveillance reports.

---

[39] Ibid.   [40] Ibid.   [41] Ibid.
[42] Marc Becker, "La historia del movimiento indígena escrita a través de las páginas de *Ñucanchic Allpa*," in *Estudios ecuatorianos: Un aporte a la discusión*, ed. Ximena Sosa-Buchholz and William F. Waters (Quito: FLACSO, Abya Yala, 2006), 133–53.

The first significant US attention to Indigenous organizing efforts came in September 1945, about a year after the founding of the FEI. Almost at the end of a thirteen-page report on Communist activities in Ecuador, the FBI included a short section with the subtitle "Activity among Indians" that reported: "the Communist Party of Ecuador is devoting increasing attention to the enlistment of Indians as Party members." The author identified the activity as significant only because Paredes, the secretary-general of the PCE, "was also the representative of the Indians in the Constitutional Assembly, and continues to work in their behalf in a governmental capacity."[43] It was in that role that he was able to amplify Indigenous demands and bring attention to rural mobilizations.

At about the same time, a Communist Party member reported that "the Indians are considered very important to the development of the Party and are being educated toward becoming a powerful factor of the movement." As a result, the PCE was seeking to establish party branches in areas of the country where Indigenous peoples lived. In addition, "The Indian Place" was a site that provided lodgings for Indigenous people who traveled to Quito, as well as training in reading, writing, and class consciousness. The number of people who would stay at this locale varied "from a handful to as many as 100 at a time." In what was a common trope among Communist activists, "once an Indian is convinced, he is an extremely loyal and fanatical Party member and becomes a very active disseminator of propaganda among his class." If the FBI source who relayed this information is to be believed, the urban left embodied subtle hints of a persistent racism. "Leaders are chosen on the basis of intelligence and good looks," the informant stated, because "the Indians as a group believe that an attractive person is also good, wise, and a person of good intentions, so that as a mass, the Indians follow a handsome man much more readily than they otherwise would." Those selected as leaders by the Party were given clothing and instructions on spreading propaganda. In return, the Communists promised the leaders land from the large estates that the Party would break up when it came to power.[44]

The short report concluded with the names of the principal Indigenous leaders: Dolores Cacuango, Agustín Vega, Vicente Vega, Manuel Ucsha, "and an individual referred to by the name of Toaquiza." Although they were identified as leaders, the FBI report did not assign agency to these

---

[43] Unsigned report, included in Hoover to Lyon, "Communist Activities – Ecuador," September 6, 1945, pp. 12–13, RG 59, 822.00B/9–645, NARA.
[44] Ibid.

figures, or give any details as to who they were or what they had done to justify inclusion in the report. Rather, the FBI was content to leave an impression that they were passive subjects whom the urban Communists could easily manipulate.[45] In contrast, the FBI maintained extensive dossiers on urban militants that included biographical data, photographs, handwriting samples, and other information gathered from covert surveillance. Indigenous activists were of little interest or concern to them.

During the same period that the FBI was conducting its investigations, the State Department solicited comment from embassy officials on a draft memo on communism in Latin America. Embassy officials in Quito collaborated on the response, and presumably the team included the FBI's legal attaché as well. The memo indicated that Communists had made little progress "in arousing a revolutionary spirit among the Indians of the Andes," even though the PCE was "devoting a great deal of attention to the Ecuadoran Indians." Party activity included organizing "strong groups of Indian Communist sympathizers in isolated regions." Communist leaders such as Paredes believed that the greatest opportunity lay in the Party's ability to organize Indigenous communities. In fact, during the recent electoral campaign Paredes had chosen to remain in Tigua, a Communist-controlled Indigenous cooperative, rather than return to Quito. From Paredes' perspective, "work among the Indians was far more important for the Party than the elections."[46] The community responded warmly to these overtures and named their local school after Paredes.[47] Perhaps these collaborative efforts were realizing more results than were readily apparent to foreign observers in Quito.

THE FEDERATION INTENSIFIES ITS ACTIVITIES

In February 1946, the FEI held its second congress in Quito, and support for the federation appeared to be spreading. Although Socialists were not nearly as engaged with Indigenous struggles as were the Communists, in the lead-up to the congress the Socialist Party newspaper *La Tierra* publicized grassroots mobilizations in support of the meeting and helped advertise the congress.[48] The FEI president Dolores Cacuango, together

---

[45] Ibid.   [46] Shaw to Byrnes, "Communism in Ecuador," 2–3.
[47] "Escuela de la cooperativa Tigua tendrá otro profesor," *La Tierra*, June 3, 1948, 1.
[48] "Congreso indigenista ecuatoriano," *La Tierra*, December 13, 1945, 4; "Del 8 a 10 de fbro. se realizará el 2°Congreso de Indios Ecuatorianos," *La Tierra*, January 30, 1946, 3, 4; "Para Congreso de Indios," *La Tierra*, January 31, 1946, 1.

with Ricardo Paredes – the FEI's representative in the national assembly –
and Luis Alvaro – the secretary-general of the Indigenous Defense
Committee – distributed a flyer written in Spanish and Kichwa calling
for people to attend the congress. The principle objectives of the meeting
were to confer about the activities of the federation, discuss legislation in
the national assembly, gather reports from local communities, support the
Tigua cooperative, and develop training courses for the organization's
members.[49] Educator and long-time FEI ally María Luisa Gómez de la
Torre published an issue of the Indigenous newspaper *Ñucanchic Allpa*
for the congress that outlined the intense labor in defense of Indigenous
interests that the FEI had undertaken since its founding eighteen months
earlier.[50] Among the proposals introduced at the congress was a plan to
draw on the technical expertise of a wide range of people to create
a National Council on Indigenous Education.[51] The FEI congress also
decided to take action against the exploitation of Indigenous communities
by *tenientes políticos*, the political lieutenants who represented the central
government at the local level. It advocated for the national government to
raise the salaries of these officials by 20 percent so that they would stop
charging Indigenous peoples for birth, marriage, and death records.[52]
Press reports indicated that the congress was a success and that the FEI
was actively engaging with many of the issues critical to Indigenous
peoples in Ecuador.[53]

In a monthly report on Communist activities in Ecuador, FBI Director
Hoover remarked that "the most important activity of the Partido
Comunista del Ecuador during the month of February was its sponsoring
of the Second Congress of the Ecuadoran Indian Federation."[54] An agent
dedicated more than two-thirds of a three-page report to an evaluation of
the FEI congress – one of the most extensive descriptions of Indigenous

---

[49] FEI and Comité Central Nacional de Defensa Indígena, *Segundo congreso de indios ecuatorianos … del 8 al 10 febrero de 1946* (Quito: Casa de la Cultura Ecuatoriana, 1946).

[50] "El II Congreso de Indios Ecuatorianos," *Ñucanchic Allpa* 3, no. 18 (February 8, 1946): 1, 8.

[51] "Segundo Congreso Indígena clausuró anoche el período de sesiones," *La Tierra*, February 13, 1946, 1.

[52] "Federación Indígena va a luchar porque no le exploten las autoridades," *La Tierra*, February 20, 1946, 5.

[53] "El Congreso de Indios del Ecuador," *Trabajadores* 1, no. 19 (February 16, 1946): 6.

[54] Hoover to Lyon, "Communist Activities in Ecuador," April 5, 1946, no. 64-200-212, RG 59, 822.00B/4-546, NARA. Unless otherwise noted, the following information on the FEI congress is from this report.

activism contained in the FBI surveillance in Ecuador. Significantly, the report includes information not contained in published newspaper articles, which indicates that it came from other sources or possibly from an informant at the meeting. At the same time, the FBI agent ignored the interests of Indigenous delegates who attended, as well as the impetus that the congress gave for renewed rural organizing.

The FBI reported that the congress proceedings "were entirely in the hands of PCE members." Socialist Party secretary-general Manuel Agustín Aguirre and Pío Jaramillo Alvarado, president of the Instituto Indígena Ecuatoriano (Ecuadorean Indigenist Institute), whom the FBI identified as "a prominent non-Communist authority on Ecuadoran Indian affairs," attended the February 8 inaugural session, but not later meetings. Paredes reported on favorable legislation that he had proposed and succeeded in getting approved in the national assembly.

Even though the FBI only noted the contents of reports from the urban *mestizo* Communist leaders, it also identified Ambrosio Lasso, Agustín Vega, Dolores Cacuango, Jesús Gualavisí, Tránsito Amaguaña, and Manuel García as "outstanding leaders from among the Indians" who participated in the congress. Except for García, all of the rest were well-known Indigenous activists and Communist Party members with long trajectories in mobilizing rural communities. In contrast to the FBI dispatch, the mainstream Quito newspaper *El Comercio* reported that FEI secretary-general Cacuango opened the assembly at the Universidad Central. Delegates elected her president of the congress, and the Indigenous leaders Lasso and Gualavisí as vice presidents. Four days later, these three Indigenous leaders closed the congress. The press accounts noted that more than 300 delegates from Indigenous communities throughout the country attended the congress, and that many of these representatives reported on local issues.[55] By all accounts, it was a large and successful assembly, which highlights yet again the relative disregard that FBI agents had for rural activists.

Rather than reporting on advances in Indigenous organizing efforts, the FBI focused instead on tensions and dissent within the urban left. The bureau identified Alvaro, head of the PCE's Indigenous Defense Committee, as the second-in-command to Paredes in charge of the federation's organizational affairs. Alvaro had printed "a considerable quantity

---

[55] "Federación de Indios del Ecuador desea el progreso mediante el orden y trabajo," *El Comercio*, February 9, 1946, 5; "Congreso de Indios eligió candidatos a la legislatura y se clausuró ayer," *El Comercio*, February 13, 1946, 1, 3.

of small posters" showing photographs of four of the Indigenous leaders, with their fists raised in a "Communist salute." He had planned to paper the walls of Quito with this flyer, but Paredes had overruled him "because of the obvious Communist impression which they conveyed." Nevertheless, the FEI and the PCE subsequently took photographs of Indigenous militants with a raised-fist salute for their own use, seemingly indicating that the problem was not with the imagery but with the person who had proposed the idea. Over the next year, Paredes and Alvaro tangled more and more, although given the available evidence it is difficult to determine how much of the conflict was ideological, strategic, or merely personal.

Rubén Rodríguez, a *mestizo* educator from Cayambe and the manager of the Communist Indian Agricultural Cooperative at Tigua, described the satisfactory progress that the members were making. The FBI reported that after the congress, Rodríguez

returned to Quito for the purpose of securing Communist Party assistance in settling a dispute which had arisen between him and Agustín Vega, the Indian who had been in charge of infiltration and PCE organization of the Indians on the Tigua Estate prior to the formation of the cooperative.[56]

According to the FBI informant, the FEI had asked Lasso to come to Quito to help settle the dispute. Significantly, the party turned to a noted Indigenous leader rather than an urban Communist ally to mediate the conflict. Lasso was no foreigner to struggle. He had shot to fame in the movement when he led an uprising on the Pull hacienda in Chimborazo in 1935. Subsequently, according to the FBI, Lasso moved "to Latacunga where, according to one PCE member, he is now doing the party more harm than good." The FBI did not elaborate on what trouble Lasso was causing, though the implication was that it was probably related to his personal behavior. Naturally it was in the FBI's interest to emphasize the most negative aspects of the FEI's organizing process. When agents did discuss Indigenous activists, it was primarily to denigrate their efforts.

The majority of the sessions at the FEI congress were dedicated to the work of a legal committee under the leadership of the *mestizo* Communist lawyer Newton Moreno. This body received "complaints of injustice and mistreatment at the hands of the landowners." The FBI reported that Newton's "committee would hurriedly judge the merits of each case and if it was decided to be well founded the committee would take complete

[56] Hoover to Lyon, "Communist Activities in Ecuador," April 5, 1946.

notes advising the complainant that the matter would be prosecuted through regular channels." Rather than congratulating the federation for pursuing their disputes through official venues rather than with strikes and other forms of protest, the FBI denigrated the legitimacy of their complaints.[57] In contrast to the FBI's interpretation of the congress, *El Comercio* quoted the Indigenous Defense Committee leader Alvaro as arguing that the FEI could never support an Indigenous uprising as had been charged, because doing so would only bring death to the Indians and destruction to their economies. Rather, Alvaro proclaimed, they sought progress through work, economic development, and social order. They would press for the application of existing legal decrees to realize these goals.[58] *El Comercio* responded positively to the FEI's legal strategy and relatively moderate demands in an editorial and called on the government to fulfill its obligation to assist rural communities.[59]

At the congress, delegate Pedro Naula complained that since coming to power Velasco Ibarra had not done anything to assist Indigenous communities. Despite hopes that the May 28, 1944 revolution would lead to solutions for problems that they were facing, "Indians in Ecuador have been completely forgotten."[60] The FEI congress hoped to change that lack of attention through renewed activism in rural communities. The FBI reported that after the congress a landholder severely beat Gualavisí when he discovered him on his land. Gualavisí had been attempting to implement a plan developed at the congress to expand the FEI's organizational efforts. The PCE's lawyer Newton Moreno announced his intentions "to prosecute the landowner vigorously."[61] This was only one of many examples of rural activists seeking to defend their interests through strategic alliances and with the assistance of urban allies.

A couple of months after the FEI congress, the police arrested Alvaro in Riobamba, where he had traveled to organize new FEI affiliates. According to the FBI, on May 22, 1946, he smuggled a letter out of the García Moreno prison in Quito where he was incarcerated, in which he resigned his position on the PCE's central committee. Alvaro said that with his imprisonment he had lost his ability to serve as a representative

---

[57] Ibid.
[58] "Federación de Indios del Ecuador desea el progreso mediante el orden y trabajo," *El Comercio*, February 9, 1946, 5.
[59] "Orden y trabajo," *El Comercio*, February 10, 1946, 4.
[60] "Congreso de Indios eligió candidatos a la legislatura y se clausuró ayer," *El Comercio*, February 13, 1946, 1.
[61] Hoover to Lyon, "Communist Activities in Ecuador," April 5, 1946.

for Indigenous communities to the PCE, and that the party should replace him. According to the FBI, Alvaro said he would explain more fully his decision to resign "when and if he should be released" from prison.[62] The government freed Alvaro in June together with other political prisoners in the lead-up to local elections, but his role in the organization remained unresolved.[63] One possible source of conflict may have related to problems the party faced in running the cooperative at Tigua.[64] Unfortunately, the archival record is unclear on the reasons for his resignation or the tensions that may have led to it.

Meanwhile, in March 1947, the FBI closed its operations in Latin America and turned over its surveillance activities to the newly formed Central Intelligence Group (CIG), a forerunner of the CIA. One of the CIG's first reports on Communist activities in Ecuador noted that the FEI held a conference in Quito from April 18 to April 20, 1947, "with the announced purpose of checking on the progress and activities of affiliated branches and presenting a new plan of action for the future." Allegedly, PCE leaders met with FEI leaders Vega and Cacuango before the conference to identify "a selected group of reliable Communist members of the FEI" who could be counted on to engage in subversive activities in case of a war between the United States and the Soviet Union, or if the PCE or FEI were forced underground.[65] Presumably this list would include Cacuango, who was a member of the party's central committee, as well as other FEI leaders who were party members. Rather than reporting on grassroots organizing efforts, the CIG framed their surveillance in terms of looming Cold War conflicts.

In November 1947, a CIG agent drafted a memo on the FEI's deterioration. Some Communists protested the party's neglect of Indigenous issues since Alvaro's resignation more than a year earlier. Some wanted Alvaro restored to his post, but Paredes as secretary-general of the party vetoed the suggestion. Some Indigenous unions threatened to withdraw from the federation if matters did not improve. Organizing Indigenous communities was so central to the Communist agenda that party leaders feared that the federation's disintegration would negatively affect the party's affairs, and for this reason must be addressed.[66] The predictions of the

---

[62] Hoover to Lyon, July 17, 1946, RG 59, 822.00B/7-1746, NARA.

[63] Hoover to Lyon, September 12, 1946, RG 59, 822.00B/9-1246, NARA.

[64] John F. Simmons to Marshall, July 31, 1947, no. 5487, RG 59, 822.00B/7-3147, NARA.

[65] CIG, "Communist Party Activities," May 21, 1947, www.cia.gov/library/readingroom/document/cia-rdp82-00457r000600140010-3 (accessed May 7, 2018).

[66] CIG, "Deterioration of Indian Federation," November 6, 1947, www.cia.gov/library/readingroom/document/cia-rdp82-00457r001000640008-6 (accessed May 7, 2018).

FEI's imminent demise, however, were exaggerated, and half a year later the federation rebounded under new leadership.

A CULTURAL TURN IN THE MIDST OF POLITICAL CONFLICT

The FEI held its third congress from April 19 to April 23, 1948, under the guidance of Modesto Rivera, who had been a member of the Communist Party since the early 1930s. As the new secretary-general of the FEI, Rivera worked closely with Cacuango, who now served as the FEI's president. Landowners complained about Rivera's actions in stirring the Indigenous masses to action, but the FEI's executive committee defended their secretary-general as a serious person who facilitated solutions to problems.[67] The collaborative efforts between urban *mestizo* militants like Rivera and rural Indigenous Communists like Cacuango would mark the organizational strategy of the FEI for decades to come.

The FEI congress began on April 19, the "Day of the American Indian," a date more commonly celebrated by *indigenistas* in commemoration of the founding of the Inter-American Indigenist Institute in Pátzcuaro, Mexico, in 1940. In order to advance the FEI's class struggle against large landholders, the congress urged "Indigenous *compañeros* on haciendas, communal lands, and all members of the race" to "form a union and affiliate with the Federation." The FEI was the "maximum organization that ties together all Indians in Ecuador." Together the struggle for liberation would gain force and achieve "its sacred mission."[68] As the FEI's new secretary-general, Rivera sent special invitations to Luis Maldonado Tamayo, the director of the Socialist newspaper *La Tierra*, and Ricardo Jaramillo, the director of the liberal newspaper *El Día*, because they had always been supportive of "the material and cultural advance of the Indigenous race."[69]

The 1948 congress received reports from the FEI leaders, starting with Rivera, who detailed plans to address the multiple problems that Indigenous peoples faced, including the low wages for their work on haciendas. Indigenous activists Neptalí Ulcuango and Luis Catucuamba

---

[67] Dolores Cacuango, "Federación Ecuatoriana de Indios," *El Día*, September 27, 1949, 8.
[68] "Las cotizaciones a la F.E.I.," *Ñucanchic Allpa* 5, no. 20 (March 1948): 3.
[69] Modesto Rivera, "Tercer Congreso de la Federación Ecuatoriana de Indios se celebrará el 19 del presente," *La Tierra*, April 18, 1948, 2; Modesto Rivera, "Lunes se inaugurará el tercer congreso de la federación e. de indios," *El Día*, April 19, 1948, 2.

also talked about the economic exploitation and inhumane treatment that agricultural workers received. Indigenous leader Tránsito Amaguaña introduced the Socialist minister of social welfare, Alfredo Pérez Guerrero. Amaguaña expressed gratitude to the minister for his support for Indigenous communities, including materials he provided to rural schools that local peasant unions had launched. Pérez Guerrero thanked the FEI for inviting him to the congress and indicated his willingness to collaborate with the federation. The minister declared that "raising the moral, biological, and education level of peasants" was one of the government's priorities. He championed efforts to create a "Junta de Cuestiones Indígenas" (Bureau of Indian Affairs) in the highlands, where most Indigenous peoples lived, to address the "Indian problem," along with a parallel bureau of peasant affairs on the coast. In an apparent attempt to pull the federation away from its Communist allies, Pérez Guerrero argued that no political party could monopolize this work in favor of Indigenous communities, since improving the lives of Indigenous workers was the responsibility of the entire country.[70]

The FEI held its congress in the midst of the ninth Pan-American conference in Bogotá, Colombia, where delegates passed an anti-communist resolution and formed the Organization of American States. The assassination of the popular liberal leader and presidential candidate Jorge Eliécer Gaitán in the middle of those debates triggered massive riots, popularly known as the *bogotazo*, that spread paranoia that communists might create similar disturbances elsewhere in the hemisphere. In Ecuador, the PCE denied that it was plotting against the government. Accusations of communist involvement in the riots in Colombia were also mistaken, the PCE declared, and were made at the behest of US imperialism and in order to serve its interests, which included the reversal of democratic reforms and "the enslavement of the people, of which the communists are the most determined defenders." From the communist perspective, these provocations were part of an imperialist plan for global domination. The party argued that communists had little to gain from the type of chaos that Gaitán's assassination had caused in Bogotá.[71]

---

[70] "En la tarde de ayer se inauguró el tercer congreso de Federación Nacional de Indios," *El Día*, April 20, 1948, 8; "Ayer se inauguró el III Congreso de la Federación Ecuatoriana de Indios; tomó la palabra el Ministro de Previsión," *El Comercio*, April 20, 1948, 12.

[71] Comité Ejecutivo del Partido Comunista del Ecuador, "Declaraciones del Partido Comunista del Ecuador, rechazando las calumnias y las provocaciones del imperialismo y sus secuaces" (Quito, April 19, 1948), Hojas Volantes, 1946–1950, D. Polit Partid., t. 1, p. 147, Biblioteca Ecuatoriana Aurelio Espinosa Pólit, Cotocollao, Ecuador. Also see

Two weeks later, *El Comercio* reported with relief on the lessening of tensions with the passing of May 1, which traditionally had been a time for large labor rallies in commemoration of International Workers' Day.[72] Despite conservative fears, the absence of any political or criminal disturbances, along with Communist statements explicitly rejecting illegal actions, would seem to corroborate the PCE's claims that it sought to pursue change through peaceful means. At the end of the FEI congress and in a move that was seemingly far removed from the PCE's prior defense of its positions in the face of a conservative onslaught, Rivera announced the inauguration of an exhibit of Indigenous art in the Casa de la Cultura in Quito.[73] Rather than engaging in serious political issues, the FEI's urban *mestizo* allies dedicated their energies instead to culturalist concerns. For a moment, the PCE and FEI appeared to be moving in two different directions.

On May 1, however, even as tensions relaxed in the cities, political discord increased in the countryside. Press reports now claimed that Indigenous agricultural workers on the government-owned Pesillo hacienda in northern Ecuador had exploited the labor holiday to lead a strike for higher wages and better working conditions. In response, the government sent in military troops and arrested the leaders. Alfonso Zambrano, the director of the government agency that oversaw the hacienda, quickly traveled to Pesillo to review the situation personally and reported that everything was calm and that the arrests had been entirely unnecessary.[74] A new image of what had happened on the hacienda now emerged in press reports. Rather than launching an uprising against landowner abuses, local educators Neptalí Ulcuango and Luis Catucuamba had been organizing a literacy campaign. A *mayordomo* had seen the assembled workers and panicked out of fear that they might be planning an uprising. Local conservatives together with the local priest had inflated these reports to turn the population against local Communist leaders, including Rubén Rodríguez.[75]

Marc Becker, "The *Bogotazo* in Ecuador," *The Latin Americanist* 62, no. 2 (2018): 160–85.

[72] "Se ha desvanecido el estado de alarma en Quito," *El Comercio*, May 1, 1948, 1; "Se ha restablecido la calma en el campamento de la 'Jones,'" *El Comercio*, May 2, 1948, 1–2.

[73] Modesto Rivera, "La primera exposición de artes manuales indígenas se inaugura el domingo," *La Tierra*, April 23, 1948, 4.

[74] "Mayordomos de hdas de asistencia propagaron rumor de levantamiento indígena," *El Día*, May 4, 1948, 7.

[75] "Indígenas del cantón Cayambe enjuiciarán al comisario nacional de esa población," *El Día*, May 4, 1948, 8; "Manera como se forjó la falsa alarma de un levantamiento indígena

While the FEI had seemingly been preoccupied with organizing an art exhibit during the political unrest associated with the *bogotazo*, Rivera now responded with a strongly worded statement condemning the arrests as an unnecessary incitement designed to alarm the general public. The FEI decried the arrests as "a provocation of people interested in causing harm to defenseless Indigenous peoples." The repression sought "to hide the tremendous exploitation of Ecuadorian Indians by wealthy land-holders." The federation blamed the government for failing to take suffi-cient responsibility in protecting the rights of rural workers. It reminded readers "that during elections it is a well-known political practice to invent all sorts of movements to discredit certain groups or parties and create confusion among the electorate." The FEI reviewed a list of mas-sacres in Indigenous communities and emphasized that "the history of Ecuador has consistently been stained with Indian blood." It called for an investigation into the true instigators of the turmoil so that they could be properly sanctioned. Rivera claimed that the FEI was not involved in subversive activities, but instead dedicated its efforts to improving the lives of Indigenous peoples through all legal channels. He pointed to its recent sponsorship of the art exhibit as an example of its positive actions, and claimed that it could not have carried out this demonstration of Indigenous culture without the work of its leaders, including Dolores Cacuango and Rubén Rodríguez, whom the police had now imprisoned in Quito. Rivera closed by arguing that to protect democracy it was necessary "to maintain peace and quiet for the majority of Ecuadorians, those who comprise the Indigenous class."[76]

Once again, the FEI and the PCE appeared to have flipped political positions. Whereas during the *bogotazo* the FEI pursued culturalist activ-ities as the PCE advanced an overtly political campaign, now it was the FEI's turn to engage in a political struggle while the PCE quietly stood by. In reality, both the party and Indigenous federation may have been fol-lowing a Soviet line of agitating for radical change through peaceful and legal means, eschewing the armed tactics that Fidel Castro would employ at the Moncada Barracks in Cuba five years later. Yet even when strategies and political lines appeared to diverge, the FEI and the PCE remained

en cantón Cayambe," *El Día*, May 6, 1948, 8, 6; Modesto Rivera, "La mano conserva-dora en los sucesos de Cayambe," *La Tierra*, May 9, 1948, 2.
[76] Modesto Rivera, "Federación Ecuatoriana de Indios se dirige al ministro de gobierno," *La Tierra*, May 5, 1948, 1, 4.

united in their support for the rights of the most marginalized people in the country.

At the time of the FEI's third congress in April 1948, the FBI had been absent from Ecuador for over a year. Even though US ambassador John Simmons admitted that the same intelligence-gathering efforts that the FBI had conducted now continued under the embassy's control, diplomatic officials seemingly took even less interest in Indigenous organizing efforts than the political police did.[77] Few traces of the meeting or the subsequent unrest at Pesillo appear in State Department cables or in declassified CIA surveillance records.

With some notable exceptions, the US government, including the State Department, the FBI, and the CIA, largely missed grassroots organizing efforts in rural communities. The true threat to the economic and political interests of the wealthy propertied classes lay in these marginalized but well-organized subaltern populations. Urban and modernizing cultural perspectives, not to mention a good deal of racism and sexism, resulted in US officials being blind to rural political dynamics. These absences point to the limits of the surveillance state and highlight that it is from the margins where the most effective challenges to exclusionary state power can be launched.

Rather ironically, a lack of surveillance of the FEI hinders the ability of historians to recover a more complete history of leftist organizing efforts in Ecuador. The racism and sexism of US officials and Ecuadorian police led them to neglect Indigenous mobilizations. In turn, their failure to document this social-movement history has helped obscure vital Indigenous contributions to the development of the Latin American left. The FEI, meanwhile, did not maintain its own archives, and the activists involved in the federation did not produce written analyses of their actions. We are left mostly with scattered manifestos and newspaper reports as sources for reconstructing this history.

Despite the partial and limited nature of the sources on the FEI, what does emerge is the importance of interethnic collaborations in pursuing the goals that rural and urban activists shared. Rural communities

---

[77] Simmons to Marshall, "Conversation with Dr. José Miguel García Moreno, Acting Foreign Minister, Concerning Disturbed Condition in Ecuador," April 21, 1948, no. 347, RG 59, 822.00B/4-2148, NARA.

experienced the economic exploitation and racial discrimination that gave meaning and urgency to a socialist agenda. Urban communists contributed an ideological orientation and a political critique that helped define and strengthen Indigenous struggles. Focusing on just one side of these exchanges results in a limited and partial understanding of these activities. Together, urban and rural activists were able to organize powerful movements for social change.

4

Friends and Comrades

Political and Personal Relationships between Members of the Communist Party USA and the Puerto Rican Nationalist Party, 1930s–1940s

Margaret Power

On June 3, 1943, Pedro Albizu Campos, president of the pro-independence Puerto Rican Nationalist Party (PNPR), walked out of the Atlanta Federal Penitentiary (AFP), where he had been imprisoned since 1937. Two other Nationalists, Julio Pinto Gandía and Juan Antonio Corretjer, met Albizu, as did Samuel Neuberger, a member of the US Communist Party (CPUSA) and an attorney sent by US Congressman Vito Marcantonio to greet him. The four traveled by train to New York City in a private compartment paid for by the CPUSA.[1] When they arrived in New York City, Earl Browder, the secretary-general of the CPUSA and Congressman Marcantonio met them. According to FBI records, the two told Albizu Campos to "lie low."[2] Albizu Campos, whose already poor health had greatly deteriorated during his five years of imprisonment, spent most of the next two years and five months in Columbus Hospital in Manhattan.[3]

* I thank Matthew Dougall Stewart for his research in the Earl Browder papers, Laura Browder for generously sharing documents about Earl Browder, and Marc Becker, Laura Browder, Barbara Epstein, Gerald Meyer, Andrae Marek, Melinda Power, Teresa Prados-Torreira, Michael Staudenmaier, Ellen Walsh, Kevin Young, and Neici Zeller for helpful comments on an earlier draft of this chapter.
1 Marisa Rosado, *Pedro Albizu Campos: Las llamas de la aurora* (San Juan: n.p., 2003), 284–85.
2 "Pedro Albizu Campos" (memo), May 11, 1954, p. 2, FBI File 105–11898, https://archive .org/stream/PedroAlbizuCampos/HQ-105–11898%20%281981%20declassification%2 9_1_01_29#page/no/mode/2up (accessed May 14, 2018).
3 The CPUSA paid Albizu's bills during the time he was confined in the hospital. For copies of those bills, see Box 2, "Albizu Campos, Pedro, 1936–1944," Earl Browder Papers, Special Collections Research Center, Syracuse University Libraries (hereafter SCRC-EB).

I begin with this anecdote because it reveals the close personal and political relationships that existed among Albizu, Corretjer, and Browder, leaders of their respective parties. The friendships between these three men, along with personal relationships between other members of both parties, have largely escaped the notice of scholars.[4] Yet these friendships offer us the opportunity to examine the crucial role that personal relationships played in the lives, thoughts, and actions of key actors in the PNPR and the CPUSA.

They also allow us to go beyond each party's public statements and written declarations to explore what lay behind or beneath the official transcript. While political ideologies guided the formulation and implementation of organizational policies, personal relationships affected the day-to-day practice and experience of these policies. For example, the warm, personal feelings that existed between Pedro Albizu Campos, Earl Browder, and Juan Antonio Corretjer contributed to the CPUSA sending one of its attorneys, Samuel Neuberger, to greet Albizu when he left the AFP, and then to purchase a private compartment on an otherwise segregated train to ensure the four could travel together to New York City. (Albizu's mother was of African descent and his father was Basque. In the US South in the 1940s, Albizu was considered black and could not have traveled with the white men.)

What is notable about this incident is that it occurred during the years after the CPUSA, like all Communist parties around the world, had adopted the Popular Front strategy. Under Browder's leadership, Popular Front politics translated into general support for the Roosevelt administration and the New Deal. This meant backing the pro-Roosevelt Popular Democratic Party (PPD) and its leader Luis Muñoz Marín in Puerto Rico and consigning what had been the CPUSA's long-time call for independence to the backburner. Once Albizu arrived in New York City, Browder visited him; the two wrote each other warm, confidential letters; and each appointed a member of his respective party to represent it to the other party. Thus, by examining the personal relationships among these three men we learn that even as the CPUSA proclaimed its support for the Roosevelt administration's policy for Puerto

---

[4] Two historians who do examine aspects of the relationship between Marcantonio and Albizu are Gerald J. Meyer, "Pedro Albizu Campos, Gilberto Concepción de Gracia, and Vito Marcantonio's Collaboration in the Cause of Puerto Rico's Independence," *Centro Journal* 23, no. 1 (2011): 87–123; Félix Ojeda Reyes, *Vito Marcantonio y Puerto Rico: Por los trabajadores y por la nación* (Río Piedras: Huracán, 1978).

Rico, it was simultaneously materially and politically backing the Nationalist Party.

In addition, the comradeship between Albizu, Corretjer, and Browder and other members of both parties refutes the suggestion that the PNPR was pro-fascist.[5] Historian Luis Ferrao has advanced this position most forcefully, claiming that "European fascism inspired more than a few of the Puerto Rican Nationalists' conceptions." As an example, Ferrao states that in 1921 Italian fascists published "a decree for the organization of young fascists. It is very like the document put out by Albizu."[6] By focusing on the comradeship among Albizu, Browder, and other members of the PNPR and CPUSA, this chapter builds on the work of Puerto Rican scholars who have challenged allegations the Nationalist Party was fascist.[7]

This story begins in the AFP in 1937 and ends in New York City in 1945, when Earl Browder was removed from the leadership of the Communist Party. The principal actors are Pedro Albizu Campos and Juan Antonio Corretjer, president and secretary-general of the PNPR; Earl Browder, secretary-general of the CPUSA; and US Congressman Vito Marcantonio. Other figures are Anna Damon, president and secretary of the CPUSA's International Labor Defense (ILD); Consuelo Lee Tapia de Lamb, a Puerto Rican member of the CPUSA; Samuel Neuberger, an attorney and member of both the ILD and CPUSA; and Julio Pinto Gandía, a leader of the PNPR. The geographic background for the first stage of this story is the AFP, where Nationalist prisoners first received backing from the ILD and later became friends and comrades with Earl Browder, who was imprisoned there from early 1941 to late 1942. After their release from the AFP, all these individuals reencountered each other in New York City, the headquarters of the CPUSA, and the nerve center of the PNPR from 1943 to 1947.

---

[5] One of the first writers to make this assertion was Gordon Lewis, who claimed the Nationalists were "dedicated to a neo-fascist *risorgimento* of violence against the American 'usurper' and regarded all peaceful means of change as a traitorous appeasement of American imperialism." *Puerto Rico: Freedom and Power in the Caribbean* (New York: Harper, 1963), 49.

[6] Luis Angel Ferrao, *Pedro Albizu Campos y el nacionalismo puertorriqueño* (San Juan: Editorial Cultural, 1990), 317.

[7] Taller de Formación Política, *Pedro Albizu Campos: ¿Conservador, fascista o revolucionario?* (Río Piedras: Taller de Formación Política, 1991); César J. Ayala and Rafael Bernabe, *Puerto Rico in the American Century: A History of Puerto Rico since 1898* (Chapel Hill: University of North Carolina Press, 2007), 109–10.

BACKGROUND

The PNPR and the CPUSA were founded in 1922 and 1919, respectively.[8] The PNPR did not affiliate with any international grouping. It was neither Marxist nor Leninist, and did not seek to establish a socialist government in Puerto Rico.[9] It recognized that Puerto Rican workers were exploited and, as a result, it sought economic justice for workers and peasants. However, it blamed their exploitation on "foreign [US] interests," not on the capitalist system. Instead of calling for workers to control the means of production, it said they should "receive the share of profits they have a right to." The Nationalist Party's priority was to end US colonial rule over Puerto Rico. Once that was achieved, the nation could work toward achieving economic justice. As the party program stated, "To resolve the economic issue, we must first obtain complete and absolute political freedom."[10] The Nationalists defined themselves as part of Latin America and advocated an end to Yankee imperialism across the Americas. They sought to reinsert Puerto Rico into the Americas so that it could rejoin its sister republics in the region, not withdraw into isolated sovereignty.

Like Communist parties around the world, the CPUSA followed the direction of the Communist International (Comintern) and shared its political program. Although the initial 1919 Congress of the Comintern devoted scant attention to the colonial issue, by the Second Congress (1920) that topic had come to the fore.[11] In that Congress, Vladimir Lenin maintained the world was divided between oppressed and oppressor nations, or colonies and colonial powers, with the clear majority of the population living in the former. "Some 70 per cent of the world population belong to the oppressed nations which are either in direct colonial

---

[8] The Puerto Rican Communist Party (PCP) was not founded until 1934 in San Juan. It worked very closely with the CPUSA, from which it received financial support and political direction. Since this chapter focuses on friendships between members of the PNPR and CPUSA in Atlanta and New York City, a discussion of relationships between the PCP and PNPR lies beyond its scope. For the politics and history of the PCP see César Andreu Iglesias, *Independencia y socialismo* (San Juan: Estrella Roja, 1951); George Fromm, *César Andreu Iglesias: Aproximación a su vida y obra* (San Juan: Huracán, 1977).

[9] The Socialist Party of Puerto Rico, led by Santiago Iglesias Pantín, affiliated with the American Federation of Labor and advocated statehood, not independence, for Puerto Rico.

[10] "El problema de Puerto Rico y el programa Nacionalista," *El Mundo*, September 21, 1932.

[11] Jean Jones, *The League against Imperialism* (Preston, UK: Lancashire Community Press, 1996,) 3–4.

dependence, or appear as semi-colonial states." Lenin argued that because peasants, not industrial workers, predominated in these colonies, Communists should support a "united front" and the "national revolutionary movements" in the colonies and abandon the fruitless attempt to work only with revolutionary proletarian movements.[12] The Comintern adopted Lenin's positions, which were published as the *Thesis on the National and Colonial Question*.[13] In it Lenin affirmed that the Comintern's policy "must be to bring into being a close alliance of all national and colonial liberation movements with Soviet Russia."[14]

The Comintern's anti-colonial position generated an increasingly sharp criticism of "Yankee imperialism." In 1928, the Communist press noted that the "severe shrinkage in the purchasing capacity of the home market" (the United States), combined with the "constantly swelling productive apparatus" encouraged, indeed propelled, "the American [US] imperialists to fight more and more sharply for a bigger share of the world market, especially in Latin America and in the East." As a result, "Yankee imperialism is intensifying its aggressive policy," as evidenced by the 150 percent increase in "US investment of capital in South America" following World War I.[15] One concrete expression of the Comintern's heightened opposition to US imperialist involvement in Latin America was the protest by Communist parties across the hemisphere against the United States' intervention in Nicaragua and its concomitant backing of Augusto César Sandino in the late 1920s and early 1930s.[16] Another was the Latin American Communist movement's widespread advocacy of Puerto Rican independence, including support for the Puerto Rican Nationalist Party, and, after 1937, for the release of Nationalist political prisoners held in US and Puerto Rican jails.[17]

---

[12] "Minutes of the Second Congress of the Communist International," Fourth Session, July 25, 1920, www.marxists.org/history/international/comintern/2nd-congress/ch04 .htm (accessed April 6, 2017).

[13] Jones, *The League against Imperialism*, 4.

[14] V. I. Lenin, *Thesis on the National and Colonial Question*, July 28, 1920, Section 6, http:// ciml.250x.com/archive/comintern/english/2_congress_theses_on_national_and_colonial_ question_29_july_1920.html (accessed April 6, 2017).

[15] *The Communist International between the Fifth and Sixth World Congresses – 1924–1928* (London: Dorrit Press, 1928), 333.

[16] Barry Carr, "Pioneering Transnational Solidarity in the Americas: The Movement in Support of Augusto C. Sandino, 1927–1934," *Journal of Iberian and Latin American Research* 20, no. 2 (2014): 141–52.

[17] For a discussion of Latin American solidarity with Puerto Rican political prisoners in the 1930s see Margaret Power, "The Puerto Rican Nationalist Party, Transnational Latin American Solidarity, and the United States during the Cold War," in *Human Rights and*

In the mid-1930s the CPUSA recognized the PNPR as an important voice of anti-colonialism on the island.[18] Harry Ward, president of the American League against War and Fascism, invited Pedro Albizu Campos to attend the World Congress against War and Fascism in Cleveland in 1935. In recognition of the important role the pro-independence party played, the invitation added, "if the Nationalist Party attends the Congress, it will have the right to send as many delegates as it can."[19] Clearly, this anti-fascist organization considered the Nationalist Party part of the anti-fascist opposition and welcomed its participation in the conference.

THE IMPRISONMENT OF NATIONALIST PARTY LEADERS

In 1930 Pedro Albizu Campos was elected president of the PNPR. Under his leadership, the party adopted a position of implacable and increasingly militant opposition to US colonial rule. The Great Depression intensified widespread poverty across the island and contributed to growing numbers of Puerto Ricans embracing the Nationalist Party's demand for independence.[20] To control and contain Puerto Ricans' heightened dissatisfaction with their colonial reality, Washington named Colonel Francis Riggs in 1933 as head of the Puerto Rican Police forces and General Blanton Winship as governor in 1934. Their mission was to manage and repress opposition to the US regime.[21] Franklin Roosevelt's Good Neighbor Policy for Latin America was neither good nor neighborly when applied to Puerto Rican Nationalists.

Transnational Solidarity in Cold War Latin America, ed. Jessica Stites Mor (Madison: University of Wisconsin Press, 2013), 25–27.

[18] For a fascinating discussion of connections between the CPUSA and the PNPR in the 1920s, see Sandra Pujals, "¡Embarcados!: James Sager, la Sección Puertorriqueña de la Liga Anti-Imperialista de las Américas y el Partido Nacionalista de Puerto Rico, 1925–1927," *Op. Cit.* (San Juan) 22 (2013–14): 105–39.

[19] *La Palabra*, December 2, 1935, p. 6. I have not been able to determine if Albizu or members of the PNPR attended the Congress. In 1933, the American League Against War and Fascism replaced the All-America Anti-Imperialist League, which the CPUSA, then known as the Workers' Party, had founded in 1925. Jim Zwick, *Confronting Imperialism: Essays on Mark Twain and the Anti-Imperialist League* (West Conshohocken, PA: Infinity, 2007), 2.

[20] In 1933, 65 percent of the labor force was unemployed. Robert David Johnson, "Anti-Imperialism and the Good Neighbour Policy: Ernest Gruening and Puerto Rican Affairs, 1934–1939," *Journal of Latin American Studies* 29, no. 1 (1997): 95.

[21] Ramón Medina Ramírez, *El movimiento libertador en la historia de Puerto Rico* (San Juan: Ediciones Puerto, 2016), 121–24.

Winship and Riggs's rule initiated an upward cycle of armed confrontations with the pro-independence forces. The clashes included the 1935 police murder of four Nationalists, the retaliatory assassination of Colonel Riggs by two Nationalists in 1936, the 1936 police murder of those two Nationalists, the 1937 police massacre of nineteen nonviolent Nationalist demonstrators,[22] and the Nationalists' failed 1938 attempt to kill Governor Winship. The US government responded to the killing of Colonel Riggs by arresting and bringing to trial the leadership of the Nationalist Party in 1936 on charges of sedition (attempting to overthrow the US government by force) and other offenses. The jury found Pedro Albizu Campos, Juan Antonio Corretjer, Luis G. Velázquez, Clemente Soto Vélez, Erasmo Velázquez, Julio H. Velázquez, Juan Gallardo Santiago, and Pablo Rosado Ortiz guilty and the eight Nationalists were imprisoned in AFP in 1937.[23]

The AFP opened in 1921 under the jurisdiction of the Superintendent of Prisons.[24] In 1930, the Federal Bureau of Prisons, which was created under the aegis of the Department of Justice, took control of the prison. In July 1938, the prison population of AFP consisted of 3,202 inmates, of whom 2,437 were white, 754 were "Colored," 10 were Indian, and one was Mexican.[25] It is probable that Albizu was classified as "Colored";

---

[22] On March 21, 1937, the Puerto Rican police, following the orders of Riggs and Winship, opened fire on a peaceful Nationalist demonstration in Ponce, a city on the southern coast of the Island, killing nineteen and wounding more than 200. For a careful analysis of what came to be known as the Ponce Massacre, see Arthur Garfield Hays, *Report of the Commission of Inquiry on Civil Rights in Puerto Rico* (New York: Commission of Inquiry on Civil Rights in Puerto Rico, 1937).

[23] Rosado, *Las llamas de la aurora*, 255; Carmelo Rosario Natal, ed., *Albizu Campos: Preso en Atlanta. Historia del reo #51298-A (Correspondencia)* (San Juan: Producciones Históricos, 2001), 17. Political prisoners housed previously at the penitentiary included Eugene Debs (1918–1921) and Marcus Garvey (1925–1927). For Debs's discussion of his years at the AFP see, Eugene Victor Debs, *Walls and Bars* (Montclair, NJ: Patterson Smith, 1973).

[24] US House of Representatives, 99th Congress, 2nd Session, "Atlanta Federal Penitentiary," (Washington, DC: US Government Printing Office, 1986), 1; Desmond King, "A Strong or Weak State? Race and the US Federal Government in the 1920s," *Ethnic and Racial Studies* 21, no. 1 (1998): 34.

[25] *The Atlantian* 1, no. 1 (1938), back page. The AFP staff published the prison newspaper *The Atlantian*, beginning in July–August 1938. I examined all the issues of the newspaper published during the years the Nationalists were imprisoned in the AFP. The racial proportions of the prison population remained basically the same during their incarceration. The last-reported racial breakdown was taken on December 28, 1940. The population was 2,218 white; 698 "Colored"; 20 Indian; 7 Mexican; 0 Oriental. "Population," *The Atlantian* 3, no. 5 (1941): 33. I thank Laura Browder for alerting me to the newspaper's existence.

however, the other Nationalists were definitely considered white within the binary system of racial classification that existed at that time.

Information about the Nationalists' time in prison is somewhat sketchy. They were not housed together, but they were able to see each other. The Bureau of Prisons classified them as common criminals, not political prisoners, and as such, they were required to work in the prison.[26] Because three of them (Albizu, Corretjer, and Soto Vélez) were highly educated (Albizu had a law degree from Harvard), they worked either in the Office of Education or the Office of Statistics. The other PNPR prisoners had more labor-intensive jobs. Three worked in the textile mill, for which they got paid, while the other three worked in the kitchen, but apparently did not get paid.[27] Neither their families, most of which were poor and/or unable to find work due to their ties to the prisoners, nor the Nationalist Party had the economic wherewithal to offer the prisoners much, if any, financial support.

Several factors explain the party's lack of funds. The exile and imprisonment of the Nationalist leadership and the wave of US government repression that washed over the island in the late 1930s and early 1940s led to disorganization, demoralization, and fear among party members and supporters, which resulted in a decrease in membership, donations, and dues. This, on top of the expenses incurred due to the trials and appeals of the prisoners, led to a general decline in party funds.[28] The Nationalists' paucity of financial resources made the International Labor Defense's monetary contributions to the prisoners even more necessary and appreciated.

INTERNATIONAL LABOR DEFENSE, THE COMMUNIST PARTY, AND THE NATIONALIST PRISONERS

Marcantonio was a key player in the relationship between the PNPR and the CPUSA.[29] In 1937 Marcantonio became president of the ILD, which was the

---

[26] Rosario Natal, *Albizu Campos*, 11.

[27] Rosado, *Las llamas de la aurora*, 269. The AFP textile mill began production in 1919. In the 1940s it produced tents and other materials for the US war effort. "Barred from Service," *The Atlantian*, 3, no. 6 (1941): 16–25.

[28] For a decline in membership see FBI, *Nationalist Party of Puerto Rico (NPPR)*, SJ 100–03, vol. 23, "Report made at San Juan," July 31, 1952, pp. 6, 42–44, 120, https://archive.org/stream/PartidoNacionalistaDePuertoRico/SJ-100-3_27_027_164_djvu.txt (accessed May 14, 2018).

[29] Meyer, "Pedro Albizu Campos," 97; Alan Schaffer, *Vito Marcantonio: Radical in Congress* (Syracuse, NY: Syracuse University Press, 1966), 57.

US branch of the Comintern's International Red Aid. He was simultaneously Albizu's attorney, the congressional representative of East Harlem (a district which included Italians and the highest concentration of Puerto Ricans in the United States), a staunch defender of Puerto Rican independence, and profoundly anti-fascist and anti-imperialist. Marcantonio was not a member of the CPUSA, but he was very close to it and in general followed and advanced its political line.[30] In August 1936, shortly after he returned from a two-week visit to Puerto Rico, Marcantonio addressed a crowd of 10,000 Puerto Ricans who had "paraded for three hours through the streets of lower Harlem ... to protest the attitudes and actions of 'Imperialistic America' in making 'slaves' of the natives of the island." Marcantonio denounced the "'political lynching' of Dr. Pedro Albizu Campos [and] said that the Puerto Rican's case 'will go down in history as another Tom Mooney or Scottsboro boys frame-up.'"[31] Marcantonio and Albizu were not only attorney and client, they were close friends. After Marcantonio was elected president of the ILD, Albizu wrote to personally congratulate him and to thank the organization for its financial support.[32]

Fortunately, the ILD regularly sent the Nationalist prisoners money to cover their basic needs.[33] The amount fluctuated between two and three dollars a month, depending on how much money the ILD had.[34] The

---

[30] Gerald Meyer, *Vito Marcantonio: Radical Politician, 1902–1954* (Albany: State University of New York Press, 1989); Annette Rubenstein, interview with author, New York, July 15, 2005. Rubenstein worked closely with Marcantonio in the American Labor Party and documented his Congressional record in *I Vote My Conscience: Debates, Speeches, and Writings of Vito Marcantonio* (New York: Vito Marcantonio Memorial, 1956).

[31] "10,000 Parade Here for Puerto Ricans," *New York Times*, August 30, 1936. The marchers received much support, as the article pointed out. "[T]housands of other residents in the area, populated mostly by Negroes and Spaniards, leaned out of windows and over the edges of roof-tops and added their protests to those of the demonstrators." Tom Mooney was a left labor leader who was imprisoned from 1916 to 1939 on what many considered "a framed-up bombing charge." The CPUSA campaigned vigorously for his release. See Dorothy Ray Healey and Maurice Isserman, *California Red: A Life in the American Communist Party* (Urbana: University of Illinois Press, 1993), 77.

[32] Pedro Albizu Campos to Vito Marcantonio, November 21, 1937, "Albizu Campos, Pedro 1936–1944," Box 2, SCRC-EB.

[33] As far as I know, the Nationalist prisoners were the only non-CPUSA-related prisoners to whom the ILD sent money.

[34] The ILD sending money to the Nationalist prisoners was what first alerted the FBI to the budding relationship between the PNPR and the CPUSA. In one of the agency's first memos on the issue, an FBI agent informed J. Edgar Hoover in 1939 that the "International Labor Defense in New York sent an air mail to the [Atlanta] prison enclosing $5.00 to each one of the seven Nationalists saying to use this money for cigarettes and to keep their spirits up." FBI, *Nationalist Party of Puerto Rico (NPPR)*,

Nationalists were understandably grateful for the ILD's support. In one of his letters to Marcantonio, Corretjer thanked the Congressman and the ILD for their monthly stipends. "Dear Vito, It was with great pleasure that I read your friendly letter, and I am again thanking you and the ILD for the money orders enclosed. You must rest assured that we appreciate in all its moral value your fraternal and inspiring attitude."[35]

Letters between the Nationalists and Marcantonio indicate the high level of frankness and trust that existed between them. For example, in one exchange Corretjer wrote to Marcantonio asking why the prisoners had received less money than expected. Marcantonio, in turn, asked Anna Damon, ILD president and secretary, why "the checks which you have been sending in [to Corretjer] and the other prisoners are smaller than the amount stipulated in the letter[s]."[36] After receiving clarification from Damon, Marcantonio responded to Corretjer informing him the smaller amount was due to the ILD having fewer funds available and that "[t]he stenographer ... slipped up in the letters and did not inform you of the changes, and continued to write the amount of three dollars instead of two dollars."[37]

Marcantonio's profound respect for Albizu and his responsibility to the Puerto Rican community that he represented in New York reinforced his commitment to the Nationalist prisoners. He not only ensured the ILD sent money to the Nationalists, but also visited Albizu and the other Nationalist prisoners five times during their imprisonment.[38] In addition, he frequently wrote to and received letters from Pedro Albizu Campos and Juan Antonio Corretjer, the secretary-general of the Nationalist Party. Anna Damon also corresponded regularly with the Nationalist prisoners.[39] The 1941 incarceration of Earl Browder, secretary-general

SJ 100–3, vol. 23, "Memo from Special Agent to J. Edgar Hoover," December 5, 1939, pp. 185–86, https://archive.org/stream/PartidoNacionalistaDePuertoRico/SJ-100-3_27 _027_164_djvu.txt (accessed May 14, 2018); Vito Marcantonio to Juan Antonio Corretjer, July 21, 1939, "Correspondence of Juan Antonio Corretjer," Marcantonio Papers, Box 46, New York Public Library (hereafter NYPL-M).

[35] Corretjer to Marcantonio, September 21, 1939, Box 46, File: Civil Liberties, Campos File, NYPL-M.

[36] Marcantonio to Anna Damon, July 19, 1939, Box 46, File: Civil Liberties, Campos File, NYPL-M.

[37] Marcantonio to Corretjer, July 21, 1939, Box 46, File: Civil Liberties, Campos File, NYPL-M.

[38] Rosado, *Las llamas de la aurora*, 271.

[39] Elizabeth Gurley Flynn, an important CPUSA member and leader, was also "[p]rominent in this work." William Z. Foster, *History of the Communist Party of the United States*

of the CPUSA, in the AFP brought the Nationalist prisoners into direct, regular contact with the Communist leader and deepened the bonds of solidarity and ties of comradeship between them and the two parties.

BROWDER AND THE AFP

In January 1940, Browder was convicted of passport fraud and sent to the AFP.[40] Director of Prisons James W. Bennett and AFP Warden Sanford consulted with each other regarding whether to send Browder to Atlanta. Sanford warned of the potential danger of housing Browder with Campos and Corretjer, an indication he was aware of the importance of personal contact and the possibility of friendship.[41] His concerns proved accurate. After Browder entered the AFP in March 1941, he met and became friends and comrades with Albizu, Corretjer, and other PNPR leaders jailed there; as a result, the links between the two parties increased.[42]

These men's shared experiences and political consonances were brought into sharp relief by the challenging prison conditions and often racist and/or anti-communist prison administration and population, which magnified the similarities between the three of them and minimized their differences. Albizu, Browder, and Corretjer were highly intelligent, well-educated men who loved to read, share ideas, and discuss politics. As the exchanges between the men after their release (when they could write to each other freely) attest, they found in each other respected and stimulating interlocutors. For example, Corretjer wrote to Browder congratulating him on a speech he had given in New York City. "As I go once again

(New York: International, 1952), n.p., http://williamzfoster.blogspot.com/2013/01/chapter-fourteen-communists-and.html (accessed August 20, 2017).

[40] "Browder is Loser in Supreme Court," *New York Times*, February 18, 1941. In 1937 and 1938, Browder used his passport when he "visited Spain to inspire and encourage the American boys in the Abraham Lincoln Brigade." However, in the 1920s he had traveled to the Soviet Union, Germany, Italy, and China for political reasons, "countries which would have been dangerous for him had he traveled under his own name." When he applied for a passport in 1934, he failed to mention he had traveled abroad on other passports, hence his conviction on passport fraud. Elizabeth Gurley Flynn, *The Man from Kansas* (New York: Workers Library, 1941), 13, 20, 22.

[41] Letter from Sanford to Bennett, December 12, 1941, Record Group 129, Series: Notorious Offenders File; 1919–1975, File: Browder, Earl Russell, 14314/60140-A; U.S. National Archives and Records Administration, https://catalog.archives.gov/id/603 7712 (accessed May 14, 2018). I thank Laura Browder for sharing this document with me.

[42] "The End of the Road for a Communist Leader," *New York Times*, March 21, 1941.

over it I can't but think that we are in the yard of Atlanta and you are simply talking your truth between two friends."[43]

While in prison, Browder wrote to his wife, Raissa, whom he addressed as Mom, about what he had been reading and his thoughts on politics.[44] His letters make clear he was very interested in Latin America and Latin American politics, one more element that drew these men together.[45] In one letter to Raissa, he wrote he was "studying a history of the Latin American wars of independence by a conservative but intelligent Latin America historian, Belaunde."[46] The combination of shared interests and difficulties that life in prison entailed served to forge a strong bond between and among the men, despite their political differences. Both parties supported Puerto Rican independence and anti-imperialism. They diverged significantly on the question of socialism, which the Nationalist Party rejected. Nor did Nationalists call for the organization and liberation of the working class, which the CPUSA did. Instead, the Nationalists concentrated on uniting as many Puerto Ricans as possible to achieve national sovereignty and, as noted above, largely failed to elaborate their economic plan for an independent Puerto Rico.[47] However, the CPUSA's embrace of Popular Front politics facilitated a closer relationship between it and the Nationalists by toning down the former's emphasis on class struggle.

---

[43] Corretjer to Browder, February 3, 1943, "Juan Antonio Corretjer, 1942–1945," Box 16, SCRC-EB.

[44] I believe Browder referred to his wife as "Mom" because that is what he called her when talking to his three sons. His use of the term underlines how close he was to his family and how much he missed them, as do his letters. I conjecture that the absence of his family encouraged the development of stronger emotional bonds with the Nationalist prisoners.

[45] Browder believed the Comintern had given him a "supervisory role" over the Latin American Communist parties, an understanding that must have heightened his interest in the political history of the region. Maurice Isserman, *Which Side Were You On? The American Communist Party during the Second World War* (Urbana: University of Illinois Press, 1993), 199.

[46] Earl Browder to Raissa Browder, May 22, 1941, Box 6, "Browder, Earl, To/From Irene Browder, Letters from Prison, 1941," SCRC-EB. Although Browder gives no further information about the book or the author, I believe he was referring to Víctor Andrés Belaúnde, *Bolívar and the Political Thought of the Spanish American Revolution* (Baltimore, MD: John Hopkins University Press, 1938).

[47] "El problema de Puerto Rico y el programa Nacionalista," *El Mundo*, September 21, 1932.

THE COMMUNIST PARTY, POPULAR FRONT POLITICS, AND PUERTO RICO

The Comintern promulgated the Popular Front political line in 1935 in response to the rise of fascism in Italy in 1922 and Germany in 1933.[48] The Popular Front defined fascism as the principal enemy and main danger to both the working class and oppressed peoples. The Comintern advocated that Communists fight fascism by seeking alliances and working with all forces that opposed fascism. During World War II, this meant that instead of denouncing Yankee imperialism and organizing the working class to fight the bourgeoisie, Communists should view their former enemies as their temporary allies in the joint struggle against the fascists. Thus, the CPUSA fully backed the US war effort, issued a no-strike pledge to ensure maximum production in the factories, declared Communists to be proud Americans, and even dissolved the party in 1944.[49]

George Charney, Chairman of the New York State Communist Party and member of the Central Committee until he resigned in 1958, described this political change in his memoirs.

Overnight we adjusted our evaluation of Roosevelt and the New Deal. Where we had been prone to damn all things American, we were now reassured that patriotism was not necessarily reactionary or "the last refuge of scoundrels," that there was a difference between bourgeois democracy and fascism, that we had to cherish democratic traditions, and, above all, that transcending the class struggle, a basis existed for common action between the USSR and the bourgeois democratic nations of the West.[50]

The CPUSA's decision to align its politics with those of the Roosevelt administration led to a shift in its position on Puerto Rico, at least publicly and temporarily. Ernest Gruening, one of Roosevelt's key advisors on Latin America and Director of the federal Division of Territories and Island Possessions, sought to maintain US control of Puerto Rico because he considered it vital to the promotion of US policies across Latin

---

[48] I have not found any evidence that the 1939 signing of the German-Soviet Nonaggression Pact and temporary abandonment of the Popular Front policy affected relations between the CPUSA and PNPR.

[49] See Louis B. Boudin, "'Seditious Doctrines' and the 'Clear and Present Danger' Rule: Part I," *Virginia Law Review* 38, no. 2 (1952): 315–56; Van Gosse, *Where the Boys Are: Cuba, Cold War America and the Making of a New Left* (London: Verso, 1993), 21. For a discussion of the Communist Political Association, the organization that replaced the CPUSA, see *The Path to Peace, Progress and Prosperity: Proceedings of the Constitutional Convention of the Communist Political Association* (New York, May 20–24, 1944).

[50] George Charney, *A Long Journey* (Chicago, IL: Quadrangle, 1968), 59.

America. The Roosevelt administration favored Luis Muñoz Marín, the leader of the PPD, because his policies paralleled theirs and he was amenable to working with them. The PPD and Muñoz Marín advocated greater autonomy for the island in the framework of an ongoing colonial relationship with the United States.[51] The CPUSA followed suit, backed Luis Muñoz Marín and the PPD, embraced the New Deal appointees and plans for the island, and downplayed, if not ignored, the demands of anticolonial Puerto Rican forces to end US rule on the island.

The CPUSA's support for the New Deal and for US rule in Puerto Rico was demonstrated during the July 1939 Youth Congress, held in New York City.[52] Julia Rivera, most likely a member of the Puerto Rican Communist Party (PCP), represented Puerto Rico at the meeting. Instead of unequivocally demanding independence, she said, "We feel it is time the present status of Puerto Rico be terminated," a statement vague enough to be open to multiple interpretations.[53] In an apparent endorsement of the New Deal, she suggested the island needed "[c]oncrete aid ... through public works programs and better educational facilities."[54] The General Resolutions of the Youth Congress called on the US government to "Give a New Deal to Puerto Rico," and did not mention independence.[55]

These positions diverged from those of the PNPR, which refused to back the US war effort or join the Popular Front. Instead it advocated resisting the draft and maintaining the fight against US colonialism.[56] Despite these differences, however, the CPUSA and the PNPR maintained close ties with each other. The comradeships developed in the AFP helped the leaders of both parties better grasp the political positions each party held and the possibilities each represented and offered to the other. According to historian Carlos Rodríguez Fraticelli, conversations with Browder contributed to Albizu's assessment that "a favorable juncture

---

[51] I thank Mike Staudenmaier for this formulation.

[52] The American Youth Congress was the US branch of the World Congress of Youth, which was "organized by the popular-front International Committee of Youth." The Congress brought together anti-fascist youth from around the world. Katherine Merino, "Pan-American Feminism and the Origins of International Women's Rights: The Confederación Continental de Mujeres por la Paz," paper delivered at the American Historical Association annual conference, Atlanta, GA, January 2016, p. 6; Richard A. Reiman, *The New Deal and American Youth: Ideas and Ideals in a Depression Decade* (Athens: University of Georgia Press, 2010), 42.

[53] It is not clear whether she meant Puerto Rico should become a US state or an independent nation.

[54] "Proceeding of Congress of Youth," July 1–5, 1939, Special Collections, Communist Party Pamphlets, 1934–1939, Box 2, University of Illinois at Chicago.

[55] Ibid.   [56] Consuelo Lee Tapia, *Apuntes* (Ciales: Casa Corretjer, 2004), 39.

had been created for the United States to peacefully withdraw from Puerto Rico."[57] As a result, Albizu decided that it was not only possible but necessary to "create in the United States a powerful solidarity movement with the independence of Puerto Rico." Albizu believed the Nationalists could count on the CPUSA, which "had committed itself to financially and organizational[ly] support the undertaking."[58]

A combination of political pragmatism and ideals explains why the CPUSA backed the PNPR. The CPUSA was the Comintern-appointed leader of the Communist movement throughout the Americas.[59] From the late 1920s through the 1950s, both the Latin American Left and the CPUSA backed the PNPR. Earl Browder wrote a memo, presumably to the CPUSA, warning that if Albizu was returned to prison following his 1943 release, due to his refusal to sign his parole papers, it would "result in serious agitation throughout Latin-America."[60] Furthermore, the CPUSA recognized that many Puerto Ricans in New York City supported the PNPR, as did anti-imperialist forces throughout the Americas.[61] The Puerto Rican vote was critical to Marcantonio's electoral victories and the radical Congressman's voice and vote in Congress and US society were valuable to the CPUSA. The CPUSA also had an ideological investment in promoting anti-colonialism, which it did by backing the PNPR. So, even as the party built relations with the FDR administration and worked to support a broad anti-fascist front, it also fostered a close relationship with the Nationalists.

Indeed, in addition to politically and financially backing the Puerto Rican Nationalists imprisoned by the FDR administration, the CPUSA joined with the PNPR and other CPUSA-affiliated organizations to form the National Committee for the Defense of Puerto Rican Political Prisoners in New York City in 1937.[62] And, as we shall see below, it worked closely with the PNPR to publish the Spanish-language paper, *Pueblos Hispanos*.

---

[57] Fraticelli does not explain on what Browder based his opinion.
[58] Carlos Rodríguez-Fraticelli, "Pedro Albizu Campos: Strategies of Struggle and Strategic Struggles," *Centro Journal* 4, no. 1 (1991–92): 29.
[59] Manuel Caballero, *Latin America and the Comintern, 1919–1943* (Cambridge: Cambridge University Press, 1986), 81.
[60] "Memorandum on the Case of Dr. Pedro Albizu Campos," n.d. (1943), "Albizu Campos, Pedro 1936–1944," SCRC-EB.
[61] Marcantonio, for example, believed that "freeing Albizu and the other prisoners would contribute greatly to winning over the people of Latin America to the Allies' cause." Meyer, "Pedro Albizu Campos," 104.
[62] "Puerto Rican Defense Group Calls Protest," *Daily Worker*, April 6, 1937.

FROM THE AFP TO NEW YORK CITY

Upon Albizu's 1943 release from the Atlanta prison, he was greeted and escorted to New York by attorney Samuel Neuberger. Neuberger had joined the Communist Party in the 1930s, when "the growing threat of Nazism became apparent." He worked with the ILD team and was good friends with Marcantonio, who asked him to meet Albizu outside the prison and "bring him up [to New York City]."[63]

The trip to New York was not easy. In 1943 racial segregation was rampant across the South, so "there was no comingling in transportation." There were two trains out of Atlanta. The Crescent train left in the afternoon, but only whites were allowed to board it. The other was the "milk train," which left very early in the morning, and was used by blacks and poor whites. How could Neuberger, who was white, travel with Albizu, who, according to racial notions of the time, was "Colored"? Neuberger devised a plan. He reserved a compartment on the Crescent and contacted two other white people to join him. Neuberger "advised each one to take Don Pedro under the arm," while he went on ahead.

When we got [to the train station], I screamed, "Step aside, take that man aboard." We [Albizu and the white men] walked right through [the station] ... to the compartment. The psychology was simple. [H]earing this ... authoritative voice that said step aside [and] had to be obeyed, [the crowd] did. We got into the compartment [and] closed the door. The porter was a Black man; he was obviously sympathetic. He acted like he saw and knew nothing, so we carried on.[64]

Albizu, Browder, and Corretjer reunited in New York City following their respective releases from the AFP.[65] When he first arrived in New York City, Albizu stayed at the home of Consuelo Lee Tapia de Lamb and Leonard Lamb, both members of the CPUSA.[66] From the Lamb house, Albizu went to Columbus Hospital, where he stayed until November 1945.[67] Albizu and Browder wrote warm letters to each other while Albizu was confined in Columbus Hospital. Albizu typically

---

[63] Samuel Neuberger interviewed by Mary Licht, December 16, 1982, Cassette 3; "Communist Party of the United States of America Oral History Collection," OH.065, Box 1, Tamiment Library/Robert F. Wagner Labor Archives, New York University.

[64] Ibid.   [65] Corretjer was released in June 1942, Browder in May 1942.

[66] Consuelo Lee was from a prominent Puerto Rican family, which did not share her political beliefs. Tapia, *Apuntes,* 12. Leonard Lamb had fought in Spain as a member of the Abraham Lincoln Brigade. "XV International Brigade in Spain," http://internatio nalbrigadesinspain.weebly.com/lincolns-in-spain.html (accessed August 20, 2017).

[67] He was diagnosed with "arteriosclerosis, coronary sclerosis, bronchial neuritis, and general weakness." Rosado, *Las llamas de la aurora,* 282.

addressed Browder as "Dear friend." In one letter to Browder, Albizu expressed "our solidarity on the occasion of your immense grief. Your beloved father has passed on living a way of duty nobly and fruitfully performed which is an inspiration for his posterity."[68] In an undated letter of the same time period, Albizu wrote to Browder, "Please come whenever you may find time. Thanks for the report and your fraternal letter."[69] In another undated letter, Albizu wrote Browder on *Daily Worker* stationary.[70] "Dear Earl, I was happy to drop in to see you. I'm sorry I miss [sic] this opportunity. You know where I'm staying for the time being ... Please offer your wonderful wife and beloved children my [illegible] friendship. Fraternally and obliged."[71]

Members of both the Nationalist and Communist parties recognized the importance of the friendship between the two leaders, as did the US government, as the correspondence between Warden Sanford and Department of Prisons head Bennett reveals. When Albizu was in the hospital, Consuelo Lee Lamb, who was Puerto Rican, asked him "to permit me to join the ranks of the Nationalist Party of Puerto Rico." She made it clear she was a communist and her "ideology would not change in this respect." She noted she had asked Browder "to release me [from her commitment to the CPUSA]." However, since this "had never been done" she anticipated that because "Earl Browder is your friend and the friend of our Motherland, I hope that an exception will be made in my case."[72] It is not clear whether Browder refused to "release" her or whether Albizu denied her membership request, but she remained a member of the CPUSA. She did, however, become the CPUSA's representative to the PNPR and Juan Antonio Corretjer was named the PNPR's representative to the CPUSA.

---

[68] Albizu Campos to Browder, November 8, 1943, Box 2, "Albizu Campos, Pedro 1936–1944," SCRC-EB.

[69] Albizu Campos to Browder, n.d., Box 2, "Albizu Campos, Pedro 1936–1944," SCRC-EB.

[70] The *Daily Worker*, the newspaper of the CPUSA, began publication in New York City in 1924.

[71] Pedro Albizu Campos Letter to Earl Browder, n.d., Box 2, "Albizu Campos, Pedro 1936–1944," SCRC-EB. Albizu left Columbus Hospital on November 9, 1945, and returned to Puerto Rico on December 12, 1947, so he must have written the letter sometime between those dates. Rosado, *Las llamas de la aurora*, 294, 296. The letter is most likely on a *Daily Worker* letterhead because Albizu had dropped by the CPUSA office to speak with Browder.

[72] Letter from Consuelo Lee Tapia de Lamb to Pedro Albizu Campos, June 16, 1943, Box 2, "Albizu Campos, Pedro 1936–1944," SCRC-EB.

Corretjer and Albizu were likewise close friends and trusted comrades; their time together in Atlanta strengthened the bonds of respect and affection between them. When Albizu was ill in Columbus Hospital, he designated Corretjer as his "substitute," due to his "heroic devotion, emotional ability and humility in service of the cause" of Puerto Rican independence. Albizu then called on the Nationalist leadership and members "to extend lovingly and with deep fraternal solidarity, all the cooperation he [Corretjer] needs to successfully fulfill such a difficult mission."[73] Corretjer reciprocated Albizu's feelings. In a note Corretjer wrote to Browder, he referred to the Nationalist leader as "our Beloved Don Pedro."[74]

Corretjer and Browder also became good friends and comrades during their time in the AFP. Corretjer's respect for Browder and admiration for the CPUSA grew, as did his differences with the PNPR.[75] Corretjer remained a fervent Nationalist, but he added a class-based analysis to his political outlook.

One direct result of the political and personal comradeship between members of the PNPR and CPUSA was the February 1943 launch of the paper *Pueblos Hispanos*. Chilean poet and communist Pablo Neruda, who happened to be in New York City when it occurred, attended the event, as did "numerous North American and Latin American personalities."[76] *Pueblos Hispanos* was a New York-based Spanish-language weekly that reported on Puerto Rico and the rest of Latin America.[77] Its goals were to

unit[e] Spanish-speaking peoples to win the war, concentrat[ing] on the Puerto Rican people [and] their problems here in the United States ... to deal with win-the-war issues affecting Spaniards in the USA and peoples of Latin American countries ... [and] to familiarize the workers and win-the-war forces of the United States with the problems of Puerto Rico and Latin American countries.[78]

---

[73] Albizu Campos to Honorable Don Natalio Quinones (*sic*), September 20, 1943, Box 2, "Albizu Campos, Pedro 1936–1944," SCRC-EB.

[74] Press statement by Juan Antonio Corretjer, New York City, June 7, 1943, Box 2, "Albizu Campos, Pedro 1936–1944," SCRC-EB.

[75] According to Gerald Meyer, Corretjer joined the CPUSA, probably in 1943, and quit it in 1945. Meyer, "Pedro Albizu Campos," 102.

[76] Lee Tapia, *Apuntes*, 40.

[77] Rosado, *Las llamas de la aurora*, 289; Meyer, "Pedro Albizu Campos," 102.

[78] "Report from James W. Ford to Earl [Browder], Gil [Green], [Israel] Amter," April 1, 1943, Box 30, "Pueblo Hispanos 1944," SCRC-EB. Green and Amter, like Browder, were leaders of the CPUSA. The publication's win-the-war position reflected the CPUSA's influence on the journal.

Members of both parties served on the editorial staff of the paper. Corretjer was the editor and Consuelo Lee de Lamb was the manager.[79] The famous Puerto Rican poet Julia de Burgos also worked on the paper, as did Clemente Soto Vélez, a Nationalist leader who had been imprisoned in the AFP in 1937 and joined the CPUSA after his release.[80] The paper was distributed to Spanish-speaking organizations in New York City, as well as to Puerto Rico, Cuba, Latin American embassies and, perhaps, other countries.[81] It ceased publication in October 1944.[82]

Around the time *Pueblos Hispanos* began, Corretjer wrote a long letter to Browder sharing his thoughts on Albizu, his growing identification with the Communist Party, and his criticisms of that party for prioritizing support for the United States instead of solidarity with anti-imperialist forces across the Americas. Corretjer expressed his profound respect for the PNPR and his conviction that Albizu would win in "any honest election in Puerto Rico," yet also pessimistically predicted "the Nationalist Party's failure as an administrative governing Party."[83] He then counseled Browder that the Communist Party "leadership needs to show itself wise, tactful and powerful enough to realize the revolutionary prestige with which the Nationalist Party will enter in the Republic, and the revolutionary potentiality of its minor leadership and its rank and file."[84] He criticized the Communist Party's policies vis-à-vis Latin America and offered suggestions as to what the party's correct political line should be. He wrote, "It seems to me that the policy followed about the Peruvian Apristas has been slightly mistaken. IN PERU [capitals in

---

[79] Ibid.

[80] Casa Corretjer, *Re: Mujer boricua* (Ciales: Casa Corretjer, 2006), 8; Meyer, "Pedro Albizu Campos," 102.

[81] "Report from James W. Ford."

[82] Corretjer told Browder that the paper "suspended publication in order to help the development of *LA VOZ DE LA CGT*, the official organ of the General Confederation of Puerto Rican Workers, which recently began publication in San Juan, Puerto Rico." Letter to Earl Browder, October 30, 1944, Box 16, "Pueblo Hispanos 1944," SCRC-EB. According to the FBI, Browder "decreed" the closing of *Pueblos Hispanos*, to "assist the Communist and Independence movements on the island." "The Independence Movement in Puerto Rico," December 8, 1944, Reel 19, FBI Reports of the Franklin D. Roosevelt White House, Center for Research Libraries.

[83] I have not been able to determine why Corretjer thought this.

[84] It is not known if Albizu would have won had elections been held, but Corretjer evidently believed he would have. However, Corretjer did not believe the PNPR leadership was capable of successfully ruling Puerto Rico. It appears that he had greater confidence in the capacity of the rank and file, working with and possibly under the leadership of the CPUSA, to implement a revolutionary agenda for the Island.

original] they should be given help – in fact they should have been given it" since they had "not been able to develop a Communist Party."[85] Corretjer continued with his advice. "Bolivia should be paid more attention. So Should [*sic*] be Paraguay and the Dominican Republic."[86] Furthermore, Corretjer backed the July 1944 overthrow of General Jorge Ubico, the pro-US dictator of Guatemala, which the CPUSA saw as "inopportune to the military effort to defeat Hitler and Mussolini."[87]

MATTERS OF THE HEART

While personal relationships generally enhanced the relationship between the PNPR and the CPUSA, they could also result in conflicts, as the following example illustrates. In February 1943 Corretjer fell ill at the *Pueblos Hispanos* office and Lee brought him home to nurse him.[88] During his illness and convalescence the two become very close. In a letter to his father, Corretjer extolled her virtues and "her behavior and her significance in my life and for the conscience of those who love me."[89] He had fallen deeply in love with her, as she had with him.[90] Their political beliefs and personal sentiments intertwined. Corretjer retained his commitment to Puerto Rican nationalism, even as he increasingly identified with the politics of the CPUSA. His divided loyalties to the

---

[85] *Apristas* refers to members of the Alianza Popular Revolucionaria Americana (American Popular Revolutionary Alliance), which Peruvian Víctor Raúl Haya de la Torre founded in exile in Mexico in 1924. The organization was anti-imperialist and initially enjoyed a close relationship with the Comintern. However, APRA developed political differences with the Comintern, which led to a falling out between the two organizations and to Communist parties throughout the Americas criticizing the Peruvian party. Lazar Jeifets and Víctor Jeifets, *América Latina en la Internacional Comunista, 1919–1943: Diccionario biográfico* (Santiago: Ariadna, 2015), 293–94.

[86] Corretjer to Browder, February 3, 1943, Box 2, "Corretjer, Juan Antonio 1942–45," SCRC-EB.

[87] Lee Tapia, *Apuntes*, 39.

[88] I have pieced this story together from letters written by Browder, Corretjer, and Lee archived in the Browder papers at Syracuse University, as well as discussions with José López, Director of the Puerto Rican Cultural Center in Chicago, who interviewed both Corretjer and Lee about this period in their lives. Although the letters to and from Albizu, Corretjer, and Lee were originally written in Spanish, the Browder archives contain translations, which is what I have used in this chapter.

[89] Juan Antonio Corretjer to Diego Corretjer, December 9, 1943, Box 2, "Corretjer, Juan Antonio 1942–45," SCRC-EB.

[90] They remained together for the rest of their lives. He died in 1985 and she in 1989. http://siluz.blogspot.com/2011/03/la-sombra-de-juan-antonio-corretjer.html (accessed May 8, 2018).

Nationalist and Communist parties led to tensions with the PNPR leadership, which came to a head, ironically, because of his relationship with Lee.

Albizu had appointed Corretjer as the PNPR's representative to the Communist Party. Browder named Lee as the CPUSA's representative to the PNPR. The fact the two fell in love with each other while Lee was married to a respected member of the CPUSA violated party discipline and, Albizu feared, could potentially create problems between the two parties. The conflict exploded in November 1943, following a phone call and visit to Lee from Julio Pinto Gandía. Pinto Gandía was a lawyer and had represented the Nationalist leaders in the 1936 trial that ended in their conviction. Following their imprisonment he had become president of the party, a position he held from 1937 to September 1943, when Albizu named Corretjer as party leader.[91] As Lee wrote to Albizu, when Pinto called her on the phone she explained to him, "Juan Antonio Corretjer couldn't have arguments" regarding their relationship or the potential negative consequences because "he had had a bad night. He [Pinto] hung up on me and arrived here" to confront them at her home. Evidently, Lee had previously attempted to present her thoughts on the affair to Albizu, who had refused to hear them. As she wrote, "I am surprised . . . you don't at least wish to hear both sides." She continued, "In view of the incident [that] occurred at my house by the visit of Julio Pinto Gandía, I have asked my Party to accept my resignation as delegate to your Party. I no longer deal with your hospital bills. Send payment with someone you won't feel uncomfortable with."[92]

Lee also wrote to Browder about what had happened. I quote the letter in full since it so clearly reveals the ramifications of Lee's and Corretjer's relationship and the "incident" with Pinto that took place.

Comrade Browder:

In view of the incident which occurred in my home with Pedro Albizu Campos's emissary Julio Pinto Gandía, I believe I should be relieved of my mission as Delegate before the Nationalist Party of Puerto Rico. I am certain that I am persona non-grata to Pedro Albizu Campos and since Juan Antonio Corretjer is no longer the General Secretary of the Nationalist Patty but has been substituted by Julio Pinto Gandía, with whom I had the incident in question[,] I find my service to the better understanding between the two groups no longer useful but detrimental.

[91] Rafael Cancel Miranda, "Julio Pinto Gandía," *Claridad*, August 21–28, 2008.
[92] Lee Tapia to Albizu Campos, November 9, 1943, Box 2, "Albizu Campos, Pedro 1936–1944," SCRC-EB.

If the Central Committee wishes an explanation of this incident I will be glad to state the case for them.

Fraternally yours, Consuelo Lee Lamb[93]

What had happened? Albizu had found out about Lee and Corretjer's relationship, although it is not clear how. Lee had attempted to explain her perspective on their relationship to him. I have found no record of what she said or how Albizu responded. It appears from her letters, though, that Albizu rejected her explanation and sent Pinto Gandía to confront Corretjer directly. Pinto Gandía apparently treated Lee in a manner she found insulting and dismissive, so she wrote to Albizu seeking his support, which she did not get. As a result, Corretjer and Lee resigned as their respective parties' representatives to the other party.[94] Pinto Gandía also replaced Corretjer as leader of the PNPR. Corretjer continued editing *Pueblos Hispanos* until it folded a little less than a year later, briefly joined the Communist Party, and quit in 1945. Lee quit the Communist Party, married Corretjer, and the two traveled together to Cuba in 1945, where they worked with the Cuban Communist Party.[95] In 1946 they returned to Puerto Rico, where they lived for the rest of their lives.

The comradeship between Browder and Albizu continued, at least until 1945 when Browder was removed as secretary-general of the Communist Party, a position then filled by William Z. Foster.[96] To avoid a repetition of what had just happened, Albizu proposed to Browder that the two discuss and mutually agree upon who should be each party's representative. "May I suggest that you and I consider candidates before any

---

[93] Lee Tapia to Browder, December 9, 1943, Box 2, "Corretjer, Juan Antonio 1942–45," SCRC-EB.

[94] Corretjer also wrote to Browder informing him of his resignation. Corretjer to Browder, December 19, 1943, Box 16, "Corretjer, Juan Antonio 1942–45," SCRC-EB.

[95] Lee Tapia, *Apuntes*, 40.

[96] The Comintern was dissolved in 1943. Browder dissolved the CPUSA in 1944 and formed the Communist Political Association as part of his effort "to impress on liberals that Communists were sincerely committed to democracy and to the best interests of the country." Fraser M. Ottanelli, *The Communist Party of the United States: From the Depression to World War II* (New Brunswick, NJ: Rutgers University Press, 1991), 208. Further, as Maurice Isserman notes, "Browder not only believed that the struggle for socialism should be shelved for the foreseeable future, he also wanted to abandon any ideological challenge to the prevailing capitalist consensus on domestic issues." *Which Side*, 188–89. Not only were Browder's positions repudiated in 1945, he was expelled from the party. Eric Arnesen, *Encyclopedia of US Labor and Working Class History* (New York: Routledge, 2007), 297; Harvey Klehr, *The Heyday of American Communism: The Depression Decade* (New York: Basic, 1984), 410–11.

exchange of delegations between our two organizations takes place. Wishing you and your beloved all the joys of the season, Brotherly, Pedro Albizu Campos."[97]

CONCLUSION

To paraphrase a feminist slogan from the 1960s, the personal enriches our understanding of the political. Although scholars of gender and sexuality have examined interpersonal relationships, most studies still overlook their importance. This chapter has argued that the relationships among political activists are crucial for understanding political history. Those relationships affect how people think about politics and what they do. This was particularly true for friendships forged in the harsh conditions of the US penal system. Both the Nationalists and Browder were imprisoned for their political beliefs, and sent far from home and loved ones. It was in prison that Albizu and Corretjer met and became friends and comrades with Browder, strengthening the links that had existed between their respective parties and influencing the relationships between them until at least 1945.

The relationships among Albizu, Browder, Corretjer, Damon, Lee, Marcantonio, Neuberger, and Pinto Gandía developed in the specific historic and political context of the late 1930s and early 1940s. These were years of heightened repression, the exile of the PNPR's leadership, and other economic and political challenges. It was a time when the CPUSA under the leadership of Earl Browder sought to build a broad, "popular front" against fascism (apart from the 1939–1941 period, when it upheld the German-Soviet Non-Aggression Pact). It allied with the Roosevelt administration, publicly backed the New Deal in both the United States and Puerto Rico, and extended its support to Luis Muñoz Marín and the PPD. At the same time, it sent money to the Nationalist prisoners, advocated their release, and worked closely with members of the PNPR. In one extraordinary example of solidarity, Earl Browder met with under-secretary of state Sumner Welles to urge him to convince President Roosevelt that "Albizu Campos be released from Atlanta without the probationary restriction."[98]

---

[97] Albizu Campos to Browder, December 23, 1943, Box 2, "Albizu Campos, Pedro 1936– 1944," SCRC-EB.

[98] Welles to Roosevelt, May 22, 1943, Box 152, Folder 4, "Roosevelt, Franklin D., April– August 1943," FDR Presidential Library. Welles adds, "I could, of course, only gain the impression that these three Nationalists [Albizu, Corretjer, and Silva, the treasurer] are of

By focusing on personal relationships, I do not mean to suggest that friendships existed outside or independent of the larger political context or the political interests of each party. They did not. Political expediency, along with each party's goals, ideals, constraints, capabilities, and resources, influenced the actions of both parties. But so, too, did the comradeships that developed, persisted, or ended among the various individuals discussed in this chapter. To better understand the left, we must consider the personalities and relationships of the individuals who make up these groups.

The left is not a political abstraction, a disembodied idea, or an impersonal response to oppressive structures in society. It is made up of people who have a variety of relationships with each other and a range of feelings about themselves, their organizations, and the other members of their or other groups. These relationships and feelings matter. They influence the attitudes, choices, policies, and practices that leftist militants and parties adopt or reject. As we have seen in this chapter, these relationships can increase members and organizations' respect for and ties with each other, or they can lead to alienation and rupture. In either case, personal relationships matter to political organizers and organizations, and ignoring them diminishes our ability to fully understand how and why the left functions.

importance to him from the standpoint of the interests of the Communist Party." I thank Aaron Coy Moulton for generously sharing this document with me.

5

Total Subversion

Interethnic Radicalism in La Paz, Bolivia, 1946–1947

Kevin A. Young

In late May 1947 a frantic telegram arrived in La Paz from Los Andes, the rural province of 20,000 located just northwest of the Bolivian capital. The Sub-Prefect of Los Andes, Luis Lahore Monje, warned of grave threats to the social order:

Since January we have witnessed a series of troubles throughout the entire province of Los Andes, given that the entire *indiada* [Indian mass] is to be found in an attitude of subversion, continually threatening to unleash across the entire *altiplano* [high plateau region], and later entering the city of La Paz, a total uprising aimed at destroying all the towns, especially in this Province, in order to then redistribute the Haciendas' lands and name their own authorities.

Lahore Monje mentioned one hacienda in particular, in Carapata, located near the eastern shore of Lake Titicaca (see Figure 5.1). He alleged that indigenous workers there had attempted an unsuccessful uprising on May 1 and had again "started to make the rounds to all the Haciendas" in preparation for a new attempt. The "*indígenas* of Carapata, who are the main instigators and leaders," were reportedly in touch with workers at about thirty-six different haciendas in the province. And the telegram made another alarming charge: the rebels were also "in direct contact with members of the Federación Obrera Local," the anarchist workers' federation in the city.[1]

* Thanks to Tarun Banerjee, Marc Becker, Forrest Hylton, Brooke Larson, Marcelo Maldonado Rocha, Hernán Pruden, Silvia Rivera Cusicanqui, Huáscar Rodríguez García, Diana Sierra Becerra, Sinclair Thomson, Juhi Tyagi, and an anonymous reader.
[1] Luis Lahore Monje to M. E. Atristaín O., May 26, 1947, Sub Fondo Administración (Los Andes), Subserie Telegramas, Caja 80, Legajo 1, Archivo de La Paz (hereafter ALP; all ALP

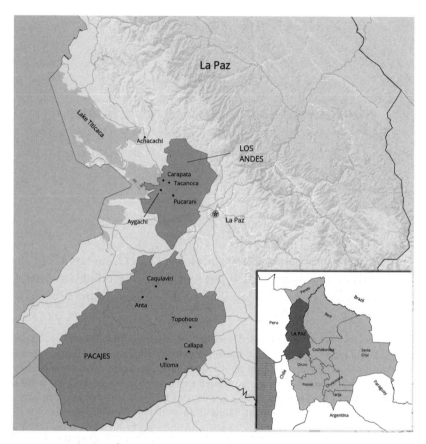

FIGURE 5.1 La Paz department.
Source: Map by author.

The telegram includes several tropes common in elite characterizations of popular rebellion. The rebels themselves are presented as a dark-skinned horde (the *"indiada"*). They are devoid of rationality, sweeping across the land like a force of nature. For the elite of La Paz this language would have conjured memories of the past indigenous uprisings that continued to haunt their dreams, from the famous 1781 siege of La Paz by the forces of Túpac Katari to the hacienda strikes and land conflicts of

documents cited herein are located in Sub Fondo Administración). Data on Los Andes from Prefectura de La Paz, "Descripción sobre las características de la provincia que debe llenarse dentro del siguiente detalle" (n.d., 1945), Los Andes, Subserie Telegramas, Caja 81, Legajo 2, ALP.

recent years. The telegram's reference to the Federación Obrera Local (Local Workers' Federation, FOL) reflects another familiar claim, implying that the unrest afflicting the province was largely the work of outside agitators.

Hysterical rhetoric aside, however, the telegram actually contained much truth. In early 1947, Los Andes and several other provinces of La Paz, along with Ayopaya and other regions of Cochabamba, were the sites of tremendous upheaval targeting hacienda owners and the racial and economic system they represented. Hacienda workers had formed dozens of unions during the year prior, while hacienda workers and "free" indigenous communities alike had also agitated for land, schools, and autonomy. And urban anarchists, most of whom would have been classified as *mestizos* or *cholos* (thus "nonindigenous"), were indeed assisting the indigenous workers in Carapata – and were doing the same throughout Los Andes and nearby provinces.[2]

Only recently has interethnic collaboration on the Latin American left begun to attract serious scholarly attention. Most commentators have instead emphasized the arrogance and ethnocentrism of urban leftists vis-à-vis rural peasants and Indians. There is certainly much evidence to support this characterization: ideology and practice on the Bolivian left, as elsewhere, have often been marred by ethnic prejudice and the assumption that urban workers and intellectuals are the vanguards of revolution.[3] Recent historical research, however, has begun to reveal a more heterogeneous set of left traditions, particularly in the 1920s, 1930s, and 1940s.[4] Several recent studies of Bolivia highlight interethnic collaboration in the 1920s through 1940s.[5] Though not totally free of traditional prejudices, the radical visions that animated these coalitions were relatively non-hierarchical compared to those that predominated on some parts of the

---

[2] The term *cholo* defies easy definition, but refers most commonly to urban residents who display cultural markers that set them apart from both the dominant creole/*mestizo* groups and from rural indigenous people.

[3] James Dunkerley, "The Crisis of Bolivian Radicalism," in *The Latin American Left: From the Fall of Allende to Perestroika*, ed. Barry Carr and Steve Ellner (Boulder, CO: Westview, 1993), 131–32; Carmen Soliz, "La modernidad esquiva: Debates políticos e intelectuales sobre la reforma agraria en Bolivia (1935–1952)," *Ciencia y Cultura* (La Paz) 29 (2012): 23–49; Kevin A. Young, *Blood of the Earth: Resource Nationalism, Revolution, and Empire in Bolivia* (Austin: University of Texas Press, 2017).

[4] See Introduction, this volume.

[5] Laura Gotkowitz, *A Revolution for Our Rights: Indigenous Struggles for Land and Justice in Bolivia, 1880–1952* (Durham, NC: Duke University Press, 2007), esp. 159–62, 247–56; Hylton, Chapter 1, this volume.

left. They were also less class-reductionist, prioritizing the struggle against racism and internal colonialism as well as the class struggle, and doing so long before the rise of the more well-known indigenous movements of the late twentieth century.

This chapter examines the alliance between La Paz anarchists and indigenous hacienda laborers in the late 1940s, focusing on the upsurge in unionization and strikes in places like Carapata in 1946–47. In 1946, rural union leaders from the provinces of Los Andes and Pacajes formed the Federación Agraria Departamental (Departmental Agrarian Federation, FAD), and in December of that year formally affiliated with the urban FOL. Three characteristics of the participants facilitated this development. First, several aspects of "Folista" politics proved particularly conducive to coalition building: their libertarian socialist vision, their attentiveness to "ethnic" as well as "class" demands, and their organizational federalism.[6]

An inclusive ideology and democratic organizational structure were not enough, however. The second prerequisite for the coalition's formation was the prior history of organizing in rural areas, which furnished local networks that formed the basis for the FAD. Past studies have often exaggerated the urban impetus behind the coalition.[7] The alliance is more properly understood as a negotiated process in which rural Indians not only helped initiate ties but also helped shape the urbanites' own discourse and priorities.

The final precondition was a series of brokers who could bridge linguistic, ethnic, cultural, and geographic divides. These individuals came from both urban and rural areas, were often bilingual, and enjoyed a certain geographic mobility stemming from their occupations and migration patterns. They acted as the proximate human links that wove the alliance together.

Together, these three elements allowed organizers to exploit, and expand, the limited opportunities offered by their external context. The postwar

[6] It is often impossible to classify a particular demand as purely ethnic- or class-based. Ethnic identities are frequently politicized given the hierarchies usually associated with ethnic typologies and their overlap with other forms of domination and resistance. For instance, a peasant struggle for land may build solidarity by labeling its participants as indigenous and large landowners as white or *mestizo*; meanwhile, "ethnic" campaigns against discrimination often involve demands for material resources.

[7] Robert J. Alexander with Eldon M. Parker, *A History of Organized Labor in Bolivia* (Westport, CT: Praeger, 2005), 61; Luis Antezana E. and Hugo Romero B., *Historia de los sindicatos campesinos: Un proceso de integración nacional en Bolivia* (La Paz: Consejo Nacional de Reforma Agraria, 1973), 159.

conjuncture of 1945–46 featured a brief but substantial relaxation of authoritarian rule, as in most Latin American countries.[8] The coalition government of Colonel Gualberto Villarroel and the Movimiento Nacionalista Revolucionario (Nationalist Revolutionary Movement, MNR), in power from 1943 to 1946, proved more willing than its predecessors to permit challenges to landlord domination in the countryside. The FAD and FOL opposed the Villarroel–MNR regime but nonetheless benefited from the relative freedom to organize. By late 1946 the government had been toppled and repression by landlords and state forces had increased, but the anarchists had seized the moment to make crucial organizational gains.

The first section below presents background on the pre-1946 political context, focusing on elite fears of an urban–rural and interethnic alliance. The second section summarizes the events of 1946–47, including FAD–FOL organizing efforts, the hacienda uprisings of early 1947, and the ensuing repression. From there, the next three sections look backward in time to examine how the coalition was possible, analyzing each of the factors identified above and how they helped La Paz radicals take advantage of the brief political opening in 1945–46. The conclusion suggests some of the broader implications for our understanding of the twentieth-century Bolivian left, social movements, and political culture.

AN INDIAN REPUBLIC VIA COMMUNIST INSTIGATION?

The growth of the FAD and its integration into the FOL seemed to confirm the worst fear of hacienda owners: an urban–rural, interethnic coalition of radicals. In the days and months following the rebellions of 1947, the establishment press sounded hysterical warnings about urban agitators in the countryside.[9] Even two years after the rebellions had been decisively repressed, the conservative Cochabamba daily *Los Tiempos* wondered whether "Bolivia and Peru will become Indian republics through communist instigation." The paper quoted a US author, Williard Price, who warned that "Indians are particularly susceptible to communist propaganda due to their long and satisfying tradition of communism."[10]

[8] Laurence Whitehead, "Bolivia," in *Latin America between the Second World War and the Cold War, 1944–1948*, ed. Leslie Bethell and Ian Roxborough (Cambridge: Cambridge University Press, 1992), 120–46.

[9] See for instance "Se organizará proceso contra los agitadores de los campesinos," *La Razón*, May 27, 1947, 4.

[10] "¿Bolivia y el Perú se convertirán en repúblicas indias bajo la instigación comunista?" *Los Tiempos*, June 21, 1949, 5.

Though hyperbolic, such warnings were partly based in reality. Cooperation between urban and rural activists had first begun in the 1920s. Urban artisans and leftist intellectuals had started providing legal and educational support to communal landholders (*comunarios*) in the mid-1920s, when struggles in defense of land and for indigenous schools became the key points of articulation. In Sucre, the socialist Ferrer School founded in 1922 had been in contact with indigenous community leaders in Chuquisaca and Potosí departments, and urban–rural collaboration played a significant role in the massive 1927 Chayanta revolt.[11] In La Paz several future leaders of the FOL had given legal advice to indigenous communities as early as 1924. Santos Marka T'ula, the most famous of the *caciques apoderados* (a network of indigenous community leaders), stayed with La Paz mechanic and anarchist Luis Cusicanqui when he was visiting the capital. The writings of people like Cusicanqui and socialist Tristán Marof also indicate that the urban left of the 1920s was starting to pay more attention to struggles against haciendas, land usurpation, and racism in the countryside.[12]

Following the Chaco War with Paraguay (1932–35), parts of the urban labor movement and the left looked to the countryside with renewed interest. Various labor federations passed resolutions condemning "exploiters of the labor of workers and of the Indian" and calling for an "alliance between workers and peasants."[13] Some supported unionization efforts and sit-down strikes among hacienda workers (*colonos*) in the late 1930s and early 1940s.[14] Between 1942 and 1944, rural organizers and Sucre socialists linked to the Partido de la Izquierda Revolucionaria (Revolutionary Left Party, PIR) held three path-breaking congresses that drew indigenous delegates from five departments. The 1944 congress set forth demands for land, unionization rights, the abolition of forced

---

[11] See Hylton, Chapter 1, this volume.

[12] Silvia Rivera Cusicanqui, "Breve historia del anarquismo en Bolivia," in *Los artesanos libertarios y la ética del trabajo*, ed. Zulema Lehm Ardaya and Silvia Rivera Cusicanqui (La Paz: THOA, 1988), 40–41; Huáscar Rodríguez García, *La choledad antiestatal: El anarcosindicalismo en el movimiento obrero boliviano (1912–1965)* (La Paz: Muela del Diablo, 2012), 55, 72.

[13] Cited in Antezana and Romero, *Historia*, 72, 87. I use "peasant" (*campesino*) in a loose sense to mean rural laboring peoples who lived near the subsistence level, including small private or communal landholders as well as estate laborers, many of whom were only semi-proletarianized. Both the structural position and subjective identity of rural wage-workers were fuzzy, since many retained communal ties and sought land in addition to labor rights.

[14] Antezana and Romero, *Historia*, 79–100; Gotkowitz, *Revolution*, 159–62.

servitude, maternity leave for female hacienda servants, literacy programs, and legal services.[15] These three congresses were important precursors to the better-known 1945 Indigenous Congress sponsored by the Villarroel–MNR regime.

The response from big landowners and the state provides some indication of the threat posed by these incipient ties. Anarchists Luis Cusicanqui, Modesto Escóbar, and Jacinto Centellas were imprisoned for writing a 1929 manifesto calling for indigenous insurrection.[16] Following the Chaco War, as many urban unions began to support rural struggles, the government responded unequivocally. A Marxist delegate to the 1938 constitutional convention was expelled for criticizing hacienda owners.[17] Various governments sought to criminalize urban–rural collaboration altogether. A 1938 executive decree by Germán Busch (1937–39) outlawed preaching to "the indigenous class." A similar decree by the Peñaranda regime in 1943 declared that urban unions "must not address issues related to agrarian activities," noting with alarm how many union statutes advocated a worker–peasant alliance.[18]

Nonetheless, by the mid-1940s the threat of such an alliance seemed more present than ever. Rural organizing efforts also received an unwitting boost from the Villarroel regime. The government-sponsored Indigenous Congress of May 1945 was intended to co-opt the growing militancy of the rural indigenous movement. Instead it had the opposite effect, raising the expectations of rural laborers and providing a set of official decrees that activists then invoked against landlords and local officials. Rural activists continued to cite the Congress as justification for their demands following Villarroel's July 1946 assassination, which brought to power a series of more repressive regimes bent on restoring rural order. While the state repression of the *sexenio* period (1946–52) would deter many urban leftists from venturing outside the city, rural

---

[15] Antezana and Romero, *Historia*, 86–92; "El problema del indio y los congresos," *Los Tiempos*, April 5, 1945, 8.

[16] Guillermo Lora, *Historia del movimiento obrero boliviano, 1923–1933* (La Paz: Los Amigos del Libro, 1970), 64–65; Rivera Cusicanqui, "Breve historia del anarquismo," 43; Rodríguez García, *La choledad antiestatal*, 79–83.

[17] Trifonio Delgado González, *100 años de lucha obrera en Bolivia* (La Paz: ISLA, 1984), 128–33.

[18] Germán Busch executive decree, March 27, 1938, Ministerio de la Presidencia, Serie Correspondencia Recibida-Enviada, Subserie Circulares, Oficios, Actas, Leyes, Decretos, Caja 198, Legajo 2, ALP; "No pueden inmiscuirse en actividades campesinas los sindicatos obreros," *La Calle*, February 3, 1943, 4.

militancy continued to spread, and some leftists continued to pursue urban–rural coalitions.[19]

THE 1946 PACT AND THE 1947 REBELLION

The FOL commenced its organizing efforts in the countryside following the federation's May 1946 decision to prioritize rural unionization. In August, the Folista Modesto Escóbar began traveling across the *altiplano*, and the FOL soon established a Center for Anarchist Union Training. The formal pact between the FAD and FOL was signed in December 1946 by FOL leaders and twenty-one FAD representatives from the provinces of Los Andes and Pacajes.[20] Most of the FAD leaders were from haciendas in the cantons of Aygachi (Los Andes) or Topohoco (Pacajes). In both provinces the haciendas greatly outnumbered the independent indigenous communities, making the haciendas the natural focus of FAD–FOL efforts.[21] Their principal demands were for unionization rights, the abolition of forced labor and other abusive practices, and the construction of new schools. Figure 5.2 shows a historic rally in La Paz on May 1, 1947, featuring both urban and rural anarchists.

In the first six months of 1947 there were several violent attacks on hacienda personnel in the La Paz and Cochabamba departments. In La Paz the two major sites of violence were the Anta hacienda in Pacajes, in May, and the Tacanoca hacienda in Los Andes in early June. At least four people were killed, including a hacienda owner, his niece, a supervisor, and a teacher. Both *colonos* and *comunarios* participated in the violence, though precise responsibility (and motives) are difficult to ascertain: the violence was partly driven by anger toward abusive owners and overseers, but inter-landlord rivalry may also have played an instigating role at Tacanoca.[22]

---

[19] Antezana and Romero, *Historia*, 101–23; Gotkowitz, *Revolution*, 192–232.

[20] FOL meeting minutes, May 1, 1946, *Libro de Actas*, Archivo Luis Cusicanqui, Tambo Colectivo Ch'ixi, La Paz (hereafter ALC); Rivera Cusicanqui, "Breve historia del anarquismo," 84; FOL-FAD joint resolution, December 22, 1946, *Libro de Actas*, ALC.

[21] Though Gotkowitz notes that "many recently formed estates remained de facto communities" (*Revolution*, 253). As of 1945, Los Andes had 121 haciendas with 5,900 *colonos* and 15 communities with 600 taxpayers; in Pacajes there were 99 haciendas and 52 communities as of 1934. See Prefectura de La Paz, "Descripción"; Subprefecto de Pacajes to Prefecto de La Paz, June 22, 1934, Pacajes, Caja 116, Legajo 1, ALP.

[22] Gotkowitz, *Revolution*, 252–53; Silvia Rivera Cusicanqui, "*Oprimidos pero no vencidos*": *Luchas del campesinado aymara y quechua, 1900–1980*, fourth ed. (La Paz: Yachaywasi, 2003), 106.

FIGURE 5.2 Anarchist rally in La Paz, May 1, 1947.
Source: Archivo Luis Cusicanqui, Tambo Colectivo Ch'ixi, La Paz.
The addition of rural affiliates in 1946–47 more than doubled the total FOL membership. Note the presence of several banners mentioning *labriegos*, or rural laborers.

However, to focus attention on the occasional acts of violence, as the press did, would be to miss most of the story. The FAD leadership explicitly opposed violence, condemning "that sinister idea that the savage Indian is only capable of protesting against arbitrary actions and taunts through violent uprisings." We "organized peasants have no need to kill, to assault, or to set fire to anyone's house."[23] While some of the violence occurred on or near haciendas that had FAD-affiliated unions, there is no evidence that the FAD leadership planned it.[24] When violent protest did occur, anarchist leaders blamed landlords' abuses for provoking "regrettable incidents that

[23] FAD, "Manifiesto: La Federación Agraria Departamental de La Paz, adherida a la Federación Obrera Local, se dirige al campesinado y a los trabajadores en general," February 4, 1947, ALC.
[24] Antezana and Romero, *Historia*, 146–55; Rodríguez García, *La choledad antiestatal*, 219–20; Gotkowitz, *Revolution*, 252–53.

neither the FAD nor anyone else could control" and argued that landlords and officials were using the violence as an excuse for repression.[25]

Most of the FAD and FOL organizers' time and energy in 1946 and 1947 went into forming unions on the haciendas, building schools, and circulating revolutionary manifestos. By May 1947, the FAD included at least twenty member unions with 20,000 total members, most of which were in Los Andes and Pacajes. The two organizations had also helped establish dozens of schools.[26] Even the confrontations in the first half of 1947 were mostly limited to work stoppages, land occupations, petitions to government officials, and other nonviolent tactics, only occasionally involving physical assaults. Just a handful of owners and administrators were killed, compared to scores of indigenous victims.

In May–June 1947 between 1,000 and 2,000 people were arrested, the FOL's office was raided and shut down, and FAD leaders like Marcelino Quispe and Evaristo Mamani were tortured. Soon after, dozens of FAD organizers were sent to a tropical prison camp in Santa Cruz department, where at least thirty of them perished of starvation and disease.[27] The FAD and FOL would survive in weakened form until around 1953, but neither organization recovered from this repression. The elite response offers an indication of the unique threat posed by the FAD–FOL alliance. One Trotskyist historian not particularly sympathetic to anarchism remarked that the May 1, 1947 march in La Paz (shown in Figure 5.2), which included thousands of FAD members, "constituted a novelty. At this moment the authorities decided to put an end to anarchist activities in the countryside."[28]

---

[25] Comité de Defensa de la Federación Obrera Local, "La verdad del 'robo' y el 'crimen,'" June 10, 1947, ALC.

[26] Robert J. Alexander, summary of interview with José Mendoza Vera, May 30, 1947, ALC; José Clavijo, interview by Silvia Rivera and Zulema Lehm, December 4, 1985, *Libro Cóndor*, ALC; Comité de Defensa, "La verdad del 'robo'"; Marcelo A. Maldonado Rocha, "'Katari irrumpiendo la paz': La escuela de Quilluma, el sueño catastrófico de la Federación Agraria Departamental," paper presented at the meeting of the Asociación de Estudios Bolivianos, Sucre, July 20–24, 2015.

[27] FAD, "Manifiesto de la Federación Agraria Departamental: ¡Inhumana masacre de campesinos en el Ichilo!" January 7, 1948, ALC. Many other violent reprisals likely happened: one statement mentioned the killing of seven of Quispe's relatives and the rape of thirty-one indigenous women by soldiers and a priest (Comité de Defensa, "La verdad del 'robo'"). Repression of peasant organizers had in fact started earlier, following Villarroel's death (Gotkowitz, *Revolution*, 256–60). The FAD did not invoke Villarroel the way many other rural Indians did, but the organization suffered the aftermath of repression all the same.

[28] Lora, *Historia del movimiento obrero*, 98.

The march was indeed a novelty: it reflected Bolivia's largest urban–rural and interethnic coalition in decades, and a remarkably horizontal one. Though the coalition was soon suppressed, its formation merits closer scrutiny.

LIBERTARIAN SOCIALISM IN LA PAZ, 1920S–1940S

Part of the background to the alliance lies in the growth of anarchism in La Paz over the prior two decades. Bolivian anarchism and Marxism both underwent substantial growth in the 1920s. Anarchism found especially strong support among the artisans, vendors, and employees in small-scale manufacturing who comprised the bulk of the pre-Chaco workforce in La Paz. Anarchist organizing reached a new level in 1927 with the foundation in La Paz of two anarchist labor federations, the FOL and a sub-federation, the Federación Obrera Femenina (Women Workers' Federation, FOF).[29] Although repressed and temporarily decimated during the war, both federations reemerged in 1935 and remained significant players on the left until the 1952 revolution, bucking the global trend of anarchism's decline relative to Marxism. As late as 1947 the FOL may have been the biggest labor federation in La Paz, largely due to the FAD's affiliation, which more than doubled the FOL's total numbers.[30]

Ideologically, La Paz anarchists' vision of a just society had much in common with the Marxists': they sought the socialized ownership of all means of production and the abolition of class distinctions. But the FOL and FOF distinguished themselves from most Marxists in two ways. First, they declared themselves "apolitical," by which they meant they abstained from electoral and party politics, but not from politics in the broader sense. Second, they advocated a greater degree of decentralization in economy, government, and revolutionary organization. Production would be controlled not by a centralized state (not even in the short term) but by the producers themselves. Politically, they envisioned a "federative system respecting the independence and autonomy of the last village and the last citizen" with "free speech and press."[31]

---

[29] Anarchist counterparts to the FOL and FOF were established in Oruro soon after (Rodríguez García, *La choledad antiestatal*, 90–93).

[30] Alexander, summary of interview with José Mendoza Vera.

[31] FOL, "Manifiesto de la Federación Obrera Local a la clase proletaria de general," May 1, 1938, ALC.

La Paz anarchists' notions of liberation were also somewhat more expansive than those of many Marxists in the Leninist, Trotskyist, and Stalinist traditions. Many defined revolution as more than just the overthrow of capitalism: it meant the end of all illegitimate hierarchy, including gender, ethnic, and political subordination as well as class exploitation. This orientation was evident in a 1946 woodworkers' manifesto, which spoke of "a better world, free of masters and executioners": "We the working class, who for the bourgeoisie are nothing but cannon fodder, fodder for exploitation, and fodder for pleasure, have to defend ourselves through the permanent political Strike, religious Strike, military Strike, and Strike of the womb."[32] A 1948 FOL statement similarly declared that "we are at the side of all the humble ones who struggle," not only "the tireless worker in the factories and workshops" but also "the laborer who fertilizes the land with their tears and their pain" and "the proletarian mother who cries in misery."[33] This expansive understanding of oppression adds another meaning to the provincial official's 1947 warning of a "total uprising."

The FOL's critiques of patriarchy were largely the result of women's leadership in the FOF, which was part of the FOL umbrella federation. After the war the FOF women emerged as a leading force within the FOL, with the formation of woman-led cooks' and flower vendors' unions in 1935–36. At the national workers' congress in late 1936, FOF delegates were central in pushing through resolutions on the eight-hour day, the six-day week, and equal pay for men and women. Over the next two decades the FOF would also spearhead struggles for day care, the right to divorce, and equal legal rights for legitimate and illegitimate children.[34] In doing so, anarchist women also pulled the men in more feminist directions. Anarchist ideology certainly frowned upon women's subordination and

---

[32] Unión Sindical de Trabajadores en Madera, "Manifiesto de la 'Unión Sindical de Trabajadores en Madera,'" December 1946, ALC.

[33] "¡En nuestro puesto!" *F.O.L.*, May 1, 1948, 1. Denunciations of women's oppression are often intended to mobilize working-class men, who understand the oppression of "their" women as an affront to their masculinity. But in the case of the FOL there was at least a strong current that denounced women's subjugation for more than simply instrumental reasons.

[34] Delgado González, *100 años*, 182–83; Ineke Dibbits, Elizabeth Peredo Beltrán, and Ruth Volgger, *Polleras libertarias: Federación Obrera Femenina, 1927–1964* (La Paz: Tahipamu, 1986), 8–9; Lehm Ardaya and Rivera Cusicanqui, eds., *Los artesanos libertarios*, 153–81; Ana Cecilia Wadsworth and Ineke Dibbits, *Agitadoras de buen gusto: Historia del Sindicato de Culinarias (1935–1958)* (La Paz: Tahipamu/Hisbol, 1989), 138–39.

domestic violence: as one male anarchist exclaimed, "How could an anarchist beat his wife?!"[35] Nonetheless, ideology alone did not eliminate all gender hierarchy. In one 1947 meeting, for instance, a FOF member accused her male comrades of refusing to help with the publication of a women's manifesto.[36] Gender relations within the FOL were relatively horizontal, but women's active pressure was necessary to make them so.

In the 1920s, some FOL members also began developing explicit critiques of racism. In a fiery manifesto Luis Cusicanqui, one of the few early Folistas who self-identified as indigenous, addressed himself to his "INDIAN brothers of the American race" and called for "revolution to do away with this vile society" led by the "powerful *mestizos* of the State."[37] He defined indigeneity in political terms, as the shared marginality of the oppressed. As analyst Silvia Rivera Cusicanqui comments, "The Indian identity that [Cusicanqui] postulates is inclusive: the manual workers of the cities and the *comunarios* and *colonos* of the countryside would make common cause against the caste system and the exclusionary and oppressive political system."[38] The manifesto reflected the loose affinity between anarchist ideology and longstanding indigenous struggles. The FOL's federalism and attacks on the national state appealed to many rural Indians seeking to defend their communal land and autonomy, while their emphasis on the dignity and freedom of the worker dovetailed with the demands of organized hacienda workers.

Anarchist organizational structure also facilitated the expression of ethnic and gender demands. The FAD retained its own decision-making power after it affiliated with the FOL in 1946, just as the FOF had done since its foundation.[39] This federative structure reflected an ideological and strategic emphasis on autonomy and self-organization. In an early article decrying "the situation of subordination and slavery" facing Bolivian women, anarchist Jacinto Centellas addressed himself directly to women, saying that "the hour of your emancipation has arrived" and "is in your hands."[40] Calls for autonomous organizing were also heard in discussions of indigenous oppression, among both anarchists and Marxists. One

---

[35] José Mendoza Vera cited in Ximena Medinacelli, *Alterando la rutina: Mujeres en las ciudades de Bolivia, 1920–1930* (La Paz: CIDEM/Hisbol, 1989), 162.

[36] FOL meeting minutes, March 23, 1947, *Libro de Actas*, ALC.

[37] Luis Cusicanqui D., "La voz del campesino: Nuestro reto a los grandes mistes del Estado" (n.d., 1929), ALC.

[38] "Breve historia del anarquismo," 42.   [39] Dibbits, et al., *Polleras libertarias*, 22.

[40] Jacinto H. Centellas, "A las mujeres en general," *Bandera Roja*, December 13, 1926, 6.

Marxist delegate to the 1927 workers' congress proclaimed that the "liberation of the Indian will be the work of the Indian himself."[41]

Such statements contrasted with the more standard Marxist and Leninist prescription for revolution under proletarian direction, which would become dominant on the left by mid-century. This "workerism" was reaffirmed by the famous 1946 Thesis of Pulacayo, adopted by the mineworkers' federation. The Trotskyist Partido Obrero Revolucionario (Revolutionary Workers' Party, POR) and Stalinist PIR espoused variants of this view, as did much of urban labor more generally. The Central Obrera Boliviana (Bolivian Workers' Central) created in 1952 would also deem the proletariat "the natural leader of the Revolution."[42] Workerism and intellectual elitism often translated into a vertical approach to organizing, which alienated many peasant activists. Peasant leader Antonio Alvarez Mamani later recalled how Trotskyist intellectuals of the 1940s sought to dictate "the orders of the party" to peasant organizers, who were invited to meetings but "without voice or vote."[43] The PIR, founded in 1940, did initially place a priority on rural organizing, but its adherence to Popular Front politics and alliance with conservative forces by the mid-1940s soon led it to oppose most agitation. Its leaders tended to view the Bolivian peasantry with caution, much as the MNR did; both parties' positions on land redistribution were ambiguous and inconsistent throughout the 1940s.[44] To be sure, the Marxist parties often spoke of the need for a worker–peasant alliance, and the POR, the PIR, and the non-Marxist MNR all had varying degrees of involvement with peasant organizing in the late 1930s and 1940s.[45] But prior to 1952, none succeeded on the scale of the FAD–FOL coalition. One reason is that workerism, ethnocentrism, and authoritarian practices were less present in the FOL than in most other left and nationalist circles.

While anarchist ideology and strategy were relatively conducive to alliance building, the Folistas' May 1946 decision to "go to the countryside" was also influenced by several conjunctural considerations.[46] At that

---

[41] Víctor Vargas Vilaseca cited in Lora, *Historia del movimiento obrero*, 25.

[42] Alberto Cornejo S., ed., *Programas políticos de Bolivia* (Cochabamba: Imprenta Universitaria, 1949), 316; Central Obrera Boliviana, *Primer Congreso Nacional de Trabajadores: Cartilla de orientación* (La Paz: Burillo, 1954), 10.

[43] Cited in Forrest Hylton and Sinclair Thomson, *Revolutionary Horizons: Past and Present in Bolivian Politics* (London: Verso, 2007), 78.

[44] Rivera Cusicanqui, "*Oprimidos pero no vencidos*," 108–09; Soliz, "La modernidad esquiva," 40–44.

[45] Gotkowitz, *Revolution*, 159–62, 215, 241; S. Sándor John, *Bolivia's Radical Tradition: Permanent Revolution in the Andes* (Tucson: University of Arizona Press, 2009), 78.

[46] José Clavijo, interview by Silvia Rivera and Zulema Lehm, December 4, 1985.

moment, the federation was facing a difficult situation in the city, due partly to regime opposition and partly to political competition from other leftists. One Folista, José Clavijo, later described a sense that "we are being isolated" and that the revolutionary struggle was "falling behind." This perception of organizational stagnation made coalition building more imperative. He recalled telling his comrades, "We are going to ossify because we no longer have organizations with which to collaborate. The only sector still open to us is the peasantry."[47]

Another fleeting circumstance further encouraged this reorientation. The aftermath of the government's 1945 Indigenous Congress opened a limited window of opportunity for rural organizing. Despite the mutual animosity between the FOL and the Villarroel–MNR regime, it seems that the Folistas enjoyed considerable "freedom to go organize" in the countryside.[48] The window was shut in the months after Villarroel's public hanging on July 21, 1946.[49] But the brief relaxation of repression was well exploited by the Folistas, whose analysis, vision, and organizing strategy (and accurate reading of the situation) helped them establish lasting rural ties.

Yet these factors are only part of the explanation for the alliance. Rural-based Indians themselves were the vast numerical majority in the strikes and mobilizations of 1947, and they would also make vital contributions to the alliance itself. In the process they helped to reinvigorate and redefine – if temporarily – the left in La Paz.

STIRRING UP THE INDIANS?

The Bolivian press of the 1930s and 1940s often featured accusations against urban radicals for "stirring up [*soliviantando*] the Indians."[50] Coming from conservative voices, these characterizations are hardly surprising. But more sympathetic observers, including both urban anarchists and historians, have also emphasized urban Folistas' initiative in forming rural unions and schools. A 1948 statement of the FOL-affiliated woodworkers' union said that FOL organizers "went to establish unions and schools for our fellow laborers" in the countryside.[51] Among historians,

---

[47] Ibid.   [48] Ibid.

[49] Paradoxically, the FOL supported the regime's overthrow in July 1946, presumably not foreseeing the possibility that successor regimes might prove more repressive.

[50] "Soliviantados los indios de Oruro por el comunismo desde hace tiempo," *La Calle*, July 29, 1942, 4.

[51] "La voz de las organizaciones," *F.O.L.*, May 1, 1948, 3.

Alexander refers to the FOL's "organization and maintenance of the Federación Agraria Departamental." Antezana and Romero go farther, arguing that the FOL "served to further awaken among the Indians the spirit of rebellion, and to *make them aware* of the system of exploitation to which they were subjected."[52]

These assessments are partly accurate: the urban Folistas did make a decision in May 1946 to prioritize rural organizing, and consistently supported that organizing for the next six years. But the growth of the FAD and the alliance of the late 1940s depended on much more than just the Folistas' views and actions. The actions of rural organizers were also central to these processes, in three ways. First, the prior history of autonomous mobilization in Los Andes and Pacajes provinces had established a series of organizations and leadership networks, both formal and informal, which served as the local foundations for FAD–FOL mobilization in 1946–47. The individuals in these networks did not require "awakening" by others. Second, the presence and participation of rural representatives within the FOL starting in 1946 helped produce a subtle shift in discourse compared to the organization's earlier periods. Third, rural-based brokers had helped forge the alliance in the first place – a process examined in the next section.

Resistance, both organized and unorganized, had been a steady feature of both provinces over the previous several decades. Pacajes was a center of organizing for the networks of *caciques apoderados* that formed in the 1910s and 1920s to combat land usurpation by haciendas and infringements on community autonomy.[53] Later, during the Chaco War, the province never ceased to frustrate state officials in charge of military recruitment. One 1934 military telegram reported that "in Pacajes province, especially in Callapa and Ulloma" – also key sites of the *apoderados* – "it has not been possible to carry out recruitment due to the rebellious spirit of the Indians."[54] Similar reports were common throughout La Paz provinces during the war. Among the locales where official telegrams warned of "night-time meetings" to plan an "indigenous uprising" were the Aygachi and Tambillo cantons of Los Andes, which would again be centers of unrest in 1947 (Aygachi featuring a strong FAD

---

[52] Alexander with Parker, *A History of Organized Labor*, 61; Antezana and Romero, *Historia*, 159 (emphasis added).

[53] Gotkowitz, *Revolution*, 46–49.

[54] Prefecto de La Paz to Subprefecto de Pacajes, September 3, 1934, Pacajes, Caja 116, Legajo 1, ALP.

presence).[55] Many future FAD organizers had reached adulthood by the early 1930s, and some were likely involved in this earlier organizing.[56] Throughout the mid-1940s, officials reported "a serious wave of discontent" throughout the department of La Paz. Even in provinces like Murillo where major unrest did not occur, authorities warned "that the indigenous class in general is to be found in a state of belligerence, directed against the owners and administrators" of the haciendas.[57] The situation intensified in the months before the much-anticipated 1945 Congress, and even more so afterward as indigenous communities and hacienda workers invoked President Villarroel's new decrees in their struggles against landlords and local officials. "The damages and the demands on the part of the indigenous population are constant," wrote the Prefect of La Paz late the following year.[58]

Union organizing in Los Andes seems to have begun prior to the FOL's May 1946 decision to promote it. An April 1945 petition testifies to the existence of a peasant union in Collantaca even before the 1945 Indigenous Congress.[59] While Folistas later helped initiate unions in other locales, rural organizing had certainly begun prior to May 1946 in many of the places where those unions eventually appeared. A September 1945 telegram reported that "the Indians of Carapata hacienda" – who would later play a key role in the FAD – "have their meetings night by night on said hacienda."[60]

Demands tended to focus on workers' rights, but also involved questions of land and self-determination. According to one local official in Sewenaki (Pacajes) just prior to the 1945 Congress, agitators had been circulating a manifesto saying that "we will rule as in past times. Starting with the *Indigenista* [*sic*] Congress, there will no longer be *mestizo* or white authorities. We will rule by ourselves."[61] The *colono–comunario*

---

[55] Subprefecto de Los Andes to Prefecto de La Paz, June 25, 1933, Los Andes, Subserie Telegramas, Caja 79, Legajo 1, ALP.

[56] Of a list of fifteen FAD members who died in captivity in 1947–48, thirteen were aged thirty-two or older, and six were over sixty; "Placa de honor," *F.O.L.*, May 1, 1948, 4.

[57] Corregidor de Cohoni to Prefecto de La Paz, April 16, 1945, and Subprefecto de Murillo to Prefecto de La Paz, January 15, 1945, Murillo, Caja 96, Legajo 1, ALP.

[58] Guillermo Arancibia R. to Ministro de Gobierno, Justicia e Inmigración, November 7, 1946, Serie Correspondencia Recibida-Enviada, Caja 171, Legajo 2, ALP.

[59] Nicolás Salinas H. and Mario Narváez A. to Prefecto de La Paz, April 26, 1945, Los Andes, Subserie Telegramas, Caja 81, Legajo 2, ALP.

[60] Carmelo Saavedra to Prefecto de La Paz, September 1, 1945, Los Andes, Subserie Telegramas, Caja 81, Legajo 2, ALP.

[61] Cited in Lino Fuentes G. to Prefecto de La Paz, April 5, 1945, Pacajes, Caja 118, Legajo 2, ALP.

boundary was often blurry, especially in the *altiplano*, where there was significant overlap between hacienda- and community-based struggles. *Comunarios* played a bigger role in the 1947 revolts in La Paz than in Cochabamba.[62] Many La Paz hacienda residents, meanwhile, had only recently seen their land taken and retained a sense of communal identity. The *colonos* on the Muncana hacienda in Aygachi, for example, still possessed the legal title to their land and were "seeking its restoration."[63]

Even on those haciendas where community restoration and land redistribution were not central to *colono* demands, the activists' actions and words reveal a desire for greater autonomy. Resistance often centered on schools, which for rural workers signified both an obligation of government and hacienda owners and an instrument for the exercise of autonomy. In early 1946 a *colono* at the Tomarapi hacienda in Topohoco filed a complaint against the owner for failing to comply with Villarroel's May 1945 decree requiring owners to build schools. At roughly the same time, *colonos* in the Caquiaviri canton of Pacajes refused to accept the teacher appointed by their hacienda owner, demanding to name their own. At other times hacienda schools were deemed instruments of oppression and boycotted, as when the FAD's Evaristo Mamani and others sought to organize a boycott of the Kella-Kella hacienda school in Caquiaviri.[64] Although the rural organizers of the 1940s focused more on labor rights than their predecessors had, their simultaneous concern for autonomy represented continuity with earlier struggles.

We do not know the exact circumstances under which rural indigenous workers came into contact with urban Folistas. Initial meetings seem to have occurred in mid-1946, and may have been facilitated by preexisting ties between rural organizers and Folistas like Modesto Escóbar. Decades later, José Clavijo suggested that it was rural leaders who had approached the FOL, though he seemed to contradict this memory in another

---

[62] Gotkowitz, *Revolution*, 253; Rivera Cusicanqui, *"Oprimidos pero no vencidos,"* 105.

[63] Felipe Iñiguez (Diputado Nacional) to Ministro de Gobierno, Justicia e Inmigración, July 4, 1947, Serie Correspondencia Recibida-Enviada, Caja 172, Legajo 1, ALP.

[64] "Denuncia sentada en el Ministerio de Gobierno," March 27, 1947, Serie Correspondencia Recibida-Enviada, Caja 172, Legajo 1, ALP; Enrique Eduardo G. (Prefecto de La Paz) to Subprefecto de Pacajes, January 23 and June 5, 1946, Pacajes, Caja 118, Legajo 2, ALP. On indigenous education see also Carlos Salazar Mostajo, *¡Warisata mía! y otros artículos polémicos* (La Paz: Juventud, 1983); Brooke Larson, "Capturing Indian Bodies, Hearths, and Minds: The Gendered Politics of Rural School Reform in Bolivia, 1920s–1940s," in *Natives Making Nation: Indigeneity, Gender and Class in the Andes*, ed. Andrew Canessa (Tucson: University of Arizona Press, 2005), 32–59.

interview.[65] What is clear is that organizers who were based primarily in the countryside were the main driving force behind the rural organizing, with urban-based Folistas playing an important but supporting role.

Elite rhetoric notwithstanding, rural Indians were also "the main instigators and leaders" in the rebellions of 1947, as Luis Lahore Monje's May 1947 telegram suggested. In fact, government and newspaper reports sometimes acknowledged rural activists' leading role in the agitation in Los Andes and Pacajes. Reportage on the January "uprisings" at the Quilloma hacienda in Topohoco and at Carapata and several other haciendas in Los Andes included no mention of urban instigators. In Los Andes, 4,000 Indians were alleged to be "threatening Pucarani [the capital] and other nearby towns."[66] Following unrest at Carapata and Caquiaviri in May, state forces took several hundred indigenous prisoners at the former and perhaps a thousand at the latter. Correspondence from the time suggests a generalized state of subversion throughout the two provinces. In May, one town resident of Los Andes wrote in terror that "the Indians from all the haciendas have risen up."[67]

In conjunction with organizing efforts on the haciendas, FAD leaders helped draft a number of public statements published in the name of the FAD, the FOL, or jointly. These statements are notable for their more explicit affirmation of Indian identity as compared with most of the earlier FOL discourse. Racism, they suggested, worked in conjunction with other systems of oppression to keep the Indian in bondage. A February 1947 manifesto observed that "when we come to the city, everyone has the right to offend us: the *chola*, the *mestizo*, the police officer, the rich, and even those Indians poisoned by capitalist values; everyone abuses the *yayas*."[68]

---

[65] Interview by Silvia Rivera and Zulema Lehm, January 6, 1986, *Libro Cóndor*, ALC. Clavijo suggested that the relationship between urban anarchists and rural organizers in the 1920s had begun similarly, when Santos Marka T'ula and another cacique approached Luis Cusicanqui. On another occasion Clavijo (December 4, 1985) stressed FOL initiative in organizing the FAD. This apparent contradiction might indicate merely a difference of emphasis, reflecting the fact that both urban and rural brokers played initiating roles.

[66] "En días pasados 4.000 indígenas de proximidades el Titicaca, irrumpieron amenazando Pucarani y otros pueblos cercanos," *Los Tiempos*, January 18, 1947, 6; "Serán enjuiciados los cabecillas de un levantamiento indígena," *Los Tiempos*, January 9, 1947, 6.

[67] "Serán aplacados tres focos de sublevaciones indígenas," *La Razón*, May 17, 1947, 5. FAD General Secretary Marcelino Quispe and his brother Esteban were singled out for arrest prior to other leaders. See Gotkowitz, *Revolution*, 258–59; "Se organizará proceso"; Simón Pando Pando (Secretario de la Prefectura de La Paz) to Subprefecto de Los Andes, May 21, 1947, Subserie Telegramas, Caja 81, Legajo 2, ALP.

[68] *Yaya* is Quechua for "father" but here probably refers to indigenous people in general; FAD, "Manifiesto: La Federación Agraria Departamental de La Paz, adherida a la

Another FAD statement emphasized the federation's Indian identity as essential to its organizing role, arguing that only the FAD, as an "organization composed of INDIANS, could understand the rebellious and just hopes and dreams of its class so long enslaved."[69] Authors would often mock the racism of elite discourse, inverting categories of civilization and barbarism. In a June 1947 manifesto following the Tacanoca uprising, the FAD and FOL referred sardonically to accusations of rebels' "theft" and "violence." Instead, it was the "civilized whites" who behaved barbarically: "The bosses are the direct descendants of the conquistadors who, having arrived in these lands, assumed their comfortable position of societal parasites, and ultimately owners, on the exclusive basis of THEFT and VIOLENCE."[70]

These documents obviously raise questions about authorship. Were urban intellectuals ghost-writing manifestos for the FAD, many of whose leaders were illiterate?[71] The FAD's short-lived newspaper, *La Voz del Campo*, was authored by its "Cultural Section," but the paper did not give names. Historian Huáscar Rodríguez suggests that urban anarchist Liber Forti was responsible for most of the FOL's own manifestos in 1947, since he worked as a typographical worker and had access to a printing press.[72] Yet rural organizers played an important role in crafting FAD statements, whether or not they themselves put pen to paper. FOL meeting records from 1946–47 confirm that rural FAD organizers were regularly present at meetings in the city.[73] Some documents were signed by specific individuals with common indigenous surnames, as with the 1948 statement stressing the FAD's identity as "an organization composed of Indians," cosigned by FAD Secretary of Relations Sebastián Choque. Other statements spoke from the perspective of "we Indians."[74] Such phrasing does not automatically prove Indian authorship, but the strong assertion of indigenous identity marks a contrast with other FOL documents. The latter often betrayed what Rodríguez calls

---

Federación Obrera Local, se dirige al campesinado y a los trabajadores en general," February 4, 1947, ALC.

[69] Salustiano Soto and Sebastián Choque, "Ante el 1° de mayo: Manifiesto de la F.A.D.," *F. O.L.*, May 1, 1948, 4.

[70] Comité de Defensa, "La verdad del 'robo.'"

[71] Seven of twenty-one FAD signers of the December 1946 pact signed with fingerprints rather than signatures (FOL–FAD joint resolution, December 22, 1946).

[72] Rodríguez García, *La choledad antiestatal*, 218.

[73] FOL meeting minutes, October 20, 1946, *Libro de Actas*, ALC.

[74] "Nuestra 'campaña de alfabetización del campesinado boliviano,'" *La Voz del Campo* (October 1950): 1.

a "civilizing tone" that reflected an assumption about "western cultural supremacy" (Cusicanqui's 1929 manifesto was a notable exception).[75] While FAD statements occasionally employed this tone as well, it was counterbalanced by a forceful ethnic consciousness. Moreover, the presence of a "civilizing tone" in some FAD statements does not necessarily indicate nonindigenous voices: Indians sometimes employed this discourse, often for strategic reasons. The FAD leader Esteban Quispe was presumably doing so when he declared from jail that "we Indians know that we are ignorant, and we are because the State and the laws have deprived us of literacy and of education from time immemorial."[76]

If authorship is difficult to verify, we can safely conclude that FAD statements were at least written with the participation of rural Indians – whether direct, through the writing or dictating of content, or indirect, through their presence in FOL circles. Either way, the struggles of rural Indians helped shape the discourse and actions of their urban comrades, infusing them with a more conscious anti-racism and a greater focus on rural exploitation, much as anarchist women infused the FOL with a more feminist orientation. The urbanites' own flexibility, meanwhile, facilitated that shift.

COALITION BROKERS

Indigenous mobilization in rural La Paz did not automatically lead to an alliance with the urban FOL. The articulation of that alliance was brokered by individual organizers who straddled the urban–rural and *mestizo*–indigenous divides. These individuals came from both sides of those divides and tended to possess characteristics that allowed them to communicate and build trust with people on the other side. Ties between the FOL and the countryside in the 1920s had largely depended on border-crossers like Luis Cusicanqui – who, as mentioned, had a close relationship with *cacique* Santos Marka T'ula. Cusicanqui's first language was Aymara and he was proudly indigenous, as his 1929 manifesto suggested. The case of the FAD–FOL alliance of the 1940s further highlights the importance of this type of organizer in interethnic and cross-sector mobilization.

One of the anarchists arrested with Cusicanqui for circulating the 1929 manifesto was plumber Modesto Escóbar. Although Cusicanqui grew disenchanted with the FOL after the war, Escóbar remained involved and played a central role in the development of relations with the FAD

---

[75] Rodríguez García, *La choledad antiestatal*, 291–92.
[76] "La voz de nuestros presos," *F.O.L.*, May 1, 1948, 4.

FIGURE 5.3 Coalition brokers.
Source: Archivo Luis Cusicanqui, Tambo Colectivo Ch'ixi, La Paz.
Modesto Escóbar (left) speaks with indigenous representative, *ca.* 1946.

in 1946–47. He was fluent in Aymara, and although he was probably raised in the city, he had many contacts in the rural *altiplano*. Within the FOL he served as one of two Secretaries of Agrarian Relations and at meetings he regularly gave reports on the situation in the countryside. In August 1946 Escóbar toured various haciendas and communities promoting union formation (Figure 5.3). After the cycle of protest and repression began in early 1947, he led FOL delegations to visit peasants jailed in the city. When the May uprisings occurred, he himself was arrested and soon imprisoned on the island of Coati, in Lake Titicaca, where he spent over two years (though he escaped the wretched fate of dozens of his rural comrades, many of whom were killed).[77] Escóbar was probably the urban Folistas' strongest link to rural workers, though several other urban FOL organizers including Juan Nieto, Santiago Ordóñez, Francisco Castro, and Hugo Aguilar were also especially active in supporting the FAD.[78]

---

[77] Data on Escóbar is from José Clavijo, interviews by Silvia Rivera and Zulema Lehm, December 4, 1985, January 6, 1986, and May 2, 1987, *Libro Cóndor*, ALC; FOL meeting minutes, October 20, 1946, February 2, 1947, and March 30, 1947, *Libro de Actas*, ALC; Rodríguez García, *La choledad antiestatal*, 76 n.52, 79–83, 228.

[78] Clavijo, interview by Rivera and Lehm, December 4, 1985; "La voz de las organizaciones"; "La voz de nuestros presos"; Rodríguez García, *La choledad antiestatal*, 206.

While the histories of rural-based coalition brokers remain more obscure, there is evidence of individuals filling a similar function on the other side of the alliance. Marcelino Llanque, a *cacique apoderado* who had led a 1921 rebellion in Ingavi province, was present at the May 1946 meeting that discussed rural organizing, and he was credentialed to "take the FOL delegation to the peasantry around the country."[79] Rural organizers like the brothers Marcelino and Esteban Quispe seem to have played a similar role. In a later interview, José Clavijo suggested that one factor in the spread of the FOL's rural visibility was that peasants who had come to the city to find work were exposed to "the FOL's message" and then helped spread word of the FOL upon return visits to their villages. He singled out construction workers, loaders, hat makers, and bakers as being particularly important. These occupations drew large numbers of rural migrants because they required little prior training, and were "jobs that are learned in practice." Workers in these industries were naturally "more linked to the countryside." Clavijo contrasted these sectors with the factory workers, who often "slipped away from the countryside."[80] Many FOL connections in rural locales were likely nurtured by prior migration, though the specific connections remain a matter of speculation.

The slow process of building mutual confidence is also apparent in Clavijo's recollections. Asked about the difficulty of urbanites "organizing unions in the countryside," Clavijo said that rural Aymaras were initially somewhat "distrustful" due to their "experiences" with the city ("the calamities they have suffered, the abuses they have received"). Folistas had "to demonstrate" their good will, and only after some time did "they have confidence in us." Clavijo felt that rural migrants, plus bilingual urbanites like Escóbar, had been crucial in this process.[81]

One notable characteristic of the formal brokers, both urban and rural, is that virtually all appear to have been male. In fact, all of the twenty-one FAD representatives who signed the 1946 pact seem to have been men. This pattern is interesting given women's relatively prominent place in the urban FOL. Anarchist women occupied formal leadership positions and frequently spoke in public, including about rural oppression. At a May Day rally of the FOL in 1938, for instance, a journalist remarked on "the speech in Aymara of an indigenous woman, who proclaimed the need to

---

[79] FOL meeting minutes, May 1, 1946.
[80] Interview by Rivera and Lehm, January 6, 1986.   [81] Ibid.

save Indians from the slavery of the haciendas."[82] There is also evidence that women were important in many instances of rural revolt.[83] In many social movements women excluded from formal leadership have played critical informal leadership roles, often serving as the primary organizers at the community level.[84] But in 1940s Bolivia nearly all of the formal leaders in rural communities were men, and it was almost always the formal leaders who were in charge of communication with the urban Folistas. Unfortunately, the role of women organizers and brokers in the rural mobilizations of 1946–47 remains unclear.

Though the evidence is fragmentary, we can conclude that the formal liaisons between city and country shared three basic characteristics: they were relatively mobile, often bilingual, and almost always men. On the urban side, most, like Modesto Escóbar, were artisans; this status would have afforded them greater freedom to travel outside the city. Fluency in Aymara also helped a great deal, both for practical purposes and because it probably helped foster trust among Aymara activists; on the rural side, Spanish-speaking ability may have been important. Urban women held formal leadership positions in the FOL, but their rural counterparts were usually confined to informal leadership roles.

CONCLUSION

The worker–peasant alliance had been a dream of leftist revolutionaries since the nineteenth century. But with few exceptions its realization had remained hampered by a lack of real commitment, the ethnic and ideological prejudices of urban leftists, and all the structural, geographic, and organizational obstacles to uniting urban workers, rural workers, and small farmers within a single coalition. These barriers were starting to erode in Bolivia in the three decades prior to 1952, however. The short-lived alliance between rural and urban anarchists in La Paz in the late 1940s suggests that the obstacles were not insurmountable.

Several factors enabled organizers to take advantage of the momentary political opening of the mid-1940s. La Paz anarchists' politics and organizing approach proved more conducive to coalition building than those

---

[82] "¡20 mil trabajadores!" *La Calle*, May 3, 1938, 8.
[83] See for instance Subprefecto de Pacajes to Prefecto de La Paz, July 25, 1934, Pacajes, Caja 116, Legajo 1, ALP.
[84] Belinda Robnett, *How Long? How Long? African-American Women in the Struggle for Civil Rights* (New York: Oxford University Press, 1997).

of certain other leftist forces. Their emphasis on the dignity and autonomy of the worker coincided with hacienda workers' desire for less abusive work conditions. Their ideological critiques of state authoritarianism and various other "non-class" forms of oppression also resonated among many rural Indians, both *colonos* and *comunarios*. And their federative organizational structure eschewed the workerist vanguardism of many Marxists and was less paternalistic vis-à-vis the peasant and the Indian.

The alliance also depended on a history of mobilization in the locales where the FAD took root. By 1947, prior struggles in La Paz provinces had already politicized many rural Indians, who did not need urbanites to "make them aware" of their oppression. Preexisting leaders and organizational networks served as the bases for the FAD. In turn, rural indigenous voices influenced anarchist discourse and practice, imbuing anarchist struggle with a more explicitly anti-racist thrust. By early 1947 FAD members comprised the bulk of the FOL and were helping to reinvigorate it after years of slow growth. In this context, whether or not rural organizers were directly writing the FAD's public statements, the urban Folistas felt compelled to listen to them.

Finally, individual brokers were central to the alliance's development. Surviving documentation provides clues about some of these border-crossers, while others remain nameless. We know little about the role of more informal brokers or women in building the coalition, though some evidence (and reasonable speculation) suggests that these groups aided with both the transmission of ideas across the urban–rural boundary and with local mobilization.

The impact of the coalition and the larger series of revolts in 1946–47 is difficult to measure, and the links to later agrarian and indigenous mobilizations are hazy. Why was this coalition so ephemeral? In explaining the rise of the FAD–FOL alliance I have emphasized the anarchists themselves, but external conditions also set limits on their ability to organize. State and landlord actions were clearly important: a brief window of opportunity appeared in 1945–46 but shut violently in 1947. Repression killed many of the key organizers and intimidated many others. A second change in the external context was the growth of a major ideological competitor, the MNR, which turned its eyes to the countryside in the late 1940s, especially after its defeat in the civil war of 1949.[85] The MNR's association with the martyred Villarroel gave it credibility

---

[85] Rivera Cusicanqui, *"Oprimidos pero no vencidos,"* 107–08. The shift toward more hierarchical organizing practices was especially apparent in the MNR, which took

among many peasants, while its control of the state after 1952 meant that it would preside over the 1953 land reform, helping it to secure peasants' allegiance and deprive leftists of potential support. Thus, while a less competitive organizational field had favored the FOL's initial inroads in the La Paz countryside, the field soon shifted against them. Here the anarchists' own antipathy to party politics and state power put them at a unique disadvantage.

Beyond its impact on Bolivia, the coalition is important for both historical and theoretical reasons. Historically, it shows that the left in twentieth-century Latin America was more diverse, both politically and ethnically, than implied by standard narratives that focus on paternalistic *mestizo* males. Theoretically, the coalition highlights the contingent nature of revolutions and other social movements. Far from being predetermined by "opportunity structures" or other external forces, these phenomena are internally contested processes shaped to a great extent by human agents whose ideologies, political cultures, social networks, and choices matter a great deal. The La Paz mobilizations of the 1940s suggest the need for close attention to movement actors and ideas, in addition to structures and external environments. External factors like repression or the presence of competitors usually play a limiting role, but movements also help determine the limits of the possible.

A related theoretical issue concerns the connection between ideology, praxis, and success. While the politics of Bolivian anarchists were especially suited to building interethnic (and inter-gender) alliances, anarchism was not the only ideology capable of doing so. Many of the most notable coalitions of the twentieth century – in Mexico, Guatemala, El Salvador, Cuba, Colombia, Ecuador, and Bolivia itself – involved Communists and Socialists. Organizers' application of ideology – their conceptual emphases, their arrogance or humility, their personal integrity and behavior – may matter at least as much as the ideology itself. In most of these cases, including the one analyzed here, urban organizers' interpretation of ideology was partly influenced by their reading of the national scene (for instance, a recognition that the urban proletariat was small or hard to crack, and that the rural poor showed signs of militancy) and by their dynamic encounters with the constituencies they sought to organize.

This case also raises a broader set of questions about coalition formation. How are coalitions constructed? How are traditional boundaries

power in the 1952 revolution. By 1952 the MNR, the Marxist parties to its left, and urban labor unions all tended to be less respectful of peasant and indigenous autonomy.

transcended? What Hylton and Thomson call the "infrequent moments of convergence" in history merit further scholarly scrutiny.[86] Conversely, the absence of popular coalitions also demands explanation. In Bolivia in the 1960s and 1970s, a stark divide between urban workers and rural smallholders helped buttress a series of right-wing military regimes, which drew substantial support from peasants. The urban–rural coalition of 1946–47 is thus all the more remarkable, and raises the question of whether later ruptures were inevitable.

[86] Hylton and Thomson, *Revolutionary Horizons*, 10. For one of the few studies of inter-sector political relations in Bolivia, see Olivia Harris and Xavier Albó, *Monteras y guardatojos: Campesinos y mineros en el norte de Potosí* (La Paz: CIPCA, 1975).

6

"Sisters in Exploitation"

The 1959 Congress
of Latin American Women and the Transnational
Origins of Cuban State Feminism

Michelle Chase

Accounts of women's incorporation and mobilization within the Cuban Revolution tend to oscillate between two contending interpretative poles. One common narrative stresses the emancipatory power of the revolution, giving special credit to Fidel Castro, leader of the revolutionary 26th of July Movement, who broke with traditional understandings of appropriate gender roles during the insurrection by recruiting women into an all-women's platoon in the Rebel Army. After the revolution he saw the need to mobilize women and offer them redress, and thereby created the mass organization the Federación de Mujeres Cubanas (Federation of Cuban Women, FMC), installing his sister-in-law Vilma Espín at its helm.[1]

Another line of interpretation questions the authenticity of the revolutionary leadership's dedication to gender equality, arguing that it largely aimed "to free women to serve the Revolution."[2] These analyses often take a dim view of the FMC, stressing its subordination to the national male leadership, its mixed success in addressing gender inequality within Cuba, and its role in transmitting government priorities to women rather than vice versa. In addition, the FMC also helped ensure the absence of an autonomous feminist movement in revolutionary Cuba, as any efforts not controlled by the leadership or official institutions were either co-opted or repressed.[3]

---

[1] For a recent reiteration of this more celebratory narrative, see Salim Lamrani, "Women in Cuba: The Emancipatory Revolution," *International Journal of Cuban Studies* 8, no. 1 (2016): 109–16.

[2] Julie Marie Bunck, *Fidel Castro and the Quest for a Revolutionary Culture in Cuba* (University Park: Pennsylvania State University Press, 1994), 89.

[3] Critical assessments of the FMC include Maxine Molyneux, "State, Gender, and Institutional Change: The Federación de Mujeres Cubanas," in *Hidden Histories of*

Despite their different conclusions, these analyses nevertheless share certain underlying assumptions and are insufficient in several ways. By implying that women's mobilization emanated from above, they erase the much more complicated story about how many Cuban women activists themselves pressed the leadership to recognize their demands. They also reinforce a common narrative about the Cuban Revolution that sees the leadership as taking the initiative and then spreading its radical ideas, or imposing them on the populace. Additionally, they tend to view these developments within a national framework, without addressing the possible influence of international processes or networks. Finally, these stories indirectly assume that the impetus for women's incorporation and gender equality – whether sincere or instrumental – emerged from the egalitarian vision of the New Left as embodied in the 26th of July Movement, ignoring the "Old," Communist-Party-based Left's vision for women's rights.

This chapter will provide a different account of women's participation in the 1959 revolution, including the formation of the FMC, by focusing on the first Congreso Latinoamericano de Mujeres (Congress of Latin American Women, CLAM) held in Santiago de Chile in November 1959.[4] This congress was initiated by the Women's International Democratic Federation (WIDF), a global, Soviet-aligned women's organization that developed an influential left-feminist vision in the early years of the Cold War, during what is often considered a lull in feminist organizing. Although few historians have explored the CLAM or its impact, it was a major meeting of leftist women that drew more than 500 delegates from 17 countries in Latin America and the Caribbean at the height of the Cold War. Cuba sent one of the CLAM's largest delegations.

The CLAM took place at a critical time for the Cuban Revolution, as the rough political consensus of 1959 was beginning to break down and new revolutionary coalitions were emerging on the island. At a time of rapid polarization and shifting alliances, the ideal of transnational

---

Gender and the State in Latin America, ed. Elizabeth Dore and Molyneux (Durham, NC: Duke University Press, 2000), 291–321, and Samuel Farber, "Gender Politics and the Cuban Revolution," in his *Cuba Since the Revolution of 1959: A Critical Assessment* (Chicago, IL: Haymarket, 2011). Despite my rough schematic characterization here, there are many complex and nuanced assessments of the FMC. See Carollee Bengelsdorf, "On the Problem of Studying Women in Cuba," *Race and Class* 37, no. 2 (1985): 35–50, and Lois Smith and Alfred Padula, *Sex and Revolution: Women in Socialist Cuba* (New York: Oxford University Press, 1996), among others.

[4] The CLAM is often referred to as the "first" Latin American women's congress, despite the fact that a similar one was held in Brazil in 1954.

women's solidarity offered by the Congress appealed to Cuban women activists of different political stripes. Many members of the anti-Batista insurrection saw their own struggle as part of a broader Caribbean Spring, and they hoped that regional dictators like the Dominican Republic's Rafael Trujillo and Nicaragua's Anastasio Somoza would soon suffer the same fate as Batista. At the same time, many women activists affiliated with the prerevolutionary Communist Party too had long seen themselves as engaged in a broader global struggle for women's equality and against imperialism. The Cuban delegation to the CLAM, rooted in this shared engagement with transnational solidarity, helped establish cooperation between women activists from the farthest-left flank of the 26th of July Movement and women affiliated with the prerevolutionary Partido Socialista Popular, or Communist Party (PSP). This process was notable given the PSP's belated cooperation during the insurrection against dictator Fulgencio Batista, and was mirrored at the national level.

The CLAM left a significant institutional legacy. Upon the Cuban delegation's return, some members decided to form a permanent group called the Congress of Cuban Women for the Liberation of Latin America (CMCLAL), whose leadership included women from the 26th of July Movement, the pro-revolutionary Catholic group Con la Cruz y con la Patria (With Cross and Country), and the prerevolutionary Communist Party. This group formed the nucleus of what would soon become the famous mass organization for women, the FMC, founded in August 1960.[5] The history of the CLAM thus helps us recover the transnational, "Latin Americanist" roots of what would eventually evolve into Cuba's state feminism – that is, the top-down policies that sought to incorporate women and alleviate some of their traditional burdens, while simultaneously eschewing more radical forms of feminism.[6]

This transnationalism was not merely present in the FMC's origins. Indeed, although it is rarely analyzed as such, the FMC was an internationalist organization that continued to pursue solidarity projects with

---

[5] Vilma Espín, Asela de los Santos, and Yolanda Ferrer offer similar if brief accounts of the formation of the Congress of Cuban Women for the Liberation of Latin America as a precursor organization to the FMC. See Espín, de los Santos, and Ferrer, *Women in Cuba: The Making of a Revolution within the Revolution* (New York: Pathfinder Press, 2012), 108–12, 196–200, 217–23.

[6] For a discussion of the term "state feminism," see Zheng Wang, "'State Feminism?' Gender and Socialist State Formation in Maoist China," *Feminist Studies* 31, no. 3 (2005): 519–51. See also Kristen Ghodsee, "Socialist Internationalism and State Feminism during the Cold War: The Case of Bulgaria and Zambia," *Clio* no. 41 (2015) 106–25.

women from the socialist bloc and the Global South for the rest of the twentieth century. The CLAM thus provided the impetus and template for subsequent FMC internationalist delegations and participation in global forums provided by the United Nations or the WIDF. Recovering the overlooked transnational origins and character of the FMC provides a fuller and more nuanced picture of state-led revolutionary women's activism.

A REVOLUTIONARY COALITION OF WOMEN: PLANNING CUBA'S CLAM DELEGATION

The 1959 CLAM was called by the WIDF, an international pro-Soviet women's group formed in the aftermath of World War II and which had affiliate groups around the world. Although the WIDF and other Communist- or Soviet-affiliated women's groups have often been dismissed as mere Soviet puppets and/or not authentically feminist, recent scholarship has challenged those assumptions. As historians such as Francisca de Haan, Jadwiga Pieper Mooney, and others have argued, the WIDF should be understood as a left-feminist group that connected women's gender oppression to broader socioeconomic questions of labor exploitation and class inequality, and sought to counter those inequalities through a mass movement that included but was not restricted to working-class women.[7]

Analyzing the rhetoric and accomplishments of the WIDF and its many national affiliates in the postwar decades, Pieper Mooney argues that although leftist women often disowned the label "feminist," considering it divisive, bourgeois, or "against" men, "outspoken orthodox communists still mixed and mingled with a wide range of women who set out to mobilize for women's citizenship rights." Ultimately groups such as the WIDF "challenged the categories of 'feminism' and 'anti-feminism'" and

---

[7] Francisca de Haan, "The Women's International Democratic Federation (WIDF): History, Main Agenda, and Contributions, 1945–1991," published in the online collection *Women and Social Movements, 1840 to the Present*, ed. Katherine Kish Sklar and Thomas Dublin (Binghamton: Center for the Historical Study of Women and Gender at the State University of New York, 2012), https://cdn.alexanderstreet.com/pdf/1006349xxx/10063 49022.pdf?e=1527797366&h=44d987be992616f2f92bedf9b4a37185 (accessed May 29, 2018). De Haan draws on the definition of left-feminism offered by Ellen DuBois, as "a sense of women's systematic oppression with a larger understanding of social inequality" (17 n. 1, citing Ellen C. DuBois, "Eleanor Flexner and the History of American Feminism," *Gender & History* 3, no. 1 [1991]: 85).

their initiatives "illustrate the ambiguity of other binary oppositions of the Cold War."[8]

At the time of its founding in 1945 the WIDF was deeply marked by the recent scars of the war in Europe, yet it also incorporated more global perspectives, partly because delegates from Latin America and elsewhere pressed the organization to move beyond the focus on European fascism and war to encompass questions of underdevelopment, national liberation, and US imperialism.[9] This global orientation of the WIDF was visible in the 1949 Congress of Asian Women in Beijing and the August 1954 Latin American women's congress, the Conferencia Nacional sobre Trabalho entre as Mulheres (National Conference on Women's Work), held in Rio de Janeiro, Brazil, which was called by the WIDF and organized primarily by the Brazilian Communist Party.[10] The decision to hold another Latin American women's congress in Chile in 1959 may have indicated the growing importance of the region within the WIDF, as some Latin American women began to take on leadership roles as vice presidents and secretaries-general after 1955.[11] The bulk of the organizational work for the 1959 CLAM was carried out by the Unión de Mujeres de Chile (Chilean Women's Union), a group formed in 1953 that was affiliated with the Chilean Communist Party and the WIDF, and headed by Lía Laffaye de Muñoz.[12]

In response to the international call, women's groups in a handful of Latin American countries began the initial planning stages. Although women from local Communist parties and local affiliates of the WIDF

---

[8] Jadwiga E. Pieper Mooney, "Fighting Fascism and Forging New Political Activism: The Women's International Democratic Federation in the Cold War," in *Decentering Cold War History: Local and Global Change*, ed. Mooney and Fabio Lanza (New York: Routledge, 2013), 52–72, quote p. 60.

[9] On the early history of the WIDF see especially Francisca de Haan, "Progressive Women's Aspirations for a Better World," published in German in *Feministische Studien* 27, no. 2 (2009): 241–57 (English version courtesy of author); Mercedes Yusta Rodrigo, "The Mobilization of Women in Exile: The Case of the Unión de Mujeres Antifascistas Españolas in France (1944–50)," *Journal of Spanish Cultural Studies* 6, no. 1 (2005): 43–58.

[10] Adriana Valobra, "'Mujeres-sombra' y 'barbudas': Género y política en el Primer Congreso Latinoamericano de Mujeres, Chile, 1959," *Anuario del Instituto de Historia Argentina* no. 14 (2014), www.anuarioiha.fahce.unlp.edu.ar/article/view/5558 (accessed May 30, 2018).

[11] Francisca de Haan, "La Federación Democrática Internacional de Mujeres (FDIM) y América Latina," in *Queridas camaradas: Historias iberoamericanos de mujeres comunistas*, ed. Adriana Valobra and Mercedes Yusta (Buenos Aires: Milo y Dávila, 2017), 17–44; Valobra, "Mujeres-sombra."

[12] Valobra, "Mujeres-sombra," 5.

predominated in the planning, the CLAM was not limited to the Marxist left. The original call for the conference specifically imagined a cross-class, politically diverse group of women who might identify variously as mothers, workers, peasants, teachers, and other professionals of various political persuasions, much as the WIDF and its national affiliates did: "Women of Latin America! Whatever your activity, your religious faith, or your political opinions; whether you live in abundance or in scarcity, this meeting is yours."[13] Appealing to the possibility of "spiritual" closeness and "ties of friendship and comprehension," the initial organizers promised that the conference would clarify women's common aspirations and would "permit us to unite our actions to realize the conquest of our rights, the welfare and happiness of our children, the sovereignty and dignity of our peoples, [and] fraternity and peace for all humanity."[14] Such rhetoric was typical of the WIDF congresses in the 1950s. Their references to maternalism or sisterhood partly reflected strategic efforts to appeal broadly to women around the globe, and the emphasis on peace reflected the global communist peace campaigns of the past decade.

The call for congressional delegations to Chile came at a time of rapid political change within Cuba. The Cuban revolutionary movement that ousted Fulgencio Batista had comprised a broad coalition from center to left, with the exception of the Cuban Communist Party, which denounced armed revolutionary tactics until mid-1958. The political diversity of the insurrectionary movement was due partly to the different positions of its component organizations. In turn, each of the major revolutionary organizations that had formed specifically to oust Batista, such as the 26th of July Movement and the Revolutionary Directorate, encompassed a variety of political leanings within their ranks, including active Catholics, anti-communists, social democrats, and dissident communists. Within this revolutionary coalition there was broad consensus over the overarching goals of social justice and true sovereignty, which might be achieved through some version of agrarian and urban reform, increased access to education and healthcare, industrial development, and diversified trading partners. Yet specific groups and actors within the revolutionary coalition did not agree on the particulars. This broad consensus began to unravel with the unveiling of the Agrarian Reform in May 1959. The details of the reform, which virtually guaranteed conflict with US-owned sugar companies like

---

[13] *1er Congreso Latinoamericano de Mujeres* (Havana: Ministerio de Relaciones Exteriores, January 1960), 4.
[14] *1er Congreso Latinoamericano de Mujeres*, 4.

United Fruit, began to turn large landowners and the US government against the revolution.[15]

At the same time, the revolution's triumph had set off a wave of excitement and grassroots mobilization, as new pro-revolutionary groups were formed and prerevolutionary organizations restructured or renamed. Some new pro-revolutionary women's groups had formed in the immediate aftermath of the 1959 victory, particularly drawing on 26th of July veterans, such as the Brigadas Femeninas Revolucionarias (Revolutionary Women's Brigades) and the Women's Section of the 26th of July Movement. At the same time, women who were predominantly, but not exclusively, affiliated with the prerevolutionary Communist Party – most of whom had not participated actively in the anti-Batista struggle due to the party's line against armed opposition – also formed a new pro-revolutionary organization, Unidad Femenina Revolucionaria (Revolutionary Women's Unity, UFR). The UFR had strong roots in the WIDF's Cuban affiliate, the Federación Democrática de Mujeres Cubanas (Democratic Federation of Cuban Women, FDMC). As I have argued elsewhere, these women with histories in the Marxist left tended to have a well-developed program demanding women's rights and women's equality, unlike many of the younger women affiliated with the 26th of July Movement. Yet without the cachet of having joined the armed struggle, they lacked the power and influence that the 26th of July wielded in 1959.[16]

The call for the CLAM undoubtedly appealed to women leaders of the Marxist left, some of whom had attended WIDF international congresses before.[17] It would allow them to forge links with increasingly powerful women like Espín from the 26th of July; emphasize a shared set of concerns and demands; and influence and raise the visibility of the "woman question" in the revolution. It was surely the UFR that brought the CLAM to the attention of the 26th of July leadership.

From the perspective of the 26th of July leaders, the CLAM presented an opportunity for international exposure on a platform that did not

[15] Excellent overviews of this process are found in Louis A. Pérez, Jr., *Cuba: Between Reform and Revolution*, fifth ed. (New York: Oxford University Press, 2015), and Lars Schoultz, *That Infernal Little Cuban Republic: The United States and the Cuban Revolution* (Chapel Hill: University of North Carolina Press, 2011).

[16] Michelle Chase, *Revolution within the Revolution: Women and Gender Politics in Cuba, 1952–1962* (Chapel Hill: University of North Carolina Press, 2015).

[17] For example María Argüelles attended the WIDF's 1948 Congress in Budapest and the 1959 Congress in Chile. See María Argüelles, "Mis impresiones sobre el Congreso Latinoamericano," *Noticias de Hoy*, December 9, 1959, 6.

include representatives from the United States. It was not meant to be a showcase for Cuban accomplishments in the area of women's rights, as WIDF congresses later in the 1960s would be, but rather a forum for Cuban women to promote and defend the young revolution, particularly in the face of growing US aggression. The broad spectrum of left-leaning groups that expressed interest in the CLAM paralleled the coalition behind the Cuban Revolution in that period. However, some of the younger Cuban delegates affiliated with the 26th of July Movement were apparently not aware of the conference's origins or did not know that the WIDF was a group supported by the Soviet Union.[18]

Cuban organizations held their first preparatory meeting, convened at the Casa de las Américas in Havana and presided over by Vilma Espín, in May 1959. This meeting represented an unprecedented encounter of women activists of different generations and political tendencies including the revolutionary movement of the 1950s, the anti-dictatorial movement and first-wave feminist movement of the 1930s, and women affiliated with the prerevolutionary Communist Party. Women known for their participation in the Rebel Army or the urban 26th of July Movement included Haydée Santamaría, Asela de los Santos, and Vilma Espín. Women affiliated with the Communist Party or the FDMC included Rosario "Charito" Guillaume, Clementina Serra, Elena Gil, Carlota Miró, Candelaria Rodríguez, and Esther Noriega. Veteran radical activists famed for opposing Cuban dictator Gerardo Machado in the 1930s included Delia Echevarría and Lía de la Torriente Brau; the latter had also participated in the first-wave feminist movement of the 1930s.

Other women who joined the planning committee included the Ortodoxo (Orthodox) Party leader Conchita Fernández; the prominent Dominican exile and anti-Trujillo activist Graciela Heureaux; and a few women better known for being the wives of famous men, such as María Caridad Molinas de Dorticós, wife of the mostly nominal Cuban president Osvaldo Dorticós, and Aleida March, Che Guevara's young wife.[19] Undoubtedly the preparation for the CLAM brought many of these women into contact with each other for the first time.

In the following months, the base of women involved in the CLAM preparations broadened to include women from Cuba's labor movement, as women from predominantly female industries began to elect

---

[18] Marel García, oral history interview, Miami, December 2011.
[19] "Congreso Latinoamericano," *Unidad Femenina*, ca. October 1959 (date illegible), 16–17, 19, 33.

delegates to represent them at the CLAM.[20] Cuba's delegation to the conference eventually included labor union representatives from other heavily female industries, such as tobacco, matches, canning, rice, and textiles.[21] Rural women also joined the final delegation, and it is likely that their participation reflected the alliance, which had begun in 1950, between some provincial chapters of the national Federación Campesina (Peasant Federation) and the FDMC.[22] Finally, Oriente Province and some municipalities also elected women to the delegation.[23]

This mobilization of women along various organizational and regional lines led to a final Cuban delegation that was enormous. In early November Vilma Espín said she hoped the delegation to the CLAM would consist of some forty or fifty women; the final delegation numbered roughly eighty.[24] Only the Chilean hosting delegation was larger, and most countries sent less than a handful of delegates. This undoubtedly reflected the surge of organizational and political activity among Cuban women in the revolution's immediate aftermath. According to PSP leader Elena Gil, the Cuban delegation's surprising size reflected the "extraordinary number of Cuban women's organizations that wanted to participate in the event." Importantly, she noted that many of them were able to raise their own funds to attend.[25] Other sources, too, suggest that the trip was largely financed by donations from individual women, associations to which they belonged, cultural fundraising events, and private businesses across the island.[26] Thus we may surmise that Cuba's

---

[20] For example, women from the food service workers' union met to elect representatives to the Congress in early November. "Elegidas delegadas a un Congreso Latinoamericano," *Revolución* (Havana), November 10, 1959, 4.

[21] *1er Congreso Latinoamericano de Mujeres*, 7.

[22] According to the pamphlet *1er Congreso Latinoamericano de Mujeres* (7), women from the "Federaciones Campesinas" formed part of the Cuban delegation. This may have referred to the Comisiones de Mujeres Campesinas – local women's sections within the Federación Campesina. Some provincial chapters of the Federación Campesina had endorsed the FDMC's 1950 congressional resolutions and urged their women members in the Comisiones de Mujeres Campesinas (Peasant Women's Commissions) to join their local FDMC chapters or to form commissions in provinces where these did not yet exist. "Las mujeres de Matanzas se unen a la lucha campesina," *Hoy*, March 10, 1950, 5; Sarah Pascual, "Georgina de Urra," *Hoy*, April 4, 1950, 11; "Programa de acción de la comisión femenina de la Fed. Campesina," *Hoy*, April 6, 1950, 11.

[23] César Martín, "Congreso," *Revolución*, November 4, 1959, 2.

[24] Martín, "Congreso," 2.   [25] "Congreso," *Revolución*, December 17, 1959, 1, 16.

[26] Espín et al., *Women in Cuba*, 219; "Congreso Latinoamericano," 16–17, 19, 33; Marel García, interview.

large CLAM delegation reflected grassroots enthusiasm more than state support.

The final delegation was also notable for its heterogeneity. It included various pro-revolutionary leftist groups, including the Brigadas Femeninas Revolucionarias, which was affiliated with the 26th of July Movement; the Movimiento de Integración Nacional (Movement for National Integration), a racial justice group affiliated with the Communist Party; and Con la Cruz y con la Patria.[27] It also included women of different generations, middle-class professionals, and labor leaders. The composition of the final Cuban delegation thus represented a sort of pro-revolutionary labor-left-feminist coalition, suggesting the possibility of a women's alliance that transcended the boundaries of generation, of social class, of Old and New Lefts, and of Catholic and secular activism.

A final striking aspect of the delegation was the presence of prominent foreign nationals who represented the anti-dictatorial and anti-imperialist movements of the Caribbean basin. Dominican exile Graciela Heureaux had formed part of the CLAM preparatory meetings, and the final Cuban delegation included Dominican exile Leda Estévez, a member of the Movimiento de Liberación Dominicana (Dominican Liberation Movement), an armed anti-Trujillo group deeply influenced by the Cuban Revolution that had formed in March 1959.[28] Their presence is not surprising since Dominican women exiles had participated actively in UFR congresses and had been highly visible in other pro-revolutionary events in Havana throughout 1959.

The two other foreign nationals who joined Cuba's delegation were Laura Meneses, wife of the Puerto Rican nationalist leader Pedro Albizu Campos, imprisoned in the United States since 1950, and María Cristina Vilanova, wife of deposed Guatemalan president Jacobo Arbenz.[29] Both were prominent and highly symbolic political figures whose presence explicitly connected the Cuban Revolution to other anti-imperialist and revolutionary movements. This connection was not lost on contemporaries. The Chilean Communist Party newspaper *El Siglo*, for example, commented that it was moving to see Espín, Meneses, and Vilanova

---

[27] "Congreso Latinoamericano," 16–17, 19, 33; Marel García, interview.

[28] Prensa Latina (Santiago), "Llegó a Chile la delegación cubana al congreso femenino," *Revolución*, November 19, 1959, 8. On this group see Piero Gleijeses, *The Dominican Crisis: The 1965 Constitutionalist Revolt and American Intervention* (Baltimore, MD: Johns Hopkins University Press, 1978), 421 n. 31.

[29] Prensa Latina, "Llegó a Chile la delegación cubana"; Yolanda Ferrer and Carolina Aguilar Ayerra, *El fuego de la libertad* (Havana: Editorial de la Mujer, 2015), 480.

together, who all embodied the same revolutionary spirit: "Our rebellious blood burns in all of them."[30] The last-minute inclusion of Meneses and Vilanova in the delegation likely reveals the hand of the national leadership of the 26th of July Movement at work. Meneses had spent time in Cuba on and off since the late 1930s, and had participated in the National Women's Congress held in Havana in 1939. The 26th of July Movement and the Puerto Rican Nationalist Party had developed some contacts throughout the 1950s and Meneses had met Fidel Castro when both were in exile in Mexico in 1955. In 1961 Meneses was included in the Cuban delegation to the United Nations, and Cuba agitated for Puerto Rican independence in international forums throughout the 1960s and 1970s.[31] Although the 26th of July Movement does not seem to have had contact with the Arbenz government in the early 1950s, Che Guevara was present in Guatemala during the coup, which deeply impacted his thinking about the US government's inevitably hostile response to Latin American revolutions. In 1959 the Cuban revolutionary government reached out to Arbenz to invite him to visit Cuba, which he did in 1960. Thus the inclusion of Meneses and Vilanova may have reflected both the authentic sense of transnational solidarity of the Cuban women delegates to the CLAM and the foreign-policy imperatives of Cuba's male leadership.

THE APPEAL OF THE TRANSNATIONAL

Most scholarly examinations of transnational politics in Cuban history focus on the post-1961 socialist internationalism that expressed itself as revolutionary militancy, encouraging either guerrilla *foco* activity (small insurrectionary groups) throughout the Americas or decolonization in Africa, or as "Tricontinentalism" which positioned Cuba as a diplomatic leader of the Global South and the Non-Aligned Movement.[32] However, it

---

[30] Quoted in Prensa Latina, "Apoyo a la revolución cubana y repulsa a las dictaduras," *Revolución*, November 23, 1959, 6.

[31] Jesus Arboleya Cervera with Raul Alzaga Manresa and Ricardo Fraga del Valle, *La contrarrevolución cubana en Puerto Rico y el caso de Carlos Muñiz Varela* (San Juan: Ediciones Callejón, 2016), 35–40.

[32] Piero Gleijeses, *Conflicting Missions: Havana, Washington, and Africa, 1959–1976* (Chapel Hill: University of North Carolina Press, 2002), and *Visions of Freedom: Havana, Washington, Pretoria, and the Struggle for Southern Africa, 1976–1991* (Chapel Hill, NC: University of North Carolina Press, 2013); Ann Garland Mahler, *From the Tricontinental to the Global South: Race, Radicalism, and Transnational Solidarity* (Durham, NC: Duke University Press, 2018); Manuel Barcia, "Locking Horns with the Northern Empire: Anti-American Imperialism at the Tricontinental

is important to recognize that while the Cuban Revolution forged new forms of solidarity across the Global South in the 1960s through the 1966 Tricontinental Conference and other means, this transnational emphasis drew on longer roots within Cuban prerevolutionary politics and was not created from scratch. In addition, scholarship has rarely studied the gendered aspects of these revolutionary forms of solidarity. The Congreso Latinoamericano de Mujeres of 1959 captures the pro-revolutionary transnational sentiment that preceded Cuba's open embrace of socialism and the alliance with the Soviet bloc, and was a form of transnational solidarity explicitly articulated around women's shared interests. Importantly, it appealed to different tendencies among the women activists on the Cuban left by drawing on and channeling their pre-1959 internationalist sensibilities. This facilitated cooperation between some segments of the "old" Marxist left – that is, women affiliated with the prerevolutionary Communist Party – and the "new" left that had emerged from the 26th of July Movement.

Cuban women affiliated with the PSP and the FDMC, the Cuban affiliate of the WIDF founded in 1948 with PSP support, were exposed throughout the late 1940s and 1950s to a specifically left-feminist internationalist agenda that focused on questions of decolonization and anti-capitalist revolution and interrogated women's roles within these processes. At times this platform was explicitly comparative, as when the FDMC promoted awareness of women's rights in the Soviet Union, China, and in the developing world through their publication *Mujeres Cubanas*, in exhibitions, and in meetings.[33] The FDMC also promoted forms of transnational women's solidarity, for example, in their crucial participation in Cuba's

---

Conference of 1966 in Havana," *Journal of Transatlantic Studies* 7, no. 3 (2009): 208–17; Sarah Seidman, "Tricontinental Routes of Solidarity: Stokely Carmichael in Cuba," *Journal of Transnational American Studies* 4, no. 2 (2012), https://escholarship .org/uc/item/owp587sj (accessed May 30, 2018); Eric Gettig, "Cuba, the United States, and the Uses of the Third World Project, 1959–1967," in *Latin America and the Third World*, ed. Thomas C. Field, Stella Krepp, and Vanni Pettinà (Chapel Hill: University of North Carolina Press, forthcoming). A growing literature also explores connections between Cuba and other sites of the African diaspora, examining the way Afro-Cubans and African Americans sought strategic alliances and informed one another's politics. On this question see Frank Guridy, *Forging Diaspora: Afro-Cubans and African Americans in a World of Empire and Jim Crow* (Chapel Hill: University of North Carolina Press, 2010); John Gronbeck-Tedesco, *Cuba, the United States, and Cultures of the Transnational Left, 1930–1975* (New York: Cambridge University Press, 2017); Devyn Spence Benson, *Antiracism in Cuba: The Unfinished Revolution* (Chapel Hill: University of North Carolina Press, 2016).

[33] Chase, *Revolution within the Revolution*.

opposition to the Korean War, which played on maternalist discourse stressing women's "natural" opposition to war and pointed out the devastation the Korean War had inflicted on North Korean women and children.[34]

A different transnational politics characterized the insurrectionary movement to oust Fulgencio Batista in the 1950s. Within this multistranded movement, particularly within the 26th of July, a regional sensibility emerged that stressed the Cuban insurrection against Batista as part of a broader Caribbean social-democratic movement, often folded within the loose concept of "Our America," a phrase used by the nineteenth-century Cuban anti-imperialist leader José Martí. This conceptualization understood Batista as one of a handful of regional dictators, including Somoza in Nicaragua, Trujillo in the Dominican Republic, Pérez Jiménez in Venezuela, and Stroessner in Paraguay. These two overlapping tendencies – a simultaneously geographical and political sense of community – were often combined into the common slogan of the 1950s, "against the dictators of our America." As historians such as Rafael Rojas have noted, Cuban revolutionaries "included positions against Latin American dictators in their various political programs ... especially the dictators of the Caribbean." Indeed, when the revolutionaries came to power on January 1, 1959, one of new president Manuel Urrutia's very first acts in office was to send messages to the UN and the Organization of American States denouncing the human-rights violations by dictators in the region.[35]

This pan-Caribbean, anti-dictatorial sensibility was nurtured in the immediate aftermath of the revolution by the flood of progressive Caribbean exiles who sought a safe haven in Havana. Dominican exiles in Havana formed new anti-Trujillo organizations inspired by the triumphant Cuban Revolution, mostly dedicated to fundraising and propaganda efforts against Trujillo. Some of these groups were founded by and were composed mostly of women.[36] According to historian Eliades

---

[34] Michelle Chase, "Hands Off Korea! Asian Decolonization and Women's Peace Activism in Early Cold War Cuba," manuscript in preparation.

[35] Rafael Rojas, *Historia mínima de la revolución cubana* (Mexico City: Colegio de México, 2015), 138.

[36] For example, the Comité Primero de Enero Pro-Liberación de Santo Domingo was founded on January 27, 1959, by Helia del Calvo. In an event to commemorate Dominican independence held in Havana on February 27, 1959, Concepción Rodríguez Díaz and Graciela Heureaux both spoke. See Eliades Acosta Matos, "La caída," in *La telaraña cubana de Trujillo* (Santo Domingo: Archivo General de la Nación, 2012), 2: 770n37.

Acosta, Cuban women were attracted to these new exile groups "to such an extreme" that one Dominican business attaché in Havana complained in February 1959 of the intense anti-Trujillo activities carried out by exiles and by Cuban citizens, "especially among women."[37]

This fervent exile agitation in the aftermath of the Cuban victory appealed both to Cubans affiliated with the 26th of July Movement and to women activists of the Marxist left. For their part, exiles took advantage of the effervescent atmosphere to broadcast their own messages. For example, at a March 1959 women's conference held by the UFR, exiles from the Dominican Republic, Nicaragua, and Spain gave speeches.[38] The UFR had also discussed forming its own group, a Comité Femenino Contra las Dictaduras de América.[39] These exile groups surely appealed to Cubans partly because they modeled themselves after the Cuban revolutionaries. Furthermore, these circum-Caribbean movements did not generate any geopolitical fault lines between Cuba's Marxist and revolutionary lefts in that period, as, say, the Soviet invasion of Hungary in 1956 might have.

This shared pro-Latin American and Caribbean sensibility was evident in the planning stages for Cuba's delegation to the Congress and helped facilitate collaboration between women of different political tendencies, despite the tensions that existed between women active in the revolutionary movement and the women of the PSP, who had opposed armed insurrection until mid-1958. For example, the Dominican exile Graciela Heureaux attended the first planning meeting at the Casa de las Américas. And it is notable that the first public statement released by the Cuban planning committee for the CLAM apparently made no mention of the demands of Cuban women or their role within the revolution; instead it focused on eliciting solidarity among Cuban women for their Latin American "sisters" who were prevented by their poverty and oppression from working, voting, exercising their proper functions as mothers, or enjoying legal protections:

Cuban women: You have Latin American sisters who cannot live with dignity, protect their children from misery or the lash, save them from premature and unjust death, educate them, work honorably when they need to, elect their rulers.

---

[37] Quoted in Acosta Matos, "La caída," 730.
[38] *Unidad Femenina*, ca. May 1, 1959.
[39] *Noticias de Hoy*, February 4, 1959.

The immense majority do not know how to read or write, they are not protected by the law [por ley alguna].[40]

This moving description of Cuban women's Latin American "sisters" resonated with the goals of the Cuban Revolution and the WIDF. Though rather vague and perhaps even paternalistic, it lent itself to the militantly anti-imperialist analysis of the ravages of foreign capital on local populations that the Cuban delegation would offer in its plenary speeches in Chile.

CONGRESSIONAL THEMES AND ACCORDS

The three main themes of the CLAM were the "dignification" of women "as mothers, workers, and citizens"; the rights of children; and the question of sovereignty in Latin America – themes that had been at the center of previous WIDF-sponsored congresses.[41] The CLAM resulted in a series of accords on the rights of women and children. The accords demanded women's right to education, including sexual education; the right to work, equal pay for equal work, and equivalency between intellectual and manual labor; support services and retraining for women sex workers; equalized *patria potestad* (custody rights over children); rights for illegitimate children; equality between formal marriages and long-term unions; the extension of legal divorce to countries that lacked it; the extension of female suffrage to countries that lacked it; access to maternal healthcare services; and adequate education for children. These demands reflected the uneven achievements in women's rights across the region. Argentine laws, for example, were blatantly unequal regarding *patria potestad*, did not permit legal divorce, and allowed discrimination against illegitimate children. Even in those countries with substantial legal equality, such as Uruguay, Cuba, Peru, Mexico, and Bolivia, congressional attendees noted that the "social reality" in these countries "does not reflect this legal equality."[42]

It may be true that the CLAM's rhetoric and demands were neither particularly radical nor particularly novel within the history of feminist mobilization and may even have reinscribed some essentializing tropes regarding women. As historian Adriana Valobra argues, the Argentine

[40] Cited in "Un poco de historia," *Mujeres*, n.d., www.mujeres.co.cu/FMC/Un_poco_de_historia.pdf (accessed May 8, 2018).
[41] "Mujeres de América Latina se dan la mano," *La Mirada* (Santiago) (November 1959): 7.
[42] *1er Congreso Latinoamericano de Mujeres*, 50–51.

delegation to the CLAM fell back on canonical models of femininity, stressing women's role as "partner (*compañera*) of the prisoner or soldier" or describing them as fundamentally motivated by familial concerns and their status as mothers or future mothers. And the CLAM overall, she argues, often subsumed the question of women's rights to "broader" economic and political problems such as development and sovereignty.[43]

Nevertheless, as Valobra notes, the tone of the conference was far from uniform. Some speakers issued strident demands for gender equality. During the opening address, WIDF President Eugenie Cotton said that "women are most of the time considered auxiliary to men, not equals," and that "there are no purely masculine or feminine problems. The real problem is that of [transforming] the relationship between men and women on bases of equality."[44] Congressional speeches referred at least obliquely to challenging gender relations and the division of reproductive labor within the private sphere. One speaker called for the dismantling of traditional gender roles as constructed within the home, calling upon mothers and fathers to require their sons and daughters to share housework burdens equally and to refrain from passing on engrained gender constructions about male bravery or women's frailty to the next generation. A young girl should be taught "that she is worth as much – not more, not less – than her brothers, male friends, and male comrades; that she is as brave as they are; that she does not [need to] depend on men [to solve] her … problems."[45]

The CLAM was also an important space for comparative conversations. The smaller thematic sessions allowed for horizontal interactions among women of the same sectors, such as peasants, youth, and labor. María Argüelles, a PSP member and longtime activist for racial justice and for women's and children's rights, described being impressed by these thematic sessions. She remarked on how intense they were, often lasting all night and into the dawn. In this way Cuban delegates were exposed to the labor challenges faced by their counterparts in other parts of Latin America, such as textile workers, bank employees, and peasants.[46] At times they were negatively impressed by the lack of legal protections their counterparts in other countries had, as when textile workers from Argentina explained "the laws they could not benefit from in comparison to us, especially in relation to maternity."[47] The CLAM also

---

[43] Valobra, "Mujeres-sombra," 10.   [44] Quoted in Valobra, "Mujeres-sombra," 9.
[45] *1er Congreso Latinoamericano de Mujeres*, 11.   [46] Argüelles, "Mis impresiones."
[47] Argüelles, "Mis impresiones."

comparatively addressed rural problems such as land hunger, low salaries, and poor educational opportunities, and raised the agrarian reforms of Cuba and Venezuela as examples of ways to give rural women lives with dignity.[48]

Although it is impossible to recover all the conversations that took place at the CLAM, the formal speeches give us some insight into the breadth of the problems delegates would have debated in thematic meetings or in informal encounters. Delegates raised the issue of single mothers, whom they argued required government support. Mexican delegates commented on the particular challenges faced by indigenous women, who struggled with societal racism, economic exploitation, and the impunity of whites and *mestizos* who abused indigenous peoples.

In the final analysis, the CLAM offered debate around important if not ground-breaking themes, laced with strands of more transgressive thinking. For a sizable part of the Cuban delegation, particularly the younger women affiliated with the 26th of July Movement, the linking of gender inequality to socioeconomic structures and the shared needs, rights, and demands of women across the continent were new insights. Marel García, a young 26th of July leader and founder of the Brigadas Femeninas, noted that she had been attracted to joining the Congress in Chile primarily because she viewed it as a way of supporting the revolution, not necessarily because of its focus on women's rights.[49] Similarly, most young women who had joined the insurrectionary movement in the 1950s had been motivated primarily by a desire to oust Batista; few of them had exposure to feminist politics or women's activism, and the 26th of July leadership never broached such issues in their manifestos. But the exposure to women activists from across the continent during the CLAM must have solidified their burgeoning interest in and awareness of women's common challenges. And special thematic panels – such as the roundtables on youth and peasant women – offered a new, gendered perspective on the constituencies most favored by Cuba's revolutionary leadership. Women like Marel García, Asela de los Santos, and other young 26th of July Movement delegates to the CLAM would become lifelong proponents of women's activism and uplift within the revolution.

---

[48] *1er Congreso Latinoamericano de Mujeres*, 15.   [49] Marel García, interview.

THE CUBAN DELEGATION, ANTI-IMPERIALISM,
AND COLD WAR POLITICS

Despite the apparent consensus within the CLAM, there were also many tensions and controversies, beginning well before the Congress took place. Due to ongoing Cold War tensions, left-sponsored congresses in Latin America were quickly contested by anti-communist groups, including the Congress for Cultural Freedom (CCF). The CCF was an international cultural organization ostensibly dedicated to freedom of speech, but also reflecting the geopolitical priorities of its clandestine sponsor, the CIA. As Patrick Iber has shown, the Chilean chapter of the CCF was the region's most active, strengthened by the influence of Carlos de Baraibar, a prominent Spanish exile journalist who wrote a column for the conservative daily *El Mercurio*. Throughout the 1950s, Baraibar and the Chilean CCF had worked to disrupt or counter left-led initiatives by promoting anti-communist youth organizations in order to rival left-leaning ones, or by demanding that opposition to Latin American dictatorships also denounce totalitarianism globally.[50]

Baraibar now initiated a campaign against the CLAM, claiming it was communist-controlled. Although women from Communist parties did figure prominently in the various delegations to the CLAM, the Congress also clearly included left-leaning women of various non-Communist political affiliations. It is also possible that the CLAM organizers had intentionally chosen to focus on relatively noncontroversial topics given the Cold War tensions they knew would erupt.[51] Nevertheless, the resulting controversy led many Catholic and some labor-based women's organizations to withdraw their support for the CLAM.[52] As word spread that Cuba would send a large delegation to the CLAM, it added to the growing sense of unease held by some Catholic women, who denounced the CLAM's alleged domination by Communists and its "extremist" positions, such as armed revolution, in reference to Cuba.[53] Although the Cuban Revolution had not yet openly embraced

---

[50] Patrick Iber, *Neither Peace nor Freedom: The Cultural Cold War in Latin America* (Cambridge, MA: Harvard University Press, 2015), 91–92, 110.

[51] Congress president Lía Laffaye commented that "luckily we'll be talking about children, which isn't too sticky of a subject. After the attacks that we've received ... any more or less progressive topic ... would have been sharply criticized." "Mujeres de América Latina se dan la mano."

[52] Valobra, "Mujeres-sombra," 6. Also see "Sin influencia comunista el congreso femenino de Chile," *Revolución*, November 4, 1959, 3.

[53] Valobra, "Mujeres-sombra," 6.

socialism, it was clear by the fall of 1959 that it had entered an escalating conflict with foreign capital and the US government, and some early defectors to the United States had begun to warn publicly of communist infiltration in revolutionary ranks. At the same time, the announcement that Cuba would participate in the CLAM also created excitement, and some groups belatedly decided to send delegations as a result.[54]

For the Cuban delegates, the CLAM served as an important early forum for the denunciation of US government subversion. It allowed them to articulate an anti-imperialist critique in the context of rising US aggression against the island and to showcase the revolution's early accomplishments in a forum not dominated by the United States.[55] In this context, the militantly anti-imperialist and openly confrontational speeches of Cuban delegates Vilma Espín and Elena Gil, as well as the presence of Laura Meneses and Cristina Vilanova within the Cuban delegation, helped establish the Cuban Revolution's anti-imperialist stance on a global stage.

The two major speeches given by Cuban delegates Elena Gil and Vilma Espín both offered anti-imperialist analyses but with different emphases. Although these speeches were purportedly prepared by the whole Cuban delegation, their content clearly reflected Gil and Espín's respective political backgrounds. Gil, a longtime PSP militant in her fifties, had become famous as a young woman for her activism in defense of the Spanish Republic, earning her the nickname "the Cuban *pasionaria*" in reference to the famous Spanish Communist leader Dolores Ibárruri.[56] Her speech reflected the Marxist left's critique of global imperialism and capitalist exploitation, a critique which the PSP and FDMC had developed during the past decade. Espín, a student leader from Santiago de Cuba who had become a leader of the 26th of July first in Santiago and then in the Sierra with the Rebel Army, reflected the revolutionary nationalism of that movement.

Gil spoke on the broad topic, "To safeguard the life of present and future generations, sovereignty, progress, and culture." She traced the ravages of Spanish colonialism and the way Britain and the United States had informally inherited this mantle in the nineteenth century. "First the caravels and galleons of the Spanish empire took our gold and

[54] Valobra, "Mujeres-sombra," 2.

[55] This was in sharp contrast, for example, to Fidel Castro's visit to the United States just six months prior, marked by accommodating public rhetoric.

[56] *Ecured* entry for Elena Gil, www.ecured.cu/Elena_Gil (accessed May 8, 2018).

silver, later they took coffee, cacao, quinine. The peoples who populated our continent were extinguished ... or fell into slavery, [and New World slavery] was later extended to ... Africa." After the end of Spanish colonialism, the new imperial powers of Britain and the United States took Spain's place, using "capital as their weapon," investing in tropical commodities, telecommunications, transportation, and energy. World War II facilitated the rise of North American capital, she explained, which sought to invade Latin American markets and the globe with US merchandise and reap harvests far greater than local investments would permit. Gil's only reference to the revolutionary leadership was a quote from a recent Fidel Castro speech in which he argued that prerevolutionary Cuba was not a democracy: it was "an empire of plantations" that exploited peasants and workers. These words, she added, could be extended to all of Latin America.[57]

Gil also denounced racial divisions, racial discrimination, and the subordination of indigenous and black populations. "This discrimination deepens further ... when it comes to indigenous and black women subjected to every kind of race and gender discrimination." She called upon the Latin American women's movement to fight tirelessly against racial segregation and inequality, advocate for the incorporation of these populations into civic life and opportunities, and work for the revitalization of indigenous cultures and the recognition and appreciation of the "black contribution to the formation of national cultures."[58] This was an agenda that the FDMC had developed since the 1940s, paralleling and fortifying the emphasis on racial justice embraced by Cuba's PSP and the WIDF.[59]

For her part, Espín gave a blistering speech in defense of the Cuban Revolution and denounced the US government's imperialist designs. Like Gil, Espín condemned the social ruination caused by US capital, highlighting the enormous plantations, monopolies, and concessions foreign investors enjoyed. Yet her speech focused much more on Cuba's history of revolutionary nationalism. She traced a now-familiar historical trajectory from the late-nineteenth-century anti-colonial activism of José Martí, through the Cuban revolution of 1933, to the rise of Batista, all culminating in the triumphant revolution of 1959. Espín praised the revolution's

---

[57] *1er Congreso Latinoamericano de Mujeres*, 25.   [58] Ibid., 26.

[59] In contrast, Vilma Espín barely touched upon the topic of race, for example, merely noting in passing that women of "our America" were familiar with "the humiliating discrimination [against their] color, [their] gender, [against] the freedom to think for themselves." *1er Congreso Latinoamericano de Mujeres*, 28.

benefits for the Cuban family, including personal and economic security, laws to benefit the popular classes such as the urban and agrarian reforms, and lower prices for foods, medicines, electricity, gas, and other goods. She showered particular praise on the agrarian reform and advances in education. She also offered copious details about US aggression toward the revolution, pleading for solidarity from the rest of the continent in Cuba's hour of danger.

Espín's speech largely eschewed specific analysis of gender inequality, but it did offer a definition of Latin American "sisterhood" based less on shared culture, language, or history than on shared forms of exploitation. The region's women were sisters, she argued,

in language, habits, customs, but especially ... in the pain of limitless exploitation, in the suffering of hunger, in misery, in the infinite desolation of ignorance. Sisters, [one and] all, in the suffering of the same problems under the same exploitation (*mano expoliadora*) [that is] implacable in daily robbing us of encouragement and the blood of our children and the richness of our countries.[60]

Although Espín did not focus on women's rights or demands, nor on their participation in the Cuban revolutionary movement, it is interesting to note that WIDF president Eugenie Cotton subsequently remembered the speech differently. In 1960, she described it as a passionate, three-and-a-half-hour address "on the role of women in the liberation of Cuba."[61] This selective memory suggests that Espín's forceful delivery and her embodiment of revolutionary commitment served to communicate powerful extra-textual messages about women in the Cuban Revolution (see Figure 6.1).

Indeed, the Cuban delegation proved to be immensely inspirational and symbolic to many women on the Latin American left. The deep support the Cuban Revolution enjoyed was visible in the delegation's effusive reception, as the Cubans drew enormous applause, both from other delegates and from crowds in the streets. Many Cuban delegates commented extensively on these spontaneous displays of solidarity. For the Afro-Cuban Communist Party member María Argüelles, "the most important [thing about the Congress] for me ... was the warmth and support that our revolution has among the people of Chile." According to Argüelles, workers, *campesinos*, and housewives alike expressed support to the delegation and shouted "*vivas*" to Fidel. Pins with the Chilean and Cuban flags, adorned with the phrase "We support the Cuban Revolution," were pinned to "thousands of

---

[60] *1er Congreso Latinoamericano de Mujeres*, 27.
[61] Cited in De Haan, "La Federación Democrática Internacional de Mujeres," 37.

FIGURE 6.1 Vilma Espín addresses the Congress of Latin American Women.
Source: Courtesy of Marel García.
Vilma Espín (standing, far right) addresses the Congress of Latin American
Women. Another Cuban delegate, Marel García, is visible in the audience
(second from left, first row, facing camera).

Chilean chests."[62] Idis Rodríguez Lambert, a prominent 26th of July member from Santiago de Cuba, was also moved by the immense support for the Cuban Revolution she found when she traveled to Chile a month before the CLAM as part of the planning committee. "In Chile they have an exceptional admiration for the Cuban revolution [and] have great hopes in it, which we can't squander," she told a journalist upon her return.[63] And in her memoirs, written nearly thirty years later, Elena Gil fondly recalled the day of the CLAM's inauguration in downtown Santiago, as the Cuban delegation walked from their hotel to the theater, singing the hymn of the 26th of July Movement to applause as they went.[64]

---

[62] Argüelles, a longtime activist for women's and children's rights, also described being impressed by the horizontal conversations that took place at the CLAM between textile workers, bank workers, and *campesinas*. Argüelles, "Mis impresiones."
[63] "Sin influencia comunista el congreso femenino."
[64] Gil, "Apuntes para mi hijo" (unpublished memoir, 1989), 98.

The passionate reception of the Cuban delegation did not go unnoticed by the WIDF's European leaders, who gained a new appreciation for the young revolution and, by extension, for the rising revolutionary fervor within the Latin American left. In 1963, Eugenie Cotton praised the 1959 CLAM as having helped the WIDF to broaden its outlook by familiarizing it with the demands of women in decolonizing and developing nations. "On the spot I obtained a better understanding than I would have been able to of the economic oppression on the one hand, which weighs down upon the whole of Latin America, and on the other of the hope roused in the hearts of the peoples of this continent by the heroic liberation of the Cuban people under the leadership of Fidel Castro."[65] In fact, historian Francisca de Haan has argued that the fact that the CLAM is often designated as the first such meeting, despite the fact that a similar congress was held in Brazil in 1954, reflects the sense that the Cuban Revolution had inaugurated a new era in Latin America. Efforts to designate the 1959 Congress as the first of its kind, de Haan argues, paid homage to the Cuban Revolution, "projecting it as the mother of leftist women's political activism throughout the Latin American continent [after] 1959," and made manifest "the WIDF's support for the political and revolutionary activism of women in Latin America after the victorious revolution in Cuba."[66]

The inspirational presence of Cuban women who had fought in the revolutionary war, rather than remaining in the rearguard, also deeply impacted the way some women on the left conceptualized gendered forms of political agency. As Adriana Valobra argues, interacting with women who had participated as combatants in the Cuban Revolution without being "masculinized" or renouncing their roles as wives and mothers disrupted traditionally binary models on the Argentine left regarding the masculinization of revolution and the preferred role of women in the rearguard. The new image of the *guerrillera* "raised the possibility of combining maternity and armed struggle." This model inaugurated a conflict and debate over gender and armed struggle that would persist in the region throughout the 1960s and 1970s.[67]

[65] WIDF, *World Congress of Women* (Berlin, 1963), 15.
[66] De Haan, "La Federación Democrática Internacional de Mujeres," 37.
[67] Valobra, "Mujeres-sombra," 10–12, quote p. 12.

THE CLAM AND THE FORMATION OF THE FMC

The CLAM established links between Cuban delegates and leftist women from throughout Latin America, as well as some delegates from Europe and a handful of delegates from the Soviet Union. For the most prominent women leaders of the Marxist left, this was not a new experience. For example, María Argüelles – veteran of the PSP, the FDMC, and the PSP-affiliated racial justice group Comité por Integración Racial (Committee for Racial Integration) – had attended the WIDF congress in Budapest in 1948. The FDMC leader Candelaria Rodríguez (who joined the planning meetings in Havana but not the delegation) had taken part in a WIDF fact-finding mission to North Korea in 1951 and had attended the 1954 Latin American women's congress in Rio de Janeiro.

For the women who came from the ranks of the 26th of July Movement or other groups, however, this was a novel experience. As Espín subsequently noted, the CLAM "helped us establish relations with many women and revolutionary organizations across Latin America and even from countries in Europe and Asia ... We made our first contact there with women from the socialist countries."[68] These encounters also took place during related travel before and after the Congress. For example, in August 1959, Vilma Espín and other members of the Cuban delegation traveled to Chile to attend the second planning meeting for the upcoming CLAM. While there, Espín and the elderly Cuban PSP member Clementina Serra toured a working-class *población* (shanty town) on the industrial outskirts of Santiago, meeting with some 200 women from the local neighborhood association.[69] After the CLAM a small group of Cuban delegates, mostly from the prerevolutionary Communist Party, traveled for several months throughout Argentina, Uruguay, Brazil, and Chile, where they met with women union leaders and their counterparts from local chapters of the WIDF.[70]

After returning to Cuba, some of the Cuban delegates to the CLAM hoped to establish a more permanent organization to reflect and

---

[68] Espín, et al., *Women in Cuba*, 220–21.

[69] "Vilma Espín con los pobres de Chile," *Unidad Femenina*, ca. October 1959 (date illegible), 14–15.

[70] Ranking Communist Party member Elena Gil described this in her unpublished memoir, "Apuntes." Other women traveling with Serra included Elena Gil, Electra Fernández, Gisela Sarmiento, and Lía de la Torriente. See Gil, "Apuntes," 99. Serra describes traveling around Latin America for four months "in preparation" for the event, but it was likely after, as described by Elena Gil. See the Gil interview in Margaret Randall, *Cuban Women Now* (Toronto: Women's Press, 1975 [1974]), 122.

implement the CLAM's goals. This may not have been a uniquely Cuban initiative; apparently many delegates to the CLAM had wanted to continue their respective delegations in a more permanent organizational form, hoping to reconvene annually or bi-annually.[71] In mid-January, Espín emitted a public call for participation in a meeting to discuss "the structure and program" that should be adopted by the permanent version of the CLAM delegation, especially requesting the continued participation of those who had been involved in the original planning meetings of fall 1959.[72]

These planning meetings resulted in the founding in March 1960 of the short-lived group called the CMCLAL. This group formed the skeletal structure for what would become the Federation of Cuban Women, which formed three months later.[73] According to Asela de los Santos, the executive committee of the CMCLAL intentionally drew on women from different political backgrounds, just as the delegation to the Chilean Congress had. The president was Vilma Espín of the 26th of July Movement; vice presidents were the 1930s anti-Machado activist Delia Echevarría, PSP member Elsa Gutiérrez, and Lula Hortsman of the pro-revolutionary Catholic group Con la Cruz y con la Patria.[74]

The stated goal of the CMCLAL was to disseminate and implement the accords of the CLAM and to continue to forge links of solidarity between Cuban women and others throughout the region. For example, Havana's March 1960 Women's Day celebrations were one of the CMCLAL's first major efforts. The group interpreted this as a day for showing solidarity with women around the world.[75] It serendipitously coincided with the Week of Solidarity with Latin American Countries, thus permitting combined celebration of the CMCLAL and women delegates from Latin America.[76] The CMCLAL also organized support efforts after the massive Chilean earthquake of May 1960. Thus the women who were loosely grouped first in the CMCLAL attempted to reinforce the networks with their regional counterparts first established in Chile in 1959.

[71] "Congreso," *Revolución*, December 17, 1959, 1, 16.
[72] "Convocan delegadas al Congreso de Mujeres," *Revolución*, January 18, 1960, 11.
[73] Espín et al., *Women in Cuba*, 108–12, 196–200, 217–23.
[74] Espín et al., *Women in Cuba*, 111.
[75] Ferrer and Aguilar Ayerra, *El fuego de la libertad*, 482.
[76] "16 organizaciones integran el Comité 'Pro Cincuenta Aniversario del 8 de Marzo,'" *Unidad Femenina, Suplemento gráfico* (March 1960): 2–4.

Throughout the spring of 1960 the CMCLAL also began to take on additional local tasks directed toward women's uplift and political mobilization, anticipating some of the future functions of the FMC. For example, due to fears of an impending invasion, the CMCLAL prioritized holding emergency medical classes to teach women to serve as paramedics. The group also began to set up small training schools, including sewing classes, as a means of training women without skills, especially poor rural women. The CMCLAL also responded to the growing atmosphere of intense mobilization, taking on an increasingly political role as opposition to the revolution grew. As demonstrations began to spread across the country, pro-revolutionary women held counterdemonstrations in response, physically confronting the growing number of street protests by Catholic women or other women critical of the revolution's policies. This became one of the tasks of the nascent CMCLAL.[77]

Throughout the spring of 1960 the group had begun to institutionalize many of the activities that had heretofore been carried out in a scattered and sporadic way by women affiliated with the 26th of July and the UFR. By April of 1960 the CMCLAL sought to make its organizational structure more permanent, issuing a call for an assembly to establish a provincial committee for Havana. It invited all existing members of the CMCLAL, as well as delegates from women's organizations and women's sections of existing organizations in every municipality of the province.[78] By the summer of 1960 Vilma Espín was presiding over a formally structured women's organization that extended across the country. In August 1960, with Fidel Castro's blessing, this group was rechristened the Federation of Cuban Women. As Espín noted subsequently, "When the federation was formally constituted on August 23, 1960, it had in reality already existed for some time."[79] The women given initial leadership positions within the FMC closely reflected the composition of the delegation to the CLAM.

Although the FMC's name removed any reference to the transnational, "Latin Americanist" origins of the organization, the CLAM Congress of 1959 nevertheless left a lasting legacy within the FMC. According to FMC leaders Yolanda Ferrer and Carolina Aguilar, the Congress in Chile was the first time most Cuban women activists had held forth on an international stage, and it served as a kind of template for their subsequent presentations on behalf of the FMC "in different tribunes, for more than

---

[77] Espín et al., *Women in Cuba*, 221.   [78] *Noticias de Hoy*, April 22, 1960, 6.
[79] Espín et al., *Women in Cuba*, 223.

half a century, conveying our message of advances on the road toward equality of rights, opportunities, and possibilities... The invaluable experiences acquired in the exchanges and congressional activities, and concepts expressed by the president ... Eugenie Cotton [and other speakers]" gave the CLAM "a transcendent importance for the Cubans, who took many of these lived experiences into account in the [subsequent] construction of the organizational and programmatic bases of the FMC."[80]

The CLAM was also foundational in establishing what Ferrer and Aguilar argue was one of Vilma Espín's long-term priorities: establishing horizontal relations with progressive and revolutionary women's organizations throughout Latin America and the Caribbean, and, more gradually, with women's organizations in the socialist bloc and the former colonial world.[81] We see this impetus reflected, for example, in the Congreso de Mujeres de Toda América (Women's Congress of the Americas), held in Havana in January 1963, which was a successor congress to the CLAM, first proposed by the Cuban delegation at the 1959 CLAM.[82]

In fact, although rarely analyzed as such, the FMC was an internationalist organization and Espín was an internationalist leader. Throughout the 1960s and 1970s, we see this internationalist impulse in various FMC expressions of solidarity with national liberation movements, including voluntary labor campaigns held to benefit Vietnam, Cambodia, and Laos, and FMC study groups devoted to global women's movements. Espín herself apparently selected a group of women who traveled to Vietnam with a brigade of hundreds of Cuban construction workers. She also supervised the creation of a joint FMC-Army unit of women volunteers who traveled to Angola in 1976, eventually forming a female anti-aerial artillery regiment that engaged in combat in the final battles between Cuban, Angolan, and South African forces.[83] If Cuban internationalism should be understood as a "defining element" of the revolution, crucial to the production of internal socialist consciousness as well as foreign-policy goals, then it is important to recognize that the FMC participated actively in such projects.[84]

[80] Ferrer and Aguilar Ayerra, *El fuego de la libertad*, 481.
[81] Ferrer and Aguilar Ayerra, *El fuego de la libertad*, 481–84.
[82] Prensa Latina, "Apoyo a la revolución cubana."
[83] Ferrer and Aguilar Ayerra, *El fuego de la libertad*, 485–87; Espín et al., *Women in Cuba*, 285, 287.
[84] Isaac Saney, "Homeland of Humanity: Internationalism within the Cuban Revolution," *Latin American Perspectives* 36, no. 1 (2009): 111–23, quote p. 112.

We also see this internationalist impulse in the FMC's long-term, active engagement within the WIDF, to which the FMC became an affiliate and in which Vilma Espín served as vice president after 1965.[85] Within the WIDF, Espín – like some other women leaders from the decolonizing world – worked to convince the organization that its historical focus on peace, derived from the foreign-policy goals of the Soviet Union, did not mesh with the reality in Latin America, which required more militant and aggressive forms of self-defense against imperialism. In 1978, the FMC founded a Regional Center of the WIDF in Havana, where hundreds of leaders from Latin American and Caribbean women's organizations were trained for international leadership roles in the late 1970s and 1980s.[86] After the collapse of the Soviet Union, which had been the WIDF's largest source of financial support, Espín played an important role in mobilizing members to work for the organization's survival, although it never regained its prominence.[87]

The FMC also actively engaged with the United Nations, as Candace Johnson has demonstrated, partly in order to reinforce domestic priorities that could be buttressed by global human-rights discourse. In particular, after the collapse of the Soviet Union, the FMC sought to protect Cuba's relatively strong indicators in reproductive rights and maternal health, partly by appealing to UN goals. It also sought to fortify UN initiatives relating to women and children. Cuba was the first country to sign the UN's Convention on the Elimination of all Forms of Discrimination against Women in 1979 and it also signed the UN Convention on the Rights of the Child (1989). In its statements to the UN Economic and Social Council, the FMC has strongly argued for the centrality of social rights to human rights – for example, arguing that the provision of free and universal health and education should be considered an indication of human-rights attainments. In general, as Johnson shows, the FMC has used its relationship with the UN strategically, to forge a broader definition of global human rights and also to seek points of confluence between global human-rights discourse and socialist or revolutionary goals. She argues persuasively, "Although the FMC might advocate feminist policies

---

[85] De Haan, "La Federación Democrática Internacional de Mujeres," 37.

[86] Ferrer and Aguilar Ayerra, *El fuego de la libertad*, 485, 490. Kirsten Ghodsee writes that the purpose of this center was "to train Latin American women on how to represent their countries at the United Nations," in response to the dearth of women-headed delegations to the 1975 UN Conference in Mexico City. Ghodsee, "Socialist Internationalism and State Feminism," 118.

[87] Ferrer and Aguilar Ayerra, *El fuego de la libertad*, 491.

and goals, but not identify itself as a feminist organization, there is no ambiguity in its human rights orientation."[88]

In considering the FMC's longer trajectory of internationalism, it makes sense to conceptualize the CLAM as a foundational event in the history of Cuba's postrevolutionary state feminism, establishing bases for those subsequent transnational efforts. The history of Cuba's delegation to the Congress of Latin American Women in Chile illuminates the diverse political tendencies and grassroots activism that eventually congealed in the CMCLAL and FMC, and thus deepens our understanding of the revolution's efforts to incorporate and liberate women. Recovering this example of women's transnational activism helps us rethink the prevalent scholarly emphasis on the Cuban national leadership, highlighting instead the connections among lesser-known actors and among women activists of different political stripes. In contrast to common depictions of the FMC as merely a top-down mass organization established by the revolutionary leadership to ensure women's support, or as an organic outgrowth of the 26th of July Movement's growing belief in women's equality and liberation, the history of the 1959 Congress of Latin American Women and its ramifications illuminates the complex transnational, left-feminist, and politically plural origins of the FMC.

[88] Candace Johnson, "Framing for Change: Social Policy, the State, and the Federación de Mujeres Cubanas," *Cuban Studies* 42 (2011): 35–51, quote p. 45.

7

Revolutionaries without Revolution

Regional Experiences in the Forging of a Radical Political Culture in the Southern Cone of South America (1966–1976)

Aldo Marchesi

Why did so many young activists from very different political traditions undergo a common process of radicalization during the 1960s in the Southern Cone of South America? A myriad of people coming from different backgrounds – Catholic activism, pro-Soviet communism, socialism, Trotskyism, anarchism, national populist traditions, and technocratic developmentalism – found in the New Left a "movement of movements" with new repertoires of contention and a tool for political mobilization more effective than old methods of traditional politics. Perhaps this was the most singular fact of the late 1960s in the Southern Cone: the emergence of a new movement that incorporated different traditions into a new political project. This movement was based on a Latin Americanist consciousness, the combination of national liberation and socialism as a single strategy, and the idea of armed struggle as the way to achieve that goal. Although in each country activists created local political organizations that assumed these perspectives, the process of their creation and development took place through an important regional dialogue.

Academic explanations, written mostly by sociologists under the influence of Marxist or functionalist structuralism during the 1970s, viewed the emergence of the New Left as just one more element in the rise of social unrest, radicalization, and the political polarization of the popular and middle sectors. They explained it as a reflection of the crisis of the import-substitution industrialization models that had helped to achieve important levels of social welfare within urban areas. These approaches correctly diagnosed the problems that Southern Cone governments faced due to the regressive economic adjustments that reduced the real incomes of middle sectors and workers in the 1960s, and showed how those changes had led to the establishment of a new kind of authoritarianism. Authoritarian reactions of the 1960s and 1970s, usually spearheaded by the military, promoted a conservative modernization model with a strongly regressive character. However, these studies offered few insights to understand the specifics of the New-Left protest that emerged during that period.[1]

In the 1980s and 1990s, a greater scholarly interest in politics and culture led to more attention being paid to the ideas of these movements. Some explanations emphasized the role of ideology in the emergence of the New Left.[2] Yet the adoption of such approaches often meant neglecting the structural, material, and social aspects of this history. These approaches conceived of ideas as an autonomous field with little link to economic and social processes. Perhaps the most prevalent argument was that ideology itself was the key factor in explaining leftist political radicalization. However, although in the late 1960s many leftist militants considered different forms of Marxism vital to their political identity, ideology did not work as a cohesive tool to promote radicalization, and did not facilitate the convergence of the diverse and even contradictory traditions within the New Left. Sometimes the disparate nature of the ideological traditions from which these different groups came inhibited their unification. Other scholars cited the impact of the Cuban Revolution as the key factor to explain the rise of the New-Left groups that took up guerrilla warfare. Although some challenged the rural *foquista* strategy promoted by Che Guevara, in which a small group of guerrillas sparked a revolution, all were extremely loyal to Cuba and recognized it as the vanguard of the Latin American revolution.

In this chapter I use the category of political culture to propose an alternative explanation of how these militants converged during the 1960s. Here I use the term "political culture" to include diverse aspects including ideology, morals, sentiments, class subjectivity, historical experience, and art, which, at the same time, cannot be reduced to just one of these individualized categories. I will examine the transnational militant political culture that emerged from the constriction of political

---

[1] For a comprehensive interpretation, see David Collier, ed., *The New Authoritarianism in Latin America* (Princeton, NJ: Princeton University Press, 1979); Guillermo O'Donnell, *Contrapuntos: Ensayos escogidos sobre autoritarismo y democratización* (Buenos Aires: Paidós, 1997).

[2] As an example see Hugo Vezzetti, *Sobre la violencia revolucionaria: Memorias y olvidos* (Buenos Aires: Siglo XXI, 2009).

space, socioeconomic crisis, and increased social polarization during the late 1960s and early 1970s in the Southern Cone. I argue that leftist political violence cannot be explained merely as a structural response to political and economic constraints; it was also a result of contingent cultural definitions articulated by a new political generation of activists inspired by the emergence of an intellectual New Left and new cultural attitudes about youth rebellion held by middle-class sectors. By tracking the historical genesis of the political ideas, clandestine practices, cultural affinities, and strong emotions that constituted this political culture, the chapter seeks to explain how this political generation, which emerged from the increased social mobilization of the 1960s, ultimately embraced guerrilla war as the sole means to achieve social change in their countries in the early 1970s.

This political culture was not merely the result of preformed ideas or ideologies. Rather, it resulted from the interaction of previously held ideas and the political circumstances that these activists had to face. It was in that process that activists gradually developed a unique political culture, which they built in the course of the regional exchanges. The uncertain historical contingency of local processes would often lead them to places that would have been inconceivable in the mid-1960s.

In my book *Latin America's Radical Left: Rebellion and Cold War in the Global 1960s*, I showed how the region's political dynamics gradually forged a shared experience among the different leftist organizations that emerged into public life in the mid-1960s and became key actors in the processes that preceded the consolidation of authoritarianism in the Southern Cone. The region was a laboratory where activists assessed each local event and drew conclusions that would influence the coming struggles. Regional dynamics also helped postpone national defeats. Regional exile was not seen as traditional exile but as a continuation of national struggles. As long as there were countries in the region that provided a safe place to retreat to, there could still be hope for a revolution. This situation changed radically after the 1976 coup in Argentina, as authoritarian regimes had spread across the region and the possibilities for organizing strategic rearguard forces were greatly limited. Leftist militants constructed a shared understanding of Latin Americanism that denied the viability of liberal democracy within a regional context of economic underdevelopment and Cold War. They promoted violent revolutionary struggle based on a conception of morality in which "politics were understood in terms of good and evil, social change was reduced to an aspect of revolutionary will, and political commitment was associated with individual sacrifice."[3] This political culture was built in dialogue with the expectations that the Cuban Revolution raised in the Southern Cone.

This political culture also expressed a common generational sensitivity toward politics, which was developed in dialogue with two global processes of the 1960s: the emergence of the "New Left" in the world and the new meanings that being young acquired among middle-class and popular sectors. The elements of this political culture can be briefly described as follows: an idea of transnational community that combined Latin Americanism and internationalism; a set of ideas initially critical of the legalism and reformist strategies of the traditional left; and, lastly, a notion of the model activist associated with the idealized figures of the revolutionary soldier and the proletarian. Below I explore these three features of this transnational political culture. To illustrate, each section begins with an account of an individual experience that reveals the contingency and uncertainty in which these processes of cultural construction developed.

A TRANSNATIONAL COMMUNITY: SOUTHERN CONE ACTIVISTS BETWEEN INTERNATIONALISM AND LATIN AMERICANISM

Svaente Graende was a young forestry technician from Sweden who came to Latin America to participate in a foreign cooperation project. In 1972, at the age of twenty-five, he decided to go work in the Panguipulli forestry complex in southern Chile. There he came into contact with a mobilized peasant population and, inspired by their actions, joined the Movimiento de Izquierda Revolucionaria (Revolutionary Left Movement, MIR). After the 1973 coup, a group of forty MIR activists attacked a police post in the region. The action failed, and the activists dispersed in an attempt to avoid persecution. A group of eleven activists soon contacted Graende, and together they tried to carry out various actions throughout the Chilean Andes until military actions made it impossible to continue. Five survivors decided to cross the Andes into Argentina. Graende set up base in Buenos Aires for four months. There he taught classes in Marxism along with the other four members of the group. After a trip back to Sweden to visit his sick father, he returned and decided to join the "Monte Rosa Jiménez"

---

[3] Aldo Marchesi, *Latin America's Radical Left: Rebellion and Cold War in the Global 1960s* (New York: Cambridge University Press, 2018), 14.

company, which the guerrilla group known as the Partido Revolucionario de los Trabajadores–Ejército Revolucionario del Pueblo (Revolutionary Workers' Party–People's Revolutionary Army, PRT-ERP) was forming in Tucumán, a province north of Buenos Aires. On October 14, 1975, Graende died during an ambush carried out by the Argentine army.[4]

Graende's story is one of the more extreme examples of activists who were involved in projects unrelated to their countries of origin. These involvements were seen by armed groups as "examples of proletarian internationalism."[5] However, the evolving concepts used by these organizations, as well as the various attitudes toward international matters, cannot be reduced to the classical Marxist concept of internationalism. Multiple identities coexisted throughout the period, and there were many "imagined communities" with respect to which the activists developed a sense of belonging. Key imaginaries included nationalism, the Southern Cone (although never explicitly conceptualized as an *ism*), Latin Americanism, Third-Worldism, and proletarian internationalism.[6]

The reworking of certain nationalist positions from a leftist perspective had a strong impact on the formation of the New Lefts in Argentina and Uruguay.[7] The intellectual development of the national left, which originated with Trotskyism and gradually permeated other political sectors, contributed to a reconsideration of the national question. In Argentina and Uruguay this meant a strong reassertion of the importance of the nineteenth-century wars of independence on the part of these countries' armed groups, who went as far as presenting their own struggle as a continuation of those wars. Although such symbolic appeals to the national past do not appear to have been as important in Chile – perhaps due to the characteristics of its political history in the nineteenth century – the most radical version of dependency theory also contributed to the growth of a national liberation discourse there.

Most of these groups initially adhered to a version of nationalism that overlapped with the Latin Americanism that predated the Cuban Revolution. In the 1950s some of the activists who would later join armed groups already shared longstanding notions of Latin Americanism, such as Víctor Raúl Haya de la Torre's Indo-Americanism, which the Santucho

---

[4] For details see "Chile: La guerrilla de Panguipulli," *Estrella Roja* 71 (March 14, 1976): 4–6, 16.

[5] Ibid.

[6] For the concept of imagined communities see Benedict Anderson, *Imagined Communities: Reflections on the Origin and Spread of Nationalism* (London: Verso, 1983).

[7] Marchesi, *Latin America's Radical Left*, chapters 1–2.

family advocated in northern Argentina in the late 1950s.[8] Others took up these legacies and reinterpreted them, proposing a specific role for Latin America in the context of the Cold War. Examples included the "third alternative" (to the United States and Soviet Union) proposed by the Uruguayan magazine *Marcha* and Uruguay's student movement, and the Latin Americanist and pro-Yugoslavian positions of some Chilean Socialists. These positions were present in various ways at the inception of the region's armed organizations.

Initially, the Cuban Revolution was read as the maximum embodiment of that Latin Americanist program. The phrase "first free territory of America," with which the vast majority of the revolutionary government's early speeches and declarations ended, evidenced its centrality. Cuba would promote revolutionary initiatives for Latin America, ranging from cultural production to support for guerrilla groups. From the Punta del Este conference in 1961 to the creation of the Organización Latinoamericana de Solidaridad (Latin American Solidarity Organization, OLAS) in 1967, this aim of serving as an example for other revolutionary projects grew in importance, reaching its highest point in 1967 with Che Guevara's Bolivia campaign and the proposal to establish a centralized command for Latin America's revolution.

However, Cuba's Latin Americanist orientation was at odds with other international alignments, and this tension influenced Southern Cone activists. Throughout the 1960s two foreign-policy approaches coexisted in revolutionary Cuba: on one hand, a complex and increasingly close relationship with the Soviet Union, and on the other, the country's efforts to play a guiding role in Latin America and the rest of the Third World. Cuba was a nerve center of East–West and North–South tensions. All of this shaped the definitions adopted by Southern Cone activists. Although most activists had been highly critical of the Soviet Union's role in the Cold War (its invasions of Hungary and Czechoslovakia, its lack of support to national liberation movements, etc.), Cuba's growing relationship with the USSR led many to more moderate positions. By the mid-1970s many leftists would even consider themselves part of the international Communist movement. It was in that context that the concept of proletarian internationalism emerged more explicitly in these organizations. For some organizations this discourse had been present earlier, as in the case of the Trotskyist sectors of the PRT. But until the late 1960s a Latin Americanist position had prevailed, as was most evident in the OLAS.

[8] Some of them were later very important in the creation of the PRT-ERP.

While the coming together of the region's activists appeared to be justified by these theoretical frameworks, in practice such encounters seemed to have much more to do with the region's political dynamics than with any preheld ideas. The decision to participate in actions in other countries was generally linked to the impossibility of returning to one's place of origin due to the advancing repression or the need to prepare a more organized return. When Argentine activists associated with revolutionary Peronist sectors participated in the forming of the Movimiento de Liberación Nacional Tupamaros (Tupamaros National Liberation Movement, MLN-T) in Uruguay, they did so because conditions were not ripe for their return to Argentina. When a group of Brazilian activists joined the Chilean MIR, they did so because they had come to accept that revolutionary projects were not viable in Brazil at that time. In Argentina, the Chilean, Uruguayan, and Bolivian activists who participated in PRT-ERP actions did so with the idea of returning to their countries of origin. These experiences were even viewed as internships of sorts, which prepared the activists for future return operations. In most cases activists' participation in revolutionary actions in other countries was not the result of a voluntary decision, but was rather due to the fact that they had been forced to flee their own countries.[9]

The regional political process itself and the exile experience in neighboring countries were much more instrumental in fueling a transnational perspective than any views on supranational political and cultural identities that may have been previously held by these activists. The need to act jointly was reinforced by the realization that the rise of authoritarianism was a regional phenomenon. Conservative sectors saw the experiences of neighboring countries as examples to follow, and national police and military forces developed similar repressive and counterinsurgency methods and coordinated their implementation under the auspices of the inter-American system of the Organization of American States. As MIR activist Bautista Van Schouwen said in 1971, the continental coordination of "counter-revolutionary reaction" pushed revolutionaries into joining together.[10]

Despite the intention of expanding coordination efforts to other countries of Latin America, the Junta de Coordinación Revolucionaria

[9] The sole exception was the first incarnation of the National Liberation Army (ELN) in Bolivia, which was organized by Guevara and where his involvement alone was surely responsible for attracting a significant number of foreign activists.

[10] Quoted in Marchesi, *Latin America's Radical Left*, 128.

(Revolutionary Coordination Board, JCR) was limited to the Southern Cone, including Uruguay's Tupamaros, Chile's MIR, Argentina's PRT-ERP, and Bolivia's Ejército de Liberación Nacional (National Liberation Army, ELN). The JCR's formation was not attributable to a previously defined identity such as Latin Americanism. No such *ism* appears to have existed in the region before the 1970s. Rather, it was simply the realization of their common political contexts and a number of demographic similarities – including social background (a predominantly middle-class or skilled-worker membership), cultural traits, and age composition (young people predominating) – that drew these organizations together in a regional network. Continental discourse notwithstanding, the revolutionary practice was confined to the Southern Cone as a result of the restrictions on these groups' activities imposed by Cuba and the JCR's own limitations. The JCR's geographic limits suggest that activist exchanges were determined less by preconceived ideas than by the regional political process.

However, after the 1976 coup in Argentina, as Southern Cone activists left for countries outside the region and came into contact with guerrilla organizations in the Andes and Central America, they began to make connections between their experiences and those of the left in these other regions. These movements of people contributed to forging a common path for various left-wing organizations that, since the 1960s, had been gradually distancing themselves from the international experiences of Socialism, Communism, and Trotskyism, and which, as a result of their decision to take up arms and their close relationship with the Cuban Revolution, had been constructing a left delimited by the historically determined space of Latin America. In this sense, the experience of the Southern Cone armed left appears to be a stage in the construction of a left identified with the continent's history, devoid of universal aspirations, and which today plays a key role in Latin American politics.

The left's Latin Americanist and internationalist declarations were, however, taken seriously by the military forces of the region, which resuscitated the traditional conservative discourse that cast the left as a foreign influence, this time in a regional context. The target had shifted from the Soviet Union and Cuba to the neighboring countries. The most dramatic example of this is perhaps Bolivia. There the ELN – which had a markedly internationalist dimension that set it apart from other organizations, most likely stemming from Guevara's initial presence – defended its internationalism, while the military redirected its accusations of conspiracy toward bordering countries with whom Bolivia had long-running conflicts. As General René Barrientos said in 1968 in reference to the ELN's ties with Chilean activists, "Insurgency and treason go through Chile."[11]

Nationalist stances that ran counter to Latin Americanism emerged timidly within leftist organizations near the end of this period. Faced with national border conflicts, activists often held diverging views. For instance, in 1976 Bolivian ELN and Chilean MIR activists clashed over negotiations between their countries' dictatorships over Bolivia's access to the sea.[12] Uruguayans and Bolivians would also protest the excessive influence that the Argentine PRT-ERP wanted to exert over their organizations. These complaints seemed to revive certain national differences that had a long history in the national political cultures of the region. What is notable is that such differences became more acute in 1976 as the regional project started to fail.

IDEAS: FROM THE NEW TO THE OLD LEFT

Arnol Kremer was born in 1941 in the city of Zárate, in Buenos Aires province. He became politically active as he was finishing high school. He was one of the many young people who felt that the New Left spoke to them. This led him to join the group MIR Praxis, headed by Silvio Frondizi. In an interview, Kremer defined the MIR Praxis as a group with a "third international position," highly influenced by the ideas of Rosa Luxemburg. After this group split up he joined the Malena (Movimiento de Liberación Nacional, or National Liberation Movement) briefly. This was a short-lived group that had a strong impact on student and intellectual circles and which brought together Marxists, nationalist sectors of the Peronist left, and sectors that came from the Unión Cívica Radical (Radical Civic Union) party. In 1968, he joined the PRT, a group he defines as Trotskyist but which by that time had already gone through some changes. In the PRT he promoted the establishment of the Ejército Revolucionario del Pueblo (ERP). In the party he was involved in trade union activities, going by the underground name "Luis Mattini." As of 1972 he occupied a high-ranking leadership position within the organization. In 1976, Kremer was the only member of the political governing committee who survived the army's persecution. All the other members had been murdered in different military operations. As a result, he had to step in as general secretary. From 1977 to

---

[11] Quoted in ibid., 105.   [12] Ibid., 173.

1978, the remaining PRT members, who had survived repression and were living in exile, went through a profound crisis. As after previous defeats, one of the explanations given was a poor understanding of Marxist-Leninist theory. It was under these circumstances that Kremer's faction in the PRT began to place more stress on certain positions that Mario Roberto Santucho, the PRT general secretary killed in 1976, had been insisting on since 1975, namely on the need for a closer relationship with the international Communist movement, and to take the Soviet and Cuban view of international conflicts.[13] The experience of defeat also had an impact on the definitions adopted by the JCR in 1977.[14] Upon Kremer's return to Argentina after the dictatorship's 1983 fall, he joined the Argentine Communist Party for a brief period. Kremer is currently an independent left-wing activist and intellectual who identifies more closely with autonomous action and social movements.[15]

Kremer's story illustrates the ideological transformations that the groups of the New Left underwent in the 1960s and 1970s. Many of these groups went through a first period marked by an attempt to build an alternative to the traditional left, and a second period in which they returned to certain practices and discourses that were typical of what they had initially set out to combat.

The concept of "New Left" is elusive and has had a range of meanings both globally and in the region. In the recent literature on the 1960s these movements have been conceptualized as global forces associated with youth identities that made vague criticisms of the Cold War order based on cultural and ethical concerns.[16] Researchers tend to agree that in Latin

---

[13] This generated resistance within the party. See, for example, "Minuta sobre la situación del partido," in *El Topo Blindado* digital archive, http://eltopoblindado.com/opm-marxistas/partido-revolucionario-de-los-trabajadores-prt/prt-exilio/minuta-sobre-la-situacion-del-partido/ (accessed May 25, 2018).

[14] "Manifiesto JCR," *Che Guevara Magazine* no. 3 (October–December 1977): 18, Archivo de la Lucha Armada "David Cámpora," Archivo del Centro de Estudios Interdisciplinarios Uruguayos, Universidad de la República, Montevideo (hereafter ADLADC).

[15] The information on Arnol Kremer is taken from "Entrevista a Luis Mattini," Archivo de Historia Oral, Instituto de Investigaciones Gino Germani, Buenos Aires; Luis Mattini, *Hombres y mujeres del PRT-ERP* (Buenos Aires: Editorial de la Campana, 1995); "Entrevista a Luis Mattini," November 1, 2007, Argentina Indymedia, http://argentina.indymedia.org/news/2007/11/560696.php (accessed May 25, 2018).

[16] Jeremi Suri, *Power and Protest: Global Revolution and the Rise of Détente* (Cambridge, MA: Harvard University Press, 2005). For alternative views, see Greg Grandin, "H-Diplo Roundtables, Grandin on Jeremi Suri," https://networks.h-net.org/pdf-h-diplo-roundtable-grandin-suri (accessed May 25, 2018), and Giovanni Arrighi, Terence

America's case the New Left was more associated with political action than in other parts of the world, and that even where there were counter-cultural expressions, such expressions did not run counter to the political ideas of the left. Rather, most were conceived as part of a broader movement for change that had specific existential, cultural, and ethical dimensions, as well as political implications.[17] Moreover, some authors have noted that in Latin America the distances separating the new from the old were less pronounced than in other parts of the world, as there were continuities in terms of the political goals pursued.[18]

Among the groups studied here, there were three ways in which the rupture between the old and the new was manifested most explicitly: (1) The violent methods of political action adopted entailed a break with the electoral practices and concerns that had been the focus of the traditional left's activity, primarily in the 1950s; (2) the new groups initially exhibited a greater pluralism in political and ideological discussions, incorporating activists from a wide range of *isms* (socialism, Soviet communism, Trotskyism, Maoism) of the left and even others who came from traditions such as popular nationalist movements and Catholicism, an open attitude which stemmed largely from a democratizing reaction against the absence of discussion within traditional left-wing parties; (3) lastly, all of these organizations were highly critical of the international polarity imposed by the Cold War. These views, which took up certain issues that had been raised since the 1950s, entailed questioning the pro-Soviet positions held by the Communist parties and the majority sectors of the Socialist parties.

These initial elements of rupture were gradually altered by the changing political dynamics in the region and by the definitions that these organizations adopted in response. Most of these groups evolved from movements into parties, a process in which the early pluralism gave way to increasing homogenization shaped by ideological concerns. In the transition into

K. Hopkins, and Immanuel Wallerstein, *Movimientos antisistémicos* (Madrid: AKAL, 1999), chapter 5.

[17] María Cristina Tortti, *El "viejo" partido socialista y los orígenes de la "nueva" izquierda* (Buenos Aires: Prometeo, 2009); Eric Zolov, "Expanding Our Conceptual Horizons: The Shift from an Old to a New Left in Latin America," *A Contracorriente* 5, no. 2 (2008): 47–73; and Vania Markarián, *El 68 uruguayo: El movimiento estudiantil entre molotovs y música beat* (Quilmes: Universidad Nacional de Quilmes, 2012).

[18] Jeffrey Gould, "Solidarity under Siege: The Latin American Left, 1968," *American Historical Review* 114, no. 2 (2009): 348; Eduardo Weisz, *El PRT-ERP, nueva izquierda e izquierda tradicional* (Buenos Aires: Centro Cultural de la Cooperación, Ediciones del Instituto Movilizador de Fondos Cooperativos, 2004).

Leninist parties, the groups developed increasingly centralized structures, with fewer spaces for democratic discussion of ideas. These changes were connected with, and justified by, the decision to go underground, which objectively limited the possibilities for democratic debate. Operating underground also involved the party imposing various forms of control over its activists, which affected all aspects of everyday life, from sexual choices to the way activists dressed, their relationships, and so on.

As military repression escalated in magnitude and intensity, these groups tended to retreat into themselves, become more hostile to internal differences, and emphasize the role played by ideology in shaping activists in the face of adverse situations. Ideology became a panacea that would solve all the problems they faced. When many of these organizations suffered major defeats, the leading explanation given was their poor understanding of Marxism-Leninism. The solution proffered was to focus more intently on studying this theory, which they believed had the capacity to shed light on reality. As the activists of the Bolivian ELN said when they decided to become the Partido Revolucionario de los Trabajadores–Bolivia (Bolivian Revolutionary Workers' Party, PRT-B), correctly incorporating Marxism-Leninism could even be an ecstatic experience:

> We are ecstatic because we have, for the time being, achieved the synthesis of theory and practice, and we are united and determined to further that synthesis with our minds focused on our people, our working class, and our first commander, and all the martyrs who have sacrificed themselves to make our dreams come true, to liberate our peoples and build socialism.[19]

The same thing happened at an individual level. As the methods of torture were systematized, more widely used, and began targeting more and more activists, ideological weakness was the explanation given for the behavior of anyone who broke under torture.[20]

Along with the underground nature of their activities and the growing authoritarianism, there were other factors that favored ideological homogenization among Southern Cone activists. On one hand, the Cuban Communist Party's gradual shift toward the sphere of Soviet influence was imitated by some Southern Cone activists who, realizing the importance that Cuba had as a rearguard base for Latin American revolutionary forces, tried to adapt their discourse and definitions to the pro-Soviet

---

[19] ELN Bolivia, "Nace el PRT de Bolivia" (April 6, 1975), ADLADC.
[20] Marchesi, *Latin America's Radical Left*, chapter 3.

climate that prevailed in Cuba in the mid-1970s. This shift somewhat jeopardized the open atmosphere for debate that had been common in Cuba in the late 1960s and which had influenced the emergence of the new Southern Cone left. On the other hand, Latin America's version of Althusserian Marxism offered instruments for a New Left that considered itself "weak" in ideological terms compared to the Communist tradition, and which found in these texts an orthodoxy about the role of ideological struggle that it could embrace.[21]

In sum, what initially emerged as a response to the more dogmatic approaches of the Cold War left was gradually transformed by regional and global dynamics and began to assume characteristics associated with the old Communist parties. Among these were an excessively structured and dogmatic view of ideology and an increasing alignment with the international Communist movement. This process was especially pronounced in the wake of a series of defeats suffered by the region's armed groups in the second half of the 1970s.

THE IDEAL REVOLUTIONARY: FROM ACTIVISTS TO SOLDIERS

Héctor Hernán González Osorio was twenty-two years old when he joined the MIR in 1970.[22] He had just earned a degree in psychology from the University of Chile. In the MIR he took on increasingly heavy responsibilities, focusing on "*poblaciones*" (villages) and trade union work. In 1974, as the first MIR leaders were captured by the repressive forces, González became a member of the central committee. That same year he was captured by the Dirección de Inteligencia Nacional (National Intelligence Directorate, DINA). In late 1974, he was separated from the other MIR activists who were in jail, most of whom would later be disappeared. The DINA decided to put him with a group of no more than ten prisoners in Villa Grimaldi for about five months. There the

---

[21] For the influence of Althusserianism in Latin America see Marta Harnecker, *Los conceptos elementales del materialismo histórico (versión corregida y ampliada)* (Mexico City: Siglo XXI, 1985). See also Marchesi, *Latin America's Radical Left*, chapter 3.

[22] Information in this and the following paragraph is drawn from María Olga Ruiz, "Historias y memorias de traición: Reflexiones en torno a la conferencia de prensa de los cuatro miristas de 1975," in *Recordar para pensar: Memoria para la democracia. La elaboración del pasado reciente en el Cono Sur de América Latina*, ed. Tania Medalla, Alondra Peirano, Olga Ruiz, and Regine Walch (Santiago de Chile: Ediciones Boll Cono Sur, 2010), 257–58.

activists were held in chains, harshly beaten, and subjected to various forms of torture. In January 1975, González was taken to see his wife. The DINA's Lieutenant Pedro Espinoza informed González in front of his wife that, since he was the highest-ranking member of the MIR in prison at that time, he would have to make a public statement calling on his party to surrender. González recalls that given the organization's devastating outlook, "We began to consider the absurd idea of using the statement to send a message to the party about how things really were, which were very different from the triumphalist image reflected in our own internal communications drafted outside prison." Seven prisoners were put in a small room next to the torture room and tasked with drafting the statement, which was then checked by Captain Miguel Krasnoff, a member of the DINA, who changed the text to convey false information regarding the fate of some murdered and disappeared activists. González was chosen to read the text before a portable film camera. The filmed statement was then broadcast by the media. In the statement, they "called on the MIR to put down their weapons and put an end to what they described as a futile and suicidal attempt to oppose the Military Junta through underground armed actions."

Two days later, the MIR issued a death sentence against the seven activists who had been involved in writing the statement. Over the coming months, the other MIR members who were in prison shunned them, accusing them of betrayal. In September 1975, González was released along with Hernán Carrasco and Humberto Menanteaux, two of the other prisoners who had participated in the statement. They all tried to leave the country but found it extremely difficult to do so: "We were told that no country would give us a visa because they couldn't guarantee our safety as a result of the MIR's death sentence." In the end, González obtained a work visa from Spain. Carrasco and Menanteaux tried to contact the MIR again to provide information on the DINA but were recaptured in the process and killed by military forces. González's ordeal continued in exile. In Spain he tried to contact the MIR and was turned away. He requested asylum in Geneva but the Chilean exile community pressured Switzerland into denying his request. He was granted asylum in Belgium but a left-wing Belgian newspaper mistakenly included him in a list of DINA torturers. He returned to Geneva, where Chilean refugees demanded that he be thrown out of the university. In 1989, the Chilean Vicariate of Solidarity offered him the possibility of telling his story. Since the 1990s, González has been a key witness in several trials for human rights abuses.

The complicated and tragic story of Hernán González evidences the weaknesses of the activist model that was constructed by the armed groups of the Southern Cone. González's case is an example of the rigid boundaries that delimited the model of activism to be followed and the consequences of trespassing such limits.

The works of Ana Longoni, Vera Carnovale, and Hugo Vezzetti on Argentina have explored the principles on which these models of activism were founded. Self-sacrifice, or placing the good of the organization completely above one's own interest, meant taking up old traditions that could be associated with Christianity and Jacobinism, as well as with the experience of the Communist world.[23] These authors also observe how the imaginary of war influenced activists' perception of their own political practice, replacing the figure of the political activist with that of a revolutionary armed soldier. According to Carnovale, this shift appears to have been an intentional consequence of an ideological and ethical paradigm that was constructed very early on and which was faithfully observed throughout this period. Longoni posits that it was the result of a sectarian attitude based on the conviction that the revolutionary cause would succeed, which precluded an understanding of the adversity of their political situation. Vezzetti has a similar argument, but he emphasizes how the imaginary of war contributed to three myths that were common among revolutionaries: the political myth (that violence exacerbates contradictions), the epistemological myth (that violence reveals power relations), and the moral myth (that violence leads individuals to action).

With some nuances and differences in emphasis, the aspects noted by these three authors are found in all the organizations examined in this chapter. These studies correctly identify the elements upon which a specific "structure of feeling" was built among activists in these armed organizations.[24] However, they do not explain how these elements were configured during the historical process studied here. How were these elements transformed over this period? And what interaction existed between these elements and state repression?

---

[23] Ana Longoni, *Traiciones: La figura del traidor en los relatos acerca de los sobrevivientes de la represión* (Buenos Aires: Grupo Editorial Norma, 2007); Vera Carnovale, *Los combatientes: Historia del PRT-ERP* (Buenos Aires: Siglo XXI, 2011); Vezzetti, *Sobre la violencia revolucionaria*. Although in fact this ethos could be linked to secular nationalism and military organizations of all kinds, they do not draw this comparison.

[24] On "structures of feeling" see Raymond Williams, *Marxism and Literature* (Oxford: Oxford University Press, 1977), 128–36.

In 1968, after Guevara's death, activism had already been linked to the characteristics of a revolutionary soldier. Guevara's death profoundly impacted the Southern Cone and in particular its new political generation, which in the late 1960s was looking for new forms of political action that would break with past practices. The texts and life of Guevara had left a legacy that combined the elements mentioned by the above authors. The unconditional commitment to the revolutionary cause entailed waging a war and joining a revolutionary army. Politics meant taking up arms. Death was always a possibility, as Guevara himself said in his 1966 message to the Tricontinental, which became his political testament.[25] But at the same time a revolutionary's death played an exemplifying role, as it would lead others to join the revolution.

While these ideas of Guevara were familiar to Southern Cone activists by late 1967, the ways in which they were interpreted changed over time. None of the leftist organizations would have the same notion of activism in 1975 as they had in 1968. They interpreted Guevara's death in the context of a Southern Cone where authoritarian practices were advancing but had not yet reached a significant level of repression.[26] While most Southern Cone groups were thinking of taking up arms, there was still a huge distance between the Spartan model proposed by Guevara and the reality of these activists, who lived primarily in cities, were connected with different urban social struggles, and were immersed in urban cultures that were radically different from the isolation imposed by Guevara's rural guerrilla model.

Moreover, while states were committing substantial human rights abuses in interrogations and in practices aimed at discouraging public mobilizations, resulting in several deaths, the practice of systematic political assassination was still limited. In this sense, Guevara's model was interpreted with a relative flexibility by the young people who started to join these organizations in the years 1968 and 1969. Doing so entailed renouncing certain individualistic values of capitalist society. But this approach had little to do with the military discipline of a professional army. The title of a book on this subject by historian Vania Markarián, *Uruguay's 1968: The Student Movement Amidst Molotov Cocktails and Beat Music*, illustrates how many students – including some who by the end of 1968 would be joining the MLN-T – saw no conflict between the hedonism of the global counterculture and Guevara's ideas.[27] However,

---

[25] Ernesto Guevara, "A crear muchos Vietnam," *Punto Final* no. 27 (April 1967): 20–26.
[26] Marchesi, *Latin America's Radical Left*, chapters 1–2.
[27] Markarián, *El 68 uruguayo*.

as state repression escalated, a greater emphasis was placed on the model proposed by Guevara, which began to be interpreted more rigidly, as an instrument to resist increasingly uncertain and adverse conditions.

The qualitative changes in repressive state practices in the Southern Cone follows a clear timeline, with each key moment involving relatively successful attempts to destroy left-wing political organizations, including armed groups, in different countries of the region. This repressive escalation was characterized by the systematic development of certain torture methods applied during interrogations and imprisonment, the rise in political assassinations by the state with no legal framework to justify such actions, the violation of the constitutional guarantees of prisoners, and the use of family members as political hostages. The first moment began with the intensification of the persecution of Brazil's student movement and armed left-wing groups in late 1968, with Institutional Act No. 5. This resulted in the defeat of most of the country's armed groups. Something similar occurred in 1972 in Uruguay, when the president declared an internal state of war and the armed forces took on a more active role in combating the guerrilla movement. By the end of the year the Tupamaros had been defeated. From 1973 to 1975, the repressive actions of the DINA in Chile practically wiped out the MIR inside the country. As of 1975, with the Argentine army's involvement in the repression against the guerrillas in Tucumán, the state began devising a strategy of forced disappearances and clandestine detention centers that after the 1976 coup was expanded to the rest of the country and which destroyed several organizations, including the PRT-ERP, which suspended its activities in Argentina in 1977.[28] Between 1976 and 1983 the Argentine military dictatorship would kill between 9,000 and 30,000 people, according to various estimates.

The new Southern Cone left paid special attention to these processes. Their newspapers used eyewitness accounts to denounce state torture and political assassinations, and cautioned that these crimes were linked to an authoritarian escalation that was becoming inevitable in the context of the Cold War and which could only be resisted through armed struggle. While shrewdly forecasting the rise of a new form of authoritarianism, the region's armed left failed to fully understand how this repression would affect their own organizations. It is striking that even though they were well aware of how torture had contributed to their "sister" organizations' defeats, they still believed that they would be able to withstand it.

---

[28] Marchesi, *Latin America's Radical Left*, chapter 4.

After the coup in Chile, the MIR ordered its activists to remain in the country and not request asylum, under the slogan "No asylum!" Nine months later, although the organization had lost 40 percent of its leaders, it still judged its "no asylum" policy a success, as it had helped keep "combatant morale" high and turned the organization into "the strongest left-wing political force in Chile" as all other parties retreated.[29] With respect to torture, a July 1974 document issued by the political committee said:

It is not historically true that torture cannot be withstood. Bourgeois movements of all kinds have had members among their ranks who have been able to withstand it; the Bolsheviks of the beginning of the century have claimed that they successfully withstood it ... Revolutionaries all over the world are currently facing and overcoming torture.

The text went on to caution activists that:

If it is confirmed that a fellow activist has given away information, even if it was under torture, his name will be reported to all other activists, to the rest of the left, and to revolutionary movements all around the world. The MIR reserves the right to apply the harshest penalties and measures, the magnitude of which will depend on how far the struggle has developed.[30]

The leadership knew of cases in which torture had had devastating effects on other organizations in the region. In 1972, more than 3,000 people had been imprisoned in Uruguay, accused of belonging to the MLN-T. This effectively wiped out the organization in the country. The defeat was associated with, among other things, the development of new torture techniques by the armed forces. The magazine *Punto Final* had followed this process closely, along with similar processes in Brazil and Bolivia. However, the MIR document that claimed it was possible to withstand torture explained the defeat of the Tupamaros as the result of "ideological weakness."[31]

Two days after the 1976 coup in Argentina, the PRT-ERP called its central committee to a meeting. In that meeting, Mario Santucho drafted a report that was later published as an editorial in *El Combatiente* under the title "Argentines, Take Up Arms!" In that report Santucho gave an extremely positive assessment of the post-coup situation:

The final defeat of Peronism and the reactionary military coup have imposed upon the Argentine people the historical responsibility of rebelling en masse, taking the

---

[29] Miguel Enríquez, "¡A fortalecer nuestro partido!" in *Con vista a la esperanza* (Santiago de Chile: Escaparate Ediciones, 1998), 347.
[30] Ibid., 338.   [31] Ibid., 340.

fate of the nation into their own hands, and heroically facing any sacrifices that may be necessary to wage a victorious revolutionary war, with our powerful working class as the backbone of this battle, to achieve our Second and final Independence.[32]

Considering the regional context, Santucho was right in warning that the new regime would not be a temporary dictatorship but a lasting one, as it was the "definitive government that imperialist bourgeois forces have adopted to fight against Argentina's revolutionary forces." However, he predicted a reaction from the popular movement that had not happened in any of the other countries in the aftermath of the coups, and which would not happen in Argentina either. With respect to the Chilean experience Santucho said:

The military government has no possibility of inflicting a profound defeat on the mass movement or of taking a strategic initiative. In this sense, the coup in Chile cannot be compared [to Argentina's] as the conditions here are not the same. The "Pinochetazo" had a strong support from the population, was backed by imperialism, and had a surprise factor that worked in its favor.

Chile's working and popular masses, so accustomed to struggling legally, were suddenly met with a new situation in which they became major targets for the enemy and were powerless to mount any meaningful organized and long-lasting opposition to military actions.

That is not the case in our country.[33]

According to Santucho, "The coup has no significant social support and far from unifying the bourgeoisie it will aggravate its differences. Imperialism is not showing any particular enthusiasm for the coup solution."[34]

Santucho's argument is paradoxical in that it points out the "definitive" nature of the new authoritarianism that was taking root while also emphasizing its supposed weakness. The reasons for this contradiction reflected his interest in justifying the viability of armed actions in that context. The supposedly weak institutional bases that Santucho saw in the new regime seemed to set Argentina apart from the counterrevolutionary processes underway in neighboring countries.

The two examples discussed above highlight a tension between denouncing the advancing continental counterrevolution and showing

---

[32] Mario R. Santucho, "Argentinos, ¡A las armas!" *El Combatiente* no. 210 (March 31, 1976): 2, 15.
[33] Quoted in Mattini, *Hombres y mujeres del PRT-ERP*, 450.   [34] Ibid.

the limits of its power in national contexts. In the Chilean case, the ideological strength of the MIR seemed to be the guarantee that would enable it to survive the increasing use of torture against its activists, in contrast to what had happened to the Tupamaros a year earlier. In the Argentine case, the connection between the social movement and its illegal activities, and the alleged weakness of the dictatorship, were used to demonstrate that things in Argentina would be different than in Chile. The predictions were wrong. Each coup entailed extreme levels of repression, the first targets of which were armed groups, which it effectively destroyed. Although the activists were aware of what was happening in nearby countries, they were unable to learn from previous experiences.

When faced with growing adversity, the activists lacked the flexibility necessary to adapt to the new authoritarian circumstances. Instead, what prevailed was a greater emphasis on the figure of the model hero and on sacrificial duty. They promoted an overly optimistic and voluntaristic image of the activist, arguing that activists were capable of withstanding and even learning from torture and imprisonment. In that context, the growing number of activists who were murdered and imprisoned by the state was not assessed as a loss that signaled the gradual defeat of the armed organizations, but rather seen as a reaffirmation of the new moral duty that should lead survivors to deepen their commitment to the struggle.

As Longoni argues, political action was understood as a renunciation that was expressed by the "sacrificing of 'personal projects,' the harsh conditions of underground life, the cult of resistance under torture, and the resignation to death."[35] These renunciations also affected the activists' families, who were often targeted by repression or used as hostages. This meant that children were among the "sacrifices" that these activists had to make, thus altering family relations and affections forever and resulting in deep emotional scars.

This policy of renunciation meant that during the most dramatic moments these organizations were significantly isolated from the outside world. As they were increasingly surrounded and their capacity for political action was further curtailed, the energy of their activists was focused on increasing their capacity for sacrifice and reaffirming their absolute commitment to the cause. They believed that that capacity would influence the political process, which they were interpreting with less and less accuracy and from more ideologically charged perspectives.

[35] Longoni, *Traiciones*, 181.

These attitudes explain the effort to return to their native countries that all of these organizations planned to carry out but very few succeeded in even attempting. Of the four groups studied here, only the MIR conducted a return operation, in 1978. The first results of this operation, however, had a catastrophic effect on the organization. From 1974 to 1977, different factions of the MLN-T tried to carry out return operations to Uruguay from Argentina. None of these plans were actually implemented because, due to the high levels of infiltration, the intelligence apparatus was quickly notified whenever any activists entered Uruguay. The PRT-ERP discussed the possibility in exile, and a faction of the organization carried out one such attempt in 1981, setting up a small group of activists in Salta that escaped detection but was dissolved in 1982 as Argentina's political situation changed following the Malvinas/Falklands War.[36] Escalating repression was also instrumental in shaping the images of activism built by these organizations. Sociological study of the relations between social movements and state repression can help explain certain behaviors, both because the ideas available to activists are shaped in part by states and because the state's actions allow limited room for action.[37] In a comparative study of social movements and state violence in Italy and Germany in the late 1960s, Donatella della Porta finds behaviors similar to those noted in this study. Her explanation does not rest on ideological factors but on the increasing isolation of certain social-movement sectors at the end of that decade. That isolation stemmed from state actions in two senses: the capacity of the state to incorporate part of the reforms demanded by social movements, and its capacity for dissuasion through repression. If the state succeeded in isolating these groups the result was inevitable: "the more isolated a group becomes, the more abstract, ritualistic, and impervious to factual arguments its ideology becomes."[38] In the Southern Cone the states had a very limited capacity to incorporate demands, but their extremely repressive response heightened these groups' isolation, limiting their relations with social movements. With the coups, repression targeted the full range of social movements, cultural organizations, and left-wing political parties. This

---

[36] Daniel de Santis, *La historia del PRT-ERP por sus protagonistas* (Temperley: Estación Finlandia, 2010), 674.

[37] Christian Davenport, Hank Johnston, and Carol Mueller, eds., *Repression and Mobilization* (Minneapolis: University of Minnesota Press, 2005).

[38] Donatella Della Porta, *Social Movements, Political Violence, and the State: A Comparative Analysis of Italy and Germany* (Cambridge: Cambridge University Press, 1995), 201.

further increased these organizations' isolation, as they no longer had a public with which to conduct their political work. From then on, their defeat seems to have been inevitable.

In sum, at each moment of authoritarian escalation the leftists' response was to place greater emphasis on the figure of the revolutionary soldier. While these images were present from the start, the context of escalating repression, which generated an adverse and uncertain scenario, boosted the appeal of this model so that by the end of the period it had become the prevailing one in what was left of these organizations.

FROM CLASS DIVERSITY TO PROLETARIANIZATION

Ana Casamayou was a young chemistry student from a typical educated and progressive middle-class family of 1960s Montevideo. Her father was a dentist and her mother was a landowner. Casamayou was drawn to politics while still in high school, where she came into contact with a small organization called Grupos de Acción Unificadora (Unifying Action Groups), formed primarily by Catholic activists. There she was first introduced to the concept of "proletarianization." This had a profound effect on her:

Ever since I became active in politics, as a student, and until the famous "proletarianization," I kept asking myself how I could be studying for a degree when there were so many people who couldn't. I felt guilty because I had the possibility of studying while I saw the conditions the rest of society was in. I felt I was in a privileged position.[39]

When she began her university studies in the School of Chemistry, Casamayou came into contact with MLN-T activists. In 1969, at age twenty-one, she joined the organization. From that moment on, her study and leisure times were reduced to meet the demands of activism. She recalls how she participated in various activities during that period, performing a range of functions, including that of guard in the "people's prison," where the MLN-T held the individuals it kidnapped for ransom. Casamayou was forced to flee to Chile in late 1972 after the defeat suffered by the organization. In exile, Casamayou decided to live in the campsites in southern Chile. While traveling to Chile she met Antonio

---

[39] Clara Aldrighi, "Entrevista a Ana Casamayou," in *Memorias de insurgencia: Historias de vida y militancia en el MLN Tupamaros, 1965–1975* (Montevideo: Ediciones de la Banda Oriental, 2009), 286.

Bandera Lima, a sugarcane cutter and MLN-T member from Bella Unión, who would become her second partner in the organization.

Her relationship with Bandera Lima entailed the meeting of two very different worlds. She was a middle-class university student and he a self-educated rural worker who already had "seven or eight kids" before he met her. According to Casamayou, these differences helped her decide to have children in the adverse conditions under which the exiled Tupamaros were living. "Because of his social background – he was a cane cutter – and because he already had children, he made it easier for me to decide to have children of my own. If I had formed a relationship with another student as rigid as me, I'm sure I wouldn't have had children for many years to come."[40]

Bandera Lima represented a small group of *peludos* (hairy men) who were highly regarded by all the activists, as he represented the proletarian origins of the organization. When the crisis within the MLN-T worsened in 1974, four sugarcane leaders were proposed as a solution to the crisis. During that same period, the Tupamaros proposed their own version of proletarianization, which they called "peludización."

In 1973, Casamayou traveled to Cuba with Bandera Lima, where they had two children. In 1978, they left Cuba for Colombia with their two children to join activists who were conducting armed actions to finance a return operation to Uruguay and to support sectors of the Colombian guerrilla movement. Casamayou decided to distance herself from the organization and left for Mexico. In 1986 she went back to Uruguay. She did not return to political activism and currently works as a professional photographer.[41]

Casamayou's story illustrates the horizontal dialogues between different social classes that were enabled by the growth of these armed groups. On one hand, the participation of middle-class activists in social organizations involving lower-class sectors entailed a transfer of cultural resources from the former to the latter. While in this interaction the MLN-T was sometimes vertical or authoritarian in its efforts to "raise the consciousness" of the lower-class sectors, it is also true that many members of these lower-class sectors were able to use these opportunities to further projects aimed at both personal and collective emancipation. These experiences forged social organizations that, in those cases in which they survived repression, continued to be active beyond the period studied. Moreover, for many individuals these experiences allowed them to enhance their

[40] Ibid., 290. [41] Ibid., 281–301.

education and gave them access to cultural capital that would have otherwise been out of their reach.

This coming together of different social classes was made possible in part through the notion of proletarianization, which involved a very critical view of middle-class life, and even of the privileges enjoyed by some within the popular sectors, and an idealization of the lifestyle of certain working-class sectors. This concept allowed revolutionary organizations to advance their political and social projects in ways that would not have been feasible otherwise.

However, this approach also limited the possibility of developing a radical political project, since it entirely rejected the middle-class origins of the vast majority of the organizations' activists. The middle class had a long and varied history of political action in the region. The first reformist political projects in the Southern Cone had been strongly connected with these sectors. By the mid-twentieth century this situation was more complex. In Argentina, the identity of the middle classes had been resignified by the conflict between Peronists and anti-Peronists, where middle sectors tended to keep their distance from the working-class groups identified with Perón.[42] But even so, in all three countries there were numerically significant middle-class sectors associated with center-left and left-wing projects, as was the case of Socialism in Argentina and Chile, and *Batllismo* and independent sectors of the National Party in Uruguay. However, young activists from radicalized middle-class sectors portrayed their origins in an increasingly negative light as the region became more polarized and radicalized.

The view expressed by the MIR's Miguel Enríquez was somewhat more flexible. In April 1968 Enríquez, the new general secretary of the party, who at twenty-four had just married and was finishing medical school, was interviewed by *Punto Final*. After accepting the criticism directed at the MIR for being an organization of students and the petite bourgeoisie, he explained that "neither students nor intellectuals are a social class and that they will only play a role in the revolution insofar as they join the battle waged by the classes that are the motor of the revolution."[43] Enríquez listed the many revolutionary leaders from a petit-bourgeois

---

[42] See Enrique Garguín, "'Los argentinos descendemos de los barcos': The Racial Articulation of Middle-Class Identity in Argentina, 1920–1960," in *The Making of the Middle Class: Toward a Transnational History*, ed. A. Ricardo López and Barbara Weinstein (Durham, NC: Duke University Press, 2012), 355–76.

[43] "Exclusivo, jefe del MIR saca la cara," *Punto Final* no. 54 (April 23, 1968): 2–4.

background who had played an outstanding role in revolutionary struggles throughout history. Among these was Guevara, the "most outstanding and heroic," who had been a doctor. He also highlighted the combatant role that students had played throughout the history of Latin America. And lastly, with respect to the traditional parties of the Chilean left, he pointed out that the "only thing the traditional left can hold against the MIR is the young age of its leaders. Because most of their leaders are petit bourgeois too, the only difference is that they're older."[44] Like Régis Debray in *Revolution in the Revolution?*, he acknowledged the enormous participation of students in Latin America's revolutionary processes and admitted that there was no inevitable correspondence between the position they occupied in the social structure and their connection to the revolutionary cause.[45] Nonetheless, it was the more dismissive approach that gradually prevailed within the armed groups of the Southern Cone. Various academic approaches noted that certain middle-class sectors were sympathetic to authoritarian processes (in Brazil, Argentina, and Chile), and this observation led the organizations to make generalizations about the middle classes, which paradoxically impeded an analysis of their own involvement in the political process.[46]

More than these academic approaches, however, what appears to have been decisive in this sense was the ideological shift toward orthodox interpretations of Marxism-Leninism that limited the possibilities of reflecting on Latin America's middle classes, which were completely different than those of 1917 Russia. This shift led to a very critical view of middle-class sectors and the explicit aim to radically root out the "petit-bourgeois deviations" of which various activists could be guilty due to their class origins. As shown above, the defeats in Brazil, Uruguay, and Bolivia were explained as the result of the ideological weaknesses of certain activists. Thus, it was considered necessary to eradicate such practices in order to successfully reconstruct the organizations. It was in this context that the MLN-T coined the term *peludización* and that a number of Brazilian activists began working as factory operators in Santiago. In the Argentine case, this approach was especially important, as various organizations had been promoting different proletarianization

---

[44] Ibid., 3.

[45] Régis Debray, "¿Revolución en la revolución?" *Cuadernos de la Revista Casa de las Américas* (Havana) 1 (1967).

[46] See José Nun, "A Latin American Phenomenon: The Middle-Class Military Coup," in *Latin America: Reform or Revolution?* ed. James Petras and Maurice Zeitlin (Greenwich, CT: Fawcett, 1968).

practices since the late 1960s, requiring that activists give up their social positions, abandon their studies, and become industrial workers. The PRT was particularly concerned with increasing the number of working-class members, and often explained its internal political conflicts as the result of a class struggle within the organization. In an internal document, the PRT-ERP claimed that 30 to 40 percent of its membership in mid-1973 was composed of factory workers.[47] Much of that percentage had been formed by activists who were not working-class in origin but had been sent by the party to work in factories. This practice was not only seen as necessary for the organization's political growth, it was also considered a moral baptism for activists who came from the petite bourgeoisie.

The PRT-ERP document *Moral y proletarización* (Morality and Proletarianization), written in 1972, provides key insight into how the organization conceptualized the "revolutionary morality" that was implicit in the idea of proletarianization. The aim of this document was to provide tools to combat the "hegemony" of the bourgeois class, which was based on individualism. Everyday life was part of the military and political battle that the revolutionaries were waging. It was thus necessary to develop an "ethics of combat" that would enable the necessary transition to the socialist ethics of tomorrow. Following the example of Vietnam, this ethics of combat entailed reorganizing "all aspects of life around war, [changing] our relations with the people, with our fellow activists, with our partners and our children, with our families and the people around us." Although all of society suffered under ruling-class hegemony, "those who have gone through the social experience of being workers will be more likely to acquire a working-class consciousness." As activists they had to "tear down [their] individualistic personality and rebuild it anew, founding it on revolutionary and proletarian bases" through a process of proletarianization that entailed taking up the "social practice of the working class, its way of life and its work . . . Taking up arms is not enough if our everyday lives are still locked in the social practices of the bourgeoisie or the petite bourgeoisie." "Subjectivism," "self-sufficiency," the "search for glory," "clique mentality," "liberalism," and "fear for one's own life" were the individualistic deviations that affected revolutionary organizations. The key to correcting these individualistic attitudes was through the practice of criticism and self-criticism, where each activist had to place "an emphasis on self-criticism over criticism."[48]

---

[47] PRT, "Anteproyecto de resolución sobre internacional, 1973," Archivo del Centro de Documentación e Investigación de la Cultura de Izquierda, Buenos Aires.

[48] Luis Ortolani, "Moral y proletarización," *Políticas de la memoria* no. 4 (2004–2005): 96.

In this sense, proletarianization was associated with a moral code that had little to do with the subjective experience of proletarians. The values upheld did not seem to fit any actual social sector. And in some cases the sacrifices demanded by the organization, which were justified as a way of abandoning individualism, were more feasible for middle-class activists who had greater economic and social resources, thus allowing them to bear the costs of giving up family and work more easily than working-class sectors. Thus, the construction of the ideal proletarian was closer to certain notions of ethical puritanism held by middle-class sectors than to the historical experience of industrial workers.

Much of this vocabulary and the insistence on practicing self-criticism appear repeatedly in the minutes of the MLN-T's central committee in Argentina, evidencing the great influence that the PRT-ERP had during this period. Something similar can be noted for the Bolivian ELN in its process of transformation into the PRT-Bolivia. The organization that was the least prone to this kind of discourse – at least during the period studied – was the MIR. The PRT-ERP leader Arnol Kremer recalls that when MIR leader Edgardo Enríquez went to Argentina to participate in JCR meetings, some activists were critical of his upper-class background and his university education, which they saw as signs of "class weakness." Their disapproval led them to put Enríquez in modest lodgings in the outskirts of Greater Buenos Aires, thus making it difficult for Enríquez to make all the political contacts he had planned in downtown Buenos Aires.[49]

In sum, what I have set out above are the key aspects of a transnational political culture of the left that was forged in the heat of the Southern Cone's political struggles in the late 1960s and early 1970s. The elements of this political culture can be briefly described as follows: a Latin Americanist view supported by regional exile experiences; a set of ideas initially critical of the traditional left; and, lastly, a model activist associated with the idealized figures of the revolutionary soldier and the proletarian. This political culture was not the result of preformed ideology. It resulted from the interaction between previous ideas and the new political circumstances that these militants faced. It was in that process that these activists gradually developed a unique political culture, which was built in the course of the regional exchanges that were born of the uncertain historical contingency of local processes that often led them to places that would have been inconceivable in the mid-1960s.

---

[49] Luis Mattini, *Los perros: Memorias de un combatiente revolucionario* (Buenos Aires: Continente-Pax, 2006), 116–25.

8

Nationalism and Marxism in Rural Cold War Mexico

Guerrero, 1959–1974

O'Neill Blacker-Hanson

On September 26, 2014, Mexicans across the country – and people throughout the world – awoke to the news of yet another massacre, this one in Iguala, in the southwest state of Guerrero. This was not about drug cartels or personal vendettas. This was the disappearance of forty-three students from the *escuela normal* (teacher-training school) in nearby Ayotzinapa. The massacre opened new and old wounds. It is widely acknowledged that the students presented no violent threat to the government, so why would anyone think they did? Or, more likely, why would they think they could portray them as either drug-related criminals or activists out to disrupt the political rally taking place? In May 2013, Guerrero's Governor Ángel Aguirre had depicted Ayotzinapa as "a place that has been used by some groups to indoctrinate these youths and cultivate social resentment amongst them."[1]

Although neither charge raised by the government and press was accurate, they had a familiar echo.[2] Mexico's legacy of radical teachers dates to the aftermath of the Revolution of 1910, when the state undertook efforts to promote a national vision through education. As part of

---

[*] My appreciation to the University of New Mexico's Latin American and Iberian Institute and, as always, the people of Guerrero who have shared their stories and lives with me.

[1] Interview with Adela Micha, *Televisa*, May 2013, www.youtube.com/watch?v=MQzG9 a8J_sM (accessed May 17, 2018). For a detailed chronology of these events see John Gibler, *I Couldn't Even Imagine That They Would Kill Us* (San Francisco, CA: City Lights, 2017).

[2] For more on the role of radical teachers, and the Cold War in Guerrero, see O'Neill Blacker-Hanson, "Cold War in the Countryside: Conflict in Guerrero, Mexico," *The Americas* 66, no. 2 (2009): 181–210.

these efforts, the Raúl Isidro Burgos School for teacher training was founded in Ayotzinapa in 1926. Yet as early as 1928, community engagement by its teachers led a wary administrator at the Secretaría de Educación Pública (Ministry of Public Education), José Manuel Puig Casauranc, to describe them as "agents of disruption and social dissolution."[3] His depiction proved prophetic: in ensuing decades, when they sought progressive change *in opposition* to the state, the very community ties that teachers had initially established and the leadership roles they had assumed *in transmitting* national doctrine provided them with a network of local alliances. Students' demands for a more just, equitable society that respected cultural traditions led to the school's reputation as a "hotbed" of radicalism.[4] Ayotzinapa graduate and activist Arturo Miranda Ramírez writes that the school became "distinguished as the seedbed of social fighters."[5] Indeed, as one walks Ayotzinapa's campus – a short ride from Chilpancingo, Guerrero's modest state capital – virtually every wall is covered by students' murals, many prominently displaying its most notorious graduate: guerrilla fighter Lucio Cabañas Barrientos (1938–74). His portrait, showing him gun in hand, stands alongside others: Marx, Engels, Lenin, Guevara, and Guerrero's Genaro Vázquez. It is this history that may explain – but never excuse – the events of 2014.

That night in Iguala also brought to the fore Mexico's often-neglected, even denied, *guerra sucia* (dirty war) of the 1970s. During the Cold War, Latin American dictatorships used military and paramilitary forces to kidnap, imprison, torture, kill and disappear perceived internal enemies; these included self-identified communists and socialists, but also other students, faculty, trade unionists, peasants, artists, musicians, and writers. While extensive documentation exists of these crimes in the Southern Cone, little was accessible in Mexico until 2000, when the newly elected president opened limited access to many – although not all – relevant documents. Numerous organizations had formed in the 1970s to demand accountability and, tragically, now serve as models for those that arose in response to the recent disappearances. By 2014, however, these historic links had been complicated with the rise of the drug cartels in the intervening decades. The cartels have thoroughly penetrated the governmental

---

3 Quoted in Mary Kay Vaughan, *Cultural Politics in Revolution: Teachers, Peasants, and Schools in Mexico, 1930–1940* (Tucson: University of Arizona Press, 1997), 147.

4 Baloy Mayo, *La guerrilla de Genaro y Lucio* (Mexico City: Diógenes, 1980), 44–45.

5 Arturo Miranda Ramírez, *El otro rostro de la guerrilla* (Mexico City: El Machete, 1996), 27.

and military apparatuses while simultaneously challenging the state's legitimacy, including its monopoly over violence against the population. Thus, while government officials had portrayed the mid-twentieth-century opposition as communists, bandits, and outsiders, the earliest government statements following the 2014 disappearances attempted to portray the students as drug cartel members. Continuing an archetype begun long before the Cold War, government rhetoric recalled the state's notorious reputation as *Guerrero bronco* (untamed Guerrero), stressing its history of violence and instability in an attempt to excuse the disappearances.[6]

Twentieth-century uprisings throughout Latin America emerged from longstanding local conditions and power relations. Earlier interpretations of the Cold War era's oppositional movements too often overemphasized external causes, notably the Cuban Revolution of 1959. Recent scholarship, however, explicitly debunks Cold War rhetoric emanating from governments keen to redirect the source of opposition from homegrown conditions of poverty, oppression, and political exclusion by faulting foreign influences.[7] First, this chapter establishes the historic and contemporary context of the opposition movements that emerged in Guerrero in the 1960s. Second, it examines the demands for democratic inclusion that created a broad-based popular movement seeking economic and social justice. Third, it argues that guerrilla leaders' transition from nationalism grounded in the Mexican Revolution of 1910 to the language of international socialism reflected their familiarity with both earlier Latin American theorists and contemporary socialist efforts. Their ideological radicalization, however, may well have resulted in increased isolation from the peasant base on which they depended and which had initially rallied behind the nationalist language. The guerrilla leaders' own missteps compounded the setbacks caused by ruthless state repression. The chapter concludes with an examination of the reign of government terror that made Guerrero the site of the gravest violence of Mexico's dirty war.

[6] A term popularized by Armando Bartra, *Guerrero bronco: Campesinos, ciudadanos y guerrilleros en la Costa Grande* (Mexico City: Era, 1996).
[7] See, for example, Gilbert M. Joseph and Daniela Spenser, eds., *In from the Cold: Latin America's New Encounter with the Cold War* (Durham, NC: Duke University Press, 2008).

A BRIEF HISTORY OF *GUERRERO BRONCO*

In the decades following the Revolution of 1910, local elites sustained authority through electoral fraud and the government-sponsored violence emblematic of state politics, prefiguring what would occur in succeeding decades. Concurrently, the federal government expanded its efforts at centralization, with benefits of land redistribution, irrigation, infrastructure, and education inequitably distributed both geographically and socially. As Guillermo de la Peña notes, "to the extent that [such programs] satisfied demands, the state machine was legitimized and strengthened," but its failure to implement many of these programs undermined that national goal.[8] The people of Guerrero, or *Guerrerenses*, experienced increasing alienation as a purportedly "revolutionary" government failed to satisfy their economic and civic expectations. As that government increased its brutality to maintain power, the populace responded with its own increased, yet unequal, militancy.

With the close of World War II national and international financial interests stimulated the expansion of modernization projects, and popular resistance intensified as rural communities lost land and cohesion to export-oriented production and the infrastructure that facilitated it. Prices and production rose, initiating the "season of the fat cows," increasing the impoverishment of those lacking land or capital.[9] Many of the state's workers migrated to emerging urban centers, notably Acapulco (Figure 8.1). Others took advantage of the Bracero Program (1942–64) to emigrate to the United States as guest workers.

By the mid-1950s the national economy began to slump into recession.[10] Further reorganization of economic relations ensued, including cutbacks in social welfare programs, resulting in a surge of protests from organized labor, peasants, and students. Conflicts erupted from the northern state of Chihuahua to the southern state of Chiapas. Groundbreaking strikes occurred in railway, electrical, telegraph, medical, educational, and oil enterprises. Students from the massively expanding Universidad Nacional Autónoma de México (National Autonomous

---

[8] Guillermo de la Peña, *Local and Regional Power in Mexico* (Austin: University of Texas, 1988), 309.

[9] Antonio Sotelo Pérez, *Breve historia de la Asociación Cívica Guerrerense, jefaturada por Genaro Vázquez Rojas* (Chilpancingo: Universidad Autónoma de Guerrero [hereafter UAG], 1991), 26–27.

[10] See, among many, John W. Sherman, "The 'Mexican Miracle' and Its Collapse," in *The Oxford History of Mexico*, ed. Michael C. Meyer and William H. Beezley (Oxford: Oxford University Press, 2000), 141–68.

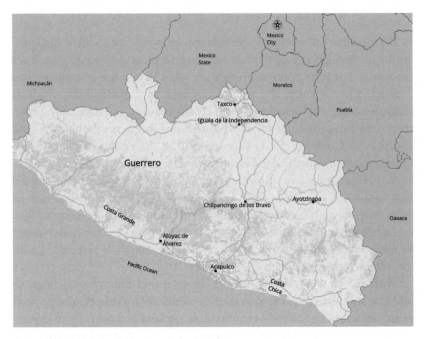

FIGURE 8.1 Guerrero state.
Source: Map by Kevin Young.

University of Mexico), the Instituto Politécnico Nacional (National Polytechnic Institute), and the national *normal* school provided ongoing support to these labor struggles, and also engaged in student strikes. Many rural regions were experiencing their own strife. The movement led by Rubén Jaramillo (1900–62) in neighboring Morelos arose to address an unresponsive political system and increasing economic inequality. Jaramillo's trajectory from legal to armed opposition would be replicated in Guerrero following his assassination and that of his family.[11]

In Guerrero, local, national, and international winds converged. Disillusionment with development programs was exacerbated by the regime's failure to ameliorate economic inequality. Entrenched resistance by powerful political factions continued to evade demands for the opening of democratic channels. The repression of labor and agrarian organizing increased. Regional *caciques* (political bosses), state authorities, and their

[11] Tanalís Padilla, *Rural Resistance in the Land of Zapata: The Jaramillista Movement and the Myth of the Pax Priísta, 1940–1962* (Durham, NC: Duke University Press, 2008).

hired gunmen maintained a "climate of terror."[12] With the 1959 arrival of a cadre of teachers, who brought with them experience honed in the capital's labor struggles – where they had been exposed to the full range of governmental response, from verbal accusations through physical intimidation to violent repression – their home state stood poised to erupt.[13] In Guerrero, they immersed themselves in the labor organizing already underway, a choice that would both secure popular support for future struggles and contribute to the philosophical radicalization of the leadership.[14]

OPPOSITION AND RESPONSE: 1959–1974

Genaro Vázquez Rojas (1933–72) was in many ways representative of his colleagues. In a 1971 interview he spoke of his childhood in the small community of San Luis Acatlán and identified his father as a *campesino* who had taken him as a young boy to community meetings.[15] In Mexico City he enrolled in the national *normal* school on a public scholarship, and although he never worked as a teacher in his home state, he taught briefly in a poor *barrio* of Mexico City.[16] His commitment to radical democratic change merged the realities of exploitation that he had witnessed as a child and the education he acquired on the streets of the capital. While these latter experiences introduced Vázquez to the theoretical and practical value of the urban working class, he returned to Guerrero committed "to fully dedicate myself to the solution to the agrarian problems" which had not been resolved despite prior struggles led by Emiliano Zapata and Rubén Jaramillo.[17]

---

[12] Francisco A. Gomezjara, *Bonapartismo y lucha campesina en la Costa Grande de Guerrero* (Mexico City: Posada, 1979), 143.

[13] For more on the Guerrerense teachers who studied in Mexico City, see Blacker-Hanson, "*¡La Lucha Sigue!* ('The Struggle Continues!') Teacher Activism in Guerrero and the Continuum of Democratic Struggle in Mexico" (Ph.D. diss., University of Washington, 2005).

[14] They included, among many, the newly formed unions of coconut industry and coffee workers. The Liga Agraria Revolucionaria del Sur (Revolutionary Agrarian League of the South) "Emiliano Zapata" emerged in March 1963 among textile workers. Its stated purpose was to "struggle for land, against exploitation, misery, injustice, poor health and cultural conditions, and the practical absence of political rights." "Declaración de principios y programa," in Sotelo, *Breve historia*, 112–19.

[15] Vázquez, in the magazine *¿Por qué?* December 16, 1971, in Miguel Aroche Parra, *El Che, Jenaro y las guerrillas: Estrategia y táctica de la revolución en México* (Mexico City: Federación Editorial Mexicana, 1974), 21.

[16] Gomezjara, *Bonapartismo*, 264.

[17] *¿Por qué?* December 16, 1971, in Aroche Parra, *El Che, Jenaro y las guerrillas*, 21.

Upon their return to Guerrero, Vázquez and the other activists from Mexico City, most of whom were native *Guerrerenses*, were joined by colleagues who had undergone their own politicization at Ayotzinapa, where students had been encouraged to link the popular yearning for democracy, in which they had been immersed all their lives, with the language of class struggle. Together, these activists pursued an end to the "terrifying crimes" perpetrated by Governor Raúl Caballero Aburto and his henchmen, against whom an extensive list of charges was lodged.[18] Their efforts would unleash the most public display of government repression yet witnessed in Guerrero: the assault on citizens gathered in the plaza of the state capital on December 30, 1960.

The activists demanded democratic transparency, community decision-making, and an end to government-sponsored violence. These demands reflected an expansion beyond the economic grievances initially raised against Caballero Aburto, to an increased focus on democratic accountability, addressing political exclusion and the dearth of Constitutional guarantees, explicitly articulated as "absolute respect for the Constitution."[19] At the same time, demands such as an end to forest exploitation, recognition of the right to unionize, attention to the educational needs of the community, and affirmation of a social orientation in the state's educational curriculum reflected the enduring grassroots expectations nurtured in the Revolution of 1910 and embodied in the Constitution of 1917. The coalition of 1960 was characterized by its allegiance to nationalist iconography and its continued expectations that the federal government would intervene as representative of popular interests vis-à-vis state elites.[20] This orientation distinguished this phase of opposition struggle from that which arose later, after the violence unleashed by national authorities had disabused activists of such allegiance.

The strategy was to build cross-class, cross-sector alliances that could bring "business as usual" throughout the state to a standstill. The umbrella Asociación Cívica Guerrerense (ACG) was formed from numerous labor organizations, eventually representing over thirty-five distinct

[18] Salvador Román Román, *Revuelta cívica en Guerrero (1957–1960): La democracia imposible* (Mexico City: INEHRM, 2003), 181. Caballero established laws centralizing authority over all state security forces, new penal codes with explicit political overtones, and new taxes that adversely affected the poor. For a complete discussion of the initial charges, see José C. Gutiérrez Galindo, *Y el pueblo se puso de pie: La verdad sobre el caso Guerrero* (Mexico City: n.p., 1961), 197–207.

[19] Andrés Rubio Zaldivar, *El movimiento social guerrerense y a la lucha armada de Genaro Vázquez Rojas* (Chilpancingo: UAG, 1994), 17–19.

[20] On the early nationalist language and strategy, see Salvador Román Román, *Revuelta cívica*, 132–35.

groups, many already led by Vázquez's colleagues. *Los cívicos*, as they were known, further brought together rural workers, small landholders, those running small commercial ventures (e.g., shopkeepers and, most prominently, market vendors), students, and teachers. Other supporters organized into the Sociedad de Padres de Familia (Parents' Association), as well as several religious affiliations, including organizations of Evangelicals, Catholics, and the Masonic Lodge of Chilpancingo.[21] Universidad Autónoma de Guerrero (Autonomous University of Guerrero, UAG) instructor and activist Saúl López López remarks that the broad, "almost monolithic" unity among distinct social forces made participants feel "like one big family."[22]

Negotiations with the state government broke down, and on October 30, a platoon of soldiers arrived in Chilpancingo. Numerous gatherings were dispersed with increasing violence and injuries, but people continued to reassemble. The movement's demands were adopted by *municipios* and lower-rung elected officials, not only in Chilpancingo, but in Iguala, Atoyac, Taxco, Tixtla, Zumpango del Rio, Apango, Huitzuco, and Tenango del Río. Numerous rural *normal* schools declared their support, as did universities in Michoacán and Nayarit. By mid-November, over 500 small merchants in Chilpancingo and an estimated 23,000 workers throughout the state were on strike. Five of the seven Chilpancingo city council members denounced the governor.[23] On November 20, celebrated nationwide as the anniversary of the Revolution of 1910, 20,000 people gathered in the Alameda "Granados Maldonado," one of the main plazas of Chilpancingo, demanding the governor's resignation.[24] Tensions grew.

The statewide closure of businesses and the resultant impasse were too great a challenge to government authority. On December 30, the standoff came to an abrupt end when the governor ordered the 24th Battalion,

---

[21] The important participation and contributions of women is evident through both discourse of participants and photographs of events. See for example Pablo Sandoval Cruz, *El movimiento social de 1960 en Guerrero*, with photographs by Jesús Salmerón, second ed. (Chilpancingo: n.p., 1999). As he notes, "If anyone thinks that woman is the weaker sex and is cowardly, he makes a mistake. In 1960, they demonstrated they are on a par with the men" (165).

[22] Saul López López, "Testimonio," in Sandoval Cruz, *El movimiento social*, 106–07.

[23] The Acapulco Chamber of Commerce reported a 750,000 pesos/day loss. Sandoval Ramírez, "Testimonio," in ibid., 31.

[24] Ibid., 7. This would be an extraordinary figure, as Chilpancingo's official population was 15,000 then.

aided by additional forces, to fire on the people maintaining a strike presence in the central plaza of Chilpancingo. Men, women, and children were among the fifteen dead and the even greater number who were injured. Testimonies suggest that the assault was premeditated: citizens reported seeing significant troop movement that morning.[25] The military intervention led to a definitive break between the state government and civil society. Immediately thereafter, President Adolfo López Mateos seized the state's political reins, and on the morning of December 31, dispatched the 50th Battalion to Chilpancingo. The remaining strikers soon joined their compatriots in the Chilpancingo jail. In an emergency session of the Senate, an interim governor was appointed to replace the disgraced Caballero.

The remarkable success of the popular sectors in bringing the governor's administration to an end stemmed from a confluence of factors. In a state with a long history of excluding popular voices from decision-making, it cannot be assumed that sheer numbers and tenacity brought political victory. The movement's demands were met by the highest authorities – the President and Senate – whose own political interests factored into the decision to remove the governor. Local, regional, and national political schisms shaped the alignment of forces on all sides of the conflict. Certainly the federal government's effort to secure capital investment in the region was a key factor: political instability would have discouraged national and international investors.

Political conflicts in Guerrero continued, with the state frequently using violence. In local elections in 1962, all the *cívico* candidates were defeated by what was widely perceived as electoral fraud. Two days later, opposition candidates and leaders of the ACG were arrested.[26] The populace mobilized in protest, and on December 30, 1962, a military attack in Iguala (site of the 2014 disappearances) resulted in 7 deaths, 23 people injured, and 280 arrests.[27]

Twenty thousand soldiers maintained order as the "winning" candidates assumed their posts. Over the next several years, the populace was subjected to military incursions, the destruction of the market booths of those who had supported the *cívicos*, and the tactic known as *tierra*

---

[25] Ibid., 69.

[26] An estimated 150 *cívicos* were arrested. Jaime López, *10 años de guerrillas en México* (Mexico City: Posada, 1974), 49.

[27] Armando Bartra, *Los herederos de Zapata: Movimientos campesinos posrevolucionarios en México, 1920–1980* (Mexico City: Era, 1985), 84.

arrasada, a "scorched earth" practice that left entire communities bereft of shelter and crops. Military attacks included the execution of *campesinos*, the wounding of others, the rape of women, and burning of communities. In the state's Costa Grande region, over 400 homes were razed or burned by government troops, leaving over 2,000 families homeless.[28] *Campesinos* fled to the mountains. Jails filled. The popular movement, while suppressed, was not entirely crushed: two campus strikes occurred, one in opposition to the newly appointed rector at the UAG, and another in Ayotzinapa in support of those at the UAG.[29] For Vázquez, the lesson of the repression was clear. His belief that the system could be made to work if democratic processes were permitted to operate had begun to erode after the massacre in Chilpancingo, and still further after the one in Iguala. He and many others concluded that there was no electoral path to democracy, and the guerrilla movement in Guerrero was reborn.

As the democratic struggles continued, their geographic focus shifted from the state capital to the town of Atoyac in the Costa Grande, and with this shift, public leadership passed from Vázquez to Lucio Cabañas Barrientos. Like Vázquez, Cabañas was initially exposed to theoretical analyses of the struggle for social justice during his years as a student at the *normal* school, and like Vázquez, Cabañas was transformed by his experiences of repression by the state. He was the child of *campesinos* and the grandson and great-nephew of revolutionary heroes. In conversation with teacher-activist Félix Hoyo Arana, Cabañas recalled that his earliest political education was witnessing "the repression, the *caciques*, the poverty and misery of the people ... [such that] when the army was sent out [into the communities], he thought of the robberies, torture, disappearances, incarcerations the army had done to the people, and with this on his mind, he could fight."[30]

After the 1960 massacre in Chilpancingo, Cabañas returned to complete his studies at Ayotzinapa, where his leadership skills had been recognized early. He had served as president of the school's strike committee and was elected to colead the Executive Committee of Students. He

---

[28] *Política*, September 15, 1963, cited in Gomezjara, *Bonapartismo*, 292–93. See also United Nations Economic and Social Council, Commission on Human Rights, "Report of the Working Group on Enforced or Involuntary Disappearances", E/CN.4/1997/34, December 13, 1996, www.ohchr.org/EN/Issues/Disappearances/Pages/Annual.aspx (accessed April 27, 2018).

[29] López, *10 años de guerrillas*, 51.

[30] Lucio Cabañas, as reported by Félix Hoyo, interview, Mexico City, May 5, 2002. Unless otherwise noted, all subsequent cited interviews were conducted by the author.

traveled to outlying communities, securing political ties with students at *normal* schools throughout the region, many of whom later became involved with his guerrilla movement either as combatants or supporters.[31] It was then that he developed into "a man of action."[32]

Following graduation, Cabañas took up a teaching post in his home-town of Atoyac, where he became immersed in local issues, including the denuding of the forests, the proposed closure of a textile cooperative, and charges of malfeasance against school administrators. Each of these foci challenged the government's economic development policies, the absence of democracy, and lack of local autonomy, yet Cabañas's tactics suggest a continued faith that the federal government would fulfill the expecta-tions of the Constitution. Despite harassment, Cabañas and colleague Serafín Núñez sustained the support of diverse sectors, including parents, students, and members of the ACG. Discussions with the government continued sporadically, punctuated by marches, rallies, and denuncia-tions. Although there were rumors of a government plan to remove the protesters from their sit-in in the central plaza of Atoyac, no one was prepared for what occurred. It was, Núñez says with understatement, "a disproportionate response."[33] The plaza was filled with demonstrators on May 18, 1967, when the police opened fire, killing seven and injuring many others. This date is still cited by activists in Guerrero as a key turning point in the struggle for democracy. Cabañas was present; Núñez, by chance, was not. These two colleagues would not see each other again.[34]

Three months later, on August 22, the state launched an assault on striking coconut workers in Acapulco demanding the right to independent organizing, leaving at least 40 dead and 500 injured.[35] And then, like Jaramillo and Vázquez before him, Cabañas abandoned public life and went to the mountains, where he formed the Partido de los Pobres (Party of the Poor, PDLP), an armed group opposing the regime. Determining that the status quo was "at least as atrocious as [the risks] of revolution, perhaps a great deal more,"[36] Cabañas said, "We were tired of the peace-ful struggle without any success. This is why we said: we will go to the

---

[31] Sandoval Ramírez, *Testimonio*, 53.   [32] Mayo, *La guerrilla*, 45.

[33] Serafín Núñez, interview, Chilpancingo, July 2003.

[34] Núñez, interview; Fausto Ávila, interview, Chilpancingo, February 21, 2003.

[35] Armando Bartra, "Donde los sismos nacen," in *El sur en movimiento: La reinvención de Guerrero del siglo XXI*, ed. Tomás Bustamente Álvarez and Sergio Sarmiento Silva (Mexico City: Laguna, 2001), 48.

[36] Barrington Moore, Jr., *Social Origins of Dictatorship and Democracy* (Boston, MA: Beacon, 1966), 103–04.

Sierras [the mountains]."[37] The region reaffirmed its reputation as *Guerrero bronco*.

Like their compatriots in the ACG, those who struggled alongside Cabañas and Núñez in Atoyac led a community-based movement that coalesced behind grassroots demands for democratic accountability (a voice in determining the exploitation of community resources, such as forest lands) and local autonomy (community involvement in the schools). Cabañas's support was a result of conscientious efforts to secure community involvement from the start. His ability to do so may well have been enhanced by his decision to remain in Guerrero for his professional studies, a choice that may partially explain the broad base of support he retained in his later years.[38] And, while such support is impossible to quantify, in 1973 the US government explained the military failure to capture him thusly: "It is apparent that Cabañas and his group operate freely in Guerrero. Implications are that local populace, for whatever reasons, continues to afford Cabañas cover."[39]

Both Vázquez and Cabañas underwent radicalization as institutional avenues of protest led to dead ends and as government repression intensified in the form of elections widely perceived as fraudulent, destruction of property, deadly assaults, disappearances, and torture. With two guerrilla fronts now opened across the *sierras*, the federal government moved to eliminate the opposition. No independent *campesino*, worker, or student organizations remained overtly active in the state. If an individual were even suspected of oppositional activities, he or she was seized and tortured, disappeared, or murdered.[40] Despite government efforts to cripple Cabañas's leadership, it required a massive military response, including

---

[37] Lucio Cabañas, "Así me fui a la sierra, habla Lucio Cabañas," in Luis Suárez, *Lucio Cabañas: El guerrillero sin esperanza* (Mexico City: Grijalbo, 1985), 57.

[38] López, *10 años de guerrillas*, 71. Hoyo, interview, and Alejandra Cárdenas also assert strong grassroots support for Cabañas, insisting he could not have survived as long as he did without it. Alejandra Cárdenas, interview, Chilpancingo, August 2, 2002, and numerous subsequent discussions.

[39] US Embassy cable, April 15, 1973, quoted in Kate Doyle, "The Dawn of Mexico's Dirty War: Lucio Cabañas and the Party of the Poor," National Security Archive (hereafter NSA), December 5, 2003, https://nsarchive2.gwu.edu/NSAEBB/NSAEBB105/index.htm #article (accessed April 23, 2018).

[40] Hoyo, Cárdenas, and Ávila, interviews. For more on the state repression of the period, see UN and NSA reports on the government's "dirty war" in Guerrero. Simón Hipólito notes that among the disappeared are likely unknown numbers of indigenous people who traveled as seasonal laborers, "many of whom joined the PDLP." The distance from family suggests that many would be among the unidentified disappeared. Simón Hipólito, *Guerrero, amnistía y represión* (Mexico City: Grijalba, 1982), 31.

over 24,000 soldiers amassed in the *sierras* – representing about one-third of the national military – to kill Cabañas on December 2, 1974.[41]

DEMOCRATIC NATIONALISM AND THE ALLURE OF INTERNATIONAL SOCIALISM

The two most prominent social leaders to emerge in Guerrero in this period, Genaro Vázquez and Lucio Cabañas, along with their colleagues, reflected the guerrilla warfare spreading elsewhere in their own country and across Latin America. Their early beliefs represented their personal experiences as sons of *campesinos*, roots that facilitated and legitimated their leadership. Their ideological principles, initially grounded in faith in the national postrevolutionary government, would be transformed by the recognition that democratic processes to secure economic and social justice were absent.

On the international stage, perhaps the single most influential event of the period was the Cuban Revolution of 1959, which demonstrated that a revolution could be won. One colleague reports that Cabañas was able to pick up the nightly radio announcements from the Sierra Maestra as the revolution progressed.[42] While many of Guerrero's activists retained their commitment to the democratic promises of Mexico's revolution, the vision of equality and opportunity broadcast from Cuba rekindled their belief that their own country could realize those promises. The Cuban revolutionaries' merging of economic and social justice encouraged the ideological fusion of Mexican democracy and Cuban-style socialism that would become a hallmark of the opposition leaders. Octaviano Santiago Dionisio, PDLP militant and longtime political prisoner, credits his own early political proclivities to three decisive influences: the "brutal repression to which the people of Guerrero were subjected," the Cuban Revolution, and disillusionment with the electoral process.[43] Thus, the analysis of these leaders reflected a rejection of the worst abuses of capitalist economic exploitation, a response to the increasingly aggressive closure of democratic political channels, socialism's utopian ideals, and the local roots of seasoned

---

[41] Bartra, *Los herederos*, 90. This may include state police in addition to federal forces.

[42] Miranda Ramírez, *El otro rostro*, 33. Alfonso Aguario also describes his strong awareness of other international resistance movements, such as that in Guatemala. Interview, Chilpancingo, February 21, 2003.

[43] Octaviano Santiago Dionicio, *Testimonio de un preso político* (Chilpancingo: Federación Estudiantil Universitaria Guerrerense, UAG, 1979), 9, 14 (interviewed in the Acapulco public jail, January 1, 1979).

leadership carrying the trust accrued by earlier generations of teachers. The rhetoric they used demonstrates these multiple influences, employing the internationalist language of anti-capitalist, anti-imperialist struggle alongside nationalist imagery and icons. Expectations that had arisen in their nation's revolution re-emerged in demands for land redistribution, employment, educational opportunities, and access to democratic processes. That fusion facilitated construction of a broad-based coalition. The coalition's effectiveness, however, was both increased and constrained by its dedication to Mexican nationalism, which encouraged reliance on a government that did not hesitate to quash their efforts.

Evidence of retention of a strong nationalist identity among the popular classes was revealed in numerous ways, and the leadership actively sought to appeal to it. Prior to the December 1960 assault in Chilpancingo, in response to a government announcement of a prohibition on gatherings of more than five people, community activists set up a permanent sit-in symbolically located at the Monument to the Flag in Iguala. Participant Pablo Sandoval Cruz describes demonstrations where "unforgettable moments of joy" were based on a shared national history: "This spirit of solidarity ... was the same ... that we had inherited from [independence-era leaders] Vicente Guerrero" and "from José María Morelos, with his heroism and his great patriotism."[44] Speeches and other communications from the leadership also employed nationalist rhetoric. Vázquez cited "our respect for the Constitution [through which] we want [legal] guarantees."[45] An ACG manifesto issued on January 19, 1963 was presented in strongly nationalist language, declaring commitment to the "revolutionary ideal of 1910 of 'Effective Suffrage.'" It closed with the capitalized slogan "MI PATRIA ES PRIMERO" ("My native land is first").[46] In an April 1964 manifesto, the ACG challenged the "bad administration of justice and the annulment of the democratic liberties granted by statute in the national Constitution."[47] Cabañas asserted the government had broken with "the highest and most sacred principles of the Constitution."[48] Despite

---

[44] Sandoval Cruz, *El movimiento social*, 38–39.
[45] Vázquez, "Anecdotario," in ibid., 130.
[46] ACG manifesto, January 19, 1963, in Gomezjara, *Bonapartismo*, 306–07.
[47] ACG manifesto, April 1964, in *Bonapartismo*, 306–07. This document represents the fusion of reliance on the language of revolutionary nationalism (demands grounded in the Constitution of 1917) and the desirability of a more radical revolutionary socialist agenda (the rescue of resources from the hands of imperialists, scientific economic planning, etc.).
[48] Cabañas, "Anecdotarios," in *Bonapartismo*, 140.

persistent government violence, the language of nationalism and rights guaranteed by the Constitution continued to color critiques of the state's betrayal.

By late 1964, Vázquez and his colleagues in the ACG were beginning to evince a new and more uncompromising analysis. An October 1964 manifesto articulated four key goals: the end of the capitalist oligarchy allied with "Yankee" imperialism; establishment of a coalition government composed of workers, *campesinos*, progressive students, and intellectuals, as a transition step toward socialism; the full political and economic independence of the country; and the establishment of a new social order for the benefit of the working majority.[49] To implement this project, they called for a network of grassroots Committees of Struggle that would comprise the new version of the ACG, now renamed the Asociación Cívica Nacional Revolucionaria (National Revolutionary Civic Association, ACNR). The Committees were intended to be locally based organizations grounded in Marxist-Leninist theory seeking "radical change of the political and economic regime" toward one that was both "democratic and popular." The statement was a declaration of independence from the current government. Yet even as he shifted toward more radical rhetoric, Vázquez would still call on the populace to send telegrams and letters to the President and Interior Ministry. Communiqués continued to employ the icons of the nation's past: "Our struggle has its inspirational roots in [our] national history and reality: our flag . . . is the same raised by Hidalgo, Morelos and Guerrero, Juárez, Zapata, and Villa."[50] The claiming of revolutionary symbols and appeals to the national government to intervene on behalf of local protesters reveals a presumption of receptivity, pointing to some level of successful post-revolutionary state legitimation at the federal level. Further, this may be indicative of the organizations' understanding of the local populace and its discomfort with the more radical, "foreign," "godless" language of international Marxism-Leninism.

Vázquez's more radical ideology as expressed in later communiqués and interviews came as no surprise to colleagues Antonio Sotelo Peréz and

---

[49] Aroche Parra, *El Che, Jenaro y las guerrillas,* 40, places the manifesto's release in October 1963. Elsewhere, the call for "clandestine committees of struggle" appears in an ACG "Manifesto" issued in August 1964 in Iguala, in Antonio Aranda Flores, *Los cívicos guerrerenses* (Mexico City: Luysil de México, 1979), 72–77.

[50] Vázquez, "La Asociación Cívica Nacional Revolucionaria acerca de la liberación de Genaro, 22 de abril de 1968 de la cárcel de Iguala, Gro.," n.d., very shortly after April 22, in Aranda Flores, *Los cívicos,* 123–26.

Arturo Miranda Ramírez, who watched Vázquez conduct study sessions among his cohorts. The *cívicos* discussed the revolutionary theory they studied with the aid of a "copious collection" of books on guerrilla warfare, with Vázquez expostulating on "seizing power for the people, armed insurrection, class warfare, and other concepts that derived from the triumphant revolutions in Africa, Asia, and Latin America."[51] Miranda Ramírez also recalls that while Vázquez was waging war in the mountains, he often shared his political thoughts with the local *campesinos*, expressing opinions on a range of issues, including "the Sino-Soviet split, the Tupamaros in Uruguay, Allende's regime in Chile," and theoreticians "Trotsky, Lenin and Stalin, [as well as the] works of Che and the Cuban Revolution."[52] In a communiqué released on July 8, 1969, the ACNR (over Vázquez's signature) called for the "re-establishment as a specific task ... the intensive study of the Revolutionary Theory of Marxism-Leninism," resulting in ongoing internal "political and ideological debate on the theoretical orientation of Marxism" and its applicability to their struggle.[53] Vázquez's goal was to both learn from and adapt the lessons of historic and contemporary international struggles. They were "not," he insisted, "the definitive inspiration ... of our struggle," which lay instead in "our own reality, both national and local." The guerrillas merely "extracted the applicable political and military" lessons from Marxist theory and practice.[54] Alongside these readings and discussions, Sotelo notes, Vázquez insisted on the study of nationalism: the history of Mexico and Guerrero, and of nationalist leaders including Hidalgo, Morelos, Villa, Zapata, and the more recent Jaramillo and Arturo Gámiz, who were all "indispensable elements on the menu."[55] Another colleague, Fausto Ávila, while having read Marxist literature, unhesitatingly noted that his primary ideological influence was the Mexican Revolution, citing, for example, Mariano Azuela's 1915 novel *Los de abajo*. He further suggested that his cohorts who self-defined as socialists did so because of the government's failure to fulfill its revolutionary promises.[56] Other activists reported being influenced by the works

---

[51] Sotelo Pérez, *Breve historia*, 128.   [52] Miranda Ramírez, *El otro rostro*, 75–76.

[53] ACNR, "Conclusiones llevadas a cabo por la ACNR en las montañas del Sur, conclusiones de la reunión llevada a cabo por la Dirección Político-Militar de la Asociación Cívica Nacional Revolucionaria, el día 8 de julio de 1969, en las montañas del Sur," in Aranda Flores, *Los cívicos*, 123–26.

[54] Vázquez, "Entrevista a Genaro Vázquez en el otoño de 1970," interviewer unidentified (unpublished, Fall 1970). In possession of author.

[55] Sotelo Pérez, *Breve historia*, 128.   [56] Ávila, interview.

of Adolfo Gilly, John Womack, Martín Luis Guzmán, Elena Poniatowska, Luis González de Alba, and José Revueltas.[57]

The ACG manifestos illustrate Vázquez's most lucid analysis of the interconnectedness of traditional *caciquismo* (boss rule) and emerging capitalism in Mexico, demonstrating the adaptation of Marxist-Leninist analysis to the conditions of twentieth-century rural Mexico.[58] For Vázquez, the "*cacique capitalista*" embodied a synthesis of traditional feudalism and encroaching modernization, combining the values of these two seemingly conflictive systems. Vázquez challenged traditional progressives who had called for the advance of capitalism with its presumptive link to democracy. He concluded, alternatively, that "residual feudalism" required open conflict between the popular classes and capitalism. He explicitly rejected the participation of the national bourgeoisie, arguing that under the contemporary Mexican state, that class – rather than the working classes – would reap the primary benefits of any reform of the state. Vázquez's political experiences in his native state progressively radicalized his ideological approach to repressive conditions in Guerrero. Earlier demands for land redistribution were ultimately replaced by calls for an end to private landholdings and the socialization of transportation and communication infrastructure.

Although it is difficult to assign relative weight to the factors that led to the demise of Vázquez's movement, his transition to more radical and internationalist language, in concert with geographic isolation and government repression, may well have contributed to lessening his movement's appeal to the masses. While he appeared to retain the admiration of many, as evidenced in interviews and the response to his death, the broad-based popular movement of 1960 would remain a high point in his efforts to secure economic and political justice. Vázquez died in a car accident in 1972. His colleagues in the ACNR dispersed, with some joining Cabañas's guerrilla movement.[59]

Lucio Cabañas's political tendencies, like those of Vázquez, initially exhibited his early influences, including those of his instructors in Ayotzinapa. Rural *normal* schools reflected their *campesino* composition, and the life experiences of its students left them predisposed to radical politicization. Ayotzinapa was renowned for its teachers' radical advocacy, with a reputation "unquestionable and envied" by other schools

[57] Eloy Cisneros, interview, Chilpancingo, July 2, 2003.
[58] ACG, "A todo el pueblo de Guerrero y México," in Gomezjara, *Bonapartismo*, 301–02.
[59] Ávila, interview.

nationwide, having produced a number of progressive and leftist fighters in its decades-long history.[60] So while his tutelage remained local, Cabañas's education was by no means provincial. He did not adhere to any single doctrine and, like Vázquez, avidly read diverse theoreticians, including not only Marx and Lenin, but Mexican anarchist Ricardo Flores Magón and later the writings of Che Guevara and German-American Herbert Marcuse.[61] As in Vázquez's case, this breadth and flexibility was evident in Cabañas's efforts to adapt the lessons of international theory and struggles to local conditions.

Cabañas's analysis had deeper roots as well, influenced by the anti-imperialism of Uruguay's José Enrique Rodó (1871–1917) and Peru's Víctor Raúl Haya de la Torre (1895–1979), and the socialism of Peru's José Carlos Mariátegui (1894–1930). Mexico's Cold War–era militants became acquainted with these early-twentieth-century activist-intellectuals at school and, in the case of Cabañas, during his early engagement with the Mexican Communist Party.[62] They took what was relevant to their struggles, seeking to combine arguments developed elsewhere with the realities of mid-century Guerrero. As Cabañas noted, "The contact with the poverty of others and my life of shortages made me unhappy, it was not Marxism-Leninism as many think."[63]

Haya de la Torre argued that the Marxism of European intellectuals overlooked the contextual specificity of Latin America, where capitalism was dominated by foreign capital, constraining the development of an indigenous bourgeoisie. He argued that a Latin American socialist revolution could further be defined as "anti-imperialist," "agrarian," or "national revolutionary."[64] These latter terms resonated with Guerrero's populace. Haya de la Torre concluded that Latin America was not ready for socialism and instead suggested an anti-imperialist state under the leadership of a cross-class alliance (a vision adopted and then rejected by Vázquez, as noted above).

Cabañas's elasticity also reflected Mariátegui's assertion that "socialism [should not] be absolute, abstract, indifferent to the facts, and to

[60] Mayo, *La guerrilla*, 44–45.
[61] Cárdenas, interview. Alfonso Aguario (interview) also recalls Cabañas reading Marx as early as 1962.
[62] Hoyo and Cárdenas, interviews.
[63] Quoted in Carlos Bonilla Machorro, *Ejercicio de guerrillero* (Mexico City: Gaceta, 1981), 108.
[64] Harry E. Vanden and Marc Becker, eds., *José Carlos Mariátegui: An Anthology* (New York: Monthly Review, 2011), 13, 18.

changing, mobile reality," but must rather adapt to "the realities of a local situation."[65] Mariátegui also believed Marxism required adaptation to Latin American conditions, notably emphasizing factors such as education and indigenous culture, not just class position, in the production of consciousness. He had been inspired by widespread student protests in Argentina (1918) and Peru (1922), which convinced him that education could and should influence students' engagement with the broader society.[66] As with these earlier examples, the popular struggles in Guerrero and Mexico City brought students and workers together "socially and ideologically."[67] This was undoubtedly Vázquez's trajectory, and it was this tradition and his own experiences at Ayotzinapa that led Cabañas to emphasize the strategic importance of education.

One former PDLP combatant, identified as "Pedro Periquito" (likely his *nom de guerre*), recalled especially enjoying the Saturdays and Sundays when Cabañas held assemblies in the mountains for the *campesinos*. "In these assemblies he spoke to the *campesinos* of a new revolution, for which they had to take up arms." When Cabañas asked if he wanted to study for a professional career (he was a young child at the time), he had answered that he could not, since he had no money. "He told me that that is why there is the struggle, for children to have the opportunity to study what we want and not grow up ignorant, that this is why we prepare for a new revolution that is gestating and in which we will participate to our utmost."[68] As had Mariátegui and Haya de la Torre, Cabañas called for the formation of preparatory schools with a popular orientation, a goal realized with the founding, among others, of the still-open "Che Guevara" popular preparatory (*prepa popular*) in Chilpancingo.[69]

In his last years, Cabañas took up the more volatile rhetoric of revolutionary socialism, influenced by his interactions with radical university faculty who joined the struggle in Guerrero after government massacres in Mexico City in 1968 and 1971. Only months before his death, Cabañas requested that UAG faculty sympathizers provide study sessions on

---

[65] Vanden and Becker, "Acknowledgements," in ibid., 13.

[66] Mariátegui, "Public Education," in *Seven Interpretive Essays on Peruvian Reality*, trans. Marjory Urquidi (Austin: University of Texas Press, 1988), 91–93, 87.

[67] Ibid., 107.

[68] Quoted in Eleazar Campos Gómez, ed., *Lucio Cabañas y el Partido de los Pobres: Una experiencia guerrillera en México* (Mexico City: Nuestra América, 1987), 150. Armando Pedraza León, *Réquiem para la guerrilla en Guerrero* (Mexico City: n.p., 1979), 14, also discusses these study sessions in the sierras.

[69] Many of these high schools are affiliated with the UAG. A "popular orientation" for the UAG had been among the student demands in 1960.

Marxist thought to his guerrilla fighters. In February 1974, faculty joined a group of perhaps twenty to thirty guerrillas (most of whom were about eighteen years old) in the mountains, where they addressed concepts of exploitation and the state.[70] Former PDLP activist Ricardo Rodríguez points to these radical ideologies as a framework with which to articulate the life experiences of the community.[71]

Cabañas's independence from orthodox Leninism was further apparent in his interpretation of the role of a vanguard party. He often eschewed strict Leninist democratic centralism in favor of a more fluid responsiveness to community input. Cabañas's style reflected his belief that the life experiences of the people had much to teach him and is evident in his oft-repeated slogan *Ser pueblo y estar con el pueblo* ("To be of the people and with the people"). This approach was augmented by his personal distaste for "authoritarianism and abuse."[72]

Not unlike Vázquez's choice to return to Guerrero to organize the agrarian sector, Cabañas's prioritizing of rural workers further reflects his rejection of a rigid Marxist analysis, which typically saw industrial wage workers as the key revolutionary actors. In August 1973 Ignacio Salas Obregón, founder of the Liga 23 de Septiembre (September 23rd League) – a key urban revolutionary group – met with Cabañas to secure organizational links between the Liga and the PDLP, arguing the greater effectiveness of a nationwide armed front.[73] Such efforts failed under the weight of differing class backgrounds, the contrasting terrains of the groups' respective struggles, and most significantly, disagreement on the relative weight of urban and rural leadership and the perception that urban militants neglected grassroots organizing. As Cabañas's colleague Miranda Ramírez noted, the urban leadership tried to "construct the tree first and then its roots, to build the guerrilla organization and then its base."[74] The failure to establish nationwide links, however, as well as the

---

[70] Cárdenas and Hoyo, interviews; Expediente 100–10-1–78-H51-L-77, File on Cárdenas, Dirección General de Investigaciones Políticas y Sociales, Archivo General de la Nación, Mexico. The source for this government assessment of the sessions is unidentified, but its specificity and rhetorical ring suggest it is the result of statements made by participants under police interrogation, most likely Cárdenas.

[71] Ricardo Rodríguez G., "Testimonio," October 27, 2001, 3, in possession of the author.

[72] Hoyo, interview.

[73] Mario Ramírez Salas, "La relación Partido de los Pobres y Liga Comunista 23 de Septiembre, en el estado de Guerrero," presentation at conference *La guerrilla en las regiones de México, siglo XX*, Zamora, Michoacán, July 2002.

[74] Quoted in José Luis Moreno Borbolla, "Testimonios sobre los movimientos armados de la década de los setenta," presentation at UNAM, October 25 and November 6, 2003.

failure of the two movements within Guerrero to unite, contributed to the ultimate demise of both.

Similarly, the ACG/ACNR and PDLP perceived themselves as struggling against a common enemy, but failed to effectively unite. Numerous obstacles, including distance, logistics, alternative strategies, and charismatic leadership, kept them apart. In an undated interview, Vázquez's right-hand man, José Bracho Campos, explains the two movements' vain attempts to unite. "More than unification, we sought coordination. We were fellow players in a united front which we sought not to dilute but to integrate into a broader front. A proposed meeting [to discuss unification] did not occur due to adverse circumstances at that time, and later, we lost contact."[75]

The guerrillas' shortcomings notwithstanding, the fluidity and evolution in the numerous public statements of the ACG and PDLP challenge the simplistic and one-dimensional identities imposed on these rebels. The government responded aggressively with patriotic rhetoric and violent repression to alienate the guerrillas from potential allies. In the context of the Cold War, and the government's interest in combating challenges from the left while maintaining its status as a leader of the "Third World independent bloc," charges of communist infiltration or socialist goals were potent weapons against the opposition's strategy of securing the participation and trust of diverse community sectors.

GUNS AND BUTTER

The government's rhetorical and military efforts to isolate and discredit the opposition increased in frequency and intensity in the early 1970s. Its rhetorical tactics relied heavily on its control of major news outlets, while military personnel conducted an estimated fourteen major, deadly, military campaigns in Guerrero from 1968 until Cabañas's death in 1974. Yet despite these efforts, the guerrillas' support, both overt and covert from significant segments of the populace, persisted. Several *campesinos* from the region later recalled, "We had no fear of Lucio, the people sympathized with him" because of his support for "those who need help."[76] An uncle suggests family

---

[75] José Bracho Campos, undated interview at the time of an arrest, in José Natividad Rosales, ¿*Quién fue Lucio Cabañas? ¿Qué pasa con la guerrilla en México?* (Mexico City: Posada, n.d.), 80.

[76] Testimony of Francisca Sánchez Romero and Cutberto Calderón Santana (2000), in Gloria Leticia Díaz, "A 27 años de una masacre, el recuerdo huele a pólvora," *Proceso* (September 30, 2000): 22.

networks provided the backbone of support, with a core of over 300 whose loyalty was based on family ties more than political affinity, as well as local peasants who engaged sporadically.[77] While such depictions may well be selective, the two guerrilla movements could not have survived as long as they did without the covert or passive support of numerous *campesinos*.

Successive administrations sought to undermine that support with a two-pronged strategy wherein they provided services while suppressing opposition. They did so by conflating the military presence with economic largesse: the army itself was the visible hand distributing benefits. In one example of many, two battalions of soldiers arrived in Atoyac with the task of suppressing any public display on the occasion of the first anniversary of the May 1967 massacre. Concurrently, the government initiated Operation Friendship in the form of 27 commandos with 500 military doctors to dispense medical care, medicines, and food throughout the Coyuca, San Jerónimo, Atoyac, and Tecpan municipalities.[78] Even so, Secretary of Defense General Hermenegildo Cuenca Díaz acknowledged that the army's presence had increased concerns among the populace. In a lengthy interview with the US Department of State that year, Cuenca unabashedly described these activities as part of government efforts to "reach the population and *control it.*"[79] In an interview with newspaper *Excélsior*, Cuenca insisted that army participation in civil projects was "to dispel the negative attitude of the civilian population which has inevitably originated as a consequence of the investigations and detentions."[80] The strategy reflects that found in manuals provided by the US School of the Americas, with recommendations including introduction of "social and economic activities in the zones of conflict" for the purpose of political indoctrination.[81] Yet tensions were kept high by the unpredictability of repression and the traumatized communities it left behind.

---

[77] Hoyo, interview. This "seasonal warrior" reflects the cyclical engagement of *campesinos* in Mexico's military past – notably, the War of Independence and Zapata's Army of the South.

[78] Fierro Armenta, *Monografía de Atoyac*, 360, records the visit as May 16, 1969.

[79] Robert McBride to Secretary of State, May 27, 1971, NSA, https://nsarchive2.gwu.edu /NSAEBB/NSAEBB105/Doc1.pdf (accessed May 17, 2018). Emphasis added.

[80] Undated interview quoted in Natividad Rosales, *¿Quién fue Lucio?*, 86. See also Dirección Federal de Seguridad (DFS), order from Cuenca Díaz of September 23, 1972, in Gustavo Castillo and Misael Habana de los Santos, "Descubren pruebas de que Cuenca Díaz ordenó 'exterminar' a Lucio Cabañas," *La Jornada*, November 27, 2003.

[81] Juan Fernando Reyes Peláez, "El largo brazo del Estado: La estrategía contrainsurgente del gobierno mexicano," presentation at conference *La guerrilla en las regiones de México*.

The necessity of securing popular support was evident, but some of the populace was not easily cajoled. Cabañas's surviving half-brother David (his *nom de guerre*) recalls the futility of the efforts: while the government was supplying foodstuffs to the people, they were often passing them along to the guerrillas.[82] Letters to the editor, anecdotes, and official discourse further confirm the failure of government efforts to win the "hearts and minds" of the populace.[83]

MEXICO'S DIRTY WAR: "GOD KNOWS WHAT THEY HAVE DONE."[84]

The Mexican state, at the highest levels of command ... abandoned the legal framework and committed crimes against humanity that culminated in massacres, forced disappearances, systematic torture, war crimes, and genocide, in its attempts to destroy sectors of society it considered its ideological enemy.[85]

Government policy against perceived dissent was most aggressive in peripheral rural states, most notably Guerrero. State and federal personnel fanned out across the state, targeting entire communities, individual *campesinos*, students and faculty, and those bearing the names Cabañas or Barrientos and, to a lesser extent, Vázquez.[86] The government justified this aggressive repression with its depiction of a cancerous threat to national security. Like its counterparts in the Southern Cone, the government drew analogies between the military and "doctors" responsible for the "national health," who were expected to employ "medications," a euphemism for torture, assassination and disappearances.[87] Military discourse dehumanized victims, describing them as "packages."[88]

---

[82] "David" Cabañas, interview, Mexico City, February 17, 2003.

[83] For additional examples of the populace subverting government outreach, see Blacker-Hanson, "*¡La Lucha Sigue!*" and "Cold War in the Countryside."

[84] Widow of dirty-war victim Ignacio Sánchez of El Quemado, in Víctor Ballinas, "Con esas *calentaditas*, cualquiera se raja," *La Jornada*, November 4, 2001.

[85] Ignacio Carrillo Prieto, *Informe General* (Fiscalía Especial para Movimientos Sociales y Políticos del Pasado, 2005), NSA, https://nsarchive2.gwu.edu//NSAEBB/NSAEBB180/010_Informe%20General.pdf (accessed May 17, 2018).

[86] Doyle, "Dawn of Mexico's Dirty War."

[87] Sergio Aguayo Quezada, *La charola: Una historia de los servicios de inteligencia en México* (Mexico City: Grijalbo, 2000), 94.

[88] General E. Jiménez, November 22, 1973, cited in Ignacio Carrillo Prieto, *Draft Report* (Fiscalía Especial para Movimientos Sociales y Políticos del Pasado, 2005), Chapter 6, pp. 73–74, NSA, https://nsarchive2.gwu.edu/NSAEBB/NSAEBB180/index.htm (accessed May 17, 2018).

Military reprisals against communities suspected of supporting or concealing guerrillas were often swift and unexpected. It is no coincidence that Atoyac municipality – home of Lucio Cabañas, his extended family, and the PDLP – was heavily targeted by authorities. One incident was the roundup of *campesinos* in the village of El Quemado in September 1972, on the presumption of their involvement in recent ambushes against the army. They were reportedly tortured and held incommunicado.[89] Accusations that local people were providing food to Cabañas's brigades brought the military to Los Piloncillos. On April 24, 1973, a reported 400 soldiers with four tanks surrounded this community of 15 homes, leaving 6 *campesinos* dead. The community learned that had the wanted men not been home, the soldiers intended to burn the village down.[90]

Among the most ruthless weapons in the state's arsenal were disappearances, which heavily targeted Atoyac and Cabañas's relatives. In 2003 the National Security Archive reported, "Mexican human rights groups say they have collected evidence of some 650 cases of civilians who disappeared from Guerrero during the dirty war – more than 400 of them from Atoyac de Alvarez alone."[91] The National Human Rights Commission notes the disappearance of a Lucio Cabañas Tabares, seized by the military from his barbershop in Atoyac in April 1974. His seizure was confirmed by Dirección Federal de Seguridad (Federal Security Agency, DFS) files, indicating that he had been detained by the army and held at Military Camp No. 1. He, too, then joined the ranks of the disappeared.[92] On another occasion, one survivor told his daughter the reason he had been tortured. She reported: "They told him to abandon his second name because they were going to finish off everyone with the last name Cabañas. He refused. He kept telling them, 'My name is Alejandro Arroyo Cabañas.'"[93] "David" Cabañas reports that over 126 members of the Cabañas and Barrientos families disappeared in the years after 1967.[94] Survivors also report

---

[89] Pedraza León, *Réquiem*, 7, attributes the formation of the PDLP's Brigada Campesina de Ajusticiamiento (Peasant Execution Brigade) to this incident.

[90] Díaz, "A 27 años de una masacre," 22.   [91] Doyle, "Dawn of Mexico's Dirty War."

[92] Witness T305, in the Report of the National Human Rights Commission, as reported in James F. Smith, "One Family Paid Dearly in 'Dirty War,'" *Los Angeles Times*, December 11, 2001. The reports of family arrests and disappearances were confirmed by "David" Cabañas, interview.

[93] Smith, "One Family Paid Dearly." For additional examples of detained, tortured, disappeared and dead relatives, see Gloria Leticia Díaz, "La familia de Lucio Cabañas reclama su cadáver," *Proceso* (May 26, 2001): 36. "David" attributes his survival to fleeing incognito to Mexico City. Cabañas, interview.

[94] "David" Cabañas, interview and Smith, "One Family Paid Dearly."

witnessing the detention of disappeared victims. Octaviano Santiago Dionisio notes that upon his arrival at a clandestine jail "common prisoners" informed him of the recent incarceration of several political prisoners who remain disappeared today.[95] Following the arrest and torture of UAG faculty members Alejandra Cárdenas and Antonio Hernández, Cárdenas testified that while held in a clandestine military "secret house" and prison she, too, personally saw other militants alive whom the government later claimed had died in armed confrontations.[96]

By October 1973, as reports proliferated of detainees being dropped in the ocean from the military base just south of Acapulco, local fishermen began to report finding articles of clothing and bones. The military responded by threatening the local population with reprisals if the information were made known, while publicly dismissing accusations of human rights violations.[97] As human rights advocates argue, disappearances could not have been perpetrated without the knowledge and at least tacit consent of the highest authorities.[98]

Despite the extent of the violence in Guerrero, most of the world turned a blind eye to Mexico's dirty war. The government's denunciation of human rights abuses elsewhere, such as its condemnation of the military coup in Chile, helped divert attention from its own ruthlessness. The exception was the publicity given the 1968 massacre in Tlatelolco Plaza by the international press gathered for the upcoming Olympic Games in Mexico City. Those few governments that chose to condemn the spread of state repression in Latin America focused on the more flagrant military dictatorships that had seized power in Central American and Southern Cone nations.

CONCLUDING THOUGHTS

This chapter has explored popular organizing in a rural context in response to the abuse of national and regional authority in Mexico. In Guerrero, both the federal and state regimes used extrajudicial, repressive

---

[95] Santiago Dionisio, *Testimonio*, 29.
[96] Cárdenas, presentation, University of Washington, November 14, 2002. See also "¿Dónde están Antonio y Alejandra?" *Proceso* (July 29, 1978); Enrique Maza, "Antonio Hernández, ex preso político, confirmó, sin conocer a Osorio, todo lo que el soldado declaró," *Proceso* (April 16, 1988).
[97] Carrillo Prieto, *Draft Report*, Chapter 6, p. 74.
[98] DFS files "confirm that [President] López Portillo (1976–82) gave instructions for the disappearance of detained guerrillas." Aguayo, *La charola*, 95.

rule to assure their hegemony over the popular classes and to try to exert power over each other. In the power struggles among elites, the general population was subjected to the violent abuse of its civil and human rights. Legitimate channels of protest were blocked by official intransigence and a willingness to use violence to maintain control. Despite their own rivalries, federal and state power contenders were united in silencing popular calls for democratic inclusion. As scholar Kate Doyle writes, "[G]iven the choice between repression and negotiation, political stasis or change, the regime predictably, inexorably chose violence to preserve the status quo."[99]

The dirty war in Mexico – indeed, throughout Latin America – was an asymmetric struggle. On the one hand stood a national government, with governmental and paramilitary forces, an extensive propaganda apparatus, and international military, intelligence, and propaganda support. Against these forces stood poor *campesinos*, teachers, and laborers, often armed with vintage weapons that had survived the decades since their revolution. The conclusion is inescapable: the most serious human rights abuses were committed by the national and state governments and sanctioned at the highest levels. As scholar Enrique Condés writes, the human rights violations committed by leftist rebels "pale in comparison with the tortures, extrajudicial executions, pillaging and violations committed by the police and military."[100]

In addition to government repression, it is also important to acknowledge the full spectrum of popular responses. Many citizens accepted or shared the government's vision for the nation – if not its tactics – while others, unable or unwilling to take up arms, attempted alternative strategies to ameliorate conditions within contained parameters. Many ceased participating in what they perceived as either a fraudulent electoral charade or risky public opposition. The majority of citizens who participated in Guerrero's rallies, marches, and sit-ins were there to demand economic rights and political access. Their behavior illustrates the entrenched belief that their government was a flawed-but-reparable embodiment of their vision. Perhaps naively, they believed their goals could be accomplished within the framework of the Mexican state. This carefully nurtured trust may well have saved the nation from a more radical revolution. Had the *caciques* of Guerrero ever granted a degree of participatory democracy, or

[99] Doyle, "Dawn of Mexico's Dirty War."
[100] Enrique Condés Lara, *Represión y rebelión en México* (Mexico City: Miguel Ángel Porrúa, 2007), 1: 22.

at least the façade of it, opposition movements may never have found the mass base they did.

It is also essential to assess the failings of the militant opposition efforts. While governmental violence undoubtedly quashed democratic participation, the guerrilla movements led by Genaro Vázquez and Lucio Cabañas made mistakes that contributed to their defeat. First, the neglect of urban centers and failure to unite with other opposition efforts likely contributed to their isolation and demise.

Additionally, the popular movement begun in 1960 demanded the fulfillment of the perceived promises of the Revolution of 1910. Both Vázquez and Cabañas initially shared this aim of improving the current system from within, but ultimately concluded that only a new socialist, revolutionary government would satisfy those demands. Their transition to the more radical argument that a new revolution was needed may well have discouraged some of their potential supporters who retained faith in the national government. Despite continued references to nationalist heroes, the leadership perhaps failed to fully fuse that historic legacy with the international language of socialism. Numerically, neither the ACNR nor PDLP ever relied on armed militants; their strength lay in the support of noncombatants. Under the weight of government repression, their ideological leap may have limited successful outreach to potential allies not ready to take up arms against the "revolutionary" government. It is important to remember, however, that their ultimate isolation and defeat were a direct result of overwhelming government violence. Guerrero attests to the government's fragile achievement in channeling the dreams of radical change into its fold – or silencing the dreamers – by the use of extraordinary savagery alongside its rhetoric.

After the military defeat of the armed combatants, and the zealous government carnage, many survivors found alternative projects to pursue, including the defense of human rights, accountability for the disappeared, environmentalism, anti-globalization, and indigenous and women's rights. They pursued their commitment to a progressive agenda through legitimate public fora, including electoral politics and widespread activism in nongovernmental organizations. This shift in strategy reflected many leftists' ideological return to nationalism and away from the socialism they had sought during the years of the dirty war.

By the 1980s popular demands increased for government accountability for the innumerable of family and friends who had suffered, disappeared, and died during the dirty war. As the new century approached, demands for rights and accountability were once again couched in the language of democratic nationalism and channeled through institutional paths. Deep community roots had proven a potent recruiting tool when family and community members joined in both public and clandestine opposition in mid-century. As the face of the movement again became public, those ties motivated demands for the return of the disappeared. This same perseverance is apparent in the demands for the return of the forty-three Ayotzinapa students. As Milan Kundera has written, "the struggle of man [*sic*] against power is the struggle of memory against forgetting."[101]

Half a century later, the question arises: did the left make a difference? It is difficult to recreate either the sense of urgency or the utopian optimism that inspired participation in grassroots movements, both armed and unarmed, in the "long 1960s" in Latin America. Although the revolution envisioned by many Mexican activists in the 1960s and 1970s did not occur, their struggles were not fruitless. Activist and *prepa* instructor Alfonso Aguario believes that the popular struggles of the 1960s and 1970s were a "grand democratic movement," concluding that while they may have been "romantic" and "utopian," they were "the only road to follow" for those who believed they had "an obligation to participate in the process of change."[102] Aguario was not alone in positioning these efforts within a vision of utopia. Former political prisoner and UAG professor Alejandra Cárdenas contends that the political currents of the 1970s are "incomprehensible without including the notion of utopia, justice, a better world." She described Cabañas's ideal as "a world without poverty and with justice and socialism." Such beliefs sustained the activists, making their efforts "worth the pain."[103]

Did the high price Guerrero's communities paid have any lasting effect? The heightened attention to human rights in Mexico, both at home and on the world platform, can be traced in large part to the people of Guerrero, who stepped forward to challenge and publicize the state's behavior. The path they cleared contributed to a worldwide outcry to protect the human rights of the Zapatistas who rose up in Chiapas in 1994. As evidenced by the ongoing efforts to locate the missing students of Ayotzinapa, the demands for government accountability continue. As one human rights report on Guerrero noted, "The people and communities maintain their resistance."[104]

---

[101] Milan Kundera, *The Book of Laughter and Forgetting*, trans. Aaron Asher (New York: HarperPerennial, 1996), 4.
[102] Aguario, interview.
[103] Cárdenas, presentation, University of Washington, and discussions with the author.
[104] Centro de Derechos Humanos Miguel Agustín Pro Juárez (Centro Prodh), *La violencia en Guerrero y Oaxaca* (Mexico City: Centro Prodh, 1999), 62.

9

The Ethnic Question in Guatemala's Armed Conflict

Insights from the Detention and "Rescue" of Emeterio Toj Medrano

Betsy Konefal

> I dare say that the *militares* understood the ethnic component and how to manipulate it better than the revolutionaries. They understood it was a very serious issue ... and that they had to disarticulate it, prevent indigenous support for revolution.
>
> – Domingo Hernández Ixcoy[1]

Questions about indigenous involvement in Guatemala's long and ultimately genocidal civil war (1960–1996) have been debated since the earliest days of the conflict. The war itself was not ethnically based. Guerrilla insurgents fought predominantly over political and economic issues, and in the name of social revolution. Armed conflict started soon after the US-sponsored overthrow of the reformist government of Jacobo Arbenz Guzmán in 1954, as insurgents explicitly challenged the reimposition of military dictatorship and repression, as well as the reversal of democracy and labor and land reforms that had been initiated by Arbenz and his predecessor, Juan José Arévalo. Over the next three decades,

---

[*] My thanks to Hernández Ixcoy, Emeterio Toj Medrano, and Gustavo Meoño for sharing their memories and interpretations of this case with me. Thanks, too, to Kevin Young and Marc Becker for their helpful feedback as this chapter developed. I first recounted this episode in a book, *For Every Indio Who Falls: A History of Maya Activism in Guatemala, 1960–1990* (Albuquerque: University of New Mexico Press, 2010). Since that time, I've learned more about its backstory and significance, which is the subject of this chapter. The case was also included as "illustrative" in the UN-sponsored truth commission report, Comisión para el Esclarecimiento Histórico (CEH), *Memoria del silencio*, 12 vols. (Guatemala: UNOPS, 1999), "Caso ilustrativo no. 98: Privación arbitraria de libertad y tortura de Emeterio Toj Medrano."
[1] Domingo Hernández Ixcoy, interview, Chimaltenango, September 7, 2002.

revolutionary groups would engage in guerrilla assaults against an intransigent and often brutal state bent on suppressing all types of reform, drawing inspiration and sometimes support from other revolutionary movements in the region and Fidel Castro's Cuba.

Yet in a society with a Maya majority, deeply entrenched histories of racism and discrimination, and a striking correlation between indigenous identity, poverty, and political marginalization, ethnicity would be central to experiences of war, and to insurgent and counterinsurgent strategies. Ethnicity became an especially important factor in the Guatemalan conflict as mobilization intensified in the mostly Maya-populated western highlands, an area where the largest of the guerrilla armies, the Ejército Guerrillero de los Pobres (Guerrilla Army of the Poor, EGP), expanded in the 1970s. The "ethnic component," as EGP member and Maya-K'iche' Domingo Hernández Ixcoy put it, was indeed "a very serious issue" for virtually all parties to the conflict: the successive Guatemalan regimes and their military strategists, the multiple revolutionary armies (to varying degrees), and their supporters. Most recognized that success or failure would likely pivot on indigenous support for revolution.[2]

Undermining and preventing such support was a central concern of Guatemalan military regimes. As the guerrilla organizations expanded, the state worked to bind indigenous communities to the army and its pacification project by forcing indigenous men and boys into the lowest ranks of the Guatemalan army and an extensive network of local civil patrols. The patrol system was onerous and coercive, compelling Maya men in the early 1980s to guard their own communities against guerrilla incursions, and at times to take part in state terror. State forces at the same time tried to preempt indigenous participation in opposition movements through a combination of targeted repression against leaders and supporters, co-optation, and psychological operations. As Hernández Ixcoy suggests in the epigraph, and as I will explore in this chapter, part of that effort involved trying to exploit fissures within the left over questions of ethnic identity.

---

[2] The four main guerrilla armies included the EGP, the Organización Revolucionaria del Pueblo en Armas (Revolutionary Organization of People in Arms, ORPA), the Fuerzas Armadas Rebeldes (Rebel Armed Forces, FAR), and the armed wing of the Partido Guatemalteco del Trabajo (Guatemalan Workers' Party, PGT), Guatemala's Communist Party. In 1982, these four groups joined together in the umbrella Unidad Revolucionaria Nacional Guatemalteca (Guatemalan National Revolutionary Unity, URNG). Of these revolutionary movements, the EGP and ORPA were generally considered to be more attuned than the FAR or the PGT to indigenous-specific concerns.

For their part, certain figures in the revolutionary movements worked to overcome such divisions and to cultivate indigenous backing. Central to that effort for the EGP was a *guerrillero* named Emeterio Toj Medrano. A Maya-K'iche' with a long history of organizing inside and outside his community of Santa Cruz del Quiché, Toj served as a bridge between the EGP and a small but important indigenous sector that came to be known as the *movimiento indígena*. Mayas affiliated with the movement tended to be relatively well educated and often at least a step removed from subsistence agriculture. In the early 1970s, they began discussion groups where they debated questions of identity and discrimination, and condemned the economic and political marginalization of Mayas. Within a few years, key members began to express support for revolution. But they also sharply criticized the guerrilla organizations' positioning on indigenous identity: a vocal sector argued vehemently for a vision of revolutionary change that did not prioritize class over race.[3]

Emeterio Toj's assignment for the EGP was not an easy one: the guerrilla groups, led predominantly by *ladinos* (a term used in Guatemala for people marked, culturally and otherwise, as nonindigenous), struggled to address the thorny relationship between class and race in a society plagued by multiple and layered forms of exclusion.[4] Toj's job involved engaging with the indigenous movement's critiques of

---

[3] For their arguments, see the periodical *Ixim: Notas Indígenas*, published from 1977 through 1979 and supported by the Maryknolls. The complicated relationships among Mayas and *ladinos* in Guatemalan opposition movements are the subject of Konefal, *For Every Indio*. For a brief overview of indigenous experiences in the war, with a timeline and relevant documents, see Betsy Konefal, "Guatemala: Mayas and the Civil War," in *Modern Ethnic Conflicts*, second ed., ed. Joseph R. Rudolph, Jr. (Santa Barbara, CA: ABC-CLIO, 2015), 237–52. For broader treatment of the civil war see Greg Grandin, *The Last Colonial Massacre: Latin America in the Cold War* (Chicago, IL: University of Chicago Press, 2004); Beatriz Manz, *Paradise in Ashes: A Guatemalan Journey of Courage, Terror, and Hope* (Berkeley: University of California Press, 2004); Diane Nelson, *A Finger in the Wound: Body Politics in Quincentennial Guatemala* (Berkeley: University of California Press, 1999); Victoria Sanford, *Buried Secrets: Truth and Human Rights in Guatemala* (New York: Palgrave Macmillan, 2003).

[4] See, for example, the 1981 publication by Mario Payeras, "Los indios guerrilleros," *Revista Compañero* 4: 16–17, for positioning of the EGP, and the documents by ORPA, *Acerca del racismo* (commonly known as *"Racismo I"*) and *Racismo II: Acerca de la verdadera magnitud del racismo*, from 1976 and 1978, respectively, in Colección Infostelle, Archivo Histórico, Centro de Investigaciones Regionales de Mesoamérica (hereafter CIRMA), Antigua, Guatemala. For the PGT see "La cuestión indígena," in *Polémica* no. 3 (1982): 63–64; and for the FAR, see Fuerzas Armadas Rebeldes, *Documentos históricos*, vols. 1 and 2 (Guatemala: Ediciones FAR, 1988 and 1989).

revolutionary theory and strengthening ties to its members in order to build a stronger and broader oppositional front.

This chapter explores ethnic dynamics both in the state's counterinsurgency war and within opposition movements, through an episode that put a glaring and very public spotlight on the subject: the army's capture and exploitation of the EGP's Emeterio Toj in 1981, followed by his remarkable escape. It's a story that begins several decades earlier, in the highlands of El Quiché and Huehuetenango.

MAYA MOBILIZATION IN THE GUATEMALAN HIGHLANDS

Guatemala's decade-long experiment with reform was a transformative period led by the governments of Arévalo and Arbenz (1944–54) that are together known as the October Revolution or "Guatemalan Spring." Arévalo introduced important changes to Guatemala's labor code and initiated ambitious public-education and health campaigns. Arbenz ushered in reform of Guatemala's inequitable land-tenure system, a process that was especially mobilizing in the countryside. The Agrarian Reform of 1952 affected hundreds of thousands of people in its meager eighteen months of existence, with local agrarian committees formed all over the country to petition for land. Approximately 100,000 families received a plot.[5] Almost all of them then lost it after the CIA-directed coup ended the October Revolution and installed Colonel Carlos Castillo Armas as Guatemala's head of state in 1954.

The Castillo Armas regime and the dictatorships that followed were intent on reversing the October Revolution's labor and land reforms and quelling the widespread urban and rural mobilization that the period had engendered.[6] But that was not easily accomplished. Highland activism re-emerged in the decades after the coup, and while the state tried to contain it through a combination of repression and the promotion of subservient organizations, that goal proved elusive. Church-based cooperatives and

---

[5] As Jim Handy writes, distribution to nearly 100,000 families "directly benefited as many as 500,000 people out of a population of close to 3 million . . . . More than 19 percent of the people eligible to benefit from the law received land before the overthrow of Arbenz." Jim Handy, *Revolution in the Countryside: Rural Conflict and Agrarian Reform in Guatemala, 1944–54* (Chapel Hill: University of North Carolina Press, 1994), 94–95.

[6] Even the era's one and only civilian administration, that of Julio César Méndez Montenegro (1966–70), quickly belied its claim to being "the third government of the Revolution" by giving security forces a free hand in quashing political mobilization. After Méndez Montenegro, the next civilian was permitted to assume office only in 1986, with the transition closely controlled by the Guatemalan military.

new state-approved options grew quickly in place of banned Revolution-era organizations, with many escaping the strict bounds that the government intended. Dismantled agrarian committees from the reform period re-emerged as *campesino* leagues, and were important precursors to the largest and most important *campesino* organization in Guatemala, the Comité de Unidad Campesina (Committee for Peasant Unity, CUC), which became public in May 1978.

The Catholic Church was an important factor in these processes. Prior to the 1954 coup, the Church had been active as an anti-Arbenz force in the region, vocally condemning what it saw as a dangerous regime sympathetic to communism. But its influence changed rather dramatically in the 1960s and 1970s, especially at the parish level. As the Church expanded its presence in the highlands after 1954, many priests and nuns began to approach their work with a new, more progressive vision forged during the Second Vatican Council meetings (known as Vatican II) of 1962–65, and especially after the Medellín conference of Latin American bishops in 1968. A theology of liberation and the religious and lay workers inspired by it placed primary importance on equipping rural Guatemalans to challenge unjust structures and conditions, and to create the conditions for their own emancipation.[7]

It was in this context that Emeterio Toj came of age. He and many like him, including his friend and *compañero* Domingo Hernández Ixcoy, helped lead highland mobilization in new directions. Toj grew up near the departmental capital Santa Cruz del Quiché, a small but bustling market and administrative hub of a region that was home to a large Maya majority (mostly K'iche's and Ixiles), over 80 percent of the department's population in the 1950s (Figure 9.1).[8] As a young man, Toj remembers with dismay, he had taken part in the Church's aggressive anti-Arbenz activities. But alongside the local Church, he, too, changed his thinking in the 1960s.[9]

Despite their preponderance in numbers, Mayas tended to be underrepresented in positions of authority and economic power in the region, with access to land and credit a particularly potent and worsening problem in the period after the 1954 coup. These were some of the first issues addressed by

---

[7] For more, see Konefal, *For Every Indio*; Diócesis del Quiché, *El Quiché: El pueblo y su iglesia, 1960–1980* (Guatemala City: Diócesis del Quiché, 1994); Oficina de Derechos Humanos del Arzobispado de Guatemala (ODHAG), *Guatemala: Nunca más*, vol. 3: "El entorno histórico" (Guatemala City: ODHAG, 1998).

[8] *Sexto censo de población* (Guatemala City: Dirección General de Estadística, 1950), 30.

[9] Emeterio Toj Medrano, interview, Guatemala City, August 24, 2002.

FIGURE 9.1 Guatemala.
Source: National Aeronautics and Space Administration/SERVIR, 2005 (with author modifications). See www.nasa.gov.

progressive Catholics in the area. Toj joined the Catholic Action catechist program in the 1950s, and took on leadership roles in the 1960s. He was among the founders of new Church-sponsored cooperatives in the area, helping to create savings-and-loan and agricultural co-ops in several towns in the department. He also became a well-known broadcaster at the parish radio station, Radio Quiché, established in 1969, and he was integral to its liberation-theology programming and literacy work. He was active in cultural events, too, part of efforts to appreciate and "rescue" K'iche' history and ethnic pride in the early 1970s. To that end he helped establish the Maya-Quiché Cultural Association in Santa Cruz, and advocated, among other things, for the community's indigenous beauty queen to gain respect – or at least prize money – on par with the town's ceremonial *ladina* queen.[10]

Domingo Hernández Ixcoy was from the same area, and also began as a catechist in and around Santa Cruz. Younger than Emeterio Toj, Hernández Ixcoy was born just before the 1954 coup, so came of age in the 1970s, when liberation-theology-inspired activism in the area was at its peak. Alongside Catholic Action leaders such as Toj, Hernández Ixcoy focused attention on questions of social exploitation, workers' rights, and land ownership, as their discussions became infused with the material concerns of liberation theology. They met Jesuit priests and students from Guatemala City, and they began to learn about the writings of Marx. In small groups, they studied labor laws and the constitution, and took on more politicized literacy work and *concientización* (consciousness-raising) around El Quiché.

This led to the founding of Guatemala's most important peasant organization, CUC. This would prove to be a vital link between Maya *campesinos* in the highlands and Mayas and *ladinos* working as wage or indebted laborers on distant coastal plantations, especially in the sugar and cotton industries. For Emeterio Toj and Domingo Hernández Ixcoy it would also lead them to join the revolutionary movement, as close connections developed between Maya leaders of CUC and the *ladino*-led EGP. In the repressive yet effervescent political context of the 1970s, both Toj and Hernández Ixcoy saw the guerrilla movement as a necessary extension of their struggle.[11]

URBAN YOUTH AND THE HIGHLAND MAYA

When the first guerrilla insurgencies began in the 1960s, their leaders did not see great potential for revolutionary mobilization in the western highlands, where most indigenous people lived. Allied with urban students and peasants from the east, and with modest support and training from the Cuban government, they concentrated their efforts in the eastern Sierra de las Minas, as well as in the capital and the agricultural zones of the southern coast. The most influential of the early guerrilla groups was the

---

[10] For more on indigenous community queens and their political roles, see Betsy Konefal, "Subverting Authenticity: *Reinas Indígenas* and the Guatemalan State, 1978," *Hispanic American Historical Review* 89, no. 1 (2009): 41–72.

[11] Domingo Hernández Ixcoy, interview; Emeterio Toj Medrano, interview, August 24, 2002.

Rebel Armed Forces (FAR), led by Luis Turcios and, after his death in 1966, César Montes. Guatemalan security forces, with the decisive use of state-sponsored death squads, had greatly weakened the FAR and the other small insurgent groups by 1968. Yet the FAR would survive, and would prove to be important to future opposition movements because it introduced the ideas and language of revolution to Guatemala-City-based students – including a young Gustavo Meoño – and to the most progressive nuns and priests in Guatemala's Catholic community. The students and *religiosos* in turn incorporated those ideas into their work in the western highlands.

Gustavo Meoño would become a leader of the EGP in the 1970s and 1980s, but in 1966, he was just finishing high school and working with a new student group in the capital that named itself "the Crater," taking inspiration from the latent power of the volcanoes that gave shape to the highlands. The group grew out of a series of Vatican-II-inspired "social promotion" workshops in the mid-1960s – *cursillos de capacitación social* – organized by a Venezuelan Jesuit, Father Manuel Aguirre Elorriaga. Aguirre's model, based on the work of Brazilian popular educator Paulo Freire, was immediately adopted by Guatemala-City-based Maryknoll Sister Marjorie Bradford. With help from several Jesuit priests, Bradford brought together students she taught at the exclusive Maryknoll girls' school Monte María, with those from the Jesuit boys' school next door, Liceo Javier.[12]

Bradford and the Crater would fundamentally change the lives of many of these students. Bradford describes herself and the students watching an eruption of an active volcano called Fuego at the close of the first *cursillo* in the capital:

The sky glowed with an eerie red-and-gray suffusion. We put our ears to the ground and heard the reverberations ... Instead of regarding this as an evil or destructive omen, we could not help but sense an identity between the eruption and the spiritual breakthrough in ourselves. What had seemed a dead crater was now blazing forth with an intensely illuminating volcanic force, revealing something of what lay hidden behind that hardened cone of a shell. It gave us at once a symbol and a promise of the forces at work in our own natures and in Guatemala.[13]

---

[12] The information in the following section is based on interviews with Marjorie (Margarita) Bradford Melville, in Guatemala City, October 22, 2017, and in San Quintín, Baja California, Mexico, March 23–26, 2018, and on the memoir she published with her husband, Thomas Melville, *Whose Heaven, Whose Earth?* (New York: Knopf, 1971).

[13] Melville and Melville, *Whose Heaven, Whose Earth?*, 134–35.

The young people held frequent discussions and, with financial support from the Maryknoll Fathers, began to rent a house for meetings and workshops, which they named the Centro de Capacitación Social (Center for Social Formation). (They later adopted the more symbolic name "Cráter," or Crater.) Students from other schools were soon invited to help diversify the group. Meoño, from a middle-class *ladino* family, was a student at Liceo Guatemala; others came from two public schools where Bradford had begun to teach sociology classes in 1965.

In social promotion workshops, Bradford and her students analyzed the teachings of the Church that emanated from Vatican II, and debated how to turn them into reality. They began working with residents, usually children, in the impoverished Guatemala City neighborhoods of Limonada and Castañas. An even more momentous step involved Bradford taking Crater students to work during weekends and vacations in the distant highlands of Huehuetenango. The department was a predominantly Maya area that was a world apart – physically and culturally – from most urban Guatemalans, and utterly unknown to the relatively privileged Crater students. Maryknoll had parishes and projects established throughout that department, and empowering local leaders was central to their mission. Several priests invited the students to lend a hand. First in small numbers and soon in groups of up to eighty, Crater students applied the ideas of Christian social justice and liberation by working in literacy and cooperatives in indigenous communities through-out Huehuetenango, vaccinating children, and leading social promotion workshops, sometimes for weeks and even months at a time.

For Meoño and others in the Crater, the experience was transforma-tive. Meoño turned eighteen years old in 1966, and graduated from high school. Against the wishes of his family, he decided to abandon his college plans in order to work full-time with Mam and Jakaltek Mayas in Huehuetenango, and he and fellow Crater students became central to Maryknoll efforts to strengthen the co-operative movement in the depart-ment. The organizing foundations they laid would also prove to be instru-mental as revolutionary mobilization expanded into the countryside in the early 1970s, some of it led by these very students.

Soon after the Crater was established, relationships between some of its members and the FAR guerrilla group developed in Guatemala City. Several of the original Crater founders were studying in 1966 and 1967 at the University of San Carlos where the FAR actively recruited, and Sister Marjorie Bradford was at the same time taking classes there in sociology. Newspapers and other materials from the FAR began to show up at the Crater center, and several students made personal connections with militants. Bradford herself befriended a university student and future FAR member named Juan Lojo Romero. After he joined the FAR, Lojo introduced Bradford to leaders Luis Turcios and later César Montes. Students and several nuns and priests began to debate the relationship between liberation and revolution, and the meaning of Vatican encyclicals given Guatemala's oppressive social system. Mostly among themselves, but sometimes with guerrilla contacts, they talked about spreading the revolution to the western highlands (an area largely ignored by guerrilla movements up to that point), where the Crater students had seen social injustices in indigenous communities up close.

They pointed specifically to Pope Paul VI's encyclical of 1967, "Progress of Peoples," as justification for their position. While the Pope warned against revolutionary mobilization, the statement offered a significant qualifier that drew the attention of Bradford and her students:

The injustice of certain situations cries out for God's attention … Everyone knows, however, that revolutionary uprisings – *except where there is manifest, longstanding tyranny which would do great damage to fundamental personal rights and dangerous harm to the common good of the country* – engender new injustices, introduce new inequities and bring new disasters. The evil situation that exists, and it surely is evil, may not be dealt with in such a way that an even worse situation results.[14]

The "except" clause spoke volumes in 1967: in the context of what seemed to be endless tyranny in post-1954 Guatemala, many of the Crater students and the nuns and priests around them felt as if the Pope himself were giving them the green light. At the time, the encyclical's warning of an "even worse situation" seemed less dire than the injustices of the status quo. Even from the vantage point of a half-century later, Marjorie Bradford's convictions remain: they could not just educate and organize people, she argues, and then abandon them to state repression. They felt that they had no choice but to work to equip Maya communities to defend themselves.[15]

---

[14] *Populorum Progressio*, Encyclical of Pope Paul VI on the Development of Peoples, March 26, 1967, paragraphs 30 and 31 (emphasis added), http://w2.vatican.va/content/paul-vi/en/encyclicals/documents/hf_p-vi_enc_26031967_populorum.html (accessed May 31, 2018).

[15] Marjorie (Margarita) Bradford Melville, interview, October 22, 2017. I am presently working on a book on the formation of the Crater in Guatemala, its members' experiences with liberation theology, and its connections to ideas of revolution. The Crater students became future leaders of opposition in many forms, much of it alongside

During an increasingly repressive 1967, Sister Bradford and several
Maryknoll priests, including Thomas Melville and his brother Arthur,
came to believe that social revolution was necessary and justified. As one
declassified CIA document described their position in early 1968, "A
growing despair is indicated by the defection of some members of
a religious organization and their followers (the Melville group), who
admit no solution to the miserable poverty of most Guatemalans except
by violent destruction of the prevailing order."[16] But the Crater students
and the Sisters and priests who worked with them defined violence somewhat differently: a statement of "Christian Revolutionary Movement
Principles" that seems to have come from the group described violence
as "the wealthy minority [taking] natural resources that rightfully belong
to all society for its own exclusive benefit." On the other hand, the
document stated, "the force that is used to oblige this minority to a just
order is not violence."[17] Two Crater students went to the Petén to explore
possibilities of establishing a revolutionary base in that department. The
head of Crater's board of directors, Gustavo Porras, went with FAR
leader César Montes to Cuba for discussions and training. Others continued their work in Huehuetenango, El Quiché, and in the capital.

In October 1967, Sister Bradford and Juan Lojo from the FAR, along
with several priests and another nun, organized a meeting in Escuintla,
Guatemala, to discuss options with several *campesino* leaders and Crater
students. On the agenda was the idea of developing a Christian revolutionary front in the highlands, an organization – armed only if necessary –
that could exist alongside the FAR and other revolutionary groups. It was
imagined as an independent revolutionary alternative that would be more
palatable than the mainstream guerrilla groups in highland areas where
the Church's longstanding anti-communism exerted a powerful force.[18]

The idea was thwarted almost immediately, when, in December 1967,
the group was reported to authorities by one of the priests who

---

indigenous community leaders. Members included the EGP's Arturo Taracena, Gustavo
Porras, and Gustavo Meoño.

[16] CIA Directorate of Intelligence, "Intelligence Memorandum: Guatemala After the
Military Shake-up," May 13, 1968, p. 2, Box 54, Country File, "Guatemala, Volume
2," Lyndon B. Johnson Presidential Library.

[17] "Christian Revolutionary Movement Principles," n.d., Box 5, Blase Bonpane collection,
Special Collections, Young Research Library, University of California Los Angeles.

[18] This idea was embraced by several nuns and priests and by their FAR contact, but most of
the Crater students themselves, it seems, were more inclined at the time to join forces with
the FAR rather than establish an independent organization. Gustavo Meoño, interview,
Guatemala City, October 15, 2017.

participated, Father Luis Gurriarán. Gurriarán informed the former and then current Maryknoll Superior, and the news quickly traveled to the Guatemalan Defense Ministry and the US embassy. Maryknoll authorities demanded that Marjorie Bradford and the Melville brothers leave Guatemala, and several Maryknoll associates and friends soon had to follow them. The expulsions were ordered in the hopes of preventing the entire Maryknoll institution from being expelled by the Guatemalan government. The episode, which shook the Maryknoll order and became an international scandal, is known as the Melville affair, after Fathers Tom and Art. It was, however, primarily the product of organizing begun by Sister Marjorie Bradford.[19]

Sister Bradford and the Melville brothers managed to delay their departure by a week, and during that time, scrambled to reach the eighty or so Crater students working in Huehuetenango, El Quiché, and the Petén to let them know what had happened. A number of the students had been singled out by security forces and placed on a "hit list" as a result of the Escuintla meeting. Gustavo Meoño, deeply involved in Crater work in Huehuetenango at the time, was one of over a dozen students who were given seventy-two hours to leave the country, after which, the Maryknoll Superior was warned by Guatemalan authorities, their security could not be guaranteed.[20] Several priests, Sisters, and friends helped those on the security forces' list leave the country. In early January, eight or nine of the students gathered in Mexico City where they met up with Marjorie and Tom (who had renounced their vows and left the Maryknoll order, and had gotten married), and Tom's brother Art.

While there is no space to recount these developments in detail, Crater leader Gustavo Porras and FAR leader César Montes, in Cuba at the time, eventually reunited with the students in Mexico. Within a few years, they would contribute to the founding of the largest of Guatemala's revolutionary groups, the EGP. In 1972, the newly formed guerrilla group entered Guatemala through the northern colonization zones established by Catholic priests, and would soon extend their base of support in significant areas of the western highlands. As described in the Church's truth commission report, "Religion was a key intermediary in the

---

[19] Interviews with Marjorie (Margarita) Bradford Melville. See also Melville and Melville, *Whose Heaven, Whose Earth?*; Blase Bonpane, *Guerrillas of Peace: Liberation Theology and the Central American Revolution* (Boston, MA: South End Press, 1985); Penny Lernoux, *Hearts on Fire: The Story of the Maryknoll Sisters* (Maryknoll, NY: Orbis Books, 1993).

[20] Gustavo Meoño, interview, October 15, 2017.

relationship between guerrilla groups led by professional revolutionaries and indigenous communities. And it enabled the guerrillas to make a qualitative leap forward from 1976 on." The guerrillas' ability to gain highland support was very much the product of organizational ground-work by the Maryknolls and Crater students in Huehuetenango, and also the consciousness-raising work done by the Maryknolls and by Jesuits and Sacred Heart priests and their catechists in El Quiché. It was the revolutionaries' combination of economic demands with liberation theology's "respect for human dignity," the truth commission observed, "that most resonated among the indigenous population."[21]

The former Crater students who went on to become *guerrilleros* would be closely involved in the formation and development of the peasant organization CUC in the second half of the 1970s, and in connecting its members to the EGP. In the process, they met and joined forces with two of the area's most active catechists and organizers, Emeterio Toj Medrano and Domingo Hernández Ixcoy.

THE KIDNAPPING OF EMETERIO TOJ MEDRANO

Emeterio Toj Medrano and Domingo Hernández Ixcoy had been involved in virtually every aspect of the mobilization growing in the highlands in the 1970s. As a broadcaster, Emeterio in particular was able to connect outside organizers to the population. As Jesuit Ricardo Falla described his role, "Emeterio opened up the *campo* [countryside]."[22] Beyond facilitating access to Maya *campesinos*, Toj became, as mentioned, an especially crucial liaison between the EGP and more urban *indígenas* on the periphery of the revolutionary movement. There were many politically engaged Mayas around Quetzaltenango and Totonicapán, for example, who supported the revolution's fundamental goals, but were not convinced that *ladino* leaders fully represented their interests. Knowing Emeterio's reach and experience, the EGP (with Gustavo Meoño playing a crucial part) designed a role specifically for him, and one that he was uniquely positioned to play. Emeterio recalls that he was eager to take part, committed to bringing more Mayas into a unified opposition.[23]

---

[21] Human Rights Office of the Archdiocese of Guatemala, *Guatemala: Never Again!* (Maryknoll, NY: Orbis Books, 1999), 225.

[22] Ricardo Falla, interview, Santa María Chiquimula, November 12, 2002.

[23] Emeterio Toj Medrano, interview, August 24, 2002; Gustavo Meoño, interview, Guatemala City, August 18, 2017.

Toj moved his family to Quetzaltenango, working clandestinely in Guatemala's second-largest city, which was home to a prosperous and well-educated K'iche' middle class. He moved around frequently, extending organizing networks to other important areas. He was making real progress, area activists remember: "We were all with him ... Here in Xela [Quetzaltenango] *indígenas* had begun to move."[24]

In the course of this work, Emeterio was captured by the Guatemalan army on July 4, 1981, in broad daylight in Quetzaltenango, taken into clandestine detention and "disappeared." It is clear that his captors were aware of who he was and what they had with Toj: a well-known community organizer, broadcaster, and CUC founder and leader. It is unclear whether they knew of his EGP membership, but intelligence services seem to have been especially interested in his connections to the incipient indigenous movement, interrogating him again and again about his Quetzaltenango-area contacts and work.

He was subjected to a horrifying range of physical and mental tortures almost constantly for two weeks.[25] Some of these were commonplace: they subjected him to the infamous *capucha*, a hood kept over a prisoner's head, often infused with chemicals and inducing feelings of suffocation; he was bound for days in an excruciating position; he was prevented from sleeping; food and water were withheld, though they were kept tantalizingly near; he was drugged; his captors threatened to kill family members and rape his wife and daughters in front of him. But he also experienced a more unusual, ethnically charged threat, which suggests that his interrogators knew of his commitment to the long and many-sided struggles in which he had been involved since his teens. As he explained to a reporter in 1982, at the same time that his captors tortured him physically and threatened his family, they also

threatened ... to do away with the *pueblos indígenas* of the western highlands themselves [*propiamente dicho*]. When I told them that that was not possible, they said to me, "Well, yes, we have a plan to colonize these areas with people from the east [*ladinos*]."[26]

---

[24] Anonymous interview, Quetzaltenango, November 13, 2002.

[25] Details can be found in his statement to the CEH truth commission and in earlier statements to Amnesty International. See CEH, *Memoria del silencio*, "Caso ilustrativo no. 98," and Amnesty International, AI Index: AMR 34/35/82, July 20, 1982, "Guatemala: Testimonio de Emeterio Toj Medrano."

[26] Amnesty International, AI Index: AMR 34/35/82, July 20, 1982, p. 3. If these were the words of one or more of his captors, it would suggest that the genocide that in fact unfolded in the next two years may have been an extreme iteration of a broader idea in

Emeterio rightly suggests that only army intelligence could explain with certainty what they were trying to accomplish with his detention. He does believe that they came to consider him to be more useful alive than dead. Instead of adhering to the typical pattern of disappearance and torture followed by execution, after a few weeks of severe mistreatment, they sought to use him as a psychological operations propaganda tool.[27] "What is certain," he suggests, "is that yes, they knew the value I had [as an interlocutor] before my *pueblo*." He describes the army using him as a means to cajole [*ablandar*] the *pueblo*:

It was an inveigling/softening up [*ablandamiento*], where your own leaders would talk to the *pueblo* . . . .They wanted me to denounce what we had done in CUC, [say] that it wasn't good . . . .They wanted me to totally retract myself, to condemn what we had been doing in CUC, and condemn the *guerrilla*, and condemn the Church . . . .[The goal was that] the force of the *guerrilla* would be diminished, that the indigenous people would not incorporate themselves into the *guerrilla* . . . that was the central point, . . . the objective . . . What they wanted was . . . to create division, create confusion.[28]

Despite intense coercion in its many forms, Emeterio Toj managed somehow to protect the individuals with whom he was working in the western highlands, naming no one in the *movimiento indígena*: "They did not succeed . . . they got nothing out of me," he told a reporter in 1982.[29]

intelligence circles of "doing away with" indigenous communities. It's unclear, and this rendition of events could have "fit" with EGP propaganda as it was developing in early 1982. But the timing suggests otherwise. At the time of his detention (July–November 1981) and even at the time of this interview (four months later, March 1982), the outlines of the state's campaign of "scorched earth" destruction of Maya communities were far from obvious; it was not yet apparent that a genocidal level of annihilation was about to unfold, so the threat stands out as bizarre, going well beyond "normal" warnings that a lack of cooperation would result in reprisals against family and community. By analyzing the victims of massacres, anthropologist Victoria Sanford dates the "implementation of a shift in army strategy from selective massacres to genocide" to mid-1982, after which massacres routinely included women, children, and elderly people. See Victoria Sanford, "Violence and Genocide in Guatemala," n.d., Institute on Violence and Survival, Virginia Foundation for the Humanities, https://gsp.yale.edu/case-studies /guatemala/violence-and-genocide-guatemala (accessed May 12, 2018).

27 Toj notes that his torture stopped and his treatment changed precisely at the moment when a new guerrilla front arose in El Quiché, the Augusto César Sandino Front, joined by his sons and other relatives and friends, members of his *pueblo* infuriated by his kidnapping. He suspects that military intelligence sought to use him as a strategic tool against that effort, so in effect, believes that the uprising may have saved his life. Emeterio Toj Medrano, interview, Guatemala City, September 29, 2002.

28 Emeterio Toj Medrano, interview, September 29, 2002.

29 The interview was published in Amnesty International, AI Index: AMR 34/35/82, July 20, 1982, p. 2. He elaborated further in an interview on September 29, 2002: he was

● **EL EXDIRIGENTE DEL CUC, Emeterio Toc Medrano** (derecha) aparece acompañado en el salón de banquetes del Palacio Nacional, por el licenciado Donaldo Alvarez. ministro de Gobernación v el ne- | riodista Carlos Toledo Vielman, secretario de Relaciones Públicas de la Presidencia, quien lo presentó en nombre del gobierno. (Foto Luis A. García).

FIGURE 9.2 "CUC Founder Turns Himself In!"
Source: "¡Fundador del CUC se entregó!" *El Gráfico*, October 23, 1981.
Emeterio Toj Medrano (right) at a government-sponsored press conference several months after his capture.

But he did give in to the army's propaganda efforts to a certain extent. After almost two months in secret detention, Toj was one of several captives that a US delegation met during a "fact-finding" trip in late August 1981. He was presented to them by Guatemala's Minister of Defense, and as instructed, he told the visitors that he was formerly of CUC and that he was renouncing the organization because it had been infiltrated by communists. He was opting instead to join the army.[30]

His biggest propaganda event was an army-orchestrated press conference almost two months later, on October 22, 1981. In Figure 9.2 he is shown seated at a table with the Minister of the Interior and the president's Secretary of Public Relations, reading a long and familiar script, one prepared over weeks under the supervision of someone his captors referred to as a "psychiatrist." In a forty-five-minute address broadcast on television and

determined that "not a single name of the *hermanos* I was working with in Los Altos [Quetzaltenango] would leave my mouth, and that is how it happened." None of his contacts were picked up or detained after his interrogations.

[30] Members of the delegation included US Congressional Representatives Patricia Schroeder and Thomas Petri.

on the radio, Emeterio Toj seemingly performed as the army wished. He recounted his personal history of working in cooperatives and in cultural organizations, and he admitted to belonging both to CUC and to the EGP.

This was in some ways a repeat performance: the tactic had been used only weeks before when the government staged a press conference in which another captured member of the EGP, the Jesuit priest Luis Pellecer Faena, had denounced the guerrillas and in his case, accused the Catholic Church of sympathy for revolutionaries. Among other implausible statements, Pellecer had claimed to have staged his own kidnapping, a falsehood obvious to those who witnessed the abduction and his press conference, clearly given under duress. Nonetheless, these performances were believed to be – and sometimes were – effective. The government's Interior Minister actually referenced the powerful example of the Pellecer case as he introduced the new featured speaker, CUC's Emeterio Toj.[31]

The message Toj was expected to deliver is revealing. State brutality against CUC leaders and members was horrific, and state forces knew that by 1981 little separated CUC from the guerrillas.[32] But with the press conference, they sought to damage the CUC–EGP multiethnic alliance not through physical repression, but through the words of CUC's most famous founder. They required Emeterio to portray CUC as an apolitical and benign indigenous organization whose interests did not coincide with those of the EGP. The CUC did not want violence, Emeterio stressed. On the contrary, it reflected the basic and justifiable desires of *indígenas*, "cultural, economic, and social." It sought better prices for agricultural products, he explained, lower prices for agricultural inputs, and better wages. The CUC also worked against racial discrimination, Emeterio read, "which has existed and continues to exist in the country."[33]

Racial discrimination was an underlying concern of CUC, to be sure, but not one that the group singled out or addressed publicly. But racism on

[31] "Presentación hizo Toledo Vielman de exactivista Toj; Que por su voluntad se acogió a las fuerzas de seguridad," *El Imparcial*, October 23, 1981.

[32] The firebombing of the Spanish embassy, occupied by twenty-seven CUC members and students in January 1980, is only the most obvious example. Nearly everyone in the building, a total of thirty-seven people, burned to death as police and security forces stood by. See CEH, *Memoria del silencio*, 6: 163–82.

[33] "Otro dirigente campesino renunció al EGP; Gobierno presentó ayer a Emeterio Toc [*sic*] Medrano," *Diario La Hora*, October 23, 1981. Coverage was extensive, with articles appearing in every major paper that day. See also "Co-fundador del CUC habla," *Diario Impacto*; "Se entrega guerrillero fundador del CUC," *Prensa Libre*; "Fundador del CUC hace llamado deponer las armas a subvertores," *Diario de Centro América*; "¡Fundador del CUC se entregó!," *El Gráfico*.

the part of the left was an issue the state expected Emeterio to highlight. (The hypocrisy cannot be overstated, as state forces were on the verge of ramping up genocidal terror in the highlands.) His statement stressed racial tensions within opposition movements, and specifically accused *ladinos* of lacking respect for *indígenas*. Outsiders (meaning *ladinos*) had infiltrated the indigenous-led CUC, Toj stated, and pushed aside its original leaders and their interests. Under the circumstances, he said, he had gone into hiding and turned himself in to the authorities. He urged his fellow *indígenas* to turn away, too, to avoid any sort of collaboration with subversion. The guerrilla groups, he warned, were not to be trusted: they were "oppressors and discriminators" who treated indigenous *campesinos* as "cannon fodder ... For them," he declared, "that is our historic function."[34] *Indígenas*, his message continued, wanted nothing to do with revolution: "We indigenous Guatemalans only want peace, work, and food," he said as he wrapped up his appeal. "Give us that and we will work the land as we have been doing until now."[35] He was instructed to deliver the same statement in his maternal language to send his message over the airwaves to his fellow K'iche's.

It was an explosive performance. Nearly everyone in activist circles in those years remembers watching or listening to it and debating: had Emeterio turned on CUC and the EGP and allied with the army?! It was inconceivable. But then again, there he was on the screen and on the radio.

The propaganda show would continue. In the weeks both before and after the press conference, the army took Emeterio Toj on a speaking tour of Maya communities. Accompanied by army officials, he met in person with local leaders, and had to urge them to turn away from opposition movements. To thousands of other highland residents, Toj was forced to speak from an army helicopter, his famous radio announcer's voice exhorting people to turn away from the guerrilla and trust security forces. To reach K'iche' audiences, the army mandated again that he deliver the message first in Spanish, and then in K'iche'. Telling me about it two decades later was still painful for him. But he explained that he had tried with his tone of voice and choice of words to signal to people in these situations that he was not sincere in what he was saying, and that his words were delivered under duress. That was more feasible, he explained, when speaking in K'iche', the subtleties of which would have been lost on his army captors.[36]

---

[34] "Otro dirigente campesino renunció al EGP"; "¡Fundador del CUC se entregó!"
[35] "Otro dirigente campesino renunció al EGP."
[36] Emeterio Toj Medrano, interview, September 29, 2002.

Gustavo Meoño, the *ladino* co-operative organizer who started as a Crater student in Huehuetenango and then helped the EGP expand in El Quiché, was by 1981 an EGP *comandante*. That October, he happened to be in southern El Quiché in the community of Chupol at the time of Emeterio's press conference. He heard Toj's message on the radio, and at the same time, he witnessed area residents' reactions to it. His memories of the episode are vivid. When people in Chupol heard Emeterio's words in Spanish, Meoño explains, they were distraught, crying, horrified by what he was saying. "The *militares* are good," he remembered Emeterio saying, "they are our friends, the Army is our friend, the Army is there to defend us ... On the contrary, the guerrillas are assassins, liars, they trick us, they are using us, so we have to renounce them."[37]

But the reaction to his comments in K'iche' was different. "When Emeterio spoke in K'iche'," Meoño recalls, "the people's expressions changed. The people who had been really pale, aggrieved hearing their leader, their friend, their teacher, their catechist Emeterio saying these barbarities in Spanish, ... when they heard it in K'iche', they changed." They started to smile, Meoño explained, and exchanged glances with each other. "'Emeterio did not change,' they said, 'he is the same Emeterio!'" Witnessing the relief of Chupol residents when they heard Emeterio's message – the one intended for them alone – convinced Meoño that Toj had not, in fact, switched sides.

This would prove to be important. On the evening of November 26, after months in army detention, Emeterio Toj managed to escape from the army barracks where he was being held in Guatemala City. He had been ordered to speak to his own community of Santa Cruz the next day, he recalls, and he could not and would not do it. He claims that army guards were accustomed to him by that time, and he managed to slip out. (It seems likely, however, that he had some degree of inside help.) Frantic and desperate to hide, he turned to CUC and EGP contacts in the city. But could they trust him? Captives did not just *escape* from the army, and everyone had heard his statements. It was difficult for people to believe he was not a spy.

An extremely nervous CUC and EGP contact hid him for the night, then managed to move him to the house of Domingo Hernández Ixcoy the next day. Emeterio and Domingo had a long history together, but they had little confidence that the EGP hierarchy would accept him back. They put

---

[37] Gustavo Meoño, interview, August 18, 2017. Unless otherwise noted, the information in this section is drawn from Meoño's account.

their trust in one *comandante*, Gustavo Meoño. As it happened, Hernández Ixcoy had just helped to set up a meeting between Meoño and some contacts in Cobán, in the country's northeastern department of Alta Verapaz, and he suspected that at that moment Meoño would be headed in that direction. Hernández Ixcoy boarded a bus to try to reach him, though he knew neither the exact time nor location of the meeting. En route, his bus pulled into a restaurant at a crossroads in San Julián, apparently famous for its delicious stews. When Domingo walked through the door, there sat Gustavo Meoño ready to eat lunch. It was a stunning bit of luck. Breaking the norms that forbade such open contact, Hernández Ixcoy quickly explained Emeterio's situation. Meoño paid his bill and jumped in his car, leaving his "delicious *caldo* and refreshing beer" on the table.

Meoño immediately moved Toj to a more secure location, and started his debriefing. As mentioned, Meoño had known and worked with Toj and CUC for several years in El Quiché, and had recently witnessed the reactions to Emeterio's words by people in Chupol. "I had heard it, but also seen it with my own eyes," he explained. That experience was on his mind as he tried to determine what had happened. "Was he lying to me, or was he telling the truth? He was telling me a story that was incredible, a story that could have been totally an invention, a lie." Maybe he hadn't escaped, reasoned Meoño, maybe the army had set him up with a mission to infiltrate the EGP, "maybe even to get to me. [Such] things ... were happening." There was in fact a strong possibility that Toj had been co-opted by military intelligence and that he was cooperating to save his life or save his family. "Who knows what they were willing to offer him to play that role. It was a possibility. *Grande.*"

Meoño continued:

But there was also the possibility that, no, that Emeterio was telling the truth, that he was recounting what had happened, that ... in this manner so incredible he had managed to escape a military prison. That is what I had to disentangle. I had to decide, knowing that if I said, "no, I'm not going to make this decision alone, I'm not going to assume that responsibility, better that I go to my *compañeros*," I knew that they would shoot Emeterio.

Before and after Toj's escape, Meoño could recall five other *guerrilleros* captured by the army and then released. The EGP had executed them all, assuming they were traitors. "I thought about all of this," he said, "through the long hours, all night, we stayed up all night [*amanecimos*]. And my conclusion was that ... Emeterio is telling the truth."

After reaching that judgment, Meoño chose not to consult higher-ups about next steps, but to handle this alone, and to do so boldly, striking a blow to the army in the process: his EGP unit commandeered four radio stations in the capital and (misleadingly) announced on the radio, using Emeterio's own famous voice, that the EGP had staged a sensational rescue of *compañero* Emeterio Toj Medrano and freed him from the army's clutches:

> With profound revolutionary satisfaction we inform the *pueblo* of Guatemala and international public opinion that on Thursday, November 26, at 5 p.m. we carried out the escape plan of *Compañero* Hemeterio [*sic*] Toj Medrano from the General Justo Rufino Barrios barracks of this capital. The escape ... constitutes one more demonstration of the incapacity ... of the army of assassins of [President Romeo] Lucas García. The detailed testimony ... [Toj] has given of his kidnapping and physical and psychological tortures during the almost five months he was in the hands of government forces constitutes the clearest ... evidence of the criminal and bloody methods the *Luquista* [Lucas García] cabal uses to try to dupe our *pueblo* .... Since they are unable to defeat the guerrilla forces and the organized *pueblo* on the battlefield, the *Luquista* army ... is resorting to farcical pronouncements ... that they cobble together with forced declarations ... The Army ... tries to compensate with supposedly successful propaganda when on the ground it is losing the war ... THE LIES OF *LUQUISTA* PROPAGANDA ARE RENDERED MEANINGLESS BY REVOLUTIONARY TRUTH![38]

The statement condemned the government's practice of manipulating and duping the public via a symbolic Emeterio Toj, just as they had done with the Church's Pellecer before him. Of course the EGP's tactic was similar, using the power of Emeterio's own voice in calling out the government's lies. And though individual EGP members had helped Toj after he escaped the army barracks, the pronouncement's "revolutionary truth" – *we rescued Emeterio!* – was in fact untrue.

Gustavo Meoño, Domingo Hernández Ixcoy, and Emeterio Toj have discussed the episode many times since it happened. They all agree, Meoño maintains, that if any other EGP *comandante* had been the one to make that call – *was Toj someone to be trusted, or a traitor?* – Emeterio would be dead.[39]

It is striking, as many of this volume's contributors argue, how important a role the personal and specific play in shaping the left's history. In many urban–rural and interethnic alliances, as Young writes, urban

---

[38] Ejército Guerrillero de los Pobres, press release, "Logramos la fuga del compañero Hemeterio Toj Medrano," n.d. (emphasis in original), Colección Infostelle, Archivo Histórico, CIRMA. See also "En una grabación, dice que no desertó del EGP," *Prensa Libre*, December 3, 1981; "Reacciones por escapatoria de líder del CUC," and "Supuesta fuga se explica," *El Imparcial*, December 3, 1981.

[39] Gustavo Meoño, interview, August 18, 2017.

organizers' interpretation of events was shaped in part "by their dynamic encounters with the constituencies they sought to organize."[40] Meoño's background and work with Crater in Huehuetenango and El Quiché helped shape the kind of *comandante* he would become, one less strident about ideology than many others, and able to interpret the countryside and rural leaders such as Emeterio. His relationships over decades with Mayas in the western highlands likely saved Emeterio Toj's life.

But is Meoño an exception who proves the rule? His familiarity with indigenous Guatemala was unusual for a *ladino*, though he had that in common with others who had been part of the 1960s Crater experience. As it happened, others in the EGP did not necessarily share his faith in Emeterio. Meoño had to face an internal EGP review for his actions, to come before the directorate for questioning. Some accused him of being a traitor himself: after hearing the things Toj had said on television, the words he had spoken from the helicopters, how could Meoño have trusted him? "And you," they charged, "with your decision, you converted a traitor into a hero!" It was difficult. Meoño is certain, however, that it was the right call: "History has demonstrated that it was the just decision, the correct decision," Meoño insists. "And Emeterio, with his life and his attitude, well, he has demonstrated that *of course* he wasn't a spy, he wasn't a traitor. He has demonstrated that to this very day."

THE ETHNIC QUESTION: WINNING BATTLES, BUT LOSING THE WAR

Meoño stands out among *ladinos* as particularly astute about the need for strong interethnic relationships among different sectors of the Guatemalan opposition. But in the view of Domingo Hernández Ixcoy (also a member of the EGP), state forces had the edge over *guerrilleros* when it came to understanding the role of ethnicity in Guatemala's armed conflict, and in exploiting the war's "ethnic component" for strategic gain. Hernández Ixcoy used the verbs "manipulate" and "disarticulate" to describe the counterinsurgency's deliberate strategy of distorting perceptions and sowing distrust to prevent indigenous support for revolution, and we see that kind of effort laid bare in the kidnapping and public display of Emeterio Toj Medrano.

---

[40] Young, page 154 in this volume.

In the 1970s and early 1980s, Guatemalan revolutionaries tried to counter state propaganda through efforts to strengthen their support among Maya communities. The EGP, especially, some of whose founders had roots in Crater, conceived of a revolution that would draw strength from, and bring change to, the highlands. In fact, real and developing connections to indigenous communities – through Crater, Catholic Action, CUC, and even the bridge-building work of Emeterio Toj – gave the revolutionaries much of their resonance in the 1970s.

The case of Toj's kidnapping and "rescue" at first glance appears to be a win for the revolutionaries, given his successful escape and Meoño's audacious public announcement declaring the EGP's triumph over government "assassins." Together they managed to counter the state's very public manipulation of indigeneity, and to blunt the effectiveness of ethnic division as a tool of counterinsurgency. But victory was fleeting, as the state had another card to play: Toj had come freely to the army, a government spokesperson told the press, and was free to go. The spokesperson actually expressed concern for Emeterio's safety since the EGP had discovered his "reinfiltration plan" and would undoubtedly subject him to so-called "revolutionary justice." Toj was in "serious danger," he warned ominously: his execution by the EGP was likely imminent.[41]

That warning was not far from the truth, as we learned from the EGP's Meoño. And while the state-mandated performance of a coerced Emeterio might not have changed many minds among K'iche' *campesinos*, the episode proved to be extremely damaging to relationships between the EGP and the indigenous sector that Emeterio had been courting around Quetzaltenango. The important task of building a strong and inclusive alliance between the EGP and an educated and vocal *movimiento indígena* was far from complete in 1981. With Emeterio's capture, trust evaporated. Toj's comments about *ladino* revolutionaries' discriminatory attitudes hit home for some in the *movimiento indígena*, participants remember, and his subsequent escape caused alarm. If he was now working for the

---

[41] "Plan de reinfiltración en la guerrilla fue descubierto, asegura comunicado oficial en torno al ex-líder campesino," *El Gráfico*, December 4, 1981. Privately, officials were reportedly furious over the escape, and the CEH truth commission was told that an officer had lost his position over the incident. Emeterio Toj, interview, September 29, 2002.

army, they were all in danger.[42] In effect, the *militares* had gotten much of what they wanted out of the kidnapping of Emeterio Toj.

But while the state may have been winning battles, it, too, was losing the larger struggle, failing in its efforts to solidify control over the highland population and prevent widespread opposition and revolutionary mobilization. When and where state control proved elusive, the military adopted more and more violent means of addressing the "ethnic question." Civil patrols were one approach, and the system expanded dramatically in the early 1980s to include almost every indigenous community in the highlands, with area men falling under the command of military commissioners and required to supply around-the-clock defense of their communities against "subversion." The army established "model villages" in conflictive zones, again under tight military surveillance. Ultimately security forces resorted to extremes involving unthinkable levels of death and destruction: targeted repression of groups and leaders gave way in 1982 and 1983 to the "scorched earth" annihilation of over 600 highland communities – men, women, children, and old people murdered, animals killed, homes and crops burned, sacred sites destroyed. In all, an estimated 200,000 people were disappeared or killed during the armed conflict, mostly at the hands of state forces; an estimated 83 percent of the dead and disappeared were of Maya descent, largely due to the state's scorched earth practices. Over a million more people fled war-ravaged communities, many of them taking refuge internally in distant "Communities of Population in Resistance," or in refugee camps in Mexico. The UN-sponsored truth commission determined that with its scorched earth tactics, the Guatemalan army had committed "acts of genocide" in areas of the Maya highlands.[43]

With counterinsurgent violence reaching such extremes, the opposition was brought to its knees. Opposition movements of all kinds were driven underground, revolutionary alliances fell into crisis, and leaders fled into exile. Disagreements among mainstream guerrilla groups and the vocal Maya sector in and near the revolutionary movements, in particular, reached a breaking point. Dramatic fractures developed

---

[42] For more on growing divisions among opposition groups, see Konefal, *For Every Indio*, chapters 6–7.

[43] For these truth commission findings and their analysis, see Daniel Rothenberg, ed., *Memory of Silence: The Guatemalan Truth Commission Report* (New York: Palgrave Macmillan, 2012), "Part I: Human Rights Violations and Acts of Violence," 61–80, and "Part IV: Conclusions and Recommendations," 177–93; for the full report in Spanish see CEH, *Memoria del silencio*.

within guerrilla groups over questions of ideology and emphasis, and some Mayas in the early 1980s formed ethnically separate revolutionary organizations. In doing so, they faced vehement charges from the mainstream guerrilla groups that they had become, in essence, counter-revolutionaries.[44]

No party to the armed conflict, in fact, could win the war. The state proved utterly incapable of building national consensus or stability, especially after resorting to genocide. The armed opposition – by that time consolidated in the Guatemalan National Revolutionary Unity, URNG – after 1982 could no longer operate effectively within Guatemala, but it maintained political pressure against a counterinsurgency state whose brutality had outraged international sensibilities. The parties slowly reached a series of accords in the 1990s that ended formal conflict (Gustavo Porras of the Crater and the EGP was central to that effort). But without legislation to implement the agreements that were reached, the peace accords did almost nothing to resolve the underlying economic, social, and political causes of the war, or address the deep wounds that resulted from it.

From the failures and devastation of war, however, a remarkably robust civil society did re-emerge and grow in strength in the 1990s and in the post-accords twenty-first century.[45] New means emerged to confront old problems. Though solutions have remained as elusive as ever, civilians (Mayas, *ladinos*, Guatemalans in multiethnic coalitions, former *guerrilleros*, returned refugees) have managed to create a range of ways to reassert their demands, through NGOs, the courts, political parties, and other civil society groups. Emeterio Toj Medrano remains active in

---

[44] The most high-profile dispute became public with a fiery document in 1982, when Maya revolutionaries voiced distrust of a would-be revolution that prioritized one form of oppression (class) over another (race): "A revolution cannot be selective," Maya revolutionaries insisted, "where some forms of oppression are destroyed and others conserved, where some are considered urgent and others deferrable." See Movimiento Indio Tojil, "Guatemala: De la república burguesa centralista a la república popular federal," Binder 125, Colección Infostelle, Archivo Histórico, CIRMA. The main guerrilla armies responded with their own damning accusations against the authors of that document: they charged that Mayas who emphasized race over class threatened the very viability of the revolution; they were in effect "counterrevolutionaries," and enemies of the struggle.

[45] On the peace process and its aftermath, see Santiago Bastos and Manuela Camus, *Entre el mecapal y el cielo: Desarrollo del movimiento maya en Guatemala* (Guatemala City: FLACSO, 2003); Susanne Jonas, *Of Centaurs and Doves: Guatemala's Peace Process* (Boulder, CO: Westview Press, 2000); Kay Warren, *Indigenous Movements and Their Critics: Pan-Maya Activism in Guatemala* (Princeton, NJ: Princeton University Press, 1998).

ongoing struggles for justice, as do Gustavo Meoño, who directed document recovery at the Historical Archive of the National Police for over a decade, and Domingo Hernández Ixcoy of the Asociación Maya Uk' U'x B'e.[46] Ethnic tensions that helped shape a long war certainly remain, but so do relationships and collective efforts that have long transcended them.

[46] Gustavo Meoño served as director of the Archivo Histórico de la Policía Nacional following its creation in 2005 until his abrupt ouster in August 2018. Probably not coincidentally, under Meoño's direction the Archive provided key documentary evidence in recent human rights trials. See National Security Archive, "Guatemala Police Archive under Threat," August 13, 2018, https://nsarchive.gwu.edu/news/guatemala/2018-08-13/guatemala-police-archive-under-threat.

10

For Our Total Emancipation

The Making of Revolutionary Feminism in Insurgent El Salvador, 1977–1987

Diana Carolina Sierra Becerra

During the 1980s, the Asociación de Mujeres de El Salvador (Association of Women of El Salvador, AMES) developed a revolutionary feminist praxis. It redefined socialist revolution to mean the overthrow of both capitalism and patriarchy, and mobilized women to shape the everyday and long-term trajectory of the revolutionary process. Composed of combatants, peasants, and militants in exile, AMES organized peasant women in the guerrilla territories in El Salvador and refugee camps in Nicaragua and Costa Rica, and coordinated solidarity work from Mexico, Costa Rica, Nicaragua, and the United States. It organized in those multiple sites to expand the role of working-class and peasant women in the armed struggle for El Salvador's national liberation. In so doing, it expanded the meaning of revolution. In this chapter I trace how a revolutionary feminist praxis – a dynamic interplay between theory and practice – emerged from the multiple sites in which AMES organized.

The development of a feminist praxis within a context of armed struggle challenges prior academic accounts that have situated feminism in opposition to socialism and armed struggle.[1] In the guerrilla territories

* This chapter is dedicated to the revolutionary women of El Salvador, past and present. A special thank you to the *compas* of the Museo de la Palabra y la Imagen and the Comité de Memoria Sobreviviente de Arcatao, Chalatenango, whose generosity made this project possible. I also thank Kevin Young for his relentless support and meticulous commentary, and Sueann Caulfield, Paulina L. Alberto, Victoria Langland, Jeffrey L. Gould, Daniel Chard, and Aldo Marchesi for their constructive feedback on various drafts.

[1] Stoltz Chinchilla claims that the FMLN discouraged women from politicizing "personal" problems, while Hipsher argues that it "was not until the end of the revolution" that women's organizations "developed a distinctly feminist agenda that emphasized women's

and refugee camps, AMES politicized reproductive labor, deepened the participation of women within the revolutionary process, and built alternative institutions that advanced women's equality. From these organizing practices emerged new ideas about the relationship between gender and class oppression, and about the role of women within the revolutionary struggle. In turn, these ideas drove women to hold men accountable and ensure that the revolution would also liberate women. This organizing took place as Salvadoran women in exile collaborated with leftist women from Latin America and the United States, who also critiqued the separation of women's liberation from socialist revolution. Those exchanges, in addition to its organizing, impacted how AMES theorized about the oppression of women under capitalism. To tell this rich story, I draw from the oral histories of former AMES members, and organizational documents from AMES and the Fuerzas Populares de Liberación Farabundo Martí (Farabundo Martí Popular Liberation Forces, FPL), the guerrilla organization that initially founded AMES.

political, economic, and sexual rights." Shayne and Kampwirth both date the rise of Salvadoran feminism to the 1990s, or "after the revolution" – the moment when many women abandoned the FMLN political party and formed self-identified feminist organizations. Viterna questions "whether women are attracted by emancipatory goals in the first place" and argues that FMLN women wrongfully believe that gender equality existed within the FMLN, thus internalizing the sexist narratives of male commanders. Navas claims that women's organizations pre-1980 were characterized by the "absence of a gender analysis within their objectives and platforms," while the 1980s witnessed an "incipient" women's (but not truly feminist) movement. In contrast, feminist organizations made "gender-specific demands" in the postwar era. Norma Stoltz Chinchilla, "Nationalism, Feminism, and Revolution in Central America," in *Feminist Nationalism*, ed. Lois. A. West (New York: Routledge, 1997), 214; Patricia Hipsher, "Right-and Left-Wing Women in Post-Revolutionary El Salvador: Feminist Autonomy and Cross-Political Alliance Building for Gender Equality," in *Radical Women in Latin America: Left and Right*, ed. Victoria González and Karen Kampwirth (University Park: Pennsylvania State University Press, 2001), 135; Julie Shayne, *The Revolution Question: Feminisms in El Salvador, Chile, and Cuba* (New Brunswick, NJ: Rutgers University Press, 2004), 46–66; Karen Kampwirth, *Feminism and the Legacy of Revolution: Nicaragua, El Salvador, Chiapas* (Athens: Ohio University Press, 2004), 75–111; María Candelaria Navas, *Sufragismo y feminismo: Visibilizando el protagonismo de las mujeres salvadoreñas* (San Salvador: Universidad de San Salvador, 2012), 79, 159; Jocelyn Viterna, *Women in War: The Micro-Processes of Mobilization* (New York: Oxford University Press, 2013), 11; Jocelyn Viterna, "Radical or Righteous? Using Gender to Shape Public Perceptions of Political Violence," in *Dynamics of Political Violence: A Process-Oriented Perspective on Radicalization and the Escalation of Political Conflict*, ed. Lorenzo Bosi, Charles Demetriou, and Stefan Malthaner (Surrey: Ashgate, 2014), 189–215.

THE FOUNDING OF AMES

Founded in 1970, the FPL was a Marxist-Leninist organization that rejected electoral politics and embraced mass organizing and anticapitalist armed struggle. It articulated three major goals: ending dependence on the United States; ending oligarchic power and capitalist exploitation; and building a grassroots base to construct socialism and eventually communism.[2] National events in the 1970s seemed to vindicate the FPL's radical analysis, as a series of US-backed military regimes engaged in repeated electoral fraud and savage repression of unarmed protest by peasants, workers, and students. By 1980 the state was killing at least 800 people a month.[3]

That year, the FPL joined the Frente Farabundo Martí para la Liberación Nacional (Farabundo Martí National Liberation Front, FMLN), becoming the largest guerrilla group within the coalition. According to conservative estimates, women constituted 27 to 34 percent of the FMLN membership.[4] From 1980 to 1992, the FMLN fought an armed struggle against the Salvadoran military regime, which received around $6 billion in US economic and military aid.[5] Self-described as Marxist-Leninist, the FMLN fought to overthrow military and oligarchic rule and US imperialism, and advocated a peasant–worker alliance to build a socialist society. The FMLN represented one of the last armed national-liberation movements of the late twentieth century.

While the FPL did not explicitly articulate an analysis of women's oppression, it promoted the political participation of peasant women and denounced sexism and the exploitation of poor women at the hands of elite men and government soldiers.[6] Rather than publicly denouncing sexism among working-class men, the organization encouraged the revolutionary participation of women and even characterized peasant women as more politically radical than men.[7] In 1977 the FPL encouraged or

---

[2] *El Rebelde*, Edición Internacional (March 1978): 16, Centro de Información, Documentación y Apoyo a la Investigación, Universidad Centroamericana José Simeón Cañas (hereafter CIDAI).

[3] Michael McClintock, *The American Connection, Volume 1: State Terror and Popular Resistance in El Salvador* (London: Zed, 1985), 266.

[4] In the FPL, women constituted 28 percent of combatants and 34 percent of the political cadre. Ilja A. Luciak, *After the Revolution: Gender and Democracy in El Salvador, Nicaragua, and Guatemala* (Baltimore, MD: Johns Hopkins University Press, 2001), 5.

[5] Benjamin C. Schwarz, *American Counterinsurgency Doctrine and El Salvador: The Frustrations of Reform and the Illusions of Nation Building* (Santa Monica, CA: RAND, 1991), 2.

[6] *Campo Rebelde* (July 1978): 4, CIDAI.

[7] *Compañera* (May 1979): 6; *Campo Rebelde* (January 1978): 10–11. Both in CIDAI.

directly assigned its members to build AMES as part of its larger strategy to organize working-class women. The association was publicly founded on September 3, 1979, in an assembly named after Isaura Gómez, a teacher and organizer who had been murdered alongside her twelve-year-old daughter by state forces.

The members of AMES represented two major groups: FPL militants living in El Salvador or in exile, and peasant civilians residing in FPL-controlled territories or in Nicaraguan and Costa Rican refugee camps. During the 1980s, all five guerrilla groups within the FMLN founded their own women's organizations to incorporate more women into the struggle, but AMES was the largest women's organization. By 1985, AMES could claim 10,000 members in El Salvador.[8] In addition, Salvadoran women in exile, including Tula Alvarenga de Carpio – an FPL founder who is often credited as the AMES founder – oversaw chapters in Managua, San José, Mexico City, Brooklyn, Chicago, Montreal, and Paris, as well as an international solidarity organization called Friends of AMES.[9] Other top FPL leaders also assisted AMES organizers. Mélida Anaya Montes, also known as Commander Ana María, the FPL's second-in-command and former general secretary of the national teachers' union, helped prepare AMES women before their speaking engagements, although it remains unclear whether she was a formal AMES member.[10]

Many rank-and-file AMES members had initially become politically active in labor and student movements. For example, as teenagers, cousins Rosa Rivera and María Helia Rivera became active in peasant organizing in the 1970s. Once the war broke out, they joined AMES, recruiting other civilian women within Chalatenango department, a stronghold of the FPL (Figure 10.1). Audelia Guadalupe López joined the FPL at the age of seventeen in the early 1970s. In 1985, she served on AMES's national executive

---

[8] "Women's Rights," *Women's Association of El Salvador* (Winter 1985), North American Congress on Latin America, New School for Social Research (hereafter NACLA-NS). All AMES documents from NACLA-NS are located on Reel 26.

[9] The US chapter of Friends of AMES led education and fundraising campaigns, and organized against US foreign policy in Central America. "Women in El Salvador Fight for Nothing Less Than Everything," *Reproductive Rights Newsletter: Newsletter of the Reproductive Rights National Network* (November 1982): 8, Barnard Center for Research on Women (hereafter BCRW).

[10] Aida Cañas, interview by Carlos Henríquez Consalvi, Havana, April 2015. Unless otherwise noted, all interviews were conducted by the author. All interviews are available in audio or transcription form at the Museo de la Palabra y la Imagen (MUPI) in San Salvador.

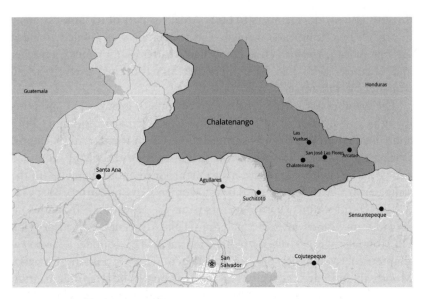

FIGURE 10.1 Chalatenango department.
Source: Map by Kevin Young.

body, using the pseudonym Rebeka Guevara.[11] The FPL women who were assigned to build AMES did not originally have an explicit awareness of their specific oppression as women. Audelia recalls that she "did not understand what we were going to do ... we began by listening to other people about the role of women."[12] In 1986 another FPL member, who later worked as an AMES organizer in a Nicaraguan refugee camp, explained that she originally "did not understand what the struggle of women was [about]."[13]

From the outset, AMES sought to organize working-class women. Given the organizing background of its membership, AMES understood its work as part of a larger history of labor organizing. For example, AMES drew inspiration from the Fraternidad de Mujeres (Fraternity of Women). Tula Alvarenga de Carpio and other Communist Party women had founded the Fraternity in 1957, organizing factory women, street

---

[11] AMES, "Entrevista a Rebeka Guevara, miembro de la dirección nacional ejecutiva de AMES," *Boletín Internacional* (January–March 1985): 3, BCRW. Rosa Rivera, interview, Arcatao, April 2015; María Helia Rivera, interview, Arcatao, April 2015.

[12] Audelia Guadalupe López, interview, San Salvador, May 2015.

[13] Quoted in Francesca Gargallo di Castel Lentini Celentani, "Las transformaciones de conducta femenina bajo el impacto del conflicto socio-militar en El Salvador" (Ph.D. diss., Universidad Nacional Autónoma de México, 1987), 180.

vendors, students, domestic workers, and housewives. Foreshadowing AMES, its slogan was "In Defense of the Woman and Child."[14] In contrast to the Fraternity, AMES explicitly linked women's rights to a revolutionary project, as evidenced by its slogan: "Winning the rights of women, we will build the new society." AMES also cited women's participation in more recent struggles, such as teacher strikes, peasant organizing, and guerrilla groups.[15] In its first three years, the association mainly organized urban-based women, demanding equal salaries for women, employment, the lowering of food prices, and an end to forced sterilizations.[16] It also denounced the economic and sexual exploitation of women street vendors, coffee pickers, and factory and domestic workers.[17]

WOMEN PLANT THE "SEEDS OF THE NEW SOCIETY"

After 1982 AMES built a stronger presence in rural areas under guerrilla control, particularly in Chalatenango department. In 1983, the FPL alone controlled twenty-eight out of thirty-three municipalities in Chalatenango.[18] That same year, the FMLN gained control over a quarter of the nation's territory, and by later in the decade it controlled a third. Although the so-called liberated territories faced constant government threats via troop invasions and aerial attacks, the FMLN held its ground, facilitating the growth of AMES within these areas since women could organize with relative freedom.

---

[14] María Candelaria Navas Turcios, "Las organizaciones de mujeres en El Salvador: 1975–1985" (Master's thesis, Universidad Nacional Autónoma de México, 1987), 127.

[15] AMES, *Participación de la mujer salvadoreña en el proceso revolucionario* (1977), 9–10, NACLA-NS. Olga Baires is listed as the author writing on behalf of AMES. Baires joined the FPL after leaving the Communist Party youth group. She participated in the Bloque Popular Revolucionario (Popular Revolutionary Bloc), a coalition of mass organizations, and worked with the Federación Cristiana de Campesinos Salvadoreños (Christian Federation of Salvadoran Peasants). She joined AMES in 1978, when she was in her mid-thirties.

[16] "Our Work, Our History" (August 1982), in *A Dream Compels Us: Voices of Salvadoran Women*, ed. Brenda Carter, Kevan Insko, David Loeb, and Marlene Tobias (San Francisco, CA: New American Press, 1989), 90.

[17] Jenny Vaughan and Jane MacIntosh, "Women's Lives in El Salvador: An Interview with Miriam Galdámez, an El Salvadoran Refugee," in *Women and War: El Salvador* (New York: WIRE, n.d.), n.p., BCRW.

[18] Jenny Pearce, *Promised Land: Peasant Rebellion in Chalatenango, El Salvador* (London: Latin American Bureau, 1986), 223.

In oral histories, former FPL women insisted on situating AMES within a context of revolutionary armed struggle. They understood the revolutionary process as the mechanism that would liberate women. María Margarita Velado, who coordinated AMES chapters in Nicaragua, recalled that AMES saw "no contradiction between the struggle for the rights of women and revolutionary change – one thing was going to depend on the other."[19] While she cautioned me against an "idealized vision" of AMES that divorced the organization from armed struggle, she also rejected reducing the revolutionary process to "only a military struggle; it was a *political*-military struggle, we were political warriors." Although AMES and FPL worked closely together, the association did not simply recruit women to join the FPL ranks. In January 1982, an AMES representative explained that their goal was to "educate and politicize women, not to arm them" (see Figure 10.2).[20]

After the FPL gained control over large portions of Chalatenango, peasants seized upon those military victories to establish new structures for local governance. As early as 1981, they began organizing popular councils to manage their immediate survival needs, such as security, food, and health. Older women, mothers with young children, and elderly persons comprised a significant portion of civilians within the liberated territories. In 1987, an AMES organizer estimated that 2,525 civilians lived in the Arcatao municipality, of whom 40 percent were women and 50 percent were children; the remaining 10 percent may have been elderly men.[21] Many civilian women had lost their male relatives to state violence, while most able-bodied men had joined the guerrilla ranks or deserted the area, and thus women alone assumed the responsibility of keeping their families alive.[22] In response to state violence, food shortages, and the absence of schools and clinics, council organizers established peasant militias and popular health clinics and schools, and collectively cultivated their own food. The clinics treated both serious injuries from government bombings and curable diseases such as diarrhea. The FMLN also actively

[19] María Margarita Velado, interview, San Salvador, April 28, 2015.
[20] Quoted in "Women in El Salvador," January 1982, BCRW.
[21] Mireya Lucero, "We Are No Longer a Community on the Run," in *A Dream Compels Us*, ed. Carter, et al., 197.
[22] Both peasant civilians and the FMLN accepted the notion that only young and elderly men would be allowed to enter refugee camps. Thus, men made choices to increase their chances of survival by either joining the guerrillas, being forcibly conscripted into the armed forces, or fleeing the country. For a discussion of how men understood their limited choices, see Viterna, *Women and War*, 109.

FIGURE 10.2 AMES political poster.
Source: Courtesy of the Museo de la Palabra y la Imagen.

promoted literacy within its camps, for both practical and ideological purposes. Sitting under trees and using sticks to write letters in the dirt, popular educators taught an entire generation to read and write, approaching education as a tool to understand and resolve collective problems.[23] While many of the peasants who participated within the councils were seasoned labor organizers, many were not, and thus the councils provided an opportunity to organize more people, deepen their political consciousness, expand their political participation, and consolidate political power over a vast territory. The self-organization of civilians was also a necessity because the FPL did not have the resources to fight against the Salvadoran military and also provide for the basic necessities of civilians.

The councils continued to grow as the FPL secured more territory. Each council oversaw one municipality that was connected to a larger regional junta made up of approximately seven municipalities. One regional junta alone oversaw the needs of 7,000 people.[24] Four regional juntas oversaw the entire Chalatenango department.[25]

The councils kept people alive but also represented a specific organizing strategy. A 1982 AMES bulletin described the councils as "an instance of local self-governance composed of representatives elected by the community."[26] A year later, an AMES organizer described the councils as "the seed of the new society."[27] Peasant organizing created a dual-power situation in which revolutionaries built institutions and relationships that challenged the existing state apparatus that upheld capitalist interests and monopolized the use of force. In directly representing their interests via the councils, peasants practiced a form of prefigurative politics, defined as the practice of building alternative institutions, political consciousness, and social relationships as a movement engages in a struggle against capitalism.[28] Despite the devastation that the war inflicted, peasants did not wait for a definitive military victory to begin

---

[23] On popular education within the guerrilla camps, see John L. Hammond, *Fighting to Learn: Popular Education and Guerrilla War in El Salvador* (New Brunswick, NJ: Rutgers University Press, 1998), esp. 52–73.

[24] Asociación de Comunidades para el Desarrollo de Chalatenango, *CCR: Organización y lucha popular en Chalatenango* (San Salvador: Algiers Impresores, 2012), 35.

[25] Ibid., 36–37.

[26] AMES, *Cómo nacemos y qué hacemos* (August 1982), 10, NACLA-NS.

[27] Azucena, "Helping Women to Participate As Equals" (1983), in *A Dream Compels Us*, 103.

[28] Carl Boggs first coined the term prefigurative politics, but as a political project it has deeper historical roots, from the Paris Commune to Spanish anarchist revolution. Boggs defined prefigurative politics as a "commitment to democratization through local, collective structures that anticipate the liberated society." Carl Boggs, "Marxism, Prefigurative Communism, and the Problem of Workers' Control," *Radical America* 11, no. 6 (1977): 103.

FIGURE 10.3 Villagers in Chalatenango after a council meeting, February 1984. *Source*: Photograph by Mike Goldwater.

building their ideal society. Rather, they used the councils to bridge the present-day movement to a revolutionary horizon (Figure 10.3).

Building the councils was no easy task. The pressing nature of the war led some to advocate prioritizing military activities over organizing efforts. A European doctor who worked in a popular clinic in Chalatenango summarized this tension in 1984:

There were people who said, we are at war and we cannot deal with too many other problems, let's win the war first and then deal with other things like health care in the villages, literacy, the situation of women ... People are very busy and therefore it is not strange if people say they can't do anything else. But finally the prevailing argument is, what is this war about? It is to improve the lives of the people, and we can't wait for that until we win the war.[29]

The councils reflected an effort to improve people's lives in the present. In line with that approach, AMES linked wartime survival to efforts to eradicate sexism.

The association intervened to ensure that women participated in the councils. Due to its efforts, a former secretary general of AMES

---

[29] The unnamed doctor is quoted in Pearce, *Promised Land*, 271.

served as the first president of the revolutionary junta government in Chalatenango. From 1982 to mid-1983, María Ofelia Navarrete had worked as AMES secretary general, coordinating its work in twenty-seven municipalities.[30] After 1983, she served as the president of the junta government and shortly after became the famous FPL Commander María Chichilco. In 1984, she explained the goals of AMES and the importance of women's political participation:

AMES is an organization that has two aims: the liberation of women as such and the liberation of the people, within which women ought to participate as a living element of the people. We struggle so that our women do not get stuck with the role of housewife who looks after the children, but also that they integrate themselves into political life. A woman has to have the opportunity to be mayor or president ... we realize that our demands as an organization are not a struggle against the other sex. On the contrary, it's our liberation and that of our *compañeros*, liberation from the machismo that the system has created.[31]

The association not only encouraged women's participation within the councils, but worked to have those bodies address women's concerns. For instance, AMES encouraged the popular clinics to address women's health needs, as one visitor to the territories noted in February 1984:

The local community governments in the area were trying to design a new health care system for thousands of people, and AMES was working with them to define the needs of women. Traditionally, things like bladder infections and gynecological problems just weren't talked about, and so they often weren't treated. Now women's needs will be incorporated into the health system.[32]

Each month, the clinic treated 200–500 patients and delivered 50 babies.[33] Older women, guardians of traditional medicine, assisted in the classification of native plants that could be used for natural remedies.[34] The same European doctor quoted earlier saw the clinics as a "system where people can participate and make decisions, feel responsible for their own health."[35] Members of AMES also collected food for civilians and for injured patients, and taught women how to bake bread

---

[30] Navarrete's political pseudonym was María Serrano. She was also known as Commander María Chichilco. "Aportes de la Asociación de Mujeres de El Salvador en el momento actual" (n.d.), 1, Folder 1, Bobbye S. Ortiz Papers (hereafter BOP), David M. Rubenstein Rare Book and Manuscript Library, Duke University.

[31] Quoted in Pearce, *Promised Land*, 274.

[32] Tracey Schear, "Popular Power in Chalatenango Province" (February 1984), in *A Dream Compels Us*, ed. Carter, et al., 185.

[33] Pearce, *Promised Land*, 269.   [34] Schear, "Popular Power," 188.

[35] Quoted in Pearce, *Promised Land*, 271.

and make candles and soap. Access to food was key for survival, perhaps explaining why many AMES members today remember food collections as a major AMES task.[36]

Collective projects provided AMES organizers with an opportunity to educate women. Those projects sought to "develop the political consciousness of women and help them to understand their 'double oppression'" and to "show [women] that they *are* capable of more, that they are capable of fighting for what they need. The problem is that men, by virtue of being men, have authority over 'their women' and this keeps women down," explained an eighteen-year-old AMES organizer in 1983.[37] In 1987, another organizer described how organizing enabled women to "understand why we were fighting and how they could participate in the process. It was a time of going from home to home, from woman to woman, and talking about these things."[38] According to this young organizer, older women wanted to limit their participation to prayers and tortillas alone, but she encouraged them to attend workshops and Bible-study groups to develop their political education.[39] Despite these obstacles, both younger and older women participated in AMES. In February 1984, the director of a US-based humanitarian-aid organization traveled to Chalatenango and commented that the "great majority of both older and younger women" participated in AMES. The older women "tended to be quieter; the younger women were bolder and more outgoing," and the latters' relationships with younger men "seemed to be on a more equal footing."[40] The younger women were mothers caring for small children, while women without children (between the ages of 18 and 25) tended to be in the FMLN.[41]

Through its political education program AMES sought to deepen women's participation. Organizers prioritized the "political and ideological training" of women in order to promote their leadership and solve "collective problems." Toward these goals, AMES held collective discussions about individual, family, and community issues, and hosted study groups about the political, economic, social, and cultural situation of the country. It outlined this work in an undated document summarizing the "contributions of the organization to the current moment."[42] This

---

[36] María Helia Rivera, interview; Ermelinda López, interview, Arcatao, April 2015; Filomena Beltrán, interview, Arcatao, September 2014.
[37] Beatriz, "Beautiful Pages of History Are Being Written" (August 1983), in *A Dream Compels Us*, ed. Carter, et al., 99.
[38] Lucero, "We Are No Longer a Community on the Run," 193.   [39] Ibid., 194.
[40] Schear, "Popular Power," 185.   [41] Ibid., 186.
[42] "Aportes de la Asociación de Mujeres de El Salvador," 1.

educational work also took place within the refugee camps. Azucena Quinteros, an AMES organizer, remembers how she organized study groups on Marx and Engels with refugee women in Nicaragua. These texts "discussed the origins of patriarchy . . . which had to do with women because they became the private property of men," she explains. To make the documents accessible, the organizers created "little drawings" that "women could understand" and discussed "why women today are oppressed a bunch of times over."[43] In other words, AMES adapted Marxism, making it accessible to rural women.

Many peasant women recall today how the association impacted their self-esteem. Esperanza Ortega remembers how her younger sister Ana Elsy, an AMES organizer and FPL member, motivated her "to do little projects to resolve some basic needs," believing "that as women we had to take initiative, that we should not hold onto the hope that the men would [financially] support us."[44] Esperanza then led a popular council. Political participation gave her "a wider vision" and taught her "to think of others" beyond her immediate circle.[45] Another peasant woman recalls her participation with pride: "it's the only thing I have ever done [outside the home] – participate in the women's meetings." She remembers how AMES organizers told her "to not merely stay at home, to not merely make the food – if you only do that you won't develop [as a person]."[46] Another notes how women's political participation resulted in "them being taken into account as if they were men."[47]

The educational work of the association also impacted its organizers. Prior to her involvement in AMES, Azucena collaborated with peasant organizations but faced resistance from her husband, who accused her of being "a loose woman who was out with men." Her husband, who was also a labor organizer, demanded that she ask permission prior to leaving the house. However, "the dialectical study" about women's realities made her "wake up" and "re-evaluate consciously" her "principles" and "family situation," she explained in 1987.[48] In 2015, she still remembered how she had explained to her children that organizing women "made her feel good; that it was a fundamental part of my life, as fundamental as they

---

[43] Azucena Quinteros, interview, San Salvador, April 2015.

[44] According to Ortega, Ayala, and the Rivera cousins, Ana Elsy was among the first to organize AMES bases in Chalatenango.

[45] Esperanza Ortega, interview, Arcatao, September 2014.

[46] Ermelinda López, interview.   [47] Filomena Beltrán, interview, Arcatao, April 2015.

[48] Quoted in Di Castel Lentini Celentani, "Las transformaciones de conducta femenina," 170, 180–81.

[her children] were."[49] In other words, she rejected her ex-husband's view that motherhood was incompatible with political participation.

As Azucena's story suggests, AMES women's insistence on their right to participate politically often faced opposition from men. A 1983 documentary about the FPL territories filmed an AMES meeting in Chalatenango in which a peasant woman called for the anti-sexist education of men. In an impassioned speech, she stressed the need to "make [the men] feel that we are a people and we have the right as *compañeras* to also fight" and not only to perform domestic tasks. To a large crowd of women and children, she implicitly responded to accusations that only morally dissolute women left their homes: "Well if [the men] are capable, if they are so confident, well they can wash their own clothes, they can make our tortillas. If we go to a meeting it is to understand the revolutionary process."[50] She mocked men who considered themselves superior to women and domestic work, and even threatened to withhold her domestic labor if men opposed her political participation. In response, the women cheered and yelled slogans, hailing "the active woman," "the dedicated and brave woman," and "the woman incorporated into the struggle."[51] Three decades later, a former AMES member remembers the slogan: *¡AMES combate, también aquí en Chalate!* ("AMES also fights in Chalatenango!").[52]

Women's organizing set limits to sexism. In 1982, a FPL woman combatant explained "how people have a better understanding of what carrying out a revolution involves ... Today in the battle zones, women may go about their duties while men take care of the children."[53] In 1983, another AMES organizer in Nicaragua defined *compañerismo* (camaraderie) as the "full integration of men into childrearing and into all family tasks." She argued that the movement needed *compañerismo* because the "Salvadoran movement cannot coexist with *machismo*."[54] The association developed measures to address men's opposition to women's political participation. In 1983, an organizer explained how AMES had confronted "serious problems" because some men had

---

[49] Azucena Quinteros, interview.

[50] *El camino de la libertad* (Instituto Cinematográfico de El Salvador Revolucionario, 1983), MUPI.

[51] Ibid.   [52] María Helia Rivera, interview.

[53] Letty, "Developing As Women within the Revolution" (June 1982), in *A Dream Compels Us*, ed. Carter, et al., 147.

[54] Malena Girón, "Breaking Down Barriers in Ideas and Practice" (May 1983), in *A Dream Compels Us*, ed. Carter, et al., 93.

threatened "to leave if their wives become politically active." In response, AMES members worked as "marriage counselors."[55] One peasant woman also remembers how the councils appointed a secretary dedicated to the resolution of community conflicts. In cases of conjugal conflicts, said person would "make [the man] see the problem that was happening in the family," she recalls.[56] The interventions of AMES seemed to improve conjugal relationships. For example, in 1983, an AMES organizer reported that a man who had initially opposed his wife's political participation now made tortillas, a supposedly feminine task.[57] In another case, a woman walked for a week to attend the first AMES Congress in 1984. Due to a government army invasion that prevented her return, her husband, who participated in the local militias, took care of their children for three months. According to the AMES organizer, he learned to better appreciate the contributions of his wife. The fact that the woman attended the Congress speaks volumes about the changes in their relationship.[58]

The work of AMES challenges the notion that vanguardism, militarism, and sexism always triumphed during the war. Writing about the revolutionary movements in Central America, Stoltz Chinchilla argues that "the very concept of the vanguard was unconsciously gendered" and that the "military predominated over the political."[59] Her characterization is partly true. But wartime conditions also imposed constraints on the FPL leadership. The self-organization of civilians became practically important within the liberated territories because the FPL did not have the resources to fight against the Salvadoran military *and* provide for the basic necessities of repopulated communities. The councils played an important role as an alternative form of government that democratically coordinated the needs of civilians, the majority of whom were women, children, and elderly persons. The association participated in the councils and its members often held leadership positions, which was part of its larger strategy for integrating women and their needs into decision-making bodies.

---

[55] Beatriz, "Beautiful Pages," 99.   [56] Esperanza Ortega, interview.
[57] Beatriz, "Beautiful Pages," 99.
[58] Lucero, "We Are No Longer a Community on the Run," 196.
[59] Stoltz Chinchilla, "Nationalism, Feminism, and Revolution," 212.

POLITICIZING PERSONAL PROBLEMS

Scholars have criticized the FMLN for discouraging the discussion of "personal" problems, which silenced women's unique grievances.[60] But the women of AMES did in fact politicize so-called private and personal problems, such as marital rape and childcare. Organizers challenged sexist notions that justified the sexual abuse of wives, and educated women about their right to deny sex. They also created childcare centers as part of a larger anti-sexist struggle to encourage women's participation, collectivize the raising of families, raise children with anti-sexist values, and resist state violence. The existence of the childcare centers, in addition to the internal discussions that were taking place about marital rape and abuse, complicates the claim that there was little discussion within the revolutionary movements regarding alternative visions of parenting, motherhood, and partnerships.

In the refugee camps, AMES educators attempted to shift how women viewed their own bodies. In 1982, Azucena began working with Salvadoran refugees in Nicaragua, where AMES organized approximately 800 women in the Nicaraguan cities of León, Chinandega, Managua, and Rivas, in addition to refugees in Costa Rica.[61] This work hoped to promote woman's participation in solidarity efforts and "prepare her for the return to her country and full incorporation into the reconstruction and formation of a new society."[62] They "organized and trained [women] who didn't know their rights ... they didn't even have knowledge about their own bodies," recalls Azucena.[63] She taught sexual education and rejected "the propaganda" of population control that "serve[d] the framework of the system" and was not "useful" for women.[64] Azucena remembers Malthusian proponents of population control, who often promoted non-consensual drug experimentation and the sterilization of women in the Global South as a means to reduce global poverty.[65] While the

---

[60] Ibid., 212.

[61] The AMES organization and the Association of Costa Rica Women in Solidarity with Salvadorean Women founded the Vocational Training Center for Refugee Women, which offered literacy, technical, and political education trainings. "Building a New Society," *Women's Association of El Salvador* (March 1984), BOP.

[62] *Desarrollo de la participación política de la mujer salvadoreña y su influencia en el proceso de la liberación nacional* (April 4, 1983), 11, Folder 2, BOP.

[63] Azucena Quinteros, interview.

[64] Di Castel Lentini Celentani, "Las transformaciones de conducta femenina," 200.

[65] Ana María Portugal, "Targets of Population Control: Latin America," *Connexions* 41 (1993): 12.

Salvadoran government did not forcibly sterilize women, it did actively promote sterilization over other means of contraception.[66] She also recalls how she facilitated discussions about rape within Nicaraguan refugee camps:

I remember that when I asked them if they had ever been raped they would say "no," you see, but when I asked them if their husbands forced them to have relations, then they said "yes," and so I told them, "that's rape" – [they replied] "oh I thought that was normal, because it's my husband, one has to service the husband."[67]

As a result of these discussions, women "began to make changes in their lives."

But it was "very complicated" to discuss marital rape "when there are people in our country dying," explains Azucena.[68] María Margarita, who worked both in Nicaragua and El Salvador, remembered having similar concerns about AMES's relationship to peasant women: "We did not look for conflicts that could break that relationship ... I have to modify that sexist behavior [but] to emphasize that situation too much could cause desertion among women."[69] In other words, characterizing the sexist behavior of poor men as the *primary* target could have alienated many peasant women who had lost their partners, sons, and male relatives to state violence. Furthermore, if some women excluded spousal sexual abuse from the category of rape, they may have framed their rape at the hands of state and paramilitary forces as the primary threat. Even if AMES had publicly denounced marital rape, a public campaign to denounce sexual violence would not be possible without survivors coming forward with their testimonies. Rather, AMES resorted to internal education about marital rape and publicly denounced state violence when survivors and relatives came forward. For example, in 1977 AMES decried the capture of pregnant women, who then gave birth inside jail, and the capture of children as a means to force women to "give information to repressive bodies."[70] It also denounced the drugging, electrocution, burning, and gagging of victims, in addition to "sexual torture, which consists of rape by one or several people." In one example, a mother testified to the murder

---

[66] Richard S. Monteith, Charles W. Warren, José Mario Caceres, and Howard I. Goldberg, "Changes in Contraceptive Use and Fertility: El Salvador, 1978–88," *Journal of Biosocial Science* 23, no. 1 (1991): 85; Jane T. Bertrand, José David Araya Zelaya, and Evelyn G. Landry, "Is Female Sterilization Voluntary in El Salvador?" *International Family Planning Perspectives* 12, no. 2 (1986): 41–43.
[67] Azucena Quinteros, interview.   [68] Ibid.   [69] María Margarita Velado, interview.
[70] AMES, *Participación de la mujer salvadoreña*, 7.

of her daughter, whose stomach was split open and stuffed with a man's decapitated head.[71] Brutal incidents such as these are almost impossible to avoid when reading AMES literature, reflecting the scale of state repression and the gendered ways in which military officials targeted their victims.

The concerns of peasant women to keep their families alive and united shaped AMES projects. In the guerrilla territories, AMES developed "common houses" or collectively run childcare centers.[72] Establishing collective childcare "was a very difficult struggle, especially when you consider the taboo against women leaving their homes ... So just getting the women to go out and leave their kids at another house was a significant breakthrough," explained Elda in 1987.[73] In Managua, AMES also established the "Luz Dilian Arévalo" childcare center for Salvadoran refugees. The center provided for the "medical, nutritional, and psycho-emotional needs" of children and promoted social skills that departed "from sexist traditions" and advanced the goals of "equality, mutual respect, and collective decision making," according to a 1984 pamphlet.[74] The association's teachers took a similar approach at popular schools within FMLN territories. They taught literacy in part as a means to "eradicate existing traditional values established as masculine or feminine."[75]

As it cared for children, AMES also strongly condemned state violence against them. In 1982, AMES denounced the military targeting of children who were "shot at point blank" and killed in attacks against the population, in addition to being "imprisoned, raped, disappeared, [and] tortured alongside their mothers in the sickest of ways."[76] To save their lives, peasants and their families dug and hid in *tatús* (underground bomb shelters). Tragically, many women accidentally suffocated their young children, hoping to muffle their cries to avoid detection from government soldiers.[77] The association frequently accompanied its denunciations with specific cases collected by the Comisión de Derechos Humanos de El

---

[71] "Situación de la mujer en material de los derechos humanos," n.d., n.p., in BOP, Folder 2. "Women in El Salvador," January 1982, BCRW.

[72] Girón, "Breaking Down Barriers," 95.

[73] Lucero, "We Are No Longer a Community on the Run," 194. Mireya Lucero was her political pseudonym.

[74] "For the Children of El Salvador (September 1984)," 4, BCRW.   [75] Ibid., 4.

[76] *La Asociación de Mujeres de El Salvador – AMES – ante las violaciones de los derechos humanos en El Salvador con relación a la niñez* (May 1982), 7. In November 1982, the AMES Mexico City chapter republished the text in *La mujer y la niñez salvadoreña, víctimas de la represión militar*. Folder 1, BOP.

[77] Pearce, *Promised Land*, 273.

Salvador (Human Rights Commission of El Salvador, CDHES), which included the state-led murder of children via machete, strangulation, and throat slitting. In 1983, AMES members also participated in a 150-person protest to denounce the use of napalm and phosphorus bombs that had left their children blind.[78]

While AMES mobilized women via their traditional identities as mothers, the organizing process also sought to change how women understood and practiced motherhood. In collectivizing childcare and food preparation, a responsibility which women mainly shouldered, AMES in 1984 encouraged women to "actively participate in the construction of a new society." Keeping children not only alive but happy "was a revolutionary contribution by women and AMES."[79] Motherhood would no longer be a mark of isolation but rather a collective struggle against the state. Decades later, former AMES members express similar views. Although childcare can "stereotype" women, "during wartime it is very important" comments María Margarita, who was among the first directors of the childcare center in Nicaragua. The center mirrored the "daily reflections" of women, including their "commitments and worries." "We go the way we are ... some of us did not have children but others did and they looked to protect them."[80] She makes an important point about how women navigated their historical constraints. The association did not choose the conditions that faced its membership, including the violent realities and unequal partnerships in which women conceived, gave birth to, and raised their children. Nonetheless, it collectivized childrearing to be inclusive of mothers who wished to participate politically, and kept children alive in a context in which the government considered them military targets. For María Margarita, that was revolutionary.

The association's organizing model compels us to reconsider the distinction that many feminist scholars have posited between "feminine" and "feminist" demands.[81] Feminine demands alleviate women's roles as

---

[78] Beatriz, "Beautiful Pages," 100.
[79] "For the Children of El Salvador (September 1984)," 4.
[80] María Margarita Velado, interview.
[81] Maxine Molyneux first coined the terms "practical" versus "gender strategic interests." Kampwirth also distinguishes between "feminine" and "feminist" organizing. Molyneux, "Mobilization without Emancipation? Women's Interests, the State, and Revolution in Nicaragua," *Feminist Studies* 11 (1985): 232; Karen Kampwirth, *Women and Guerrilla Movements: Nicaragua, El Salvador, Chiapas, Cuba* (University Park: Pennsylvania State University Press, 2002).

caretakers, while feminist demands explicitly challenge sexism. The former include demands for things like communal kitchens, clinics, and daycare centers that benefit women as workers, wives, and mothers, while an example of the latter is the demand for abortion rights. While the distinction between feminine and feminist organizing can be analytically useful, a binary opposition between the two can obscure their intimate relationship. As previously argued, AMES linked childcare to the structural transformation of capitalist patriarchy, situating that reform demand within a revolutionary project. The complexity of this organizing process is overlooked if we focus only on the immediate demand. Often, narrow visions of feminism dismiss the demands of poor women in the Global South as not sufficiently feminist. A better approach to understanding women's struggles involves paying attention to how organizers frame an issue and how the organizing process itself can shape understandings about oppression, give rise to new demands and leadership, strengthen the long-term viability of the movement, and disrupt existing gender hierarchies and intersecting oppressions.

TRANSNATIONAL DEBATES AND EXCHANGES IN EXILE

As AMES organized within the guerrilla camps, it also sent organizers abroad to coordinate solidarity work. While living in exile, AMES organizers, many of whom were university-educated women, wrote the organization's bulletins to mobilize support for peasant women, and in the process collaborated with other leftist women who also attempted to bridge women's liberation and socialism. The women of AMES redefined key concepts of the FPL in order to develop an anticapitalist feminism that could address the needs of rural women. These theoretical interventions need to be contextualized within a larger debate taking place within the left in the Americas. In the 1970s and 1980s, Latin American and US women fought to integrate a feminist praxis within national-liberation and working-class movements and reconceptualized the relationship between capitalism and patriarchy.[82] While the association's revolutionary feminist praxis emerged in part from local conditions within El Salvador, it also reflected a larger trend in Latin American feminism.

During the fight against dictatorial regimes in the 1970s, Latin American women questioned the separation of gender and class

---

[82] Norma Stoltz Chinchilla, "Marxism, Feminism, and the Struggle for Democracy in Latin America," *Gender and Society* 5 (1991): 296.

oppression.[83] Leftist women everywhere faced similar conditions, such as capitalist inequality and political repression, with specific forms and intensities varying by country.[84] In the process of organizing against state violence in its many manifestations, leftist women developed new understandings about women's oppression under capitalism.[85] In addition, the Women's International Year (1975) and the United Nations Decade of Women (1975–85), which included three international conferences in Mexico City, Copenhagen, and Nairobi, created an opening for academic research about discrimination against women.[86] In the 1980s, as authoritarian states transitioned to liberal democracies, women in Southern Cone countries also questioned their subordination to political parties that marginalized anti-sexist struggle.[87] These experiences led to a growing current of socialist feminism in Latin America that identified women's liberation as central to anticapitalist revolution.

Conversations and contacts with leftist women in the Americas shaped the association's perspective on the relationship between patriarchy, capitalism, and imperialism. For example, during her exile in Mexico City – a key site of refuge for Latin American exiles – María Candelaria Navas formed relationships with Chilean women exiles from the Movimiento de Izquierda Revolucionario (Revolutionary Left Movement, MIR) who also questioned the separation of women's liberation from class struggle. Decades later, she recalls how she and the association developed its theories in conversation with other radical women's groups.[88]

The women of AMES also worked with socialist-feminist organizations in the United States such as the Women's International Resource

---

[83] Leni Silverstein, "First Feminist Conference in Latin America," *International Supplement to the Women's Studies Quarterly* 1 (1982): 35.

[84] Cornelia Butler Flora, "Socialist Feminism in Latin America," *Journal of Women, Politics, & Policy* 4 (1984): 69–93.

[85] Jadwiga E. Pieper Mooney, "Forging Feminism under Dictatorship: Women's International Ties and National Feminist Empowerment in Chile, 1973–1990," *Women's History Review* 19 (2010): 620–21.

[86] Fanny Tabak, "UN Decade and Women's Studies in Latin America," *Women's Studies International Forum* 8, no. 2 (1985): 103–06.

[87] Sonia Álvarez, "The (Trans)formation of Feminism(s) and Gender Politics in Democratizing Brazil," in *The Women's Movement in Latin America: Participation and Democracy*, ed. Jane Jaquette (Boulder, CO: Westview Press, 1994), 32.

[88] José Miguel Castillo Mora, "'También luchábamos, también caíamos': Aproximación a la represión sufrida por las militantes femeninas del MIR en la dictadura del Pinochet," *Contrastes* 13 (2004): 139–55; María Candelaria Navas, interview, San Salvador, April 2015.

Exchange (WIRE), which also rejected sexism within the revolutionary left.[89] Bobbye Ortiz, a Jewish Marxist feminist and the editor of *Monthly Review*, founded WIRE in 1979. The organization recognized the "gender-specific ways" that "imperial powers" oppress "Third World" women.[90] It had published and translated several MIR documents in which Chilean exiles critiqued the sexism of leftist political parties, and its founder carefully archived leftist literature written by Latin American women.[91] In 1985, Ortiz identified AMES' theory as a "departure" from the linear conception of revolutionary priorities in which women's emancipation is subordinated to anticapitalist revolution. She felt assured that "when a revolutionary transformation of society is achieved in El Salvador," AMES will provide "an available body of organized, experienced, and conscious women who can play an important role in building a society free not only of class oppression but also of gender oppression."[92]

The politics of WIRE reflected the political climate of the feminist movement in the United States. The 1980s witnessed a rich period of feminist theorizing and organizing by US women of color and socialist-feminists (often overlapping groups), who aimed to create a theory and praxis capable of confronting multiple and intersecting forms of racial, gender, sexual, and class oppression.[93] In this context, groups like WIRE supported groups like AMES, which advanced a broad vision of revolution, while denouncing US intervention in Central America.

Part of AMES' support in the United States came from reproductive rights organizers. The Reproductive Rights National Network advocated

---

[89] Similarly, MIR exiles in the United States worked closely with the Boston Women's Health Book Collective, which published the classic feminist text *Our Bodies Ourselves* (1971). The book has been translated into several dozen languages. Pieper Mooney, "Forging Feminism under Dictatorship," 622.

[90] Lindsey Churchill, "Transnational Alliances," *Latin American Perspectives* 36, no. 6 (2009): 2.

[91] Gladys Díaz, *Roles and Contradictions of Chilean Women in the Resistance and in Exile: Collective Reflections of a Group of Militant Prisoners* (New York: WIRE, 1979).

[92] Bobbye Ortiz, "Changing Consciousness of Central American Women," *Economic and Political Weekly* 20 (1985): 7.

[93] These groups presented a new praxis of leftist organizing; they rejected the racist, heterosexist, and capitalist politics of liberal feminists, many nationalists, and many orthodox Marxists. They theorized intersecting oppressions to challenge the allegedly universal categories of "worker" and "woman." For these feminists, addressing the multiple sources of oppression was central, not divisive, to liberation movements. See especially Cherríe Moraga and Gloria Anzaldúa, eds., *This Bridge Called My Back: Writings by Radical Women of Color* (New York: Kitchen Table, 1983).

a broad vision of reproductive justice, defending access to abortion and contraception, while simultaneously denouncing forced sterilizations and cutbacks of social services that pushed pregnant mothers into poverty. In a 1981 bulletin, the network reported on the forced-sterilization campaigns of the US government against both American and Salvadoran women. A year later, the network publicized an advertisement for Friends of AMES, which invited US women to mobilize in support of the Salvadoran struggle.[94] Such reporting hoped to bridge the struggles of women against state violence across national borders.

Feminist and gay and lesbian organizations in the United States also hosted AMES on speaking tours. Organizers attempted to bridge queer liberation and anti-imperialism, connecting domestic struggles to struggles against US intervention abroad. For instance, a multiracial feminist group of lesbian and straight women based in San Francisco drew inspiration from the role of women in revolutionary movements in Nicaragua and El Salvador. The group hosted AMES at a 500-person conference in the Mission District in 1984.[95]

The association's members confronted questions about lesbianism while working in exile, and the exchanges resulted in individual reflections about sexuality. Through national speaking tours, Elda, an AMES representative, spoke to US-based progressives and leftists who participated in the Central America solidarity movement. Her work led her to attend a 3,000-person lesbian conference in Chicago in 1984 or 1985. She recalls that she did "not perfectly understand what it meant to be a lesbian or lesbianism," and so a lesbian comrade who worked in the Friends of AMES chapter explained to her the goals of lesbian organizations. These exchanges led Elda to believe that "the FMLN should also respect [this work]," she recounts. To this day, Elda remembers fondly "the respect [the women] had toward our work" and how AMES members "recognize[d] their way of being and their work." However, solidarity work did not always produce an understanding about sexual oppression. One former FPL member recalls with embarrassment how lesbian and gay attendees at an AMES presentation asked her what "the revolution thinks about them." She remembers having responded, "I think

[94] *Reproductive Rights Newsletter: Newsletter of the Reproductive Rights National Network* (Fall 1981): 5, BCRW; *Reproductive Rights Newsletter: Newsletter of the Reproductive Rights National Network* (Fall 1982): 8, BCRW.

[95] Emily K. Hobson, *Lavender and Red: Liberation and Solidarity in the Gay and Lesbian Left* (Berkeley: University of California Press, 2016), 115, 130.

that's inadmissible at the moment, [the lesbian and gay movement] is a deviation."[96] The attendees said nothing. This exchange demonstrates the limits of AMES' revolutionary feminism in relation to sexuality. Since the end of the war, she has changed her views and now sees sexual liberation as an important component of working-class and feminist movements.

RETHINKING REVOLUTIONARY THEORY

Organizing abroad and within the guerrilla territories and refugee camps informed the theoretical contributions of AMES, which expanded on and even departed from FPL politics. In contrast to the FPL, AMES explicitly bridged socialism and women's liberation. It intervened in Marxist debates, pointing to the role of sexism in upholding capitalist oppression, and critiquing arguments that sought to postpone the liberation of women until a revolutionary victory. It rejected the assumption that a transformation in the economy alone would automatically liberate poor women. Simultaneously, the association also critiqued Western liberal feminists who did not reject capitalism and ignored the class divisions among women.

The women of AMES pointed to the gendered workings of capitalist exploitation. Both AMES and the FPL agreed upon the necessity of armed struggle and socialism for achieving national liberation, and upon the importance of incorporating women into a class struggle that improved daily conditions while working to overthrow capitalism. In contrast to the FPL, however, AMES explicitly argued that patriarchy fundamentally shaped how working-class women experienced their oppression under capitalism. At a 1981 conference in Costa Rica, AMES explained how capitalism reproduces itself through the exploitation of women's unpaid domestic labor, which upheld "the male monopoly of political power" and forced women into unskilled jobs.[97] Influenced by the writings of Russian socialist Alexandra Kollontai, AMES insisted that housewives were members of the working class, and also denounced gender hierarchies within the working class, a departure from orthodox Marxism and the FPL.[98] While the FPL recognized that different sectors, including

[96] Azucena Quinteros, interview; Elda Ortiz, interview, San Salvador, May 2015.
[97] AMES, *Participation of Latin American Women in Social and Political Organizations: Reflections of Salvadoran Women* (New York: WIRE, n.d.), 2, BCRW.
[98] Olga Baires, email to author, April 2015.

women, made up the working class, it tended to emphasize the common class oppression between men and women, and downplay the unique oppression of women.

The association re-conceptualized women's relationship to class struggle and socialism. According to AMES, nineteenth-century Marxists had argued that the "abolition of capitalism would immediately free women from economic dependence on men, and consequently from subordination."[99] For AMES, the overthrow of capitalism was a "necessary but not sufficient condition" to achieve "our total emancipation."[100] In 1983, it wrote: "We seek the liberation of our countries from imperialism, dictatorship, and the local bourgeoisie – although we work simultaneously around the question of the specific condition of women and our oppression within the capitalist and patriarchal system."[101] Situating the liberation of women within a "context of [the] total transformation of society" was the "hallmark of revolutionary feminism."[102]

The group measured revolutionary progress through the lens of women's emancipation, stating that no "genuine social transformation" can take place "without women's emancipation."[103] A "true revolution" is "accompanied by the conquest of [women's rights] in all social spheres."[104] This analysis overlapped with, yet departed from, that of the FPL. Both organizations actively recruited women into anticapitalist movements. But whereas FPL literature suggested that women would no longer be exploited in a post-capitalist society, AMES added that women's liberation would not be automatic – rather, it would be contested even after the taking of state power. Drawing from the FPL synthesis that bridged reform struggles to revolution, the association argued that women "cannot wait for socialism or a change of structures" to solve their immediate, everyday problems.[105]

The association evaluated the maturity of other political organizations based on the extent to which those groups seriously advanced women's participation. It critiqued the Latin American "parties and movements of the democratic left" for not consistently addressing "the problems of women" and recognizing that women's "integration in the struggle" is "a key factor in the liberation of our societies." Those unnamed groups assumed that "feminism and socialism are opposed to each other." Nonetheless, AMES saw progress in the *frentista* or mass-front model because it facilitated

---

[99] AMES, *Participation of Latin American Women*, 2.   [100] Ibid., 2.   [101] Ibid., 1.
[102] Ibid., 7.   [103] Ibid., 3.
[104] Olga Baires writing on behalf of AMES, in *Participación de la mujer salvadoreña*.
[105] AMES, *Participation of Latin American Women*, 7.

women's mass participation to expose "prevailing contradictions" and expose "the true nature of military regimes." In the case of El Salvador, AMES recognized that women were participating on an unprecedented mass scale. However, women's participation alone was not sufficient. It argued that the problem of women's leadership could not be resolved through "stipulated quotas" but rather by scrutinizing "male–female relationships" and re-conceptualizing both the goals and daily practice of revolution.[106]

The organization's analysis of capitalism also set it apart from Western liberal feminists. The latter sought to incorporate elite and middle-class women into capitalist institutions without questioning how capitalism is built on the exploitation of working-class women and the imperial domination of the Global South. For these reasons, AMES argued that all women do not share a common interest, because "unquestionably our class interests transcend those of gender."[107] It rejected women's incorporation into capitalism, because obtaining a "bigger piece of pie does not constitute liberation" if one does not transform the "kind of development."[108] Only "national liberation" could facilitate "our liberation from a *machista* society," it argued.[109] Women's emancipation depended on a "collective consciousness" that would arise "with the restructuring of society without private property and exploitation."[110] In addition, AMES also critiqued essentialist views of women as innately revolutionary, pointing to women's roles "as reproducers" of the "dominant ideology," a departure from FPL discourse that tended to characterize women as inherently revolutionary and noble.[111]

CONCLUSION

The women of AMES – refugees, peasants, and FPL militants and exiles – strategically fought their feminist struggle within a revolutionary armed movement. Rank-and-file women critiqued and expanded upon Marxism and revolutionary strategy, developing a revolutionary feminist praxis that emerged from multiple sites of struggle: liberated territories, refugee camps, and chapters in exile. Audelia López recalls how AMES members "constructed a theory but from a practice and not only from our own practice but from that of other women – that gave life to AMES."[112]

---

[106] AMES, *Participation of Latin American Women*, 4–7.
[107] AMES, *Participation of Latin American Women*, 1.   [108] Ibid., 3.
[109] Vaughan and MacIntosh, "Women's Lives in El Salvador," 3.
[110] AMES, *Cómo nacemos y qué hacemos*, 5.
[111] AMES, *Participation of Latin American Women*, 5; *Compañera* (May 1979): 8.
[112] Audelia Guadalupe López, interview.

Exiled women wrote the literature of the organization and developed their theories within a larger transnational network of socialist-feminists in the Americas. But they alone did not dominate the production of AMES theory. Peasant women themselves also shaped the demands and organizing model of the association. In short, women intervened to make the revolution relevant to their own lives and dreams. For these reasons, we cannot speak of a singular monolithic understanding of Marxism within the revolutionary left in El Salvador. In other words, the top FMLN leadership did not monopolize the goals of the revolution.

Scholars are correct to argue that participation in class-based movements does not *inevitably* lead to feminist consciousness or a change in gender hierarchies.[113] While the FPL insistence on mass organizing benefited women, AMES organizers made deliberate choices to reframe FPL theories and practices, and Marxism more broadly, in order to confront the specific forms of oppression that impacted the lives of rural women. As María Margarita says, the revolutionary process needed "women to be able to express their interests," and so the "class struggle led me to understand that there were other types of oppression that women faced due to their gender oppression."[114] The members of AMES contributed to the meaning and practice of revolution. In the postwar period they have continued to apply that vision as feminist organizers, elected officials, and popular historians.[115]

Understanding the wartime making of revolutionary feminism allows us to understand the dramatic rise of self-identified feminist organizations in the early 1990s. After the 1992 signing of the Chapultepec Peace

[113] Stoltz Chinchilla, "Nationalism, Feminism, and Revolution," 216; Molyneux, "Mobilization without Emancipation?"; Sandra McGee Deutsch, "Gender and Sociopolitical Change in 20th Century Latin America," *Hispanic American Historical Review* 71 (1991): 259–306; Margaret Randall, *Gathering Rage: The Failure of Twentieth Century Revolutions to Develop a Feminist Agenda* (New York: Monthly Review, 1992).

[114] María Margarita Velado, interview.

[115] María Candelaria and Azucena are long-time members of the Asociación Movimiento de Mujeres Mélida Anaya Montes, Las Mélidas (Mélida Anaya Montes Women's Movement Association), a self-identified feminist organization founded in July 1992. Other women, such as Audelia, fight for the rights of women as FMLN political officials. Rosa and María Helia are self-identified feminists and founders of the Comité de Memoria Sobreviviente, Arcatao, Chalatenango, a committee composed mainly of older women who transmit their insurgent memories to younger generations. For a discussion of how the committee challenges sexist historical narratives, see chapter four in Diana Carolina Sierra Becerra, "Insurgent Butterflies: Gender and Revolution in El Salvador, 1964–2015" (Ph.D. diss., University of Michigan, 2017).

Accords, which finally ended the twelve-year civil war and allowed the FMLN to become a political party, many women left the party to establish their independent feminist organizations. Others opted to stay in the party and organize within it.[116] In both cases, the militant feminists of the postwar era did not emerge from thin air. Decades of struggle cultivated seasoned women organizers who had developed their own ideas of what it meant to be free.

[116] Dominant narratives date the rise of Salvadoran feminism to the early 1990s – after the revolution. For a discussion of its emergence and appeal, see ibid., 21–29. For a discussion of feminist splits from the FMLN, see Kampwirth, "Feminists Break Away in El Salvador," in *The Legacy of Revolution.*

Index